Gander · Hřebíček

Solving Problems in Scientific Computing Using
Maple and MATLAB®

Walter Gander · Jiří Hřebíček

Solving Problems in Scientific Computing Using Maple and MATLAB®

Second, Expanded Edition

With 106 Figures and 8 Tables

Springer

Walter Gander

Institute of Scientific Computing
ETH Zürich
CH-8092 Zürich, Switzerland

Jiří Hřebíček

Department of Information Technology
Faculty of Informatics
Masaryk University of Brno
Burešova 20
CZ-602 11 Brno, Czech Republic

The cover picture shows a plane fitted by least squares to given points (see Chapter 6)

Mathematics Subject Classification (1991):
00A35, 08-04, 65Y99, 68Q40, 68N15

ISBN 3-540-58746-2 Springer-Verlag Berlin Heidelberg New York

ISBN 3-540-57329-1 1. Auflage Springer-Verlag Berlin Heidelberg New York

CIP data applied for

MATLAB® is a registered trademark of The MathWorks Inc. The trademark is being used with the written permission of The MathWorks Inc.

The use of general descriptive names, registered names, trademarks etc. in this publication does not imply, even in the absence of a specific statement, that such names are exempt from the relevant protective laws and regulations and therefore free for general use.

© Springer-Verlag Berlin Heidelberg 1993, 1995
Printed in Germany

Typesetting: Camera-ready copy from the authors
SPIN 10489395   41/3143-5 4 3 2 1 0 – Printed on acid-free paper

Preface

Modern computing tools like MAPLE (a symbolic computation package) and MATLAB® (a numeric and symbolic computation and visualization program) make it possible to use the techniques of scientific computing to solve realistic nontrivial problems in a classroom setting. These problems have been traditionally avoided, since the amount of work required to obtain a solution exceeded the classroom time available and the capabilities of the students. Therefore, simplified and linearized models are often used. This situation has changed, and students can be taught with real-life problems which can be solved by the powerful software tools available. This book is a collection of interesting problems which illustrate some solution techniques in Scientific Computing. The solution technique for each problem is discussed and demonstrated through the use of either MAPLE or MATLAB. The problems are presented in a way such that a reader can easily extend the techniques to even more difficult problems.

This book is intended for students of engineering and scientific computing. It is not an introduction to MAPLE and MATLAB. Instead, it teaches problem solving techniques through the use of examples, which are difficult real-life problems. Please review the MAPLE[1] and MATLAB[2] documentation for questions on how to use the software.

All figures in the book were created either by using graphic commands of MAPLE and MATLAB or by direct use of *xfig* on a SUN workstation. Occasionally changes were made by Dr. S. Bartoň in the postscript files to improve the visual quality of the figures. These changes include different font sizes, line types, line thicknesses, as well as additional comments and labels.

This book was written as a collaboration between three institutes:

- the Department of Theoretical Physics and Astrophysics of Masaryk University, Brno, Czech Republic,

---

[1] B.W. CHAR ET AL., *Maple V Language/Reference Manual*,
Springer Verlag, New York, 1991
[2] MATLAB *User's Guide*, The MathWorks, Inc.,
24 Prime Park Way, Natick, MA 01760, 1993.

- the Institute of Physics of the University of Agriculture and Forestry, Brno, Czech Republic, and

- the Institute of Scientific Computing ETH, Zürich, Switzerland.

The authors are indebted to the Swiss National Science Foundation which stimulated this collaboration through a grant from the "Oststaaten-Soforthilfeprogramm". An additional grant from the ETH "Sonderprogramm Ostkontakte" and support from the Computer Science Department of ETH Zürich made it possible for Dr. S. Bartoň to spend a year in Zürich. He was the communication link between the two groups of authors and without him, the book would not have been produced on time. We would also like to thank Dr. L. Badoux, Austauschdienst ETH, and Prof. C.A. Zehnder, chairman of the Computer Science Department, for their interest and support.

Making our Swiss- and Czech-English understandable and correct was a major problem in producing this book. This was accomplished through an internal refereeing and proofreading process which greatly improved the quality of all articles. We had great help from Dr. Kevin Gates, Martha Gonnet, Michael Oettli, Prof. S. Leon, Prof. T. Casavant and Prof. B. Gragg during this process. We thank them all for their efforts to improve our language.

Dr. U. von Matt wrote the LATEX style file to generate the layout of our book in order to meet the requirements of the publisher. We are all very thankful for his excellent work.

D. Gruntz, our MAPLE expert, gave valuable comments to all the authors and greatly improved the quality of the programs. We wish to thank him for his assistance.

The programs were written using MAPLE V Release 2 and MATLAB 4.1. For MAPLE output we used the ASCII interface instead of the nicer XMAPLE environment. This way it was easier to incorporate MAPLE output in the book. The programs are available in machine readable form. We are thankful to The MathWorks for helping us to distribute the software.

Included in this book is a postcard addressed to The MathWorks, Inc., 24 Prime Park Way, Natick, MA 01760, USA, with which the reader may request a free copy of all the programs on diskette. Readers connected to Internet can also obtain the programs from ftp.inf.ethz.ch using anonymous ftp.

Zürich, September 13, 1993   Walter Gander, Jiří Hřebíček

Preface to the second edition

The first edition of this book has been very well received by the community, and this has made it necessary to write a second edition within one year. We added the new chapters 20 and 21 and we expanded chapters 15 and 17. Some typographical errors were corrected, and we also rephrased some text. By doing so we hope to have improved our English language.

All programs were adapted to the newest versions of the software i.e. to MAPLE V Release 3 and to MATLAB Version v4. In order to simplify the production of the book we again chose the *pretty print* output mode for the MAPLE output.

As in the first edition, this book contains a postcard which the reader may return to The MathWorks[3] to request a free copy of all the MAPLE and MATLAB programs on diskette. The programs are also available via anonymous ftp from ftp.inf.ethz.ch.

We dedicate the second edition to our late colleague František Klvaňa. We all mourn for our friend, a lovely, friendly, modest person and a great scientist.

Druhé vydání je věnováno památce našeho zesnulého kolegy Františka Klvani. Všichni vzpomínáme na našeho drahého přítele, milého a skromného člověka a velkého vědce.

Zürich, October 7, 1994   Walter Gander, Jiří Hřebíček

---

[3]The MathWorks, Inc., 24 Prime Park Way, Natick, MA 01760
phone: (508) 653-1415, fax: (508) 653-2997, email: info@mathworks.com

List of Authors

Stanislav Bartoň
Institute of Physics and Electronics
University of Agriculture and Forestry Brno
Zemědělská 1
613 00 Brno, Czech Republic
barton@vszbr.cz

Jaroslav Buchar
Institute of Physics and Electronics
University of Agriculture and Forestry Brno
Zemědělská 1
613 00 Brno, Czech Republic

Ivan Daler
Air Traffic Control Research Department
Smetanova 19
602 00 Brno, Czech Republic

Walter Gander
Institute of Scientific Computing
ETH Zürich
8092 Zürich, Switzerland
gander@inf.ethz.ch

Dominik Gruntz
Institute of Scientific Computing
ETH Zürich
8092 Zürich, Switzerland
gruntz@inf.ethz.ch

Jürgen Halin
Institute of Energy Technology
ETH Zürich
8092 Zürich, Switzerland
halin@iet.ethz.ch

Jiří Hřebíček
> Faculty of Informatics Masaryk University Brno
> Burešova 20
> 602 00 Brno, Czech Republic
> hrebicek@informatics.muni.cz

František Klvaňa †

Urs von Matt
> Department of Computer Science
> University of Maryland
> College Park, MD 20742, USA
> vonmatt@umiacs.umd.edu

Rolf Strebel
> Institute of Scientific Computing
> ETH Zürich
> 8092 Zürich, Switzerland
> strebel@inf.ethz.ch

Jörg Waldvogel
> Seminar of Applied Mathematics
> ETH Zürich
> 8092 Zürich, Switzerland
> waldvoge@math.ethz.ch

Contents

Chapter 1. The Tractrix and Similar Curves

W. Gander, J. Hřebíček and S. Bartoň

1.1 Introduction

In this section we will use MATLAB to solve two similar systems of differential equations. First we generalize the classical tractrix problem to compute the orbit of a toy pulled by a child, and then we compute the orbit of a dog which attacks a jogger. We also show how the motions may be visualized with MATLAB.

1.2 The Classical Tractrix

In the 17th century Gottfried Wilhelm Leibniz discussed the following problem, see [2, 1]. *Given a watch attached to a chain, what is the orbit in the plane described by the watch as the endpoint of the chain is pulled along a straight line?*

Let a be the length of the chain. The problem is easily solved if we assume that the point-like watch is initially on the x-axis at the point $(a, 0)$, and that starting at the origin we pull in the direction of the positive y-axis, [2], (cf. Figure 1.1).

From Figure 1.1 we immediately obtain the following differential equation for the unknown function $y(x)$:

$$y' = -\frac{\sqrt{a^2 - x^2}}{x}. \tag{1.1}$$

To solve Equation (1.1) we only need to integrate:

```
> assume(a>=0);
> y = -int(sqrt(a^2 - x^2)/x, x);
```

$$y = -(a\tilde{\ }^2 - x^2)^{1/2} + a\tilde{\ }\ \text{arctanh}\left(\frac{(a\tilde{\ }^2 - x^2)^{1/2}}{a\tilde{\ }}\right)$$

MAPLE did not include the constant of integration. Because $y(a) = 0$ this constant is zero anyway, therefore the solution to our problem is

$$y(x) = a \operatorname{arctanh}\left(\frac{\sqrt{a^2 - x^2}}{a}\right) - \sqrt{a^2 - x^2}. \tag{1.2}$$

FIGURE 1.1. *Classical Tractrix.*

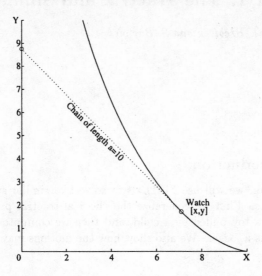

Let us now assume that the object to be pulled is initially on the y-axis at the point $(0, a)$ and that we start pulling again at the origin, but this time in the direction of the positive x-axis.

Consider the point $(x, y(x))$ on the orbit of the object. The endpoint of the chain on the x-axis is at the point $(x - y(x)/y'(x), 0)$, that is where the tangent intersects the x-axis (this is the same point which would be obtained for one step of Newton's iteration!). Therefore, the condition that the chain has the constant length a, leads to the differential equation

$$\frac{y(x)^2}{y'(x)^2} + y(x)^2 = a^2, \tag{1.3}$$

which can no longer be solved directly by quadrature. Therefore we need to call the differential equation solver dsolve,

```
> restart;
> assume(a>0);
> eq := (y(x)/diff(y(x), x))^2 + y(x)^2 = a^2;

                        2
                    y(x)              2     2
         eq :=  ------------- + y(x)     = a
                /  d      \2
                |---- y(x)|
                \ dx      /

> p:=dsolve(eq,y(x));
```

```
 p :=
                                              2    2 1/2
           2    2 1/2             (- y(x)  + a~ )
  - (- y(x)  + a~ )    + a~ arctanh(------------------) + x = _C1.
                                          a~


                                              2    2 1/2
           2    2 1/2             (- y(x)  + a~ )
    (- y(x)  + a~ )    - a~ arctanh(------------------) + x = _C1
                                          a~
```

and we obtain two solutions. From the initial condition $y(0) = a$ and from physics it follows for $a > 0$ that $y(x) > 0$ and $y'(x) < 0$. Thus the second solution is the correct answer to our problem:

```
  > p[2];
```

```
                                            2    2 1/2
         2    2 1/2             (- y(x)  + a~ )
  (- y(x)  + a~ )    - a~ arctanh(------------------) + x = _C1
                                        a~
```

We obtain the solution $y(x)$ in implicit form. Since $y(0) = a$, we obtain $\_C1 = 0$. So the solution $y(x)$ satisfies the equation

$$\sqrt{a^2 - y(x)^2} - a\operatorname{arctanh}\left(\frac{\sqrt{a^2 - y(x)^2}}{a}\right) + x = 0.$$

We could, of course, have obtained this equation also by interchanging the variables x and y in Equation (1.2). Note that it would be difficult to solve Equation (1.3) numerically, since for $x = 0$ there is a singularity: $y'(0) = \infty$.

1.3   The Child and the Toy

Let us now solve a more general problem and suppose that a child is walking on the plane along a curve given by the two functions of time $X(t)$ and $Y(t)$.

Suppose now that the child is pulling or pushing some toy, by means of a rigid bar of length a. We are interested in computing the orbit of the toy when the child is walking around. Let $(x(t), y(t))$ be the position of the toy. From

FIGURE 1.2. *Velocities* $\mathbf{v}_C$ *and* $\mathbf{v}_T$.

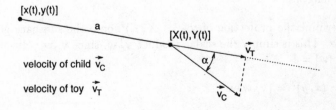

Figure 1.2 the following equations are obtained:

1. The distance between the points $(X(t), Y(t))$ and $(x(t), y(t))$ is always the length of the bar. Therefore

$$(X - x)^2 + (Y - y)^2 = a^2. \tag{1.4}$$

2. The toy is always moving in the direction of the bar. Therefore the difference vector of the two positions is a multiple of the velocity vector of the toy, $\mathbf{v}_T = (\dot{x}, \dot{y})^T$:

$$\begin{pmatrix} X - x \\ Y - y \end{pmatrix} = \lambda \begin{pmatrix} \dot{x} \\ \dot{y} \end{pmatrix} \quad \text{with} \quad \lambda > 0. \tag{1.5}$$

3. The speed of the toy depends on the direction of the velocity vector $\mathbf{v_C}$ of the child. Assume, e.g., that the child is walking on a circle of radius a (length of the bar). In this special case the toy will stay at the center of the circle and will not move at all (this is the final state of the first numerical example, see Figure 1.3).

From Figure 1.2 we see that *the modulus of the velocity $\mathbf{v_T}$ of the toy is given by the modulus of the projection of the velocity $\mathbf{v_C}$ of the child onto the bar.*

Inserting Equation (1.5) into Equation (1.4), we obtain

$$a^2 = \lambda^2(\dot{x}^2 + \dot{y}^2) \quad \longrightarrow \quad \lambda = \frac{a}{\sqrt{\dot{x}^2 + \dot{y}^2}}.$$

Therefore

$$\frac{a}{\sqrt{\dot{x}^2 + \dot{y}^2}} \begin{pmatrix} \dot{x} \\ \dot{y} \end{pmatrix} = \begin{pmatrix} X - x \\ Y - y \end{pmatrix}. \tag{1.6}$$

We would like to solve Equation (1.6) for $\dot{x}$ and $\dot{y}$. Since we know the modulus of the velocity vector of the toy $|\mathbf{v}_T| = |\mathbf{v}_C| \cos \alpha$, see Figure 1.2, this can be done by the following steps:

- Normalize the difference vector $(X - x, Y - y)^T$ and obtain a vector $\mathbf{w}$ of unit length.

- Determine the projection of $\mathbf{v}_C = (\dot{X}, \dot{Y})^T$ onto the subspace generated by $\mathbf{w}$. This is simply the scalar product $\mathbf{v}_C^T\mathbf{w}$, since $\mathbf{v}_C^T\mathbf{w} = |\mathbf{v}_C||\mathbf{w}| \cos \alpha$ and $|\mathbf{w}| = 1$.

- $\mathbf{v}_T = (\dot{x}, \dot{y})^T = (\mathbf{v}_C^T\mathbf{w})\mathbf{w}$.

Now we can write the function to evaluate the system of differential equations in MATLAB.

ALGORITHM 1.1. *Function f.*

```
function zs = f(t,z)
%
[X Xs Y Ys] = child(t);
v =[Xs; Ys];
w =[X-z(1); Y-z(2)];
w = w/norm(w);
zs = (v'*w)*w;
```

The function `f` calls the function `child` which returns the position $(X(t), Y(t))$ and velocity of the child $(Xs(t), Ys(t))$ for a given time `t`. As an example consider a child walking on the circle $X(t) = 5\cos t; Y(t) = 5\sin t$. The corresponding function `child` for this case is:

ALGORITHM 1.2. *Function Child.*

```
function [X, Xs, Y, Ys] = child(t);
%
  X  =  5*cos(t);   Y  =  5*sin(t);
  Xs = -5*sin(t);   Ys =  5*cos(t);
```

MATLAB offers two M-files `ode23` and `ode45` to integrate differential equations. In the following main program we will call one of these functions and also define the initial conditions (Note that for t= 0 the child is at the point $(5, 0)$ and the toy at $(10, 0)$):

```
>> % main1.m
>> y0 = [10 0]';
>> [t y] = ode45('f',0,100,y0)
>> axis([-6 10 -6 10])
>> axis('square')
>> hold
>> plot(y(:,1),y(:,2))
```

If we plot the two columns of y we obtain the orbit of the toy (cf. Figure 1.3). Furthermore we add the curve of the child in the same plot with the statements:

```
>> t = 0:0.05:6.3
>> [X, Xs, Y, Ys] = child(t);
>> plot(X,Y,':')
```

Note that the length of the bar a does not appear explicitly in the programs; *it is defined implicitly by the position of the toy, (initial condition), and the position of the child (function child) for $t = 0$.*

We conclude this section with some more examples. Let the child be walking along the graph of a sine function: $X(t) = t$ and $Y(t) = 5\sin t$. The child's curve is again plotted with a dotted line. With the initial conditions $x(0) = 0$ and $y(0) = 10$ we obtain Figure 1.4.

FIGURE 1.3. *Child Walks on the Circle.*

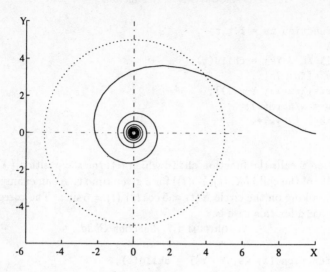

In the next example, the child is again walking on the circle $X(t) = 5\cos t$, $Y(t) = 5\sin t$. With the initial condition $x(0) = 0$ and $y(0) = 10$, we obtain a nice flower-like orbit of the toy (cf. Figure 1.5).

1.4   The Jogger and the Dog

We consider the following problem: a jogger is running along his favorite trail on the plane in order to get his daily exercise. Suddenly, he is being attacked by a dog. The dog is running with constant speed w towards the jogger. Compute the orbit of the dog.

The orbit of the dog has the property that the velocity vector of the dog points at every time to its goal, the jogger. We assume that the jogger is running on some trail and that his motion is described by the two functions $X(t)$ and $Y(t)$.

Let us assume that for $t = 0$ the dog is at the point (x_0, y_0), and that at time t his position will be $(x(t), y(t))$. The following equations hold:

1. $\dot{x}^2 + \dot{y}^2 = w^2$: The dog is running with constant speed.

2. The velocity vector of the dog is parallel to the difference vector between the position of the jogger and the dog:

$$\begin{pmatrix} \dot{x} \\ \dot{y} \end{pmatrix} = \lambda \begin{pmatrix} X - x \\ Y - y \end{pmatrix} \quad \text{with } \lambda > 0.$$

FIGURE 1.4. *Example 2.*

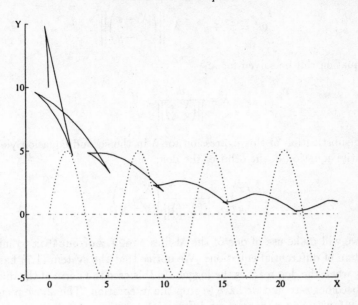

FIGURE 1.5. *Flower Orbit.*

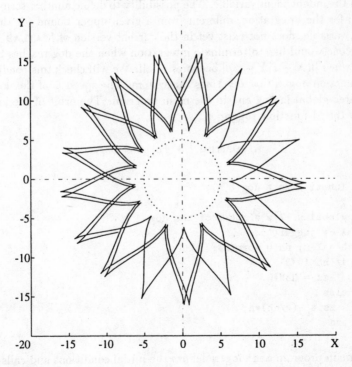

If we substitute this in the first equation we obtain

$$w^2 = \dot{x}^2 + \dot{y}^2 = \lambda^2 \left\| \begin{pmatrix} X - x \\ Y - y \end{pmatrix} \right\|^2.$$

This equation can be solved for λ:

$$\lambda = \frac{w}{\left\| \begin{pmatrix} X-x \\ Y-y \end{pmatrix} \right\|} > 0.$$

Finally, substitution of this expression for λ in the second equation yields the differential equation of the orbit of the dog:

$$\begin{pmatrix} \dot{x} \\ \dot{y} \end{pmatrix} = \frac{w}{\left\| \begin{pmatrix} X-x \\ Y-y \end{pmatrix} \right\|} \begin{pmatrix} X - x \\ Y - y \end{pmatrix}. \tag{1.7}$$

Again we will make use of one of the M-files ode23.m or ode45.m to integrate the system of differential equations. We notice that the system (1.7) has a singularity when the dog reaches the jogger. In this case the norm of the difference vector becomes zero and we have to stop the integration. The above mentioned MATLAB functions for integrating differential equations require as input an interval of the independent variable. The possibility to define another termination criterion for the integration, different from a given upper bound for the independent variable, does not exist yet in the current version of MATLAB. In our example one would like to terminate integration when the dog reaches the jogger, i.e. when $\|(X - x, Y - y)\|$ becomes small. We will check this condition in the M-function dog.m that describes the system. The speed w of the dog must be declared global in dog and in the main program. The orbit of the jogger is given by the M-function jogger.m.

ALGORITHM 1.3. *Function Dog.*

```
function zs = dog(t,z);
%
global w  % w = speed of the dog
X  = jogger(t);
h = X-z; nh = norm(h);
if nh<1e-3
   zs = NaN*h
else
   zs =  (w/nh)*h;
end
```

The main program maindog.m defines the initial conditions and calls ode23 for the integration. We have to provide an upper bound of the time t for the integration.

```
>> % main program for the dog orbit (main2.m)
>> global w
>> y0 = [60;70]   % initial conditions, starting point of the dog
>> w = 10;        % w  speed of the dog
>> [t,Y] = ode23('dog',0,20,y0,1e-5);
>> axis([0,100,-10,70])
>> hold on
>> plot(Y(:,1),Y(:,2))
>> J=[];

>> for h= 1: length(t),
>>    w  = jogger(t(h));
>>    J = [J; w'];
>> end
>> plot(J(:,1), J(:,2),':')
```

The integration will stop either if the upper bound for the time t is reached or if the dog catches up with the jogger. In the latter case we assign the value NaN (not a number) to the velocity vector in order to gracefully terminate the integration. After the call to ode23 the variable Y contains a table with the values of the two functions $x(t)$ and $y(t)$. We plot the orbit of the dog simply by the statement plot(Y(:,1),Y(:,2)). In order to show also the orbit of the jogger we have to compute it again using the vector t and the function jogger.

Let us now compute a few examples. First we let the jogger run along the x-axis:

ALGORITHM 1.4. *First Jogger Example.*

```
function s = jogger(t);
s    = [8*t; 0];
```

In the above main program we chose the speed of the dog as $w = 10$, and since here we have $X(t) = 8t$ the jogger is slower. As we can see in Figure 1.6 the dog is catching the poor jogger. The computation stops with the error message Singularity likely at t = 12.275326. This means that the difference between the two positions has become small, i.e. the dog has reached the jogger and because we assign NaN to the velocity vector we get the error message. If we wish to indicate the position of the jogger's troubles, *(perhaps to build a small memorial)*, we can make use of the following file cross.m

ALGORITHM 1.5. *Drawing a Cross.*

```
function cross(Cx,Cy,v)
% draws at position  Cx,Cy  a cross of height 2.5v
% and width 2*v
```

FIGURE 1.6. *Jogger Running on the Line* $y = 0$.

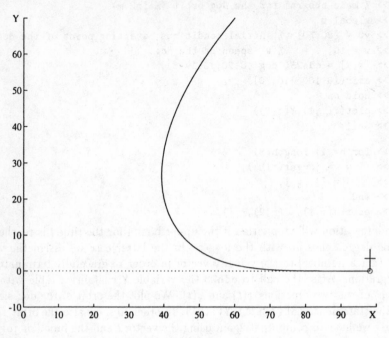

FIGURE 1.7. *Jogger Returning Back.*

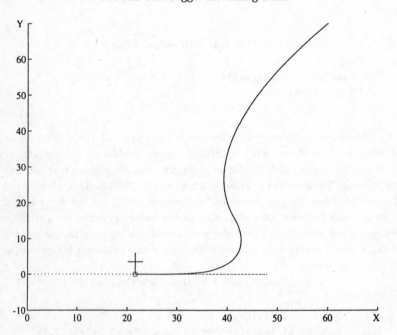

```
Kx = [Cx Cx Cx Cx-v Cx+v];
Ky = [Cy Cy+2.5*v Cy+1.5*v Cy+1.5*v Cy+1.5*v];
plot(Kx,Ky);
plot(Cx,Cy,'o');
```

The cross in the plot was generated by appending the statements

```
>> p = max(size(Y));
>> cross(Y(p,1),Y(p,2),2)
```

to the main program. The next example shows the situation where the jogger turns around and tries to run back home:

ALGORITHM 1.6. *Second Jogger Example.*

```
function s = jogger(t);
%
if t<6
    s    = [8*t; 0];
else
    s    = [8*(12-t) ;0];
end
```

However, using the same main program as before the dog catches up with the jogger at time $t = 9.3$ (cf. Figure 1.7). Let us now consider a faster jogger running on an ellipse

ALGORITHM 1.7. *Third Jogger Example.*

```
function s = jogger(t);
s    = [ 10+20*cos(t)
         20 + 15*sin(t)];
```

If the dog also runs fast ($w = 19$), he manages to reach the jogger at time $t = 8.97$ (cf. Figure 1.8). We finally consider an old, slow dog ($w = 10$). He tries to catch a jogger running on a elliptic track. However, instead of waiting for the jogger somewhere on the ellipse, he runs (too slow) after his target, and we can see a steady state developing where the dog is running on a closed orbit inside the ellipse (cf. Figure 1.9).

1.5   Showing the Motions with MATLAB

It would be nice to show simultaneously the motions of the child and the toy or the dog and the jogger instead of just plotting statically their orbits. This

FIGURE 1.8. *Jogger on an Ellipse.*

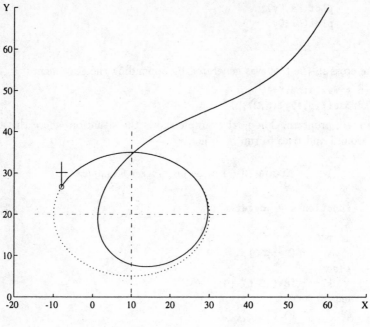

FIGURE 1.9. *Slow Dog.*

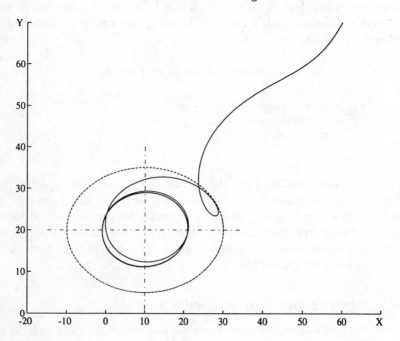

is possible using the new *handle graphics* commands in MATLAB. The main program for the child and its toy now looks as follows:

```
>> % main3.m
>> clf;
>> y0 = [0 20]';
>> [t y] = ode45 ('f', 0, 40, y0, 1E-10);
>> [X, Xs, Y, Ys] = child (t);

>> xmin = min (min (X), min (y (:, 1)));
>> xmax = max (max (X), max (y (:, 1)));
>> ymin = min (min (Y), min (y (:, 2)));
>> ymax = max (max (Y), max (y (:, 2)));

>> axis ([xmin xmax ymin ymax]);
>> axis('equal')
>> hold on;
>> title ('The Child and the Toy.');
>> stickhandle = line ('Color', 'yellow', 'EraseMode', 'xor', ...
>>              'LineStyle', '-', 'XData', [], 'YData', []);

>> for k = 1:length(t)-1,
>>    plot ([X(k), X(k+1)], [Y(k), Y(k+1)], '-', ...
>>         'Color', 'yellow', 'EraseMode', 'none');
>>    plot ([y(k,1), y(k+1,1)], [y(k,2), y(k+1,2)], '-', ...
>>         'Color', 'green', 'EraseMode', 'none');
>>    set (stickhandle, 'XData', [X(k+1), y(k+1,1)], ...
>>         'YData', [Y(k+1), y(k+1,2)]);
>>    drawnow;
>> end;
```

We define the variable `stickhandle` as a handle to a graphical object of type *line* associated with the stick. In the loop, we draw new segments of the child and toy orbits and move the position of the stick. The `drawnow` command forces these objects to be plotted instantaneously. Therefore, we can watch the two orbits and the stick being plotted simultaneously.

In the case of the jogger and the dog we do not even have to define a handle. All we have to do is to draw the segments of the two orbits in the proper sequence:

```
>> % main4.m
>> clf;
>> global w;
>> y0 = [60; 70]; % initial conditions, starting point of the dog
>> w = 10;        % w  speed of the dog
>> [t,Y] = ode23 ('dog', 0, 20, y0, 1e-5);
```

```
>> J=[];
>> for h= 1:length(t),
>>   w = jogger(t(h));
>>   J = [J; w'];
>> end

>> xmin = min (min (Y (:, 1)), min (J (:, 1)));
>> xmax = max (max (Y (:, 1)), max (J (:, 1)));
>> ymin = min (min (Y (:, 2)), min (J (:, 2)));
>> ymax = max (max (Y (:, 2)), max (J (:, 2)));
>> axis ([xmin xmax ymin ymax]);
>> axis ('equal');
>> hold on;
>> title ('The Jogger and the Dog.');

>> for h=1:length(t)-1,
>>    plot ([Y(h,1), Y(h+1,1)] , [Y(h,2), Y(h+1,2)], '-', ...
>>          'Color', 'yellow', 'EraseMode','none');
>>    plot ([J(h,1), J(h+1,1)] , [J(h,2), J(h+1,2)], ':', ...
>>          'Color', 'green', 'EraseMode','none');
>>  drawnow;
>> end
```

Acknowledgments:

The authors thank Dominik Gruntz and Urs von Matt for their help and advice in using MATLAB's handle graphics.

References

[1] E. HAIRER, S.P. NØRSETT and G. WANNER, *Solving Ordinary Differential Equations I*, Springer-Verlag Berlin Heidelberg, 1987.

[2] H. HEUSER, *Gewöhnliche Differentialgleichungen*, B. G. Teubner, Stuttgart, 1989.

Chapter 2. Trajectory of a Spinning Tennis Ball

F. Klvaňa

2.1 Introduction

Consider a tennis ball with mass m and diameter d, moving in air near the earth surface. The ball is spinning with angular velocity $\vec{\omega}$ (the vector $\vec{\omega}$ has the direction of the axis of rotation and magnitude $\omega = d\varphi(t)/dt = \dot{\varphi}(t)$, where $\varphi(t)$ is an angle of rotation). We will impose a Cartesian coordinates system (xyz) on the surface of the earth with the z axis directed vertically.

FIGURE 2.1. *Spinning Ball Moving in Air.*

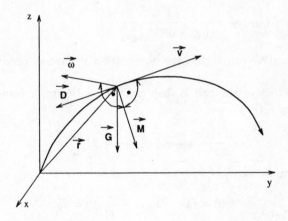

As a model of the ball we can then take a mass point, which is moving under influence of the following forces (cf. Figure 2.1)

- The weight force $\vec{G} = m\vec{g}$, where $\vec{g} = (0, 0, -g)$ is a vector of the gravitational acceleration.

- The drag force $\vec{D} = -D_L(v)\vec{v}/v$, which has opposite direction to the velocity $\vec{v}$.

- The Magnus force $\vec{M} = M_L\vec{\omega}/\omega \times \vec{v}/v$; this force is orthogonal to $\vec{v}$ and $\vec{\omega}$.

The magnitudes of the drag force $D_L(v)$ and the Magnus force $M_L(v)$ are usually supposed to have a form given by the theory of ideal fluids [1]:

$$D_L(v) = C_D \frac{1}{2} \frac{\pi d^2}{4} \rho v^2$$

$$M_L(v) = C_M \frac{1}{2} \frac{\pi d^2}{4} \rho v^2$$

(2.1)

where ρ is air density. The coefficients C_D and C_M depend for real fluids (air) on the velocity v, the ball revolution and the material of the surface of the ball. Usually we have to find this coefficients experimentally.

In [2] results of experiments with a spinning tennis ball are reported. It is shown that for a tennis ball in the regions of velocity $v \in [13.6, 28]$ $[m\ s^{-1}]$ and a ball revolution $n \in [800, 3250]$ rpm, the coefficients C_D and C_M depend on v/w only, where $w = d/2 \cdot |\vec{\omega} \times \vec{v}/v|$ is in some sense the projection of the equatorial velocity $\omega d/2$ of the spinning ball onto the velocity vector $\vec{v}$. The following expressions for the coefficients were obtained:

$$C_D = 0.508 + \left(\frac{1}{22.053 + 4.196 \left(\frac{v}{w} \right)^{5/2}} \right)^{2/5}$$

$$C_M = \frac{1}{2.022 + 0.981 \left(\frac{v}{w} \right)}$$

(2.2)

For a tennis ball we can neglect the deceleration of the ball revolution, so w is constant.

The trajectory of the ball is then defined by Newton's equations for the position vector $\vec{r}(t)$

$$m \frac{d^2 \vec{r}(t)}{dt^2} = -m\vec{g} - D_L \frac{\vec{v}}{v} + M_L \frac{\vec{\omega}}{\omega} \times \frac{\vec{v}}{v}$$

(2.3)

with initial conditions

$$\vec{r}(0) = \vec{r}_0 \qquad \text{and} \qquad \frac{d\vec{r}}{dt}(0) = \vec{v}_0.$$

The Equation (2.3) is a nonlinear system of three differential equations and no analytical solution exists for it, so we have to solve it numerically.

In practice, the most usual case is the topspin lob, for which the vector of angular velocity lies in a horizontal plane and is orthogonal to the vector $\vec{v}_0$, and, as follows from Equation (2.3), is also orthogonal to $\vec{v}(t)$ for $t \geq 0$; so the trajectory lies in the vertical plane. Let us choose the x axis in this plane. Then the final form of Equations (2.3) is

$$\ddot{x} = -C_D \alpha v \dot{x} + \eta C_M \alpha v \dot{z}$$

$$\ddot{z} = -g - C_D \alpha v \dot{z} - \eta C_M \alpha v \dot{x}$$

(2.4)

where $v = \sqrt{\dot{x}^2 + \dot{z}^2}$ and $\alpha = (\rho \pi d^2)/(8m)$. The parameter $\eta = \pm 1$ describes direction of rotation (for topspin $\eta = 1$).

As initial conditions for $t = 0$ we take

$$x(0) = 0, \quad z(0) = h, \quad \dot{x}(0) = v_0 \cos(\vartheta), \quad \dot{z}(0) = v_0 \sin(\vartheta) \qquad (2.5)$$

where v_0 is the magnitude of the initial velocity vector $\vec{v_0}$ and ϑ is an angle between $\vec{v_0}$ and $x-$axis.

2.2 MAPLE Solution

In order to demonstrate the influence of drag and Magnus forces on a trajectory of a ball, we will consider three models: a ball in vacuum, a ball in air without spin and a spinning ball.

Ball in Vacuum

In vacuum, the only force acting on the ball is gravity and the Equations (2.4) have a very simple form

$$\ddot{x} = 0, \quad \ddot{z} = -g \qquad (2.6)$$

MAPLE can find a general solution of (2.6) using function dsolve:

```
>                    # motion of ball in vacuum
> eqnid := diff(x(t), t$2) = 0, diff(z(t),t$2) = -g:
> varid := {x(t), z(t)}:
> initcid := x(0) = 0, z(0) = h,
>              D(x)(0) = v0*cos(theta), D(z)(0) = v0*sin(theta):
>              #solution for ball in vacuum
> resid := dsolve({eqnid, initcid}, varid);

resid :=

                                                               2
      {x(t) = v0 cos(theta) t, z(t) = h + v0 sin(theta) t - 1/2 g t }
```

Notice that function dsolve returns the solution $< result >$ in the form of a set of equations

$$< varname >=< expression >,$$

so there is no defined order of these equations. In order to access of individual solutions corresponding to $< varname >$ we will use the function

$$subs(< result >, < varname >).$$

Ball in the Air

For the models of a ball in the air we cannot solve Equations (2.4) analytically and we have to use a numeric solution. Since we want to use Netwon's method later to calculate a flight time, we need the derivative of $z(t)$ and hence we transform the differential equation system of second order (2.4) into a differential equation system of first order, (as the velocities $\dot{x}$ and $\dot{z}$ we use variables v_x and v_z),

$$
\begin{aligned}
\dot{x} &= v_x \\
\dot{v}_x &= -C_L\,\alpha\,v \cdot v_x + \eta\,C_M\,\alpha\,v \cdot v_z \\
\dot{z} &= v_z \\
\dot{v}_z &= -g - C_L\,\alpha\,v \cdot v_z - \eta\,C_M\,\alpha\,v \cdot v_x
\end{aligned}
\tag{2.7}
$$

where $v = \sqrt{v_x^2 + v_z^2}$. The initial conditions (2.5) have the form

$$
x(0) = 0, \quad z(0) = h, \quad v_x(0) = v_0\cos(\vartheta), \quad v_z(0) = v_0\sin(\vartheta). \tag{2.8}
$$

We will use the SI system of units. The numeric values of the parameters are $g = 9.81\ [m\,s^{-1}]$, diameter of the tennis ball $d = 0.063\ [m]$, its mass $m = 0.05\ [kg]$, and air density $\rho = 1.29\ [kg\,m^{-3}]$. As initial conditions we choose

$$
h = 1\ [m], \quad v_0 = 25\ [m\,s^{-1}], \quad \vartheta = 15°
$$

and as the parameters of the spin of a ball we take $w = 20\ [m\,s^{-1}]$ and $\eta = 1$ (top spin). The MAPLE statements to solve the problem follow.

```
>                    # numeric solution of ball in air
>                    # Basic constants in SI units
> g := 9.81:    # gravitational acceleration:
> d := 0.063: m := 0.05: # diameter and mass of ball
> rov := 1.29:  # density of air
> alpha := evalf(Pi*d^2/(8*m)*rov):
> v := (dx^2 + dz^2)^(1/2): # definition of velocity
> Cd := .508+1/(22.503 + 4.196/(w/v(t))^(5/2))^(2/5):
> Cm := eta/(2.202 + .981/(w/v(t))):
>                    # eta =+-1  defines direction of rotation,
>                    # for top spinning eta = 1
> var := {x(t), z(t), dx(t), dz(t)}:
>                    # initial conditions
> initc := x(0) = 0, z(0) = h,
>          dx(0) = v0*cos(theta), dz(0) = v0*sin(theta):
>                    # equations of motion of ball in air
>                    # rotation (drag force only)
> eqnt0:= diff(x(t),t) = dx(t),
>          diff(dx(t),t)= -0.508*alpha*dx(t)*v(t),
>          diff(z(t),t) = dz(t),
>          diff(dz(t),t)= -g-0.508*alpha*dz(t)*v(t):
>                    # equations of motion of rotating ball in air
>                    # (influence of Magnuse efect)
> eqnt1:= diff(x(t),t) = dx(t),
>          diff(dx(t),t)= (-Cd*dx(t) + Cm*dz(t))*alpha*v(t),
>          diff(z(t),t) = dz(t),
>          diff(dz(t),t)= -g-(Cd*dz(t) + Cm*dx(t))*alpha*v(t):
```

```
>                #numeric values of initial parameters
> h := 1: v0 := 25:   theta := Pi/180*15: # theta= 15 degrees
> w := 20:   eta := 1:
>                # solution for non rotating ball
> res0 := dsolve({eqnt0,initc},var,numeric);

res0 := proc(rkf45_x) ... end

>                # result is a set of equations
> res0(0.5);

   {dx(t) = 19.31511755, z(t) = 2.745476716, x(t) = 10.76902244,

       dz(t) = .7584804988, t = .5000000000}

>                # solution for rotating ball
> res1 := dsolve({eqnt1, initc}, var, numeric);

res1 := proc(rkf45_x) ... end
```

Function `dsolve(...,numeric)` returns as result a function with one parameter (independent variable). The result of a call of this function is a set of equations

$$< variable >=< value >$$

(in our case the variables are $t, x(t), z(t), v_x(t), v_z(t)$). For an access of numeric values we can again use the function **subs**.

Plotting the Graphs

As the final part of our solution we will plot the graphs of the trajectories for all three models in the same picture. For this we have to solve the subproblem of finding the flight time (solution of equation $z(t) = 0$).

To compute the flight time for the ball in vacuum t_{maxid}, we can use the symbolic solution of (2.6) in res_{id} and the function **fsolve**.

```
>                # calculation of tmax - time of falling to earth
>                # for ball in vacuum
> tmaxid := fsolve(subs(resid, z(t)) = 0, t, t = 0..5);

                      tmaxid := 1.458903640
```

In the other cases we can easily use Newton's method to solve equation $z(t) = 0$, because by integrating the differential equations we obtain also the derivative of z in variable v_z. Then the recurrence relation for the sequence of approximations of the solution of equation $z(t) = 0$ will be

$$t_{n+1} = t_n - \frac{z(t_n)}{v_z(t_n)}. \tag{2.9}$$

As the initial approximation t_0 we can use t_{maxid}. See the MAPLE function **zzero**, which implements this Newton iteration (cf. Algorithm 2.1).

ALGORITHM 2.1. *Function* zzero.

```
zzero := proc (u, t0, z, dz) local tn, ts, up;
        # find root of z(t) = subs(u(t), z) = 0
        # using Newton method
        # using diff(z, t) = subs(u(t), dz)
    tn := t0; ts := 0.0;
    while abs((tn - ts)/tn) > 10^(-4) do;
        ts := tn;
        up := u(ts);
        tn := ts - subs(up, z)/subs(up, dz);
    od;
    tn;
end:
```

```
>            # calculation of the flight time for the other models
> tmax0:= zzero(res0, tmaxid, z(t), dz(t));
```

$$tmax0 := 1.362022988$$

```
> tmax1:= zzero(res1, tmaxid, z(t), dz(t));
```

$$tmax1 := .9472277855$$

The simplest, (and probably the fastest) method for creating the graphs of our ball trajectories in air (from a numeric solution) is to use an array $[x(t_i), z(t_i)]$ as an input parameter for the function plot. To create this array from the result of dsolve(..., numeric) for a time interval with constant time step we define the simple function *tablepar*. The rest of the MAPLE statements for the creation of the graphs in red, blue and black color will then be

```
>            # making graphs:
> Gid := plot([subs(resid, x(t)), subs(resid, z(t)),
>            t=0..tmaxid], color=red):
>            # for models with numeric solution
>            # calculation of tables [x(t),z(t)]  for plotting
> tablepar := proc(u, x, y, xmin, xmax, npoints) local i,Step;
>     Step := (xmax - xmin)/npoints;
>     [seq([subs(u(xmin + i*Step), x), subs(u(xmin + i*Step) ,y)],
>         i = 0 .. npoints)]
> end:
> G0 := plot(tablepar(res0, x(t), z(t), 0, tmax0, 15),
>         color = blue):
> G1 := plot(tablepar(res1, x(t), z(t), 0, tmax1, 15)):
>            # plotting of all graphs
> plots[display]({Gid, G0, G1});
```

MAPLE cannot generate graphs with different type of lines. So to show the different graphs we have used MATLAB to plot the trajectories (cf. Figure 2.2).

ALGORITHM 2.2. *A Set of Needed m-Functions.*

```
function xdot= tennisip(t,x)
global g
    xdot(1) = x(3);
    xdot(2) = x(4);
    xdot(3) = 0;
    xdot(4) = -g;

function xdot= tennisOp(t,x)
global g alpha
    v= sqrt(x(3)^2+x(4)^2);
    xdot(1) = x(3);
    xdot(2) = x(4);
    xdot(3) = -alpha*0.508*x(3)*v;
    xdot(4) = -g-alpha*0.508*x(4)*v;

function xdot= tennis1p(t,x)
global g alpha w etha
    v = sqrt(x(3)^2 + x(4)^2);
    Cd = (0.508 + 1/(22.503 + 4.196*(v/w)^0.4))*alpha*v;
    Cm = etha*w/(2.022*w + 0.981*v)*alpha*v;
    xdot(1) = x(3);
    xdot(2) = x(4);
    xdot(3) = -Cd*x(3) + Cm*x(4);
    xdot(4) = -g-Cd*x(4) - Cm*x(3);
```

2.3   MATLAB **Solution**

Because of the nonlinear nature of our problem we have to use numerical methods to solve it. A numerical system like MATLAB appears to be more adequate than a symbolic one. So we will now try to solve our problem in MATLAB.

To solve an initial value problem of a system of n differential equations

$$\frac{d\vec{x}}{dt} = \vec{f}(t, \vec{x}), \tag{2.10}$$

where $\vec{x} = (x_1, x_2, ..., x_n)$, we can use the MATLAB function **ode23** (or **ode45**), which implements an embedded Runge-Kutta method of order 2 and 3 (respectively 4 and 5).

We have to define a m-function for each model to implement the system of differential Equations (2.10). To transfer the parameters g, α, w, η into the m-files we define them as global in our program. Let we use the following mapping of variables

$$x \longrightarrow x(1), \quad z \longrightarrow x(2), \quad v_x \longrightarrow x(3), \quad v_z \longrightarrow x(4).$$

Needed m-files are in Algorithm (2.2). In the following main program we compute and plot the trajectories for all three models (cf. Figure 2.2). To compute a sufficient dense table $[x_i, z_i]$ to plot the ball trajectories for the models in the air, we interpolate by a spline function 100 points of the solution $z = z(x)$, using the functions spline.

```
>>          % Trajectory of spinning tennis ball
>>          % initialization
>> global g alpha w etha
>>          % basic constants im MKS units
>> g = 9.81; d = 0.063; m = 0.05; rho = 1.29;
>> alpha=pi*d^2/(8*m)*rho;
>> etha = 1;
>> w = 20;
>>          % initial conditions
>> h = 1; v0 = 25; theta = pi/180*15;
>> xin = [0, h, v0*cos(theta), v0*sin(theta)];
>>          % flight time for vacuum
>> tmaxid = (xin(4) + sqrt(xin(4)^2 + 2*g*xin(2)))/g;
>>          % solution in vacuum
>> [tid, xid] = ode23('tennisip', 0, tmaxid, xin);
>>          % solution without spin
>> [t0, x0] = ode23('tennis0p', 0, tmaxid, xin);
>>          % solution with spin
>> [t1, x1] = ode23('tennis1p', 0, tmaxid, xin);
>> N = max(xid(:, 1)); x = 0:N/100:N;
>> axis([0,max(xid(:,1)), 0, max(xid(:,2))])
>> hold
>> plot(x, spline(xid(:,1), xid(:, 2), x), ':r');
>> plot(x, spline(x0(:,1), x0(:, 2), x), '--b');
>> plot(x, spline(x1(:,1), x1(:, 2), x), '-w');
```

Note that we did not have to compute the flight time for the two models in the air. By using the axis statement for the largest trajectory (the ball in vacuum) followed by a hold statement the trajectories are truncated and not plotted below the x-axis.

If we wish to actually compute the flight times we could proceed similarly as shown in the MAPLE solution. This solution is rather costly in terms of computing time, since for each evaluation of the function and the derivative we have to integrate numerically the system of differential equations from the beginning.

It is simpler, however, to compute an approximation of the flight time using inverse interpolation. In order to do so we need to find a time interval in which the function is invertible. For this we take those values in the table where the z-values of the trajectory are monotonically decreasing. This can be done with the min and max function:

```
>>          % Determine flight time  by inverse interpolation
>> [z, j] = min(x0(:, 2)); [y, i] = max(x0(:, 2));
>> tmax0 = spline(x0(i + 1:j, 2), t0(i + 1:j), 0)
>> [z, j] = min(x1(:, 2)); [y, i] = max(x1(:, 2));
>> tmax1 = spline(x1(i+1:j,2), t1(i+1:j), 0)
```

We have to take as the first point of the monotonic region of z the point with the index $(i + 1)$ in order to ensure the region $z(i + 1 : j)$ is monotonic. We then obtain for the flight times the approximate values $t_{max0} = 1.3620$ and $t_{max1} = 0.9193$ which compare well with the MAPLE results.

FIGURE 2.2.

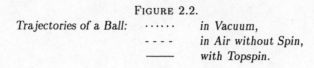

Trajectories of a Ball:	· · · · ·	*in Vacuum,*
	- - - -	*in Air without Spin,*
	————	*with Topspin.*

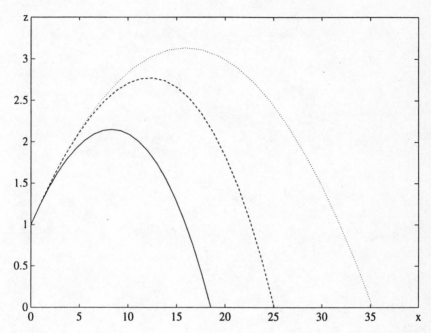

References

[1] E. G. RICHARDSON, *Dynamics of Real Fluids*, Edward Arnold, 1961.

[2] A. ŠTĚPÁNEK, *The Aerodynamics of Tennis Balls - The Topspin Lob*, American Journal of Physics, 56, 1988, pp. 138 – 142.

Chapter 3. The Illumination Problem

S. Bartoň and D. Gruntz

3.1 Introduction

In this article we consider a horizontal road illuminated by two lights, where P_i is the illumination power and h_i the height of a lamp. The coordinates of the lamps are $(0,\ h_1)$ and $(s,\ h_2)$ where s is the horizontal distance between the two light sources. Let $X = (x,0)$ be a point on the road somewhere between the two lights. In this chapter we will look for a point X which is minimally illuminated. In Figure 3.1 we have made a sketch of the situation we will refer to later in this chapter.

FIGURE 3.1. *Illumination Problem Description.*

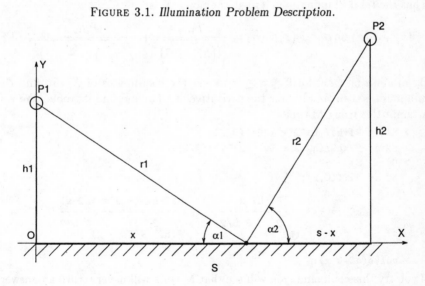

In the first section we will find X given the height and the intensity of both lamps. In the second section we will maximize the illumination at X by varying the height of the second lamp. In the last section we will go even further and optimize the illumination at X with respect to the heights of both lamps. In effect, we will optimize the illumination of the road by varying the heights of the lamps.

3.2 Finding the Minimal Illumination Point on a Road

In this section we look for the minimal illuminated point X between the two light sources. It is known from physics, that the light intensity depends on the inverse value of the square of the distance to the light source and on the impact angle of the light rays, see [1, 2].

The distance from X to the first light source is x and to the second one $s-x$. Using the Pythagorean theorem we can determine r_1 and r_2, the distances from X to the two light sources,

$$r_1{}^2 = h_1{}^2 + x^2, \quad r_2{}^2 = h_2{}^2 + (s-x)^2.$$

The light intensities from the two lamps at X are given by

$$I_1(x) = \frac{P_1}{r_1{}^2} = \frac{P_1}{h_1{}^2 + x^2}, \quad I_2(x) = \frac{P_2}{r_2{}^2} = \frac{P_2}{h_2{}^2 + (s-x)^2}.$$

If the impact angles of the light rays are α_1 and α_2, the road illumination depends on $\sin\alpha_1$ and $\sin\alpha_2$ which are given by

$$\sin\alpha_1 = \frac{h_1}{\sqrt{h_1{}^2 + x^2}}, \quad \sin\alpha_2 = \frac{h_2}{\sqrt{h_2{}^2 + (s-x)^2}}.$$

Thus the total illumination $C(x)$ at the point X is

$$C(x) = I_1(x)\sin\alpha_1 + I_2(x)\sin\alpha_2 = \frac{P_1 h_1}{\sqrt{\left(h_1{}^2 + x^2\right)^3}} + \frac{P_2 h_2}{\sqrt{\left(h_2{}^2 + (s-x)^2\right)^3}}. \quad (3.1)$$

By minimizing $C(x)$ for $0 \le x \le s$ we get the coordinates of X. To find the minimum we can simply take the derivative of $C(x)$ and find its roots. We will attempt this using MAPLE.

```
> S1 := P1*h1/(h1^2 + x^2)^(3/2):
> S2 := P2*h2/(h2^2 + (s - x)^2)^(3/2):
> C := S1 + S2:
> dC := diff(C,x);

                 P1 h1 x              P2 h2 (- 2 s + 2 x)
     dC := - 3 --------------- - 3/2 --------------------
                 2      2 5/2          2            2 5/2
               (h1  + x )            (h2  + (s - x) )
```

```
> solve(dC=0,x):
```

If you try this command, you will see that MAPLE will never return an answer. Using algebraic manipulations, the equation dC=0 can be transformed into a polynomial in x. In particular we will move one of the terms of the equation to the right hand side, square both sides, move the right hand side back to the left and write the expression over a common denominator. We observe that the numerator must be zero.

```
> eq := diff(S1,x)^2 - diff(S2,x)^2;
```

$$eq := 9 \; \frac{P1^2 \; h1^2 \; x^2}{(h1^2 + x^2)^5} - \frac{9}{4} \; \frac{P2^2 \; h2^2 \; (-2s + 2x)^2}{(h2^2 + (s-x)^2)^5}$$

```
> eq := collect(primpart(numer(eq)), x);
```

The result of the last command is a degree 12 polynomial in x,

$$(P_1^2 h_1^2 - P_2^2 h_2^2)x^{12} + (2P_2^2 h_2^2 s - 10 P_1^2 h_1^2 s)x^{11} + \cdots - P_2^2 h_2^2 h_1^{10} s^2 = 0. \qquad (3.2)$$

This polynomial is difficult to solve in closed form without specifying the constants.

We consider the following numerical values: $P_1 = 2000 \; [W]$, $P_2 = 3000 \; [W]$, $h_1 = 5 \; [m]$, $h_2 = 6 \; [m]$ and $s = 20 \; [m]$. The functions $C(x)$, $C'(x) \equiv \mathrm{dC}$, $S_1(x)$ and $S_2(x)$ (the illumination intensities on the road implied by each lamp separately) can be plotted using MAPLE, see Figure 3.2. An interval containing the zero of the function $C'(x)$ can be picked off from this graph. We will use this interval to determine X using `fsolve`.

FIGURE 3.2. *Illumination as a Function of the Position.*

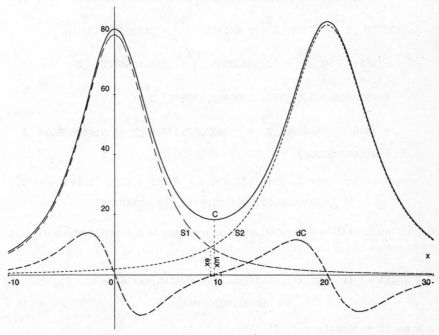

```
> P1 := 2000:  P2 := 3000:  s := 20:  h1 := 5:  h2 := 6:
> plot({C, S1, S2, dC}, x=-s/2..s*3/2);
> xm := fsolve(dC = 0, x, 5..10);
```

```
                              xm := 9.338299136

> Cmin := subs(x=xm,C);

                              Cmin := 18.24392572

> xe := fsolve(S1 = S2, x, 0..s);

                              xe := 9.003061731

> dx := xm - xe;

                              dx := .335237405
```

It is interesting to note, that the position X differs from the point x_e which is equally illuminated from both lamps.

For this numerical example we can also determine the point X directly. We can apply the `solve` command to Equation (3.2) and obtain an algebraic number defined by a degree 12 polynomial with integer coefficients. Real (physical) solutions correspond to points between the two light sources.

```
> solve(eq,x);

             12            11            10            9
RootOf(56 _Z   + 1760 _Z   - 411975 _Z   + 24315000 _Z

            8               7                 6
  - 886167750 _Z + 22194630000 _Z - 388140507750 _Z

                  5                 4
  + 4698666870000 _Z - 37664582848875 _Z

                    3                  2
  + 180676117955000 _Z - 393823660188775 _Z - 31640625000 _Z

  + 316406250000)

> select(t -> type(t, numeric) and t > 0 and t < s, [allvalues(")]);
              [.02848997038, 9.338299136, 19.97669581]
```

MAPLE returned three extremas, and it is necessary to determine which solution is a minimum.

```
> map(t -> if subs(x=t, diff(dC, x))<0 then max else min fi, ");
                         [max, min, max]

> map(t -> subs(x = t, C), "");
              [81.98104008, 18.24392572, 84.47655488]
```

As can be seen the same result was obtained for X, namely $x = 9.338299136$. Notice that the maximal illuminated points are located nearby the two lamps and not immediately beneath them.

3.3 Varying h_2 to Maximize the Illumination

In this section we use the same numerical values as in the previous one but consider the height of the second light source as a variable and maximize the illumination at X. Hence $C(x, h_2)$ is a function of two variables.

As a first step, we find the function $x(h_2)$ such that

$$C(x(h_2), h_2) = \min_{0 \le x \le s} C(x, h_2).$$

To do so, we vary h_2 from 3 $[m]$ to 9 $[m]$ and resolve the problem for each value of h_2 as in the last section.

```
> h2 := 'h2':
> H2 := array(0..30):  # array for the values of h2
> X  := array(0..30):  # array for the values of x(h2)
> for i from 0 to 30 do
>     H2[i] := 3 + 6*i/30:
>     X[i] := fsolve(subs(h2=H2[i], dC), x, 0..s):
> od:
> H2 := convert(H2, list):
> X  := convert(X, list):
```

Figure 3.3 is a plot of $x(h_2)$ generated with the following command:

```
> plot(zip((h2,x)->[h2,x], H2, X), 3..9);
```

FIGURE 3.3.
x-Coordinate of the Minimal Illuminated Point for
$$3 \le h_2 \le 9.$$

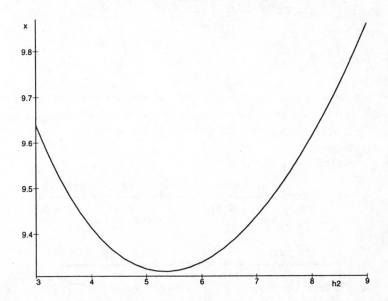

We will plot $C(x, h_2)$ as a 3-dimensional plot and overlay it with the space curve $C(x(h_2), h_2)$ of the points with minimal illumination. As expected, the space curve lies in the valley of $C(x, h_2)$.

```
> f := unapply(C, x, h2):
> P := [seq([X[i], H2[i], f(X[i], H2[i])], i=1..31)]:
> PL1 := PLOT3D(CURVES(P), STYLE(LINE)):
> PL2 := plot3d(C, x=-s/2..3*s/2, h2=3..9, style = WIREFRAME):
> plots[display]([PL1,PL2]);
```

FIGURE 3.4. *Illumination Function* $C(x, h_2)$.

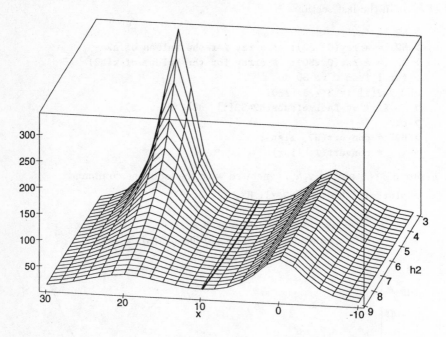

As a second step we find the point of maximal illumination on the curve $x(h_2)$. This point is among the stationary points of the function $C(x, h_2)$, i.e. among the points where the gradient of $C(x, h_2)$ becomes zero.

```
> with(linalg):
> g := grad(C, [x, h2]);
```

$$g := [\, -30000 \frac{x}{(25 + x^2)^{5/2}} - 4500 \frac{h2\,(-40 + 2x)}{(h2^2 + (20 - x)^2)^{5/2}},$$

$$\frac{3000}{(h2^2 + (20 - x)^2)^{3/2}} - 9000 \frac{h2^2}{(h2^2 + (20 - x)^2)^{5/2}}\,]$$

```
> Sol := fsolve({g[1]=0,g[2]=0}, {x,h2}, {x=0..s, h2=3..9});
```

$$Sol := \{h2 = 7.422392890, \ x = 9.503151310\}$$

In order to verify that this solution is a maximum we look at the eigenvalues of the Hessian of $C(x, h_2)$ at the above point.

```
> H := subs(Sol, hessian(C, [x,h2]));
```

$$H := \begin{bmatrix} 1.056539134 & -.1793442077 \\ -.1793442077 & -.2536310107 \end{bmatrix}$$

```
> eigenvals(H);
```

$$-.277737220, \ 1.080645343$$

The different signs of the eigenvalues tell us that we have found a saddle point. Since $H[1,1] = \partial^2 C/\partial x^2 \doteq 1.06 > 0$ we have a minimum in x-direction, and since $H[2,2] = \partial^2 C/\partial h_2{}^2 \doteq -0.25 < 0$ we have a maximum in h_2-direction, hence we found what we were looking for, namely the maximal illuminated point among all minimal illuminated points $(x(h_2), 0)$.

Note that we can analytically solve the second equation g[2]=0 for h2 in our numerical example.

```
> {solve(g[2] = 0, h2)};
```

$$\{1/2 \ 2^{1/2} \ (s - x), \ - 1/2 \ 2^{1/2} \ (s - x)\}$$

This means that for the optimal height of the second lamp, the impact angle α_2 is given by

```
> tan(alpha2) = normal("[1]/(s-x));
```

$$tan(alpha2) = 1/2 \ 2^{1/2}$$

```
> evalf(arctan(rhs(")));
```

$$.6154797085$$

```
> evalf(convert(", degrees));
```

$$35.26438965 \ degrees$$

or $\alpha_2 = 35° \ 15' \ 51.8028''$.

3.4 Optimal Illumination

It is very important to have a homogeneous illumination on a road. This problem cannot be solved using point-light sources. We will always obtain a maximal illumination beneath the light sources and a minimum somewhere between them. But for lamps of a given illumination and a given separation we can maximize the illumination of the minimally illuminated point by adjusting the heights of the light sources. We will consider this problem in this section.

The total illumination $C(x, h_1, h_2)$ is now a function of three variables. The minimal illuminated point is again, as in lower dimensions, determined by the roots of the gradient of C. We try to find a general solution; in MAPLE this means unassigning the variables we used for the numerical example.

```
> P1 := 'P1': P2 := 'P2': h1 := 'h1': h2 := 'h2': s := 's':
> g := grad(C, [x, h1, h2]);

                P1 h1 x              P2 h2 (- 2 s + 2 x)
    g := [ - 3 -------------- - 3/2 --------------------,
               2     2 5/2           2          2 5/2
            (h1  + x )              (h2  + (s - x) )

                                         2
            P1                       P1 h1
    -------------- - 3 --------------,
     2     2 3/2        2     2 5/2
    (h1  + x )         (h1  + x )

                                             2
            P2                       P2 h2
    -------------------- - 3 -------------------- ]
     2          2 3/2         2          2 5/2
    (h2  + (s - x) )         (h2  + (s - x) )
```

MAPLE cannot analytically solve for the roots of equation $\mathbf{g} = 0$. However, we can solve the second equation for h_1 and the third for h_2.

```
> sh1 := {solve(g[2] = 0, h1)};

               1/2            1/2
    sh1 := {1/2 2    x, - 1/2 2    x}

> sh2 := {solve(g[3] = 0, h2)};

                       1/2                1/2
    sh2 := {1/2 (s - x) 2   , - 1/2 (s - x) 2   }
```

We are interested in positive values only since it is rather unusual to illuminate a road from below.

```
> h1o := sh1[1];

              1/2
    h1o := 1/2 2    x

> h2o:= sh2[1];

                       1/2
    h2o := 1/2 (s - x) 2
```

Note that the optimal height for each lamp is independent of the illumination powers. This result defines the geometry! Hence the impact angles are the same as the one we computed in Section 3.3, namely

$$\tan \alpha_1 = \tan \alpha_2 = \frac{\sqrt{2}}{2} \quad \Rightarrow \alpha_1 = \alpha_2 = 35° \ 15' \ 51.8028''.$$

By substituting the optimal heights into g[1] we can find the overall solution. We assign the real solution to the variable xo since it is the only physically realistic solution.

```
> G := subs(h1 = h1o, h2 = h2o, g[1]);
```

$$G := -\frac{4}{9} \frac{P1\ x^2\ 3^{1/2}}{(x^2)^{5/2}} - \frac{2}{9} \frac{P2\ (s-x)\ 3^{1/2}\ (-2s+2x)}{((s-x)^2)^{5/2}}$$

The equation g[1] = 0 can be solved directly using the command

```
> Xsols := {solve(G=0,x)};
```

$$Xsols := \{$$

$$RootOf((P2 + P1)\ \_Z^3 - 3\ P1\ \_Z^2\ s + 3\ P1\ \_Z\ s^2 - P1\ s^3),$$

$$RootOf((P2 - P1)\ \_Z^3 + 3\ P1\ \_Z^2\ s - 3\ P1\ \_Z\ s^2 + P1\ s^3)\}$$

A geometrical determination of the optimal illumination and its physical interpretation for given values of P1, P2 and s can be found with some simple manipulations.

```
> eq1 := op(1,G)^2 = normal(op(2, G))^2;
```

$$eq1 := \frac{16}{27}\frac{P1^2}{x^6} = \frac{16}{27}\frac{P2^2}{(s-x)^6}$$

```
> eq2 := eq1*27*x^6*(s-x)^6/16;
```

$$eq2 := (s-x)^6\ P1^2 = x^6\ P2^2$$

```
> eq3:= simplify(map(u->u^(1/6), eq2), symbolic);
```

$$eq3 := (s-x)\ P1^{1/3} = x\ P2^{1/3}$$

The last simplification is valid since we know that all the values P1, P2, x are positive and $x < s$. The obtained equation can be interpreted as follows: The maximum illumination of the minimally illimunated point is received if the quotient of the distances x and $s - x$ is equal to the quotient of the cube roots of the light powers. In other words: The maximum possible illumination of the minimum illuminated point is reached if the volume densities of the illuminating powers are equal.

```
> xo := normal(solve(eq3, x));
```

$$\text{xo} := \frac{P1^{1/3}\, s}{P1^{1/3} + P2^{1/3}}$$

Let us plot the optimally illuminated point xo as a function of the power of the light sources for the case $s = 20$. We will then determine the optimal heights for the case $P_1 = 2000$ and $P_2 = 3000$

```
> s := 20:
> plot3d(xo, P1=0..2000, P2=0..3000, orientation=[110,60],
>          axes=BOXED);
> P1 := 2000: P2 := 3000: x := xo:
> h1 := h1o;
```

$$h1 := 10\,\frac{2^{1/2}\, 2000^{1/3}}{3000^{1/3} + 2000^{1/3}}$$

```
> evalf(");
```

$$6.593948668$$

```
> h2 := h2o;
```

$$h2 := \frac{1}{2}\left(20 - 20\,\frac{2000^{1/3}}{3000^{1/3} + 2000^{1/3}}\right)^{1/2} 2$$

```
> evalf(");
```

$$7.548186950$$

As we can see from Figure 3.5, for a wide range of power values the optimal illuminated point xo is around $s/2 = 10$. This can also be seen by comparing the values of xo and xm, the position of minimal illumination computed in the first section. The relative difference is

```
> evalf( (xm-xo)/xm );
```

$$.0013972025$$

but the relative difference of the illuminations is

```
> evalf( (C - Cmin)/Cmin );
```

$$.040658247$$

which is about 30 times larger.

Finally in Figure 3.6 we will compare the optimal solution Cop with that of Section 3.2 where we used the fixed heights $h_1 = 5$ and $h_2 = 6$.

```
> Copmin := evalf(C);
```

FIGURE 3.5. xo *as a Function of P_1 and P_2.*

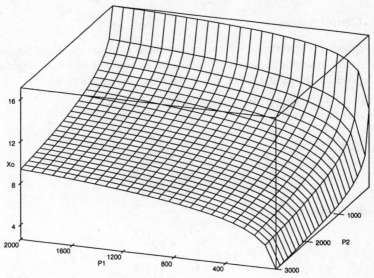

FIGURE 3.6. *The Optimal Illumination.*

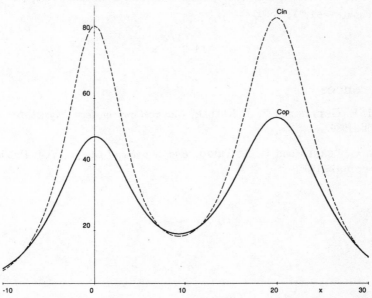

```
                        Copmin := 18.98569176

> x := 'x': Cop := C: h1 := 5: h2 := 6:
> plot({C, Cop}, x = -s/2..3*s/2);
```

3.5   Conclusion

Based on our computations we can make some recommendations to persons
involved with road illumination. If we insert xo into the optimal heights then
they depend on the light powers P_1, P_2 and the distance s only.

```
> P1 := 'P1': P2 := 'P2': s := 's':
> subs(x=xo, h1o);
```

$$\frac{1}{2} \frac{2^{1/2} P1^{1/3} s}{P2^{1/3} + P1^{1/3}}$$

```
> normal(subs(x=xo, h2o));
```

$$\frac{1}{2} \frac{2^{1/2} s P2^{1/3}}{P2^{1/3} + P1^{1/3}}$$

For the special case $P_1 = P_2$ the optimal height for both lamps is $s/\sqrt{8}$.

```
> subs(P1=P2,");
```

$$\frac{1}{4} 2^{1/2} s$$

References

[1] M. E. GETTYS and F. J. KELLER, *Classical and modern Physics*, Mc. Graw
    Hill, 1989.

[2] R. G. LERNER and G. L. TRIGG, *Encyclopedia of physics*, VCH Publishers,
    New York, 1991.

Chapter 4. Orbits in the Planar Three-Body Problem

D. Gruntz and J. Waldvogel

4.1   Introduction

The planar three-body problem is the problem of describing the motion of three point masses in the plane under their mutual Newtonian gravitation. It is a popular application of numerical integration of systems of ordinary differential equations since most solutions are too complex to be described in terms of known functions.

In addition, the three-body problem is a classical problem with a long history and many applications (see e.g. the exhaustive accounts by Szebehely [9] or by Marchal [4]). Nevertheless, the sometimes complicated interplay of the three bodies can often be described in terms of two body interactions and is therefore qualitatively simple to understand. About 100 years ago the French Academy of Sciences set out a prize for the solution of the problem which was awarded to Sundman [7] for a series solution convergent at all times. However, due to the excessively slow convergence of Sundman's series it is of no practical value for discussing orbits.

In this article we will demonstrate how MAPLE and MATLAB can be used efficiently to construct and display numerical solutions of the planar three-body problem. In Section 4.2 we will straight-forwardly use the differential equations of motion and the numerical integrator of MATLAB. Although for most initial conditions this approach will quickly produce an initial segment of the solution, it will usually fail at a sufficiently close encounter of two bodies due to the singularity at the corresponding collision.

In classical celestial mechanics the regularizing transformation by T. Levi-Civita [3] is an efficient technique to overcome the problems of numerically integrating over a collision or near-collision between two bodies. Since three different pairs can be formed with three bodies it was suggested by Szebehely and Peters [8] to apply Levi-Civita's transformation to the closest pair if the mutual distance becomes smaller than a certain limit.

In Section 4.3 we will use a set of variables suggested by Waldvogel [10] that amounts to automatically regularizing each of the three types of close encounters whenever they occur. Due to the complexity of the transformed equations of motion the Hamiltonian formalism will be used for deriving these equations. Then MAPLE's capability of differentiating algorithms (automatic differentiation) will be used to generate the regularized equations of motion.

4.2   Equations of Motion in Physical Coordinates

Let $m_j > 0$ $(j = 0, 1, 2)$ be the masses of the three bodies, and let $x_j \in \mathbb{R}^2$ and $\dot{x}_j \in \mathbb{R}^2$ be their position and velocity (column) vectors in an inertial coordinate system (dots denoting derivatives with respect to time t). For the mutual distances of the bodies the notation of Figure 4.1 will be used:

$$r_0 = |x_2 - x_1|, \quad r_1 = |x_0 - x_2|, \quad r_2 = |x_1 - x_0|. \tag{4.1}$$

FIGURE 4.1. *The Three-Body Problem in Physical Coordinates.*

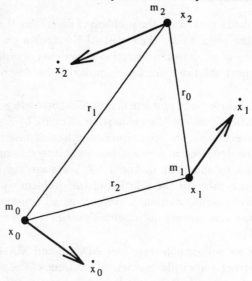

Next we notice that the Newtonian gravitational force F exerted onto m_0 by m_1 is given by

$$F = -m_0\, m_1 \frac{x_0 - x_1}{|x_0 - x_1|^3}$$

if the units of length, time and mass are chosen such that the gravitational constant has the value 1. Therefore the Newtonian equations of motion (in their most primitive form) become

$$
\begin{aligned}
\ddot{x}_0 &= m_1 \frac{x_1 - x_0}{r_2{}^3} + m_2 \frac{x_2 - x_0}{r_1{}^3} \\
\ddot{x}_1 &= m_2 \frac{x_2 - x_1}{r_0{}^3} + m_0 \frac{x_0 - x_1}{r_2{}^3} \\
\ddot{x}_2 &= m_0 \frac{x_0 - x_2}{r_1{}^3} + m_1 \frac{x_1 - x_2}{r_0{}^3}.
\end{aligned}
\tag{4.2}
$$

This system of 12 degrees of freedom may be integrated by MATLAB in a straight-forward manner by defining the (column) vector $Y \in \mathbb{R}^{12}$ of dependent variables as, e.g.,

$$Y = [x_0; \; \dot{x}_0; \; x_1; \; \dot{x}_1; \; x_2; \; \dot{x}_2].$$

The system (4.2) may then be coded by the MATLAB function Ydot = f(t,Y) presented as Algorithm 4.1.

ALGORITHM 4.1. *Function* Ydot.

```
function Ydot = f(t, Y)

global m0 m1 m2 % masses of the three bodies

x0 = Y(1:2); x1 = Y(5:6); x2 = Y(9:10);
d0 = (x2-x1)/norm(x2-x1)^3;
d1 = (x0-x2)/norm(x0-x2)^3;
d2 = (x1-x0)/norm(x1-x0)^3;

Ydot( 1: 2) = Y( 3: 4);
Ydot( 5: 6) = Y( 7: 8);
Ydot( 9:10) = Y(11:12);
Ydot( 3: 4) = m1*d2 - m2*d1;
Ydot( 7: 8) = m2*d0 - m0*d2;
Ydot(11:12) = m0*d1 - m1*d0;
```

A call to MATLAB's integrator ode45 together with a few additional lines of MATLAB code produces the orbits of the three bodies.

```
>> m0 = 5; m1 = 3; m2 = 4; global m0 m1 m2
>> x00 = [1;-1]; x10 = [1;3]; x20 = [-2;-1]; xp0 = [0;0];
>> [T1,Y1] = ode45('f', 0, 63, [x00;xp0;x10;xp0;x20;xp0], 1e-10);
```

In the above example the so-called Pythagorean initial data

$$m_0 = 5, \quad m_1 = 3, \quad m_2 = 4,$$
$$x_0 = \begin{pmatrix} 1 \\ -1 \end{pmatrix}, \quad x_1 = \begin{pmatrix} 1 \\ 3 \end{pmatrix}, \quad x_2 = \begin{pmatrix} -2 \\ -1 \end{pmatrix}, \qquad (4.3)$$
$$\dot{x}_0 = 0, \quad \dot{x}_1 = 0, \quad \dot{x}_2 = 0$$

were used for historical reasons (see also Figure 4.2). These data were first considered in 1913 by Burrau [1], but the final evolution of the system was only settled in 1967 by Szebehely and Peters [8] by careful numerical integration. An account of the history of this problem, which has no direct astronomical or physical significance, is also given in [4].

FIGURE 4.2. *Initial Configuration of the Pythagorean Problem.*

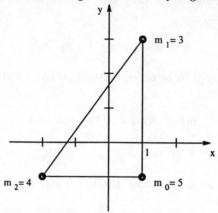

For the time interval $0 \leq t \leq 63$ 12002 integration steps were carried out in about an hour of CPU time on a Sparc 10 workstation. In Figures 4.3 and 4.4 we show the orbits of the three bodies in the intervals $0 \leq t \leq 10$ and $10 \leq t \leq 20$, and finally in Figure 4.5 the orbits in the interval $50 \leq t \leq 63$ are shown.

```
>> R1 = 1:2105;
>> plot(Y1(R1,1),Y1(R1,2),'-', ...
        Y1(R1,5),Y1(R1,6),':', Y1(R1,9),Y1(R1,10),'-.')
>> R2 = 2105:4103;
>> plot(Y1(R2,1),Y1(R2,2),'-', ...
        Y1(R2,5),Y1(R2,6),':', Y1(R2,9),Y1(R2,10),'-.')
>> R3 = 9780:12002;
>> plot(Y1(R3,1),Y1(R3,2),'-', ...
        Y1(R3,5),Y1(R3,6),':', Y1(R3,9),Y1(R3,10),'-.')
```

In the above example the smallest step size used was

```
>> [m,k] = min(diff(T1));
>> m

m =

   7.0891e-08

>> T1(k)

ans =

   15.8299
```

This small step was needed at $t = 15.8299$ where a near-collision between m_0 and m_2 occurred. The integrator barely managed to overcome this near-collision. However, the accuracy of the orbit for $t > 15.83$ is rather poor, as is seen by comparing Figure 4.5 with Figure 4.9 and with the results in [8], in spite of the small error tolerance of $1e-10$.

FIGURE 4.3.

Orbits in $0 \leq t \leq 10$. Solid Line: m_0, Dotted Line: m_1, Dashdotted Line: m_2.

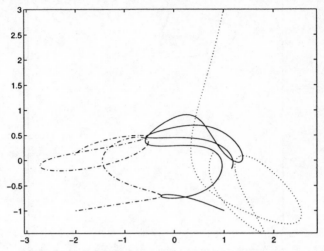

FIGURE 4.4. *Orbits in $10 \leq t \leq 20$.*

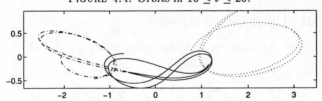

In fact, the final evolution predicted by this numerical integration is incorrect. To compensate for the high velocities at the near-collisions the integrator has to dramatically reduce the step size, sometimes rather near the level of the accuracy tolerance leading to inaccurate results. These problems will be overcome in the next section by introducing new variables such that the singularities due to all possible binary collisions are regularized.

FIGURE 4.5. *Orbits in* $50 \leq t \leq 63$.

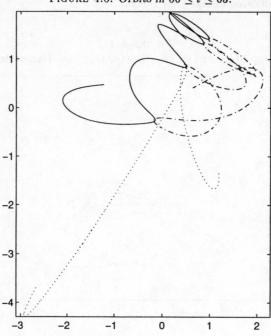

4.3   Global Regularization

For simplicity we will assume that the center of mass is initially at rest at the origin, i.e.

$$\sum_{j=0}^{2} m_j x_j = 0, \quad \sum_{j=0}^{2} m_j \dot{x}_j = 0; \tag{4.4}$$

then the equations of motion (4.2) imply that (4.4) is satisfied throughout the motion. This fact will be used to eliminate one of the variables x_j. This is best done in Hamiltonian formalism by introducing the relative coordinates

$$X = x_1 - x_0, \quad Y = x_2 - x_0 \tag{4.5}$$

with respect to x_0 as well as the canonically conjugated momenta [6]

$$P = m_1 \dot{x}_1, \quad Q = m_2 \dot{x}_2. \tag{4.6}$$

The mutual distances between the point masses expressed in the relative coordinates become

$$r_0 = |Y - X|, \quad r_1 = |Y|, \quad r_2 = |X|. \tag{4.7}$$

The equations of motion may then be derived from the Hamiltonian

$$H = \frac{|P+Q|^2}{2m_0} + \frac{|P|^2}{2m_1} + \frac{|Q|^2}{2m_2} - \frac{m_1 m_2}{|Y-X|} - \frac{m_0 m_1}{|X|} - \frac{m_0 m_2}{|Y|} \quad (4.8)$$

as

$$\dot{X} = \frac{\partial H}{\partial P}, \quad \dot{Y} = \frac{\partial H}{\partial Q}, \quad \dot{P} = -\frac{\partial H}{\partial X}, \quad \dot{Q} = -\frac{\partial H}{\partial Y}. \quad (4.9)$$

The coordinates x_0, x_1, x_2 of the three bodies may be recovered by

$$x_0 = -\frac{m_1 X + m_2 Y}{m_0 + m_1 + m_2}, \quad x_1 = x_0 + X, \quad x_2 = x_0 + Y, \quad (4.10)$$

as follows from Equations (4.4) and (4.5).

In the following the complex number $v_1 + i v_2$ associated with a vector $v = (v_1, v_2)^T \in \mathbb{R}^2$ will be denoted by the same symbol $v \in \mathbb{C}$ for convenience. Incidentally, the conventional symbol for the modulus, $|v| = \sqrt{v_1{}^2 + v_2{}^2}$, agrees in both notations.

To regularize the equations of motion at the collision between m_0 and m_1 Levi-Civita's method calls for introducing the new complex coordinate $x \in \mathbb{C}$ instead of $X \in \mathbb{C}$ according to the conformal map $X = x^2$. Furthermore, a new (fictitious) time s must be introduced according to the relation $dt = |X| \, ds$ between the differentials [3].

A generalization of this transformation due to Waldvogel [10] will be used in order to simultaneously regularize all three types of collisions in the three-body problem. Instead of the complex coordinates X, Y and time t we will use new coordinates $x \in \mathbb{C}, y \in \mathbb{C}$ and the fictitious time s that relate to X, Y, t by

$$X = \left(\frac{x^2 - y^2}{2}\right)^2, \quad Y = \left(\frac{x^2 + y^2}{2}\right)^2, \quad dt = r_0 r_1 r_2 \, ds. \quad (4.11)$$

The key for the regularizing effect of the transformation (4.11) is the relation

$$Y - X = (x\,y)^2; \quad (4.12)$$

hence all three complex relative coordinates, $X, Y, Y - X$, are written as complete squares in the new complex coordinates.

The mechanism for transforming the equations of motion (4.9) to the new variables calls for introducing new momenta $p \in \mathbb{C}, q \in \mathbb{C}$ such that the transformation from the set (X, Y, P, Q) of variables to (x, y, p, q) is canonical. The relations defining the new momenta turn out to be [10]

$$\begin{pmatrix} p \\ q \end{pmatrix} = \overline{A}^T \begin{pmatrix} P \\ Q \end{pmatrix} \quad (4.13)$$

where

$$A = \begin{pmatrix} \frac{\partial X}{\partial x} & \frac{\partial X}{\partial y} \\ \frac{\partial Y}{\partial x} & \frac{\partial Y}{\partial y} \end{pmatrix} = \begin{pmatrix} x\,(x^2 - y^2) & -y\,(x^2 - y^2) \\ x\,(x^2 + y^2) & y\,(x^2 + y^2) \end{pmatrix} \quad (4.14)$$

and $\overline{A}^T$ denotes the complex conjugate transpose of A.

Then the regularized equations of motion are

$$\frac{dx}{ds} = \frac{\partial K}{\partial p}, \quad \frac{dy}{ds} = \frac{\partial K}{\partial q}, \quad \frac{dp}{ds} = -\frac{\partial K}{\partial x}, \quad \frac{dq}{ds} = -\frac{\partial K}{\partial y}, \quad \frac{dt}{ds} = r_0\, r_1\, r_2, \quad (4.15)$$

where

$$K = r_0\, r_1\, r_2\, (H - E) \qquad (4.16)$$

is the regularized Hamiltonian, expressed in terms of the new variables, and E is the initial value of H, i.e. the total energy. Since $H(t) = E = $ constant on an orbit there follows $K(s) = 0$ on this orbit.

For the further manipulations the capabilities of MAPLE will be used as much as possible. However, the use of symbolic differentiation to form the gradient of K will produce too many terms resulting in an inefficient evaluation of the right-hand sides of (4.15).

The following method proved successful. In a first step the expression for K is written as elegantly as possible by using naturally occurring auxiliary quantities such as r_0, r_1, r_2, etc.. Then the gradient of K is evaluated by means of automatic differentiation thus generating efficient code for it.

Let $x = x_1 + i\, x_2$, $y = y_1 + i\, y_2$ with $x_1 \in \mathbb{R}$, $x_2 \in \mathbb{R}$ in a new meaning. Then we obtain according to (4.11) and (4.7)

```
> x := x1 + I*x2:
> y := y1 + I*y2:
> X := ((x^2-y^2)/2)^2:
> Y := ((x^2+y^2)/2)^2:
> r0 := factor(evalc(abs(Y-X))):
> r0 := simplify(r0, power, symbolic);

                    2     2     2     2
          r0 := (y1  + y2 ) (x2  + x1 )

> r1 := factor(evalc(abs(Y)));

            2            2     2          2
r1 := 1/4 (y1  + 2 x2 y1 + x2  + y2  - 2 y2 x1 + x1 )

        2            2     2          2
      (y1  - 2 x2 y1 + x2  + y2  + 2 y2 x1 + x1 )

> r2 := factor(evalc(abs(X)));

            2            2     2          2
r2 := 1/4 (y1  - 2 x1 y1 + x1  + y2  - 2 x2 y2 + x2 )

        2            2     2          2
      (y1  + 2 x1 y1 + x1  + y2  + 2 x2 y2 + x2 )
```

It is easy to see that the factors of r_1 and r_2 are sums of squares. We have written a small MAPLE procedure reduce (see Algorithm 4.4 on page 56) to simplify such expressions, since there exists no direct MAPLE command to perform this operation.

```
> r1 := reduce(r1);
```

$$r1 := 1/4 \ ((y1 + x2)^2 + (y2 - x1)^2) \ ((y1 - x2)^2 + (y2 + x1)^2)$$

```
> r2 := reduce(r2);
```

$$r2 := 1/4 \ ((y1 - x1)^2 + (y2 - x2)^2) \ ((y1 + x1)^2 + (y2 + x2)^2)$$

According to (4.16), (4.8) and (4.7) we obtain for K

$$K = \frac{L_0}{2m_0} + \frac{L_1}{2m_1} + \frac{L_2}{2m_2} - (m_0\,m_1\,r_0\,r_1 + m_1\,m_2\,r_1\,r_2 + m_2\,m_0\,r_2\,r_0) - E\,r_0\,r_1\,r_2.$$

$$\text{(4.17)}$$

For the auxiliary quantities L_j a simple calculation yields

$$
\begin{aligned}
L_0 &= r_0\,r_1\,r_2\,|P + Q|^2 = \frac{r_0}{16}\,|\overline{x}\,p - \overline{y}\,q|^2 \\
L_1 &= r_0\,r_1\,r_2\,|P|^2 = \frac{r_1}{16}\,|\overline{y}\,p - \overline{x}\,q|^2 \qquad\qquad \text{(4.18)} \\
L_2 &= r_0\,r_1\,r_2\,|Q|^2 = \frac{r_2}{16}\,|\overline{y}\,p + \overline{x}\,q|^2.
\end{aligned}
$$

One way of writing these expressions in mostly factored form while using real notation with $p = p_1 + i\,p_2$, $q = q_1 + i\,q_2$ is

$$
\begin{aligned}
L_0 &= \frac{r_0}{16}\left(|p|^2\,|x|^2 + |q|^2\,|y|^2 - A - B\right) \\
L_1 &= \frac{r_1}{16}\left(|p|^2\,|y|^2 + |q|^2\,|x|^2 - A + B\right) \\
L_2 &= \frac{r_2}{16}\left(|p|^2\,|y|^2 + |q|^2\,|x|^2 + A - B\right)
\end{aligned}
$$

where

$$
\begin{aligned}
A &= 2(x_1\,y_1 + x_2\,y_2)(p_1\,q_1 + p_2\,q_2) \\
B &= 2(x_2\,y_1 - x_1\,y_2)(p_2\,q_1 - p_1\,q_2).
\end{aligned}
$$

In Algorithm 4.2 a MAPLE procedure computing the regularized Hamiltonian K is given, where the meaning of L_j has been slightly modified and EE is used for the total energy E.

To compute the partial derivatives of K with respect to all its arguments we use the automatic differentiation capability of MAPLE. For an introduction to automatic (or algorithmic) differentiation we refer to [2, 5]. It is well known that the so-called *reverse mode* of automatic differentiation is best suited for computing gradients. Applying the *forward mode* to K leads to a procedure with about 300 multiplications (after optimization), whereas the reverse mode leads to a procedure with only about 200 multiplications. This number can still be reduced if we first split up the products in the procedure K in order to avoid

ALGORITHM 4.2. *Procedure K.*

```
K := proc(x1,x2,y1,y2,p1,p2,q1,q2)
    local xx,yy,pp,qq,r0,r1,r2,A,B,L0,L1,L2,m01,m12,m20,apb,amb;

    xx:=x1^2+x2^2; yy:=y1^2+y2^2;
    pp:=p1^2+p2^2; qq:=q1^2+q2^2;

    r0:=xx*yy;
    r1:=((x1-y2)^2+(x2+y1)^2)*((x1+y2)^2+(x2-y1)^2)/4;
    r2:=((x1+y1)^2+(x2+y2)^2)*((x1-y1)^2+(x2-y2)^2)/4;

    A:=2*(p1*q1+p2*q2)*(x1*y1+x2*y2);
    B:=2*(p2*q1-p1*q2)*(x2*y1-x1*y2);

    apb:=A+B:
    amb:=A-B:
    L0:=r0*(pp*xx+qq*yy-apb);
    L1:=r1*(pp*yy+qq*xx-amb);
    L2:=r2*(pp*yy+qq*xx+amb);

    m01 := m0*m1;
    m12 := m1*m2;
    m20 := m2*m0;

    L0/32/m0+L1/32/m1+L2/32/m2-m01*r0*r1-m12*r1*r2-m20*r2*r0
        -EE*r0*r1*r2;
end:
```

the generation of common subexpressions when computing the derivatives.

```
> SK   := SPLIT(K):
> RSK  := REVERSEMODE(SK):
> ORSK := readlib(optimize)(RSK):
> COST(ORSK);
```

> 141 multiplications + 132 assignments + 81 subscripts
>
> + 86 additions + 3 divisions + functions

The procedures we used here are available from the MAPLE share library. They can be obtained from neptune.inf.ethz.ch using anonymous ftp. The final result is the MAPLE procedure ORSK to evaluate the right-hand sides of Equations (4.15) with only 144 multiplicative operations (multiplications and divisions). One of the authors [10] has written a hand-optimized procedure which requires roughly 100 multiplicative operations and 50 additions, so the result obtained by MAPLE is almost optimal.

Notice that MAPLE can also be used to *prove* that the procedure ORSK is in fact correct. For that we compute the gradient using the `gradient` function of the `linalg` package and compare it element by element with the result generated by the procedure `ORSK` on symbolic input arguments.

```
> G1 := linalg[grad](K(x1,x2,y1,y2,p1,p2,q1,q2),
>                        [x1,x2,y1,y2,p1,p2,q1,q2]):
> G2 := [ORSK(x1,x2,y1,y2,p1,p2,q1,q2)]:
> zip((g1,g2)->expand(g1-g2), convert(G1, list), G2);
```

$$[0, \ 0, \ 0, \ 0, \ 0, \ 0, \ 0, \ 0]$$

For convenience numerical integration and graphical output of the orbits will again be done in MATLAB. To convert the MAPLE procedure `ORSK` into a MATLAB procedure we have to make some syntactical changes which can be done with the help of a simple editor. First, the MAPLE assignments ":=" must be converted to the MATLAB notation "=", and array references must be converted from square brackets (`a[1]`) to round parentheses (`a(1)`). Additionally a procedure head must be added and the result must be stored in an array. This leads to a MATLAB procedure of about 150 lines which is shown in Algorithm 4.3.

Since in regularized variables time t is a dependent variable the orbit itself is obtained from the first 8 differential equations of the system (4.15), whereas the temporal evolution of the three-body system may be obtained from the last equation.

When integrating this system of differential equations the time-critical part is the computation of the derivative, i.e. the evaluation of the above procedure, which is executed for every step at least once. Since procedures in MATLAB are interpreted it is a good idea to write a C program (again some syntactical changes) to perform this computation and to link it dynamically to MATLAB. This way a speed-up factor of about 10 is achieved. For a more detailed description of the mechanism of linking C code to MAPLE we refer to Section 9.3.4 on page 133.

4.4 The Pythagorean Three-Body Problem

For integrating an orbit in regularized variables the initial values of x, y, p, q at $s = t = 0$ must be calculated by inverting the transformation (4.11),

$$x = \sqrt{\sqrt{Y} + \sqrt{X}}, \quad y = \sqrt{\sqrt{Y} - \sqrt{X}},$$

and by applying (4.13). For the Pythagorean initial data (see Equation (4.3) and Figure 4.2) we may again use MAPLE to obtain these initial values. The function `evalc` splits a complex expression into its real and imaginary parts,

ALGORITHM 4.3. *Function* `threebp`.

```
function yprime = threebp(s, y)

    global m0 m1 m2 EE

    x1 = y(1); x2 = y(2); y1 = y(3); y2 = y(4);
    p1 = y(5); p2 = y(6); q1 = y(7); q2 = y(8);

    % here comes the Maple generated code
    t1 = x1^2;
    ...
    ...
    t137 = t43*xx+t44*xx+t45*yy;

    grd(1) = -y2*t96+y1*t98+t100+t101+t102+t103+2*x1*t104;
    grd(2) = y1*t96+y2*t98+t109+t110+t111+t112+2*x2*t104;
    grd(3) = x2*t96+x1*t98-t100+t101-t111+t112+2*y1*t117;
    grd(4) = -x1*t96+x2*t98-t109+t110+t102-t103+2*y2*t117;
    grd(5) = -q2*t124+q1*t126+2*p1*t128;
    grd(6) = q1*t124+q2*t126+2*p2*t128;
    grd(7) = p2*t124+p1*t126+2*q1*t137;
    grd(8) = -p1*t124+p2*t126+2*q2*t137;

    yprime(1:4)= grd(5:8);
    yprime(5:8)=-grd(1:4);
    yprime(9)=r0*r1*r2;
end
```

and the function `radnormal` simplifies radicals.

```
> Digits := 20: readlib(radnormal):
> X := 4*I:
> Y := -3:
> x := sqrt(sqrt(Y)+sqrt(X));

                      1/2    1/2       1/2 1/2
              x := (I 3    + 2    + I 2    )

> x := map(t->map(radnormal,t),evalc(x));

  x :=

                1/2       1/2 1/2                  1/2       1/2 1/2
    1/2 (2 + 2 6    + 2 2    )    + 1/2 I (2 + 2 6    - 2 2    )

> evalf(");

        1.5594395315555318362 + 1.0087804965427521214 I
```

```
> y := sqrt(sqrt(Y)-sqrt(X));

                    1/2     1/2       1/2 1/2
              y := (I 3     - 2     - I 2   )

> y := map(t->map(radnormal,t),evalc(y));

y :=

         1/2       1/2 1/2          1/2       1/2 1/2
1/2 (- 2 + 2 6   - 2 2  )  + 1/2 I (- 2 + 2 6   + 2 2  )

> evalf(");

        .13280847188730666477 + 1.1966000386838271257 I
```

Since the bodies are at rest initially, $p = q = 0$. The total energy E can be obtained from the condition $K(0) = 0$.

```
> m0 := 5: m1 := 3: m2 := 4:
> radnormal(solve(K(Re(x), Im(x), Re(y), Im(y), 0, 0, 0, 0), EE));

                           769
                         - ---
                           60
```

We now switch to MATLAB to integrate the system of differential equation using ode45.

```
>> m0 = 5; m1 = 3; m2 = 4;
>> p10 = 0; q10 = 0; p20 = 0; q20 = 0;
>> x10 = 1.5594395315555318362;   x20 = 1.0087804965427521214;
>> y10 = 0.13280847188730666477; y20 = 1.1966000386838271256;
>> EE = -769/60;
>> global m0 m1 m2 EE
>> [S,Z] = ode45('threebp', 0, 8, ...
                    [x10,x20,y10,y20,p10,p20,q10,q20,0], 1e-10);
```

For the above integration with the accuracy tolerance 10^{-10} 4442 integration steps were needed (about 3 minutes on a Sparc 10). The interval $0 \leq s \leq 8$ in fictitious time corresponds to $0 \leq t \leq t_f = 63.0218$.

```
>> size(Z)

ans =

        4442              9

>> Z(4442,9)

ans =

    63.0218
```

Next we recover the coordinates x_0, x_1, x_2 of the three bodies by means of Equations (4.11) and (4.10).

```
>> x = Z(:,1)+i*Z(:,2);
>> y = Z(:,3)+i*Z(:,4);
>> X = (x.^2-y.^2).^2/4;
>> Y = (x.^2+y.^2).^2/4;
>> x0 = - (m1*X+m2*Y) / (m0+m1+m2);
>> x1 = x0 + X;
>> x2 = x0 + Y;
```

We now may look at the orbits of the three bodies in animated graphics with the following commands.

```
>> clg
>> axis([-3.3361 3.4907 -4.9904 8.5989])
>> hold on
>> [n,e]=size(x1);
>> for k=1:n-1,
>>     plot(x0(k:k+1),'-','EraseMode','none');
>>     plot(x1(k:k+1),':','EraseMode','none');
>>     plot(x2(k:k+1),'--','EraseMode','none');
>>     drawnow
>> end
>> hold off
```

FIGURE 4.6. *Orbits in $20 \le t \le 30$.*

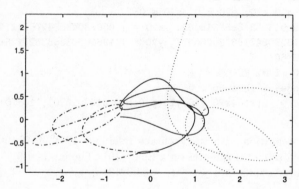

A few snapshots of this animation will be given in the following. The orbits for $0 \le t \le 20$ are the same as those shown in Figures 4.3 and 4.4. The remaining time interval is covered by Figure 4.6, Figure 4.8 and Figure 4.9. In these figures the motion of the mass m_1 is shown by a dotted line, the dashes represent the orbit of m_2 and the solid line illustrates the motion of the body with the largest mass m_0.

FIGURE 4.7. *Distances* r_2 *and* r_1.

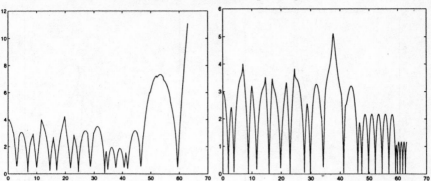

Since we have all data of the orbits available, it is possible to discuss the orbits further. We may for example find the times of near-collisions of two bodies. This can be visualized by plotting the distances r_2 and r_1 which are the absolute values of X and Y according to (4.7). We plot these distances versus the physical time t:

```
>> T2=Z(:,9);
>> plot(T2, abs(X))
>> plot(T2, abs(Y))
```

The smallest distance between any two bodies at any time $t \geq 0$ during the evolution of this three-body system occurs at $t = 15.8299$ between m_0 and m_2: $r_1 = 9.1094e-04$. This near-collision can be seen in Figure 4.4 and in more detail in Figure 4.10.

```
>> [m,k]=min(abs(Y))

m =

   9.1094e-04


k =

       1103

>> T2(k)

ans =

   15.8299
```

A simple way to discuss the velocity vectors of the three masses is to use the forward difference quotients between two consecutive integration steps as an approximation, e.g.

$$\dot{x}_0 = \text{diff}(x0) ./ \text{diff}(T).$$

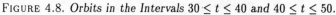

FIGURE 4.8. *Orbits in the Intervals* $30 \le t \le 40$ *and* $40 \le t \le 50$.

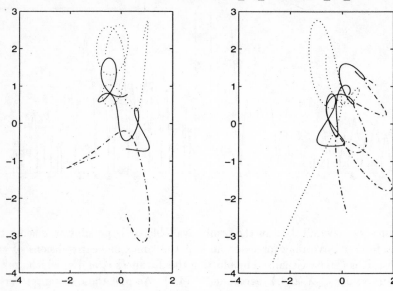

However, it is also possible to obtain the true velocity vectors from the orbital data by using Equation (4.13) and (4.6). First we prepare the symbolic expressions for P and Q by means of MAPLE (suppressing the complex conjugations for the moment):

```
> x := 'x': y := 'y':
> A := linalg[matrix](2,2,[[x*(x^2-y^2), -y*(x^2-y^2)],
>                          [x*(x^2+y^2), y*(x^2+y^2)]]);
```

$$
A := \begin{bmatrix}
x\,(x^2 - y^2) & -y\,(x^2 - y^2) \\
x\,(x^2 + y^2) & y\,(x^2 + y^2)
\end{bmatrix}
$$

```
> invA := linalg[inverse](transpose(A)):
> pq := linalg[vector]([p,q]):
> PQ := linalg[multiply](invA,pq);
```

$$
PQ := \left[-\frac{1}{2}\,\frac{-p\,y + q\,x}{x\,(x^2 - y^2)\,y},\; \frac{1}{2}\,\frac{p\,y + q\,x}{x\,(x^2 + y^2)\,y} \right]
$$

FIGURE 4.9. *Orbits in* $50 \le t \le 63$.

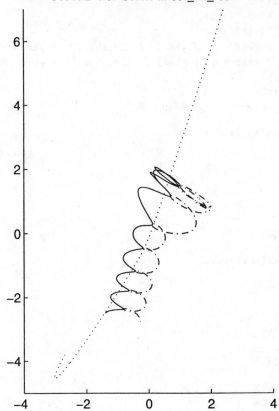

This agrees, apart from the bars, with the results given in [10], namely

$$P = \frac{p\,\overline{y} - q\,\overline{x}}{2\overline{x}\,\overline{y}\,(\overline{x}^2 - \overline{y}^2)}, \quad Q = \frac{p\,\overline{y} + q\,\overline{x}}{2\overline{x}\,\overline{y}\,(\overline{x}^2 + \overline{y}^2)}. \tag{4.19}$$

Again we may look for the maximum speeds. It turns out that m_0 and m_2 have their maximum speeds at $t = 15.8299$, the near-collision we found in Section 4.2. At this time, the velocity of m_1 is very small.

```
>> xbar = Z(:,1)-i*Z(:,2);
>> ybar = Z(:,3)-i*Z(:,4);
>> p = Z(:,5)+i*Z(:,6);
>> q = Z(:,7)+i*Z(:,8);
>> P = (p ./ xbar - q ./ ybar) ./ (2*(xbar.^2 - ybar.^2));
>> Q = (p ./ xbar + q ./ ybar) ./ (2*(xbar.^2 + ybar.^2));
>> vx1 = P/m1;
>> vx2 = Q/m2;
>> vx0 = - (m1*vx1+m2*vx2)/m0;

>> [v,k]=max(abs(vx0))

v =

   62.4819


k =

        1103

>> [v,k]=max(abs(vx2))

v =

   78.0783


k =

        1103

>> abs(vx1(k))

ans =

    0.0404
```

The near-collision at $t = 15.8299$ has a special significance. Notice that the three bodies describe approximately the same orbits before and after this close encounter (see Figure 4.4). This trend continues through Figure 4.6, and at $t \approx$ 31.66 the three bodies approximately occupy their initial positions with small velocities (see left plot in Figure 4.8). This means that near the Pythagorean initial conditions a periodic solution exists. In Figure 4.10 we show a detail of Figure 4.4 which was generated from the data obtained in Section 4.2 by the following commands:

```
>> [m,k] = min(diff(T1));
>> R = k-200:k+200;
>> plot(Y1(R,1),Y1(R,2),'-', ...
        Y1(R,5),Y1(R,6),':', Y1(R,9),Y1(R,10),'-.')
```

FIGURE 4.10. *Orbits of m_2 and m_0 near $t = 15.8299$.*

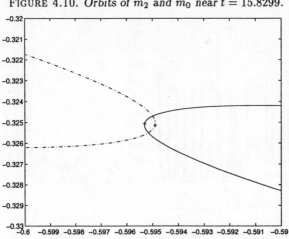

```
>> hold on
>> plot(Y1(k,1), Y1(k,2), '+')
>> plot(Y1(k,9), Y1(k,10), '+')
>> axis([-0.60 -0.59 -0.33 -0.32])
>> hold off
```

Finally, Figure 4.9 shows the asymptotic behavior of the three orbits after a close encounter of all three bodies. Notice that the final evolution obtained in Section 4.2 (Figure 4.5) with the direct approach is incorrect.

Another interesting plot is the size of the steps used during the integration. The maximum step used with the global regularization was 0.0186 and the minimum step was $2.9128e-05$ at $t = 63.0177$. For the direct approach described in Section 4.2 the minimum step used was $7.0891e-08$ (see page 40). In Figure 4.11 we show the step size used for the integrations with the direct approach (left) and with the global regularization (right). Notice that the two pictures are scaled differently.

```
>> plot(diff(T1))              >> plot(diff(S))
>> axis([0,12001,0,0.06])      >> axis([0,4441,0,0.02])
```

4.5   Conclusions

Experiments show that the long-term evolution of the three-body system is extremely sensitive to the initial data and to the accuracy of the numerical integration. Typically, neighboring orbits deviate exponentially in time. This means that systems like the one at hand are not predictable over a long time span (like the weather).

Nevertheless, the mathematical problem has a well defined, unique solution

FIGURE 4.11. *Step Sizes During the Integrations.*

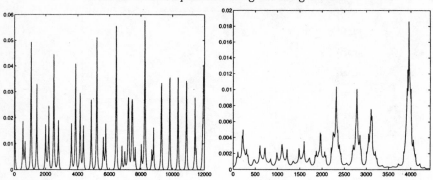

which can be approximated over a finite time interval $0 \leq t \leq t_f$ if the numerical integration is done with sufficient accuracy.

A rough check of the achieved accuracy in the interval $[0, t_f]$ is provided by the Hamiltonian $K(s)$ which theoretically vanishes on the entire orbit. In our example the maximum value of $K(s)$ for $s \in [0, 8]$ is

```
>> for k=1:n, KK(k) = K(Z(k,1:8)); end;
>> norm(KK,inf)

ans =

    1.0337e-06
```

A more reliable check is obtained by integrating the same orbit with different accuracy tolerances. The orbit is valid at least as long as the different approximations agree to sufficient accuracy. Alternatively, the validity of an orbit may be checked by integrating it backwards.

In the Pythagorean problem of three bodies it is found that the motion begins with a long interplay involving many close encounters of all three types. At time $t = 46.6$ the smallest mass, m_1, shoots through a newly formed binary of m_0 and m_2 and is accelerated to a near-escape in the third quadrant. However, m_1 comes back, just to receive another kick at $t = 59.4$ after which it is definitely expelled in the first quadrant, whereas the binary escapes in the opposite direction. Possibly, this is one of the mechanisms at work in the formation of binaries and of halos in galaxies.

Maple Code of the procedure reduce

The procedure reduce in Algorithm 4.4 tries to write a given expression a as a sum of squares.

ALGORITHM 4.4. *Function* reduce.

```
reduce := proc(a) local p,P,S,c,i,j,f;
  if type(a,{name,constant}) then a
  elif type(a,'+') then p := a; P := convert(p,list);
    S := map(t -> if (type(t,'^') and type(op(2,t),even))
                  then op(1,t)^(op(2,t)/2) fi, P);
    for i to nops(S) do
      for j from i+1 to nops(S) do
        if   has(p, 2*S[i]*S[j]) then
          p := p - (S[i]^2+2*S[i]*S[j]+S[j]^2)
                 + (S[i]+S[j])^2
        elif has(p,-2*S[i]*S[j]) then
          p := p - (S[i]^2-2*S[i]*S[j]+S[j]^2)
                 + (S[i]-S[j])^2
        fi
      od;
    od;
    p
  else map(reduce, a)
  fi
end:
```

References

[1] C. BURRAU, *Numerische Berechnung eines Spezialfalles des Dreikörperproblems*, Astron. Nachr. 195, 1913, p. 113.

[2] A. GRIEWANK and G.F. CORLISS editors, *Automatic Differentiation of Algorithms: Theory, Implementation, and Application*, Proceedings of the SIAM Workshop on Automatic Differentiation, held in Breckenridge, Colorado,1991, SIAM Philadelphia, 1991.

[3] T. LEVI-CIVITA, *Sur la régularisation du problème des trois corps*, Acta Math. 42, 1920, pp. 99-144.

[4] CH. MARCHAL, *The Three-Body Problem*, Elsevier, 1990.

[5] M.B. MONAGAN and W.M. NEUENSCHWANDER, *GRADIENT: Algorithmic Differentiation in Maple*, Proceedings of the 1993 International Symposium on Symbolic and Algebraic Computation, ISSAC'93, 1993, p. 68.

[6] C.L. SIEGEL and J.K. MOSER, *Lectures on Celestial Mechanics*, Springer, 1971.

[7] K.F. SUNDMAN, *Mémoire sur le problème des trois corps*, Acta Math. 36, 1912, pp. 105-179.

[8] V. SZEBEHELY and C.F. PETERS, *Complete Solution of a General Problem of Three Bodies*, Astron. J. 72, 1967, pp. 876-883.

[9] V. SZEBEHELY, *Theory of Orbits,* Academic Press, 1967.

[10] J. WALDVOGEL, *A New Regularization of the Planar Problem of Three Bodies,*
     Celest. Mech. 6, 1972, pp. 221-231.

Chapter 5. The Internal Field in Semiconductors

F. Klvaňa

5.1 Introduction

Let us consider a semiconductor of length l in x-direction, which is doped with a concentration of electrically active impurities $C(x) = C_D^+(x) - C_A^-(x)$. The C_A^-, C_D^+ are the acceptor and donor impurity concentrations respectively and are independent on y and z. Let this semiconductor be connected to an external potential $U(x)$ with $U(0) = U_0$ and $U(l) = 0$. Then, if the semiconductor has sufficiently large dimensions in y- and z-directions, all physical properties will depend only on x, and we can study it as a one-dimensional object.

We consider the problem of finding the internal potential in this semiconductor for a given carrier (electrons and holes) concentration $C(x)$. To simplify the problem we will assume that we can neglect recombination and generation of carriers.

Under the standard conditions we can assume the system of electrons and holes to be a classical system. Then the equilibrium concentrations of electrons $n(x)$ and of holes $p(x)$ in an internal potential field $\psi(x)$ are given by the Boltzmann statistics ([2])

$$n(x) = n_i \, e^{\frac{q}{\theta}(\psi(x) - \varphi_F)}, \qquad p(x) = n_i \, e^{\frac{-q}{\theta}(\psi(x) - \varphi_F)}, \tag{5.1}$$

where n_i is an intrinsic concentration of electrons. φ_F is the so-called Fermi potential, which is constant over the whole semiconductor, and is taken as a reference level for the potential ($\varphi_F = 0$). q is the charge of an electron, $\theta = kT$ is the statistical temperature.

Assuming that the above conditions hold, the internal potential $\psi(x)$ is given as a solution of the Poisson equation, which for our one-dimensional problem has the form

$$\frac{d^2\psi(x)}{dx^2} = \frac{q}{\varepsilon}\left(n(x) - p(x) - C(x)\right), \tag{5.2}$$

where ε is the dielectric constant.

It is useful to represent the concentration $C(x)$ by the so-called builtin potential $\psi_D(x)$ using the definition

$$C(x) = n_i \left(e^{\frac{q}{\theta}\psi_D(x)} - e^{-\frac{q}{\theta}\psi_D(x)}\right). \tag{5.3}$$

The boundary conditions for Equation (5.2) are of Dirichlet type and have the form

$$\psi(0) = \psi_D(0) + U_0 \quad , \qquad \psi(l) = \psi_D(l). \tag{5.4}$$

Finally we introduce the dimensionless quantities

$$\varphi(X) = \frac{q}{\theta}\,\psi(x)\,, \quad \varphi_D(X) = \frac{q}{\theta}\,\psi_D(x)\,, \quad u_0 = \frac{q}{\theta}\,U_0\,, \quad c(X) = \frac{C(x)}{n_i} \tag{5.5}$$

with the scaling transformation $x = \lambda_D \cdot X$, where $\lambda_D = \sqrt{\varepsilon\theta/q^2 n_i}$ is the Debye length. From Equations (5.3) and (5.5) follows that

$$\varphi_D(X) = \operatorname{arcsinh}\left(\frac{c(X)}{2}\right) = \ln\left(\frac{1}{2}\left(\sqrt{c(X)^2 + 4} + c(X)\right)\right) . \tag{5.6}$$

Equation (5.2) is transformed to

$$\frac{d^2\varphi(X)}{dX^2} = e^{\varphi(X)} - e^{-\varphi(X)} - c(X), \tag{5.7}$$

with the boundary conditions

$$\varphi(0) = \varphi_D(0) + u_0\,, \qquad \varphi(L) = \varphi_D(L)\,, \quad \text{where } L = \frac{l}{\lambda_D}. \tag{5.8}$$

5.2 Solving a Nonlinear Poisson Equation Using MAPLE

Equation (5.7) together with boundary conditions (5.8) represents a nonlinear boundary value problem which has to be solved numerically. MAPLE cannot solve a boundary value problem directly, an appropriate numerical method must be implemented for its solution. We choose the method of finite differences (see e.g. [1]).

Let us define a mesh of $N+1$ points $X_0 = 0, X_1, ..., X_N = L$ on the interval $[0, L]$ and denote $h_i = X_{i+1} - X_i$ ($i = 0, 1, ..., N-1$) and $\varphi_i = \varphi(X_i)$, $\varphi_{Di} = \varphi_D(X_i)$, $c_i = c(X_i)$. Then the discretized form of Equation (5.7) in interior points is

$$\frac{1}{h_i^*}\left(\frac{\varphi_{i+1} - \varphi_i}{h_i} - \frac{\varphi_i - \varphi_{i-1}}{h_{i-1}}\right) = e^{\varphi_i} - e^{-\varphi_i} - c_i\,, \qquad i = 1, ..., N-1, \tag{5.9}$$

where $h_i^* = \frac{1}{2}(h_{i-1} + h_i)$. Together with the boundary conditions

$$\varphi_0 = \varphi_{D0} + u_0 \quad , \qquad \varphi_N = \varphi_{DN}, \tag{5.10}$$

this is a system of nonlinear equations for the unknowns $\varphi_1, ..., \varphi_{N-1}$:

$$\begin{aligned} a_1\,\varphi_1 + b_1\,\varphi_2 &= F_1(\varphi_1) \\ b_{i-1}\,\varphi_{i-1} + a_i\,\varphi_i + b_i\,\varphi_{i+1} &= F_i(\varphi_i) \qquad \text{for} \quad i = 2, ..., N-2 \\ b_{N-2}\,\varphi_{N-2} + a_{N-1}\,\varphi_{N-1} &= F_{N-1}(\varphi_{N-1}) \end{aligned} \tag{5.11}$$

where

$$
\begin{aligned}
b_i &= \tfrac{1}{h_i} \ , \quad a_i = -(b_{i-1} + b_i) \ , \\
F_1 &= h_1^* \left(e^{\varphi_1} - e^{-\varphi_1} - c_1 \right) - b_0 \, \varphi_0 \ , \\
F_{N-1} &= h_{N-1}^* \left(e^{\varphi_{N-1}} - e^{-\varphi_{N-1}} - c_{N-1} \right) - b_{N-1} \, \varphi_N \ , \\
F_i &= h_i^* \left(e^{\varphi_i} - e^{-\varphi_i} - c_i \right) \quad \text{for} \quad i = 2, \ldots, N-2 \ .
\end{aligned}
\tag{5.12}
$$

We rewrite the above system of Equations (5.11) in matrix form as

$$
\hat{A} \cdot \hat{\varphi} = \hat{F}(\hat{\varphi})
\tag{5.13}
$$

where $\hat{A}$ is a symmetric tridiagonal matrix with the nonzero elements

$$
A_{ii} = a_i \ , \quad A_{i,i-1} = b_{i-1} \ , \quad A_{i,i+1} = b_i \ ,
\tag{5.14}
$$

and $\hat{\varphi}$ is the column vector with the elements $\varphi_1, \ldots, \varphi_{N-1}$. To solve this system of nonlinear equations we use Newton's method (see for example [1]).

Let us define the vector function

$$
\hat{G}(\hat{\varphi}) = \hat{A} \cdot \hat{\varphi} - \hat{F}(\hat{\varphi}).
\tag{5.15}
$$

Newton's method defines a sequence

$$
\hat{\varphi}^{(0)}, \, \hat{\varphi}^{(1)}, \, \hat{\varphi}^{(2)}, \cdots
\tag{5.16}
$$

of approximate solutions of the system $\hat{G}(\hat{\varphi}) = 0$ by the recurrence relation

$$
\hat{\varphi}^{(k+1)} = \hat{\varphi}^{(k)} + \hat{H}^{(k)}.
\tag{5.17}
$$

The correction $\hat{H}^{(k)}$ is the solution of the system of equations

$$
\hat{G}(\hat{\varphi}^{(k)}) + \hat{J}(\hat{\varphi}^{(k)})\hat{H}^{(k)} = 0,
\tag{5.18}
$$

where the Jacobian $\hat{J}(\hat{\varphi}^{(k)})$ contains the partial derivatives of the vector function $\hat{G}(\hat{\varphi}^{(k)})$. The i-th equation of the system is given by

$$
G_i(\hat{\varphi}^{(k)}) + \sum_{j=1}^{N-1} \frac{\partial G_i(\hat{\varphi}^{(k)})}{\partial \varphi_j^{(k)}} \cdot H_j^{(k)} = 0 \quad \text{for} \quad i = 1, \ldots, N-1 \ .
\tag{5.19}
$$

Since

$$
\frac{\partial G_i}{\partial \varphi_j} = A_{ij} - \frac{\partial F_i}{\partial \varphi_j} = A_{ij} - h_i^* \left(e^{\varphi_i} + e^{-\varphi_i} \right) \cdot \delta_{ij} \ ,
\tag{5.20}
$$

the Jacobian splits into a constant matrix $\hat{A}$ and a diagonal matrix $\hat{D}(\varphi_j^{(k)})$ depending on the current iterate. The system of linear equations for the correction becomes

$$
(\hat{A} - \hat{D}(\varphi_j^{(k)}))\hat{H}^{(k)} = \hat{F}(\hat{\varphi}^{(k)}) - \hat{A} \cdot \hat{\varphi}^{(k)},
\tag{5.21}
$$

where $D_{ii} = h_i^*(e^{\varphi_i} + e^{-\varphi_i})$. As an initial guess $\hat{\varphi}^{(0)}$, it is recommended for physical reasons to use the builtin potential $\hat{\varphi}_D$. The iteration process is stopped if

$$\|\hat{\varphi}^{(k+1)} - \hat{\varphi}^{(k)}\|_{max} = \|\hat{H}^{(k)}\|_{max} = \max_i |H_i^{(k)}| < \epsilon \qquad (5.22)$$

where ϵ is an error tolerance for the result.

It is a complicated task to prove convergence of our iteration process. But for physically realistic values of the parameters ([2]), Newton's method gives a unique solution of the problem and has good convergence properties.

For this problem in MAPLE we will take a model semiconductor with a P-N jump in the middle of the region $[0, L]$, where $L = 10$, with the impurity distribution

$$c(X) = \tanh(20\,(\frac{X}{L} - \frac{1}{2})). \qquad (5.23)$$

For simplicity, we choose a uniform grid with step $h_i = h = 1/N$, where N is the number of points of the mesh. For the quantities $\hat{\varphi}$, $\hat{\varphi}_D$, $\hat{h}^*$, $\hat{F}$ we will use arrays phi , phiD , hp , Fp . Tridiagonal matrices will be represented by the vectors of the diagonal and off-diagonal elements A , Ap and B where

$$A_i = a_i\,, \quad Ap_i = a_i - h_i^*(e^{\varphi_i} + e^{-\varphi_i})\,, \quad B_i = b_i\,. \qquad (5.24)$$

The first part of the MAPLE program follows:

```
>        #dimensionless formulation, x,L in units of Debye's length
> N:=20: L:=10.0: h:=L/N:
> U0:=0: #normalized potential on the boundary
>        #concentration of impurities - region of N-P jump
> c:=tanh(20.0*(x/L-0.5)):
>        #mesh of N+1 point for region 0..L
> xp:=array(0..N):
> for i from 0 to N do xp[i]:=i*h od:
>        #array of concentrations Ca and builtin potential phiD
> phiD:=array(0..N):
> Ca:=array(0..N):
> for i from 0 to N do
>     Ca[i]:=evalf(subs(x=xp[i],c));
>     phiD[i]:=arcsinh(Ca[i]/2)
> od:
```

To solve the tridiagonal System (5.21) we could use the standard library function linsolve , but it appears to be slow, since it does not take into account the sparsity of the matrix. So we implement the standard LU decomposition for tridiagonal systems without pivoting, which is very fast and economical in storage. The function solvetridiag(n,A,B,F) solves the symmetric tridiagonal system of n linear equations; A is the vector of the main diagonal, B contains the off-diagonal elements, and F is the vector of the right-hand sides. This function returns the solution as an array [0..n+1] . The indices 0 and n+1 refer to the corresponding elements of the vector F (see Algorithm (5.1)).

ALGORITHM 5.1.
MAPLE *Functions* solvetridiag *and* norma.

```
solvetridiag:=proc(N, A, B, F) local alfa, beta, pom, x, i;
    # solution of a linear system of  N equations
    # with tridiagonal symmetric matrix, where
    # A is a vector diagonal of elements,
    # B is a vector of off-diagonal elements and
    # F is a vector of right hand site,
    #result is a vector (0..N+1)
    x:=array(0..N+1,[(0)=F[0],(N+1)=F[N+1]]);
    alfa[1]:= -B[1]/A[1]; beta[1]:= F[1]/A[1];
    for i from 2 to N-1 do
        pom:= A[i]+B[i-1]*alfa[i-1];
        alfa[i]:= -B[i]/pom;
        beta[i]:= (F[i]-B[i-1]*beta[i-1])/pom
    od;
    x[N]:= (F[N]-B[N-1]*beta[N-1])/(A[N]+B[N-1]*alfa[N-1]);
    for i from N-1 by -1 to 1 do
        x[i]:= alfa[i]*x[i+1]+beta[i]
    od;
    eval(x)
end;  #solvetridiag

norma:= proc(N, X) local mx,i,pom;
    #calculation of a infinity norm for 1-D array X, i=1..N
    mx:=0;
    for i to N do
        pom:=abs(X[i]);
        if pom > mx then mx := pom fi
    od;
    mx
end;
```

The implementation of the Newton method is now straightforward. We define the function iterate(), which performs the iterations calculating the new potential phi from the old one, until the norm of the correction H is less than a tolerance epsilon. iterate() also returns the norm of the difference of the last two iterations. We will choose epsilon = 0.001.

```
>     #generation of vectors A,B and average step hp
> B := array(0..N-1): A := array(1..N): hp := array(1..N-1):
> for i from 0 to N-1 do B[i] := 1/(xp[i+1]-xp[i]) od:
> for i from 1 to N-1 do A[i] := -(B[i-1]+B[i]) od:
> for i from 1 to N-1 do hp[i] := (xp[i+1]-xp[i-1])/2 od:
> phi := array(0..N):
```

ALGORITHM 5.2. *Definition of the Iteration Function.*

```
iterate:=proc(phi) local i, nor, H, ex, Ap, Fp;
   #iterations for phi begin
   nor:=1;
   while nor > epsilon do
      for i to N-1 do
          ex := exp(phi[i]);
          Ap[i] := A[i] - hp[i]*(ex+1/ex);
          Fp[i] := Fpoc[i] + hp[i]*(ex-1/ex) - A[i]*phi[i];
          if i = 1 then Fp[1] := Fp[1] - B[1]*phi[2]
             elif i = N-1 then Fp[N-1] := Fp[N-1] - B[N-2]*phi[N-2]
             else Fp[i] := Fp[i] - B[i-1]*phi[i-1] - B[i]*phi[i+1]
          fi;
      od;
      H:=solvetridiag(N-1,Ap,B,Fp);
      for i to N-1 do
         phi[i] := H[i] + phi[i];
         nor := norma(N-1,H);
      od;
   od;
end; #iterate
```

```
>      #initial approximation of phi
> phi := eval(phiD):
>      #introducing of boundary condition
> phi[0] := phi[0]+U0:
>      #generation of vectors of right hand side Fpoc and Fp
> Fpoc := array(0..N): Fp := array(0..N):
> for i to N-1 do Fpoc[i] := -hp[i]*Ca[i] od:
> Fpoc[1] := Fpoc[1] - B[0]*phi[0]:
> Fpoc[N-1] := Fpoc[N-1] - B[N-1]*phi[N]:
>      #introducing the boundary conditions into Fp
> Fp[0] := phi[0]: Fp[N] := phi[N]:
> epsilon := 0.001:   #error of the result
>      #solution for  phi
> iterate(phi);  #returns a value of norm for iteruj:=proc(phi)
                                              -6
                        .1899345025*10
```

```
>      #graph of builtin potential phiD
> GphiD:=plot(arcsinh(c/2),x=0..L, color=red):
>      # plot of resulting phi and phiD
>  plot({[seq([xp[i],phi[i]],i=0..N)],GphiD});
>      #end
```

The graph of the internal and builtin potentials is in Figure 5.1.

FIGURE 5.1. *Internal and Builtin Potentials for* $u_0 = 0$.

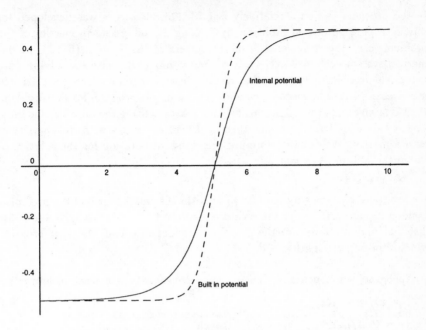

FIGURE 5.2. *Internal and Builtin Potentials for* $u_0 = 0.3$.

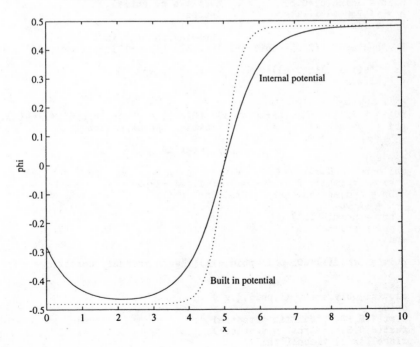

5.3   MATLAB Solution

In the previous section a relatively fast MAPLE algorithm was developed for solving a pure numerical problem, by making use of special properties of the problem (e.g. the tridiagonality of the matrix of the System (5.21)). A numerical system such as MATLAB is of course more adequate for solving pure numerical problems. By using the standard mechanism for dealing with sparse matrices in MATLAB, we can formulate a very simple program for our problem.

MATLAB allows the definition of sparse matrices using the function spdiags. The standard matrix operations then deal very efficiently with the sparsity of such a matrix. We can therefore use the standard notation for the solution of the linear system $A \cdot x = f$:

```
>> x = A\f
```

We again use Newton's method for solving the discretized form of the nonlinear Poisson Equation (5.9). In the definitions of the tridiagonal matrix $\hat{A}$ and the diagonal matrix $\hat{D}$ we use the function spdiagsx. The MATLAB program which results is straightforward:

```
%program for computing the internal potential in a semiconductor

l = 10; n = 40;
u0 = 0.3                        %external potential
xl = (0:l/n:l)'                 %mesh
cl = tanh(20.0.*(xl./l-0.5))    %concentration of impurities
phid = asinh(cl*0.5)            %builtin potential
h = xl(2:n+1)-xl(1:n)           %steps
b = 1 ./h
                                %tridiagonal matrix A
A = spdiags([b(2:n) -(b(1:n-1)+b(2:n)) b(1:n-1)],-1:1,n-1,n-1)

hs = (h(1:n-1)+h(2:n))*0.5      %average steps
c = cl(2:n)

f0 = -hs.*c
f0(1) = f0(1)-(phid(1)+u0)*b(1); f0(n-1) = f0(n-1)-phid(n+1)*b(n);
phi =  phid(2:n)                %initial approximation

                                %iteration
nor = 1
while nor > 0.001
  ex = exp(phi); f =  f0+hs.*(ex-1./ex)-A*phi
  Dp = spdiags(hs.*(ex+1./ex),0,n-1,n-1)
  H = (A-Dp)\f
  nor = norm(H,inf)
  phi = phi+H
end

phiv = [phid(1)+u0; phi; phid(n+1)] %with boundary conditions

clg;
plot(xl,phiv,'-r', xl,phid,':g')
hold;
text(4.6,-0.4,'Builtin potential');
text(6,0.3,'Internal potential');
xlabel('x'); ylabel('phi');
                    %end
```

The plot of the results for the external potential $u_0 = 0.3$ are given in Figure 5.2.

References

[1] W.H. PRESS, B.P. FLANNERY, S.A. TEUKOLSKY and W.T. VETTERLING, *Numerical Recipes*, Cambridge University Press, 1988.

[2] S. SELBERHERR, *Analysis and Simulation of Semiconductor Devices*, Springer, 1984.

Chapter 6. Some Least Squares Problems

W. Gander and U. von Matt

6.1   Introduction

In this chapter we will consider some least squares problems, that arise in quality control in manufacturing using coordinate measurement techniques [4], [5]. In mass production machines are producing parts, and it is important to know, if the output satisfies the quality requirements. Therefore some sample parts are usually taken out of the production line, measured carefully and compared with the nominal features. If they do not fit the specified tolerances, the machine may have to be serviced and adjusted to produce better parts.

6.2   Fitting Lines, Rectangles and Squares in the Plane

Fitting a line to a set of points in such a way that the sum of squares of the distances of the given points to the line is minimized, is known to be related to the computation of the main axes of an inertia tensor. In [1] this fact is used to fit a line and a plane to given points in the 3d space by solving an eigenvalue problem for a 3×3 matrix.

In this section we will develop a different algorithm, based on the singular value decomposition, that will allow us to fit lines, rectangles, and squares to measured points in the plane and that will also be useful for some problems in 3d space.

Let us first consider the problem of fitting a straight line to a set of given points P_1, P_2, ..., P_m in the plane. We denote their coordinates with (x_{P_1}, y_{P_1}), (x_{P_2}, y_{P_2}), ..., (x_{P_m}, y_{P_m}). Sometimes it is useful to define the vectors of all x and y coordinates. We will use $\mathbf{x}_P$ for the vector $(x_{P_1}, x_{P_2}, \ldots, x_{P_m})$ and similarly $\mathbf{y}_P$ for the y coordinates.

The problem we want to solve is not *linear regression*. Linear regression means to fit the linear model $y = ax + b$ to the given points, i.e. to determine the two parameters a and b such that the sum of squares of the residual is minimized:

$$\sum_{i=1}^{m} r_i^2 = \min, \quad \text{where} \quad r_i = y_{P_i} - a x_{P_i} - b.$$

This simple linear least squares problem is solved in MATLAB by the following statements (assuming that $x = x_P$ and $y = y_P$):

```
>> p = [ x ones(size(x))]\y;
>> a = p(1); b = p(2);
```

In the case of the linear regression the sum of squares of the differences of the y coordinates of the points P_i to the fitted linear function is minimized. What we would like to minimize now, however, is the *sum of squares of the distances of the points from the fitted straight line.*

In the plane we can represent a straight line uniquely by the equations

$$c + n_1 x + n_2 y = 0, \quad n_1^2 + n_2^2 = 1. \tag{6.1}$$

The unit vector (n_1, n_2) is orthogonal to the line. A point is on the line if its coordinates (x, y) satisfy the first equation. On the other hand if $P = (x_P, y_P)$ is some point not on the line and we compute

$$r = c + n_1 x_P + n_2 y_P$$

then $|r|$ is its distance from the line. Therefore if we want to determine the line for which the sum of squares of the distances to given points is minimal, we have to solve the constrained least squares problem

$$||\mathbf{r}|| = \sum_{i=1}^{m} r_i^2 = \min$$

subject to

$$\begin{pmatrix} 1 & x_{P_1} & y_{P_1} \\ 1 & x_{P_2} & y_{P_2} \\ \vdots & \vdots & \vdots \\ 1 & x_{P_m} & y_{P_m} \end{pmatrix} \begin{pmatrix} c \\ n_1 \\ n_2 \end{pmatrix} = \begin{pmatrix} r_1 \\ r_2 \\ \vdots \\ r_m \end{pmatrix} \quad \text{and } n_1^2 + n_2^2 = 1. \tag{6.2}$$

Let $\mathbf{A}$ be the matrix of the linear system (6.2), $\mathbf{x}$ denote the vector of unknowns $(c, n_1, n_2)^T$ and $\mathbf{r}$ the right hand side. Since orthogonal transformations $\mathbf{y} = \mathbf{Q}^T \mathbf{r}$ leave the norm invariant ($||\mathbf{y}||_2 = ||\mathbf{r}||_2$ for an orthogonal matrix $\mathbf{Q}$), we can proceed as follows to solve problem (6.2).

First we compute the QR decomposition of $\mathbf{A}$ and reduce our problem to solving a small system:

$$\mathbf{A} = \mathbf{QR} \implies \mathbf{Q}^T \mathbf{Ax} = \begin{pmatrix} r_{11} & r_{12} & r_{13} \\ 0 & r_{22} & r_{23} \\ 0 & 0 & r_{33} \\ 0 & 0 & 0 \\ \vdots & \vdots & \vdots \\ 0 & 0 & 0 \end{pmatrix} \begin{pmatrix} c \\ n_1 \\ n_2 \end{pmatrix} = \mathbf{Q}^T \mathbf{r} \tag{6.3}$$

Since the nonlinear constraint only involves two unknowns we now have to solve

$$\begin{pmatrix} r_{22} & r_{23} \\ 0 & r_{33} \end{pmatrix} \begin{pmatrix} n_1 \\ n_2 \end{pmatrix} \approx \begin{pmatrix} 0 \\ 0 \end{pmatrix}, \quad \text{subject to } n_1^2 + n_2^2 = 1. \tag{6.4}$$

ALGORITHM 6.1. *Function* cslq.

```
function [c,n] = clsq(A,dim);
% solves the constrained least squares Problem
% A (c n)' ~ 0 subject to norm(n,2)=1
% length(n) = dim
% [c,n] = clsq(A,dim)
[m,p] = size(A);
if p < dim+1, error ('not enough unknowns'); end;
if m < dim, error ('not enough equations'); end;
m = min (m, p);
R = triu (qr (A));
[U,S,V] = svd(R(p-dim+1:m,p-dim+1:p));
n = V(:,dim);
c = -R(1:p-dim,1:p-dim)\R(1:p-dim,p-dim+1:p)*n;
```

Problem (6.4) is of the form $\|\mathbf{B}\mathbf{x}\|_2 = \min$, subject to $\|\mathbf{x}\|_2 = 1$. The value of the minimum is the *smallest singular value of* $\mathbf{B}$, and the solution is given by the corresponding singular vector [2]. Thus we can determine n_1 and n_2 by a singular value decomposition of a 2-by-2 matrix. Inserting the values into the first equation of (6.4), we then can compute c by equating to zero. As a slight generalization we denote the dimension of the normal vector $\mathbf{n}$ by dim. Then, the MATLAB function to solve problem (6.2) is given by Algorithm 6.1. Let us test the function clsq with the following main program:

```
>> % mainline.m
>> Px = [1:10]'
>> Py = [ 0.2 1.0 2.6 3.6 4.9 5.3 6.5 7.8 8.0 9.0]'
>> A = [ones(size(Px)) Px Py]
>> [c, n] = clsq(A,2)
```

The line computed by the program mainline has the equation $0.4162 - 0.7057x + 0.7086y = 0$. We would now like to plot the points and the fitted line. For this we need the function plotline, Algorithm 6.2. The picture is generated by adding the commands

```
>> axis([-1, 11 -1, 11])
>> hold
>> plotline(Px,Py,'o',c,n,'-')
```

to the program mainline. The result is shown as Figure 6.1.

Fitting two Parallel Lines

To fit two parallel lines, we must have two sets of points. We denote those two sets by $\{P_i\}, i = 1, \ldots, p$, and $\{Q_j\}, j = 1, \ldots, q$. Since the lines are parallel, their normal vector must be the same. Thus the equations for the lines are

ALGORITHM 6.2. *Function* plotline.

```
function plotline(x,y,s,c,n,t)
% plots the set of points (x,y) using the symbol s
% and plots the straight line c+n1*x+n2*y=0 using
% the line type defined by t
plot(x,y,s)
xrange = [min(x) max(x)];
yrange = [min(y) max(y)];
if n(1)==0, % c+n2*y=0  => y = -c/n(2)
   x1=xrange(1); y1 = -c/n(2);
   x2=xrange(2); y2 = y1
elseif n(2) == 0, % c+n1*x=0  => x = -c/n(1)
   y1=yrange(1); x1 = -c/n(1);
   y2=yrange(2); x2 = x1;
elseif xrange(2)-xrange(1)> yrange(2)-yrange(1),
   x1=xrange(1); y1 = -(c+n(1)*x1)/n(2);
   x2=xrange(2); y2 = -(c+n(1)*x2)/n(2);
else
   y1=yrange(1); x1 = -(c+n(2)*y1)/n(1);
   y2=yrange(2); x2 = -(c+n(2)*y2)/n(1);
end
plot([x1, x2], [y1,y2],t)
```

FIGURE 6.1. *Fitting a Straight Line.*

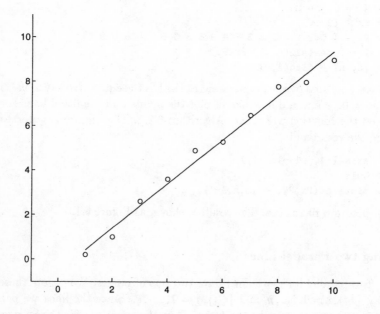

$$c_1 + n_1 x + n_2 y = 0,$$
$$c_2 + n_1 x + n_2 y = 0,$$
$$n_1^2 + n_2^2 = 1.$$

If we insert the coordinates of the two sets of points into these equations we get the following constrained least squares problem:

$$\|\mathbf{r}\| = \sum_{i=1}^{m} r_i^2 = \min$$

subject to

$$
\begin{pmatrix}
1 & 0 & x_{P_1} & y_{P_1} \\
1 & 0 & x_{P_2} & y_{P_2} \\
\vdots & \vdots & \vdots & \vdots \\
1 & 0 & x_{P_p} & y_{P_p} \\
0 & 1 & x_{Q_1} & y_{Q_1} \\
0 & 1 & x_{Q_2} & y_{Q_2} \\
\vdots & \vdots & \vdots & \vdots \\
0 & 1 & x_{Q_q} & y_{Q_q}
\end{pmatrix}
\begin{pmatrix} c_1 \\ c_2 \\ n_1 \\ n_2 \end{pmatrix}
=
\begin{pmatrix} r_1 \\ r_2 \\ \vdots \\ r_{p+q} \end{pmatrix}
\quad \text{and } n_1^2 + n_2^2 = 1.
\tag{6.5}
$$

Again, we can use our function `clsq` to solve this problem:

```
>> % mainparallel.m
>> clg
>> Px = [1:10]'
>> Py = [ 0.2 1.0 2.6 3.6 4.9 5.3 6.5 7.8 8.0 9.0]'
>> Qx = [ 1.5 2.6 3.0 4.3 5.0 6.4 7.6 8.5 9.9 ]'
>> Qy = [ 5.8 7.2 9.1 10.5 10.6 10.7 13.4 14.2 14.5]'
>> A = [ones(size(Px))  zeros(size(Px)) Px Py
>>       zeros(size(Qx))  ones(size(Qx)) Qx Qy ]
>> [c, n] = clsq(A,2)
>> axis([-1 11 -1 17])
>> hold
>> plotline(Px,Py,'o',c(1),n,'-')
>> plotline(Qx,Qy,'+',c(2),n,'-')
```

The results obtained by the program `mainparallel` are the two lines

$$0.5091 - 0.7146x + 0.6996y = 0,$$
$$-3.5877 - 0.7146x + 0.6996y = 0,$$

which are plotted as Figure 6.2.

Fitting Orthogonal Lines

To fit two orthogonal lines we can proceed very similar as in the the case of the parallel lines. If (n_1, n_2) is the normal vector of the first line, then the second

FIGURE 6.2. *Fitting Two Parallel Lines.*

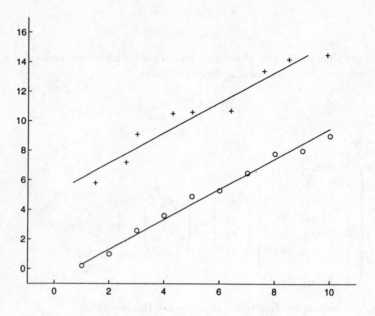

FIGURE 6.3. *Fitting Two Orthogonal Lines.*

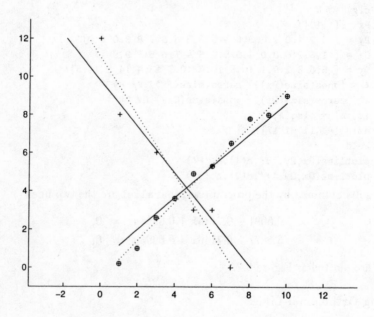

line must have the normal vector $(-n_2, n_1)$ in order to be orthogonal. Therefore again we will have four unknowns: c_1, c_2, n_1 and n_2. If the P_i's are the points associated with the first line and the Q_j's are the points associated with the second line, we obtain the following constrained least squares problem:

$$\|\mathbf{r}\| = \sum_{i=1}^{m} r_i^2 = \min$$

subject to

$$
\begin{pmatrix}
1 & 0 & x_{P_1} & y_{P_1} \\
1 & 0 & x_{P_2} & y_{P_2} \\
\vdots & \vdots & \vdots & \vdots \\
1 & 0 & x_{P_p} & y_{P_p} \\
0 & 1 & y_{Q_1} & -x_{Q_1} \\
0 & 1 & y_{Q_2} & -x_{Q_2} \\
\vdots & \vdots & \vdots & \vdots \\
0 & 1 & y_{Q_q} & -x_{Q_q}
\end{pmatrix}
\begin{pmatrix}
c_1 \\
c_2 \\
n_1 \\
n_2
\end{pmatrix}
=
\begin{pmatrix}
r_1 \\
r_2 \\
\vdots \\
r_{p+q}
\end{pmatrix}
\quad \text{and } n_1^2 + n_2^2 = 1. \qquad (6.6)
$$

We only have to change the definition of the matrix A in `mainparallel` in order to compute the equations of the two orthogonal lines. To obtain a nicer plot we also chose different values for the second set of points.

```
>> % mainorthogonal.m
>> clg
>> Px = [1:10]'
>> Py = [ 0.2 1.0 2.6 3.6 4.9 5.3 6.5 7.8 8.0 9.0]'
>> Qx = [ 0 1 3 5 6 7]'
>> Qy = [12 8 6 3 3 0]'
>> A = [ones(size(Px))   zeros(size(Px)) Px  Py
>>       zeros(size(Qx)) ones(size(Qx))  Qy -Qx ]
>> [c, n] = clsq(A,2)
>> axis([-1 11 -1 13])
>> axis('equal')
>> hold
>> plotline(Px,Py,'o',c(1),n,'-')
>> n2(1) =-n(2); n2(2) = n(1)
>> plotline(Qx,Qy,'+',c(2),n2,'-')
```

The Program `mainorthogonal` computes the two orthogonal lines

$$
\begin{aligned}
-0.2527 - 0.6384x + 0.7697y &= 0, \\
6.2271 - 0.7697x - 0.6384y &= 0.
\end{aligned}
$$

We can also fit two lines individually to each set of points:

```
>> [c, n] = clsq([ones(size(Px)) Px Py],2)
>> plotline(Px,Py,'+',c,n,':')
>> [c, n] = clsq([ones(size(Qx)) Qx Qy],2)
>> plotline(Qx,Qy,'+',c,n,':')
```

The individually computed lines are indicated by the dotted lines in Figure 6.3.

Fitting a Rectangle

Fitting a rectangle requires four sets of points:

$$P_i, i = 1, \ldots, p, \quad Q_j, j = 1, \ldots, q, \quad R_k, k = 1, \ldots, r, \quad S_l, l = 1, \ldots, s.$$

Since the sides of the rectangle are parallel and orthogonal we can proceed very similar as before. The four sides will have the equations

$$
\begin{aligned}
a: \quad c_1 + n_1 x + n_2 y &= 0 \\
b: \quad c_2 - n_2 x + n_1 y &= 0 \\
c: \quad c_3 + n_1 x + n_2 y &= 0 \\
d: \quad c_4 - n_2 x + n_1 y &= 0 \\
n_1^2 + n_2^2 &= 1.
\end{aligned}
$$

Inserting the sets of points we get the following constrained least squares problem:

$$\|\mathbf{r}\| = \sum_{i=1}^{m} r_i^2 = \min$$

subject to

$$
\begin{pmatrix}
1 & 0 & 0 & 0 & x_{P_1} & y_{P_1} \\
\vdots & \vdots & \vdots & \vdots & \vdots & \vdots \\
1 & 0 & 0 & 0 & x_{P_p} & y_{P_p} \\
0 & 1 & 0 & 0 & y_{Q_1} & -x_{Q_1} \\
\vdots & \vdots & \vdots & \vdots & \vdots & \vdots \\
0 & 1 & 0 & 0 & y_{Q_q} & -x_{Q_q} \\
0 & 0 & 1 & 0 & x_{R_1} & y_{R_1} \\
\vdots & \vdots & \vdots & \vdots & \vdots & \vdots \\
0 & 0 & 1 & 0 & x_{R_r} & y_{R_r} \\
0 & 0 & 0 & 1 & y_{S_1} & -x_{S_1} \\
\vdots & \vdots & \vdots & \vdots & \vdots & \vdots \\
0 & 0 & 0 & 1 & y_{S_s} & -x_{S_s}
\end{pmatrix}
\begin{pmatrix}
c_1 \\ c_2 \\ c_3 \\ c_4 \\ n_1 \\ n_2
\end{pmatrix}
=
\begin{pmatrix}
r_1 \\ r_2 \\ \vdots \\ r_{p+q+r+s}
\end{pmatrix}
\quad \text{and } n_1^2 + n_2^2 = 1.
$$

$$(6.7)$$

Instead of explicitly giving the coordinates of the four sets of points, we will now enter the points with the mouse using the ginput function in MATLAB. [X,Y] = ginput(N) gets N points from the current axes and returns the x- and y-coordinates in the vectors X and Y of length N. The points have to be entered clock- or counter clock wise in the same order as the sides of the rectangle: the next side is always orthogonal to the previous.

```
>> % rectangle.m
>> clg
>> axis([0 10 0 10])
>> axis('equal')
>> hold
>> p=100; q=100; r=100; s=100;
```

```
>> disp('enter points P_i belonging to side A')
>> disp('by clicking the mouse in the graphical window.')
>> disp('Finish the input by pressing the Return key')
>> [Px,Py] = ginput(p); plot(Px,Py,'o')
>> disp('enter points Q_i for side B ')
>> [Qx,Qy] = ginput(q); plot(Qx,Qy,'x')
>> disp('enter points R_i for side C ')
>> [Rx,Ry] = ginput(r); plot(Rx,Ry,'*')
>> disp('enter points S_i for side D ')
>> [Sx,Sy] = ginput(s); plot(Sx,Sy,'+')

>> zp = zeros(size(Px)); op =  ones(size(Px));
>> zq = zeros(size(Qx)); oq =  ones(size(Qx));
>> zr = zeros(size(Rx)); or =  ones(size(Rx));
>> zs = zeros(size(Sx)); os =  ones(size(Sx));

>> A = [ op zp zp zp Px  Py
>>       zq oq zq zq Qy -Qx
>>       zr zr or zr Rx  Ry
>>       zs zs zs os Sy -Sx]

>> [c, n] = clsq(A,2)

>> % compute the 4 corners of the rectangle
>> B  = [n  [-n(2) n(1)]']
>> X = -B* [c([1 3 3 1])'; c([2 2 4 4])')']
>> X = [X X(:,1)]
>> plot(X(1,:), X(2,:))

>> % compute the individual lines, if possible
>> if all([sum(op)>1 sum(oq)>1 sum(or)>1 sum(os)>1]),
>>    [c1, n1] = clsq([op Px Py],2)
>>    [c2, n2] = clsq([oq Qx Qy],2)
>>    [c3, n3] = clsq([or Rx Ry],2)
>>    [c4, n4] = clsq([os Sx Sy],2)

>>    % and their intersection points
>>    aaa = -[n1(1) n1(2); n2(1) n2(2)]\[c1; c2];
>>    bbb = -[n2(1) n2(2); n3(1) n3(2)]\[c2; c3];
>>    ccc = -[n3(1) n3(2); n4(1) n4(2)]\[c3; c4];
>>    ddd = -[n4(1) n4(2); n1(1) n1(2)]\[c4; c1];

>>    plot([aaa(1) bbb(1) ccc(1) ddd(1) aaa(1)], ...
>>         [aaa(2) bbb(2) ccc(2) ddd(2) aaa(2)],':')
>> end
```

The Program `rectangle` not only computes the rectangle but also fits the individual lines to the set of points. The result is shown as Figure 6.4. Some comments may be needed to understand some statements. To find the coordinates of a corner of the rectangle, we compute the point of intersection of the two lines of the corresponding sides. We have to solve the linear system

$$n_1 x + n_2 y = -c_1 \atop -n_2 x + n_1 y = -c_2 \quad \Longleftrightarrow \quad C\mathbf{x} = -\begin{pmatrix} c_1 \\ c_2 \end{pmatrix}, \quad C = \begin{pmatrix} n_1 & n_2 \\ -n_2 & n_1 \end{pmatrix}$$

Since C is orthogonal, we can simply multiply the right hand side by $B = C^T$ to obtain the solution. By arranging the equations for the 4 corners so that the matrix C is always the system matrix, we can compute the coordinates of all 4 corners simultaneously with the compact statement

```
>>  X = -B* [c([1 3 3 1])'; c([2 2 4 4])'].
```

FIGURE 6.4. *Fitting a Rectangle.*

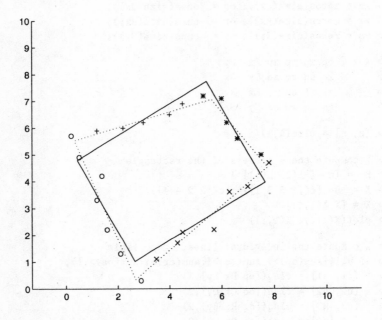

Fitting a Square

If $|d|$ denotes the length of the side of a square, then the four sides, *oriented counter clock wise*, have the equations

$$\begin{aligned}
\alpha : \qquad c_1 + n_1 x + n_2 y &= 0 \\
\beta : \qquad c_2 - n_2 x + n_1 y &= 0 \\
\gamma : \quad d + c_1 + n_1 x + n_2 y &= 0 \\
\delta : \quad d + c_2 - n_2 x + n_1 y &= 0 \\
n_1^2 + n_2^2 &= 1.
\end{aligned} \qquad (6.8)$$

The orientation is important: the parameter d in the third and fourth equation should have the same sign. If we want to orient the sides clockwise, then the normal vector in the equations for lines β and δ must have the other sign, i.e. we have to use the equations.

$$\begin{array}{rl} \beta: & c_2 + n_2 x - n_1 y = 0, \\ \delta: & d + c_2 + n_2 x - n_1 y = 0. \end{array}$$

We will assume in the following, that the four sets of points

$$P_i, i = 1, \ldots, p, \quad Q_j, j = 1, \ldots, q, \quad R_k, k = 1, \ldots, r, \quad S_l, l = 1, \ldots, s$$

belong to the four sides which are oriented counter clockwise. Then our problem becomes

$$||\mathbf{r}|| = \sum_{i=1}^{m} r_i^2 = \min$$

subject to

$$\begin{pmatrix} 0 & 1 & 0 & x_{P_1} & y_{P_1} \\ \vdots & \vdots & \vdots & \vdots & \vdots \\ 0 & 1 & 0 & x_{P_p} & y_{P_p} \\ 0 & 0 & 1 & y_{Q_1} & -x_{Q_1} \\ \vdots & \vdots & \vdots & \vdots & \vdots \\ 0 & 0 & 1 & y_{Q_q} & -x_{Q_q} \\ 1 & 1 & 0 & x_{R_1} & y_{R_1} \\ \vdots & \vdots & \vdots & \vdots & \vdots \\ 1 & 1 & 0 & x_{R_r} & y_{R_r} \\ 1 & 0 & 1 & y_{S_1} & -x_{S_1} \\ \vdots & \vdots & \vdots & \vdots & \vdots \\ 1 & 0 & 1 & y_{S_s} & -x_{S_s} \end{pmatrix} \begin{pmatrix} d \\ c_1 \\ c_2 \\ n_1 \\ n_2 \end{pmatrix} = \begin{pmatrix} r_1 \\ r_2 \\ \vdots \\ r_{p+q+r+s} \end{pmatrix} \quad \text{and } n_1^2 + n_2^2 = 1. \quad (6.9)$$

We can reuse a lot of the program `rectangle`. The only change is the new definition of the matrix A and the vector c which is used to plot the square. When entering the points we have to arrange the sides counter clockwise.

```
>> A = [ zp op zp  Px  Py
>>        zq zq oq  Qy -Qx
>>        or or zr  Rx  Ry
>>        os zs os  Sy -Sx]
>> [cc, n] = clsq(A,2)
>> % compute the vector of constants for the four lines
>> c(1) = cc(2); c(2) = cc(3); c(3) = c(1)+cc(1);
>> c(4) = c(2)+cc(1);  c=c(:);
>> % compute the 4 corners of the square
>> B   = [n  [-n(2) n(1)]']
>> X = -B* [c([1 3 3 1])'; c([2 2 4 4])']
>> X = [X X(:,1)]
>> plot(X(1,:), X(2,:))
```

In Figure 6.5 the best rectangle and the best fitted square are shown. Notice that in extreme cases, we may not obtain a result that we may wish. Consider

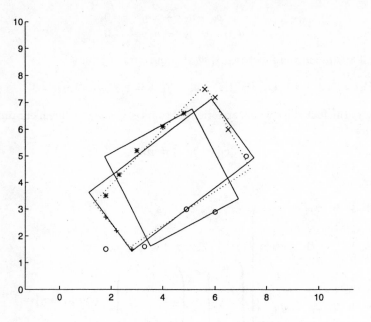

FIGURE 6.5. *Fitting a Rectangle and a Square.*

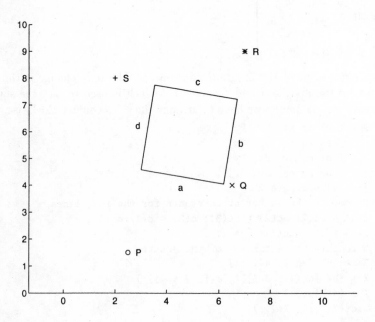

FIGURE 6.6. *"Best" Square for Four Points.*

Figure 6.6, where we computed the "best square" for the four points $P = (2.5, 1.5)$, $Q = (6.5, 4)$, $R = (7, 9)$ and $S = (2, 8)$. It seems that the square is not well fitted. However, notice that point P belongs to the first side a, point Q to b, point R to c and S to d. The four points lay perfectly on the lines through the sides so that the sum of squares of their distances is zero!

6.3 Fitting Hyperplanes

Function clsq can be used to fit an $(n-1)$-dimensional hyperplane in R^n to given points. Let the rows of the matrix $X = [\mathbf{x}_1, \mathbf{x}_2, \ldots, \mathbf{x}_m]^T$ contain the coordinates of the given points, i.e. point P_i has the coordinates $\mathbf{x}_i = X(i,:)$, $i = 1, \ldots, m$. Then the call

```
>> [c, N] = clsq ([ones(m,1) X], n);
```

determines the hyperplane in normal form $c + N_1 y_1 + N_2 y_2 + \ldots + N_n y_n = 0$.

In this section, we will show how, we can compute also best fit hyperplanes of lower dimensions s, where $1 \leq s \leq n-1$. We follow the theory developed in [3]. An s dimensional hyperplane α in R^n can be represented in parameter form:

$$\alpha: \quad \mathbf{y} = \mathbf{p} + \mathbf{a}_1 t_1 + \mathbf{a}_2 t_2 + \cdots \mathbf{a}_s t_s = \mathbf{p} + At. \tag{6.10}$$

In this equation $\mathbf{p}$ is a point on the plane and $\mathbf{a}_i$ are linear independent direction vectors, thus the hyperplane is determined by the data $\mathbf{p}$ and $A = [\mathbf{a}_1, \ldots, \mathbf{a}_s]$.

Without loss of generality, we can assume that A is orthogonal, i.e. $A^T A = I_s$. If we now want to fit a hyperplane to the given set of points X, then we have to minimize the distance of the points to the plane. The distance d_i of point $P_i = \mathbf{x}_i$ to the hyperplane is given by

$$d_i = \min_{\mathbf{t}} \|\mathbf{p} - \mathbf{x}_i + At\|_2.$$

To determine the minimum we solve grad $d_i^2 = 2A^T(\mathbf{p} - \mathbf{x}_i + At) = \mathbf{0}$ for $\mathbf{t}$, and, since A is orthogonal, we obtain

$$\mathbf{t} = A^T(\mathbf{x}_i - \mathbf{p}). \tag{6.11}$$

Therefore the distance becomes

$$d_i^2 = \|\mathbf{p} - \mathbf{x}_i + AA^T(\mathbf{x}_i - \mathbf{p})\|_2^2 = \|\mathcal{P}(\mathbf{x}_i - \mathbf{p})\|_2^2,$$

where we denoted by $\mathcal{P} = I - AA^T$ the projector onto the complement of the range of A, i.e. on the nullspace of A^T.

Our objective is to minimize the sum of squares of the distances of all points to the hyperplane. We want to minimize the function

$$F(\mathbf{p}, A) = \sum_{i=1}^{m} \|\mathcal{P}(\mathbf{x}_i - \mathbf{p})\|_2^2. \tag{6.12}$$

A necessary condition is grad $F = \mathbf{0}$. We first consider the first part of the gradient, the partial derivative

$$\frac{\partial F}{\partial \mathbf{p}} = -\sum_{i=1}^{m} 2\mathcal{P}^T \mathcal{P}(\mathbf{x}_i - \mathbf{p}) = -2\mathcal{P}(\sum_{i=1}^{m} \mathbf{x}_i - m\mathbf{p}) = \mathbf{0},$$

where we made use of the property of a projector $\mathcal{P}^T \mathcal{P} = \mathcal{P}$. Since $\mathcal{P}$ projects the vector $\sum_{i=1}^{m} \mathbf{x}_i - m\mathbf{p}$ onto $\mathbf{0}$, this vector must be in the range of A, i.e.

$$\mathbf{p} = \frac{1}{m} \sum_{i=1}^{m} \mathbf{x}_i + A\tau. \tag{6.13}$$

Inserting this expression into Equation (6.12), the objective function to be minimized simplifies to

$$G(A) = \sum_{i=1}^{m} \|\mathcal{P}\hat{\mathbf{x}}_i\|_2^2 = \|\mathcal{P}\hat{X}^T\|_F^2, \tag{6.14}$$

where we put

$$\hat{\mathbf{x}}_i = \mathbf{x}_i - \frac{1}{m} \sum_{i=1}^{m} \mathbf{x}_i,$$

and where we used the *Frobenius norm* of a matrix ($\|A\|_F^2 := \sum_{i,j} a_{ij}^2$). Now since $\mathcal{P}$ is symmetric, we may also write

$$G(A) = \|\hat{X}\mathcal{P}\|_F^2 = \|\hat{X}(I - AA^T)\|_F^2 = \|\hat{X} - \hat{X}AA^T\|_F^2. \tag{6.15}$$

If we define $Y := \hat{X}AA^T$, which is a matrix of rank s, then we can consider the problem of minimizing

$$\|\hat{X} - Y\|_F^2 = \min, \quad \text{subject to} \quad rank(Y) = s.$$

It is well known, how to approximate in the Frobenius norm a matrix by a matrix of lower rank (cf. e.g. [2]):

1. Compute the singular value decomposition of $\hat{X} = U\Sigma V^T$, with

$$U, V \quad \text{orthogonal and} \quad \Sigma = diag(\sigma_1, \sigma_2 \ldots \sigma_n)$$

   and $\sigma_1 \geq \sigma_2 \geq \cdots \geq \sigma_n$.

2. The minimizing matrix is then given by $Y = U\Sigma_s V^T$, where

$$\Sigma_s = diag(\sigma_1, \sigma_2 \ldots, \sigma_s, 0, 0, \ldots, 0).$$

Now if $Y = U\Sigma_s V^T$, we have to find an orthogonal matrix A such that $\hat{X}AA^T = Y$. It is easy to verify, that if we choose $A = V_1$ where $V_1 = V(:, 1:s)$, then

ALGORITHM 6.3. *Computation of Hyperplanes.*

```
function [V,p ] = hyper(Q);
% Fits a hyperplane of dimension s <n
% to a set of given points Q(i,:) belonging
%  to R^n.
% The hyperplane has the equation
% X = p + V(:,1:s)*tau (Parameter Form) or
% is defined as solution of the linear
% equations  V(:,s+1:n)'*(y - p)=0 (Normalform)
m = max(size(Q));
p = sum(Q)'/m;
Qt = Q - ones(size(Q))*diag(p);
[U S V] = svd(Qt, 0);
```

$\hat{X}AA^T = U\Sigma_s V^T$. Thus the singular value decomposition of $\hat{X}$ gives us all the lower dimensional hyperplanes that fit best the given points:

$$\mathbf{y} = \mathbf{p} + V_1 \mathbf{t}, \quad \text{with} \quad \mathbf{p} = \frac{1}{m}\sum_{i=1}^{m} \mathbf{x}_i.$$

Notice that $V_2 = V(:, s+1:n)$ gives us also the normal form of the hyperplane: Here the hyperplane is described as the solution of the linear equations

$$V_2^T \mathbf{y} = V_2^T \mathbf{p}.$$

In order to compute the hyperplanes we therefore essentially have to compute one singular value decomposition. This is done by the MATLAB function hyper.m (Algorithm 6.3). The reader should note that the statement [U S V] = svd(Qt, 0) computes the "economy size" singular value decomposition. If Qt is an m-by-n matrix with $m > n$, then only the first n columns of U are computed, and S is an n-by-n matrix.

Fitting a Plane in Space

Suppose that we are given the m points $P_1, \ldots, P_m$ in space, and that we want to fit a plane through these points such that the sum of the squares of the distances from the points to the plane is minimized. We can described a plane implicitly by the equations

$$c + n_1 x + n_2 y + n_3 z = 0, \quad n_1^2 + n_2^2 + n_3^2 = 1. \tag{6.16}$$

In this case the distance r from a point $P = (x, y, z)$ to the plane is given by

$$r = |c + n_1 x + n_2 y + n_3 z|.$$

84   *W. Gander and U. von Matt*

Consequently, we want to minimize

$$||\mathbf{r}|| = \sum_{i=1}^{m} r_i^2 = \min$$

subject to

$$\begin{pmatrix} 1 & x_{P_1} & y_{P_1} & z_{P_1} \\ 1 & x_{P_2} & y_{P_2} & z_{P_2} \\ \vdots & \vdots & \vdots & \vdots \\ 1 & x_{P_m} & y_{P_m} & z_{P_m} \end{pmatrix} \begin{pmatrix} c \\ n_1 \\ n_2 \\ n_3 \end{pmatrix} = \begin{pmatrix} r_1 \\ r_2 \\ \vdots \\ r_m \end{pmatrix} \quad \text{and } n_1^2 + n_2^2 + n_3^2 = 1. \quad (6.17)$$

In MATLAB this problem is easily solved by calling the function clsq:

```
>> [c, n] = clsq ([ones(m,1) P'], 3);
```

Alternatively, a point P on the plane can always be represented explicitly by

$$P = \mathbf{p} + c_1\mathbf{v}_1 + c_2\mathbf{v}_2. \quad (6.18)$$

If we use the procedure hyper to compute $\mathbf{p}$, $\mathbf{v}_1$, and $\mathbf{v}_2$, then $\mathbf{p}$ denotes the center of gravity of the data points, and $\mathbf{v}_1$ and $\mathbf{v}_2$ denote two orthogonal base vectors of the plane. Additionally, the straight line given by the equation

$$L = \mathbf{p} + c_1\mathbf{v}_1 \quad (6.19)$$

is also the least squares line through the given data points. We can generate a set of sample data points by the MATLAB statements

```
>> % mainhyper.m
>> m = 100;
>> rand ('seed', 10);
>> randn ('seed', 0);
>> P = rand (2, m) - 0.5;
>> P (3, :) = 0.5 * P (1, :) + 0.5 * P (2, :) + ...
>>             0.25 * randn (1, m);
```

These points lie approximately on the plane $x + y - 2z = 0$. The plane, that goes through these points in the least squares sense, is computed by the call

```
>> [V, p] = hyper (P');
```

We can now compute the projections of the points P_j onto this plane by

```
>> proj = p * ones (1, m) + ...
>>             V (:, 1:2) * V (:, 1:2)' * (P - p * ones (1, m));
```

In order to plot a square part of the plane we need to know the coordinates of four corner of the square. They can be computed by the following MATLAB statements:

```
>> corners = [1 -1 -1  1
>>             1  1 -1 -1];
>> corners = p * ones (1, 4) + V (:, 1:2) * corners;
```

In the same way, we can compute two points of the least squares line as follows:

```
>> straight = p * ones (1, 2) + V (:, 1) * [-1 1];
```

We are now ready to plot the least squares line and the least squares plane together with the projections of the data points onto the plane. The resulting static picture, however, would only give an inadequate representation of the three-dimensional situation. It would be hard to tell the relative position of all the different objects.

A moving picture, on the other hand, can create a much more realistic impression. In our example we can have the plane slowly revolve around the z-axis. This will also give us a good opportunity for introducing MATLAB's movie command.

A movie in MATLAB consists of a sequence of precomputed frames. The command frames = moviein (nframes) allocates the matrix frames which will store all the frames of our movie as its columns. By nframes we denote the number of single frames that we want to generate. We have to precompute all the frames of the movie and store them in frames by calls of getframe. Afterwards, we can display our animated pictures by the command movie.

In order to rotate the lines and the plane we introduce the rotation matrix

$$R := \begin{pmatrix} \cos\varphi & -\sin\varphi & 0 \\ \sin\varphi & \cos\varphi & 0 \\ 0 & 0 & 1 \end{pmatrix}, \tag{6.20}$$

where $\varphi = 2\pi/n_{\text{frames}}$. If we apply R to a point P we rotate P by the angle φ around the z-axis.

We want to use an orthographic projection to display our three-dimensional pictures on the two-dimensional computer screen, where the observer is located on the y-axis at $-\infty$. This is easily achieved by the MATLAB command view (viewmtx (0, 0, 0)).

The projection of the data points onto the plane, the least squares line, and the least squares plane must be plotted in the right sequence in order to achieve the desired effect. First, we plot the projection lines behind the plane. They can be identified by the condition P (2, j) > proj (2, j). Next, we plot the plane by a call of the patch primitive. Such a patch object supports the shading of its surface by prescribing the colors in its corners. If we make use of the gray-colormap we can color the surface of the plane such that it becomes darker along the y-axis. This trick leads to the convincing three-dimensional appearance of the picture. Then, we draw the least squares line by a call of line. Finally, the projection lines before the plane are plotted. We can avoid the automatic replotting of the picture elements, which is undesirable in this application, by setting the option EraseMode to none. In this way the default hidden line removal in MATLAB is disabled.

These considerations lead us to the following MATLAB program, which first precomputes all the frames and then displays the movie infinitely many times:

```
>> nframes = 36;  phi = 2 * pi / nframes;
>> rot = [cos(phi) -sin(phi) 0
>>         sin(phi)  cos(phi) 0
>>            0         0      1];
>> clf; axis ('off');  colormap (gray);
>> frames = moviein (nframes);

>> for k = 1:nframes,
>>    clf;
>>    axis ([-1.25 1.25 -1.25 1.25 -1.25 1.25]);  axis ('off');
>>    view (viewmtx (0, 0, 0));  caxis ([-1.3 1.3]);

>>    % plot points behind the plane
>>    for j = 1:m,
>>      if P (2, j) > proj (2, j),
>>        line ([P(1,j) proj(1,j)], ...
>>              [P(2,j) proj(2,j)], ...
>>              [P(3,j) proj(3,j)], ...
>>              'Color', 'yellow', 'EraseMode', 'none');
>>      end
>>    end
>>    drawnow;

>>    % plot plane
>>    patch (corners (1, :), corners (2, :), corners (3, :), ...
>>           -corners (2, :), ...
>>           'EdgeColor', 'none', 'EraseMode', 'none');
>>    drawnow;

>>    % plot least squares line
>>    line (straight (1, :), straight (2, :), straight (3, :), ...
>>          'Color', 'red', 'EraseMode', 'none');
>>    drawnow;

>>    % plot points before the plane
>>    for j = 1:m,
>>      if P (2, j) <= proj (2, j),
>>        line ([P(1,j) proj(1,j)], ...
>>              [P(2,j) proj(2,j)], ...
>>              [P(3,j) proj(3,j)], ...
>>              'Color', 'yellow', 'EraseMode', 'none');
>>      end
>>    end
>>    drawnow;

>>    frames (:, k) = getframe;
```

```
>>    % rotate points
>>    P = rot * P;  proj = rot * proj;
>>    corners = rot * corners;  straight = rot * straight;
>> end;
>> clf;  axis ('off');  movie (frames, inf);
```

References

[1] G. GEISE und S. SCHIPKE *Ausgleichsgerade, -kreis, -ebene und -kugel im Raum*, Mathematische Nachrichten, 62, 1974.

[2] G.H. GOLUB and CH. VAN LOAN, *Matrix Computations*. 2nd ed., John Hopkins University Press, Baltimore, 1989.

[3] H. SPÄTH, *Orthogonal least squares fitting with linear manifolds*. Numer. Math., 48, 1986, pp. 441–445.

[4] VDI BERICHTE 761, *Dimensional Metrology in Production and Quality Control*. VDI Verlag, Düsseldorf, 1989.

[5] H.J. WARNECKE und W. DUTSCHKE, *Fertigungsmesstechnik*, Springer, Berlin, 1984.

Chapter 7. The Generalized Billiard Problem

S. Bartoň

7.1   Introduction

We consider the following problem: *Given a billiard table (not necessarily rectangular) and two balls on it, from which direction should the first ball be struck, so that it rebounds off the rim of the table, and then impacts the second ball?* This problem has previously been solved for a circular table in [1, 2, 4].

Let the billiard table be parametrically described by $X = f(t)$ and $Y = g(t)$. These functions may be arbitrary, with the single requirement being that their first derivatives exist. We aim at the rim points described by the coordinates $[X(t_i),\ Y(t_i)]$. To solve the given problem, we shall use two different methods; *the generalized reflection method* and *the shortest trajectory method*. We use both methods to derive functions of the parameter t, whose roots are the points $t_1, \ldots, t_n$; i.e. the solution to the given problem. We shall first find the analytic solution in the first part of the chapter. In the second part we intuitively check this solution by solving some practical examples. In more complicated cases we shall use numerical methods to solve the final equation.

7.2   The Generalized Reflection Method

The solution of the problem can be divided into two main steps. First, the trajectory of the ball reflected by the general point on the billiard rim is found. Second, the point on the billiard rim is found such that the second ball lies on this trajectory.

The first step can be solved by a generalization of the plane mirror problem, i.e. find the path touching line l from point P to point Q, according to the mirror condition. The mirror condition is satisfied when the impact angle is equal to the reflection angle.

In the second step we calculate the distance between the reflected trajectory and the position of the second ball. This distance is a function of the impact position point. The problem is solved once the point has been found with corresponding distance equal to zero.

7.2.1 Line and Curve Reflection

To begin, we construct point M as a *mirror point* of P, using the line l as an axis of symmetry. The line l' connecting points M and Q intersects line l at point T. Now, the required path passes through point T as shown in Figure 7.1). From point P one must aim at point T in order to hit the ball located at point Q. As the mirror line we use a tangent line of the table boundary. It is possible to

FIGURE 7.1. *The Line Reflection.*

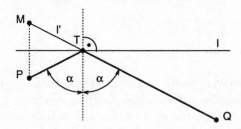

describe this line implicitly:

$$l \equiv l_1 \equiv y - T_y = k(x - T_x), \quad k_1 \equiv k = \frac{\frac{d\,X(t)}{d\,t}}{\frac{d\,Y(t)}{d\,t}}\bigg|_T \qquad (7.1)$$

where

$$T \equiv [T_x,\ T_y] = [X(t),\ Y(t)],$$

and where T_x, T_y are the coordinates of the common point on the billiard table boundary and k is the derivative of the boundary function at this point. The ball hitting the boundary is reflected just as if it were reflected by this line. To find the mirror image of the position of one ball we use l as a mirror line. The solution of the generalized billiard problem is shown in Figure 7.2. We can aim the ball located at P toward a point T on the billiard boundary. We use the line l_1, tangent to the boundary at point T, to find point M, the mirror image of point P. l_2 is the line segment connecting points P and M. l_1 is perpendicular to l_2, intersecting l_2 in its midpoint C.

If point M is known, then it is possible to draw the line segment l_3 by connecting points M and Q, and the ray l_4 (beginning at point M and going through point T). The ball located at point P will move along this ray after its reflection. Now we can calculate the distance d_2 between point Q and ray l_4. If this distance is equal to zero, i.e., $d_2 = 0$, then the position of the second ball lies on the trajectory of the first ball after its reflection. Hence, the balls must collide. A second possibility is to calculate the distance d_1 between points T and W, the intersection of lines l_1 and l_3. To hit the ball located at point Q, this distance must also be equal to zero, i.e. $d_1 = 0$, since in this case T and W must coincide; i.e., l_4 will then coincide with l_3. The calculation of the distance

FIGURE 7.2. *The Curve Reflection.*

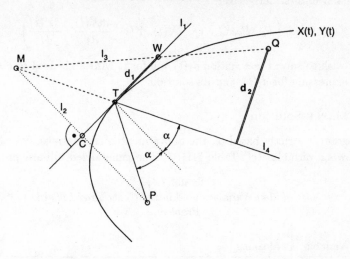

d_1 is simpler than the calculation of d_2. To determine the distance between two points is simpler as to calculate the distance between a point and a line. The problem is thus reduced to finding point T; for which the corresponding distances d_1, or d_2 respectively, are equal to zero.

7.2.2 Mathematical Description

For the analytic solution, let us again consider Figure 7.2. To simplify the process it is useful to describe all lines using the same type of formula. A line can be described by the coordinates of one point on it and a direction. For the first line, l_1, we use Equation (7.1). The other lines are described by

$$l_2 \equiv y - P_y = k_2(x - P_x), \quad \text{where} \quad k_2 = -\frac{1}{k_1}$$
$$l_3 \equiv y - Q_y = k_3(x - Q_x), \quad \text{where} \quad k_3 = \frac{M_y - Q_y}{M_x - Q_x}. \tag{7.2}$$

The simplest way to obtain the coordinates of point M is to find the point C at the intersection of lines l_1 and l_2, and to use the mirror condition

$$C_x = \frac{P_x + M_x}{2}, \quad C_y = \frac{P_y + M_y}{2}. \tag{7.3}$$

Subsequently, it is possible to calculate the coordinates of point W as the intersection of lines l_1 and l_3, and to determine the *aiming error distance* d_1,

$$d_1 = \sqrt{(W_x - T_x)^2 + (W_y - T_y)^2}. \tag{7.4}$$

Using Equations (7.1) through (7.4) we can calculate d_1 as a function of the known coordinates of the positions of the balls, and the billiard cushion shape function and its first derivative

$$d_1(t) = d_1\left(P_x,\ P_y,\ Q_x,\ Q_y,\ X(t),\ Y(t),\ \frac{dX(t)}{dt},\ \frac{dY(t)}{dt}\right). \qquad (7.5)$$

We now wish to solve the equation $d_1(t) = 0$ for t. MAPLE is used to obtain an explicit expression for $d_1(t)$, and its solution.

7.2.3 MAPLE Solution

The program is strictly based on the above mentioned relations. We shall use the following variables (cf. Table 7.1).   The generalized billiard problem is

TABLE 7.1.

List of Main Variables used in the Generalized Billiard
Problem.

Variable	Meaning
Tx, Ty	$T_x = X(t)$ and $T_y = Y(t)$, description of the shape of the cushion
k1	slope of the tangent of the cushion function in point $[T_x, T_y]$ (line l_1)
k2	slope of line l_2, which is perpendicular to the l_1, $[P_x,\ P_y]$ is a point of line l_2
k3	slope of the line l_3, connecting the points $[Q_x, Q_y]$ and $[M_x, M_y]$
Aimerr	square of the distance between points $[W_x,\ W_y]$ and $[T_x,\ T_y]$, ("aiming error")
DAA,DB	numerator and denominator of the Aimerr
Px, Py	coordinates of the first ball
Qx, Qy	coordinates of the second ball
Mx, My	mirror point of the point $[P_x,\ P_y]$, mirror line is l_1
Cx, Cy	coordinates of the intersection point of lines l_1 and l_2
Wx, Wy	coordinates of the intersection point of lines l_1 and l_3

solved when $[W_x,\ W_y] \equiv [T_x,\ T_y]$, i.e. if DAA $= 0$.

```
> E1 := solve({Wy - Qy = k3*(Wx-Qx), Wy - Ty = k1*(Wx - Tx)},
>                 {Wx, Wy}):
> assign(E1):
> E2 := solve({Cy - Py = k2*(Cx - Px), Cy - Ty = k1*(Cx - Tx)},
>                 {Cx, Cy}):
> assign(E2):
```

```
> Mx := Px + 2*(Cx - Px):   My := Py + 2*(Cy - Py):
> k3 := (My - Qy)/(Mx - Qx):
> Ty := Y(t):   Tx := X(t):
> k2 := -1/k1:
> k1 := diff(Y(t), t)/diff(X(t),t):
> Aimerr := normal((Tx - Wx)^2 + (Ty - Wy)^2):
```

We now have to solve the equation `Aimerr` $= 0$. If the parametrical description of the billiard rim $X(t)$, $Y(t)$ is used, the expression for `Aimerr` becomes a fraction. This can be used to simplify the solution, because we only need to find the zeros of the numerator. But to check if such a zero is a correct solution, we must be sure that there are no common zeros of the `Aimerr` numerator and denominator.

We now attempt to simplify the `Aimerr` numerator.

```
> DA := op(1, numer(Aimerr)):
> DB := denom(Aimerr):
> DA1 := factor(select(has, DA, {diff(X(t), t)^2,
>                                diff(Y(t), t)^2})):
> Da2 := select(has, DA, diff(X(t), t)):
> DA2 := factor(select(has, Da2, diff(Y(t), t))):
> DA - expand(DA2 + DA1);
```

$$0$$

```
> DAA := DA1 + DA2;
```

```
        / d    \ / d    \           2        2
DAA := 2 |---- X(t)| |---- Y(t)| (- X(t)  + Y(t)  + Qy Py
        \ dt   / \ dt   /

    - Qy Y(t) + Px X(t) + Qx X(t) - Px Qx - Y(t) Py) -

    // d    \   / d    \\ // d    \   / d    \\
    ||---- Y(t)| - |---- X(t)|| ||---- Y(t)| + |---- X(t)|| (
    \\ dt   /   \ dt   // \\ dt   /   \ dt   //

    Qy Px - Qy X(t) - X(t) Py + 2 X(t) Y(t) + Py Qx - Y(t) Px

    - Y(t) Qx)
```

The result of the MAPLE code is the variable `DAA`, which depends on the specific function used for the billiard cushion shape. For any given problem instance these functions must be provided as input.

7.3   The Shortest Trajectory Method

From physics [3] it is known that the trajectory of a light beam from one point to another minimizes the length of the path. In case of a reflection this curve consists of two line segments. The first line segment connects the point of the light source, *(in our case: the position of the first ball)*, with the point of reflection, *(the point on the billiard table boundary)*. The latter point is connected by the second line segment to the point of observation, *(the position of the second ball).* Using this, we can also solve the generalized billiard problem.

We can construct the first line segment l_P connecting the point P with the reflection point T on the billiard table boundary, and the second line segment l_Q connecting Q with T. Now we must find the smallest sum of the lengths of both line segments S as a function of T. Remember that T is the point on the billiard table boundary.

With $T \equiv [X(t), Y(t)]$, our problem is to solve equation

$$\frac{d\left(\sqrt{(T_x(t) - P_x)^2 + (T_y(t) - P_y)^2} + \sqrt{(T_x(t) - Q_x)^2 + (T_y(t) - Q_y)^2}\right)}{dt} = 0$$

for the parameter t.

7.3.1 MAPLE Solution

```
> LP := sqrt((X(t) - Px)^2 + (Y(t) - Py)^2):
> LQ := sqrt((X(t) - Qx)^2 + (Y(t) - Qy)^2):
> lP := diff(LP,t): lQ := diff(LQ,t):
> dl1 := numer(lP)*denom(lQ) + numer(lQ)*denom(lP);
```

```
               /  d      \          /  d      \       /  d      \
dl1 := (- |---- X(t)| Px + X(t) |---- X(t)| - Py |---- Y(t)|
               \ dt      /          \ dt      /       \ dt      /

           /  d      \                         2                 2 1/2
    + Y(t) |---- Y(t)|) ((X(t) - Qx)  + (Y(t) - Qy) )      + (
           \ dt      /

        /  d      \   /  d      \        /  d      \
  X(t) |---- X(t)| - |---- X(t)| Qx + Y(t) |---- Y(t)|
        \ dt      /   \ dt      /        \ dt      /

        /  d      \                    2                 2 1/2
   - Qy |---- Y(t)|) ((X(t) - Px)  + (Y(t) - Py) )
        \ dt      /
```

For the final solution of equation dl = 0 we first have to specify the billiard table shape functions X(t) and Y(t).

7.4 Examples

We now compare the reflection method with the shortest trajectory method. Both should produce the same result. As a first example we consider the circular billiard table, whose solution is well known [1, 2, 4].

7.4.1 The Circular Billiard Table

To check our program we will recompute the solutions given in [1, 2, 4] with the same assumptions: i.e., $R = 1$ and $Q_y = 0$.

We can simply continue the computations with the MAPLE programs presented in Sections 7.2.3 and in 7.3.1 by defining

```
> X(t) := cos(t): Y(t) := sin(t): Qy := 0:
```

Because the shape of the billiard cushion is well defined, the position of the balls is completely general. First, we shall solve DAA = 0 (cf. Section 7.2.3).

```
> DA := simplify(DAA);
```

$$DA := 2\ \cos(t)\ \sin(t)\ Px\ Qx + \cos(t)\ Py - 2\ \cos(t)^2\ Py\ Qx + Py\ Qx$$
$$- \sin(t)\ Px - \sin(t)\ Qx$$

```
> SolDA := solve(DA,t);
```

$$SolDA := 2\ \arctan(RootOf((Py + Qx\ Py)\ \_Z^4$$
$$+ (2\ Qx + 4\ Qx\ Px + 2\ Px)\ \_Z^3 - 6\ Qx\ Py\ \_Z^2$$
$$+ (2\ Qx - 4\ Qx\ Px + 2\ Px)\ \_Z - Py + Qx\ Py))$$

Using the command solve we can calculate an *analytic* value of the parameter t such that DA = 0. The solution details are not presented here for the sake of brevity. To compare our result with the results of [1, 2, 4] we shall substitute the general variables Px, Py and Qx by their numerical values. We shall check if the zeros of DA are the correct solutions of the Aimerr. If they are substituted into DB its value must not be zero.

```
> Px := 1/2: Py := 1/2: Qx := -3/5:
> DA := simplify(DA):
> SolDA := solve(DA, t);
```

$$SolDA := 2\ \arctan(RootOf(\_Z^4 - 7\ \_Z^3 + 9\ \_Z^2 + 5\ \_Z - 4))$$

```
> SolDA := allvalues(SolDA);
```

$$SolDA := 2\ \arctan(7/4 + 1/4\ 17^{1/2} + 1/4\ (58 + 6\ 17^{1/2})^{1/2}),$$
$$2\ \arctan(7/4 + 1/4\ 17^{1/2} - 1/4\ (58 + 6\ 17^{1/2})^{1/2}),$$
$$2\ \arctan(7/4 - 1/4\ 17^{1/2} + 1/4\ (58 - 6\ 17^{1/2})^{1/2}),$$
$$2\ \arctan(7/4 - 1/4\ 17^{1/2} - 1/4\ (58 - 6\ 17^{1/2})^{1/2})$$

```
> FSolDA := evalf(SolDA);
```

$$FSolDA := 2.750972642,\ .9380770508,\ 2.274796770,\ -1.251457484$$

```
> for i from 1 by 1 to nops([FSolDA]) do:
>     tA[i] := FSolDA[i];
>     DBi := evalf(subs(t = tA[i], DB));
>     if DBi = 0 then print('Root',i,' unusable!'); fi;
>     print('i =',i, ' tA = ', tA[i],' ==> DB = ', DBi);
> od:
```

```
i =, 1,   tA = , 2.750972642,   ==> DB = , 2.948610256

i =, 2,   tA = , .9380770508,   ==> DB = , 2.742080136

i =, 3,   tA = , 2.274796770,   ==> DB = , 2.415361451

i =, 4,   tA = , -1.251457484,  ==> DB = , 6.280614814
```

Note that the position angles (*in radians*) of the aiming points are the same as in [1, 2, 4], i.e., evalf(tA[4]+2*Pi) = 5.031727826. The coordinates of the four aiming points are computed for $t = t_{A1}, \ldots, t_{A4}$ by $T_x = \cos(t)$ and $T_y = \sin(t)$.

We now check the second method dl = 0 (cf. Section 7.3.1). We again use MAPLE to find the general analytic solution:

```
> Px := 'Px': Py := 'Py': Qx := 'Qx': Qy := 0:
> dl := simplify(dl1);
```

$$
\begin{aligned}
\text{dl} := &\ (-\ 2\ \cos(t)\ Qx + Qx^2 + 1)^{1/2}\ \sin(t)\ Px \\
&- (-\ 2\ \cos(t)\ Qx + Qx^2 + 1)^{1/2}\ \cos(t)\ Py \\
&+ \sin(t)\ Qx\ (-\ 2\ \cos(t)\ Px + Px^2 + 1 - 2\ \sin(t)\ Py + Py^2)^{1/2}
\end{aligned}
$$

```
> Sol1l := solve(dl, t):
```

The analytic solution exists, but is more complicated than in the preceding example, because the variable dl contains square roots. In such cases it is better to modify the equation first i.e. to remove the square roots before the solution.

```
> eq := op(1, dl) + op(2, dl) = -op(3, dl):
> eq := expand(map(u -> u^2, eq)):
> eq := lhs(eq) - rhs(eq) = 0:
> Sol1l := solve(eq, t):
```

The result is not to complicated, but still is not shown here for the sake of brevity. But we can reassign values for Px, Py and Qx and solve eq again:

```
> Px := 1/2: Py := 1/2: Qx := -3/5:
> Sol1l := solve(eq,t);
```

$$
\begin{aligned}
\text{Sol1l} := &\ 2\ \arctan(-\ 11/2 + 1/2\ 137^{1/2}), \\
&\ 2\ \arctan(-\ 11/2 - 1/2\ 137^{1/2}), \\
&\ 2\ \arctan(\text{RootOf}(-\ 4 + \_Z^4 + 5\ \_Z^3 - 7\ \_Z^2 + 9\ \_Z^2))
\end{aligned}
$$

As shown, both solutions are the same. Note that two zeros of the second solution result from modifying the equation. Thus they are of no practical use for us.

FIGURE 7.3. Dan and dln Functions.

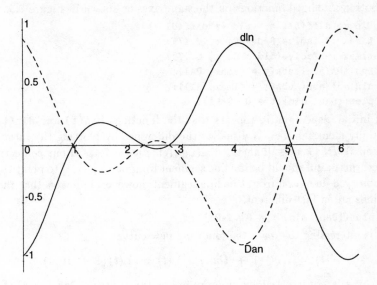

FIGURE 7.4. *Graphical Comparison of* Dan *and* dln.

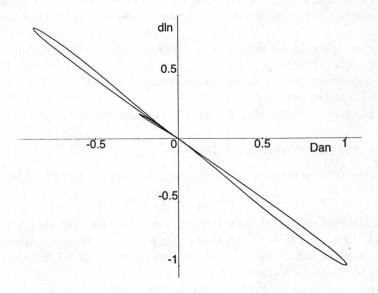

Let us compare the functions DA(t) and dl(t). Because they were signifi-cantly simplified they have lost their initial physical meaning. We first normalize the functions by dividing each of them by their largest absolute value. Then we plot both normalized functions on the same axes as shown in Figure 7.3.

```
> DAd := diff(DA, t): dld := diff(dl, t):
> tamax := fsolve(DAd = 0, t, 6..7):
> tlmax := fsolve(dld = 0, t, 6..7):
> Dan:=DA/abs(subs(t = tamax, DA)):
> dln:=dl/abs(subs(t = tlmax, dl)):
> plot({Dan, dln},t = 0..2*Pi);
```

Upon initial inspection, it appears that the functions Dan(t) and dln(t) are essentially identical. Let us visualize the difference by plotting the rather un-usual curve $PF(x,y) \equiv [\text{Dan}(t), \text{dln}(t)]$, (cf. Figure 7.4). If our conjecture is correct, this graph should be the line segment from point $[-1,1]$ to point $[1,-1]$. The observed deviation from this line segment, however, indicates that the two functions are in fact different.

```
> plot([Dan, dln, t = 0..2*Pi]);
```

It is interesting to create the following new curve:

$$\tilde{X}(t) = X(t)(1 + Dan), \quad \tilde{Y}(t) = Y(t)(1 + Dan). \qquad (7.6)$$

This curve is constructed by superimposing the function Dan (or dln) as a "perturbation" to the table shape function. Since at the aim points the functions DA, Dan are equal to zero, the coordinates of these points are on the cushion (cf. Figure 7.5). The aim points, therefore, can be found graphically as the points of intersection of the cushion shape function and the disturbed shape function (7.6).

Because graphical output will be used several times, we shall create a MAPLE procedure ResultPlot (see Algorithm 7.1), which will be used for plotting the graphical solution. Procedure ResultPlot is easy to use. For example, Figure 7.5 was created via

```
> ResultPlot(Px, Py, Qx, Qy, X(t), Y(t), Dan, 0, 2*Pi, tA, 4);
```

7.4.2 The Elliptical Billiard Table

An ellipse with the semi-axes a and b is described in parametric form by:

$$X(t) = a \cos(t), \quad Y(t) = b \sin(t). \qquad (7.7)$$

We consider the ellipse with the major semi – axis $a = 1$ and with the minor semi – axis $b = 0.8$. Let $P \equiv [-0.6, -0.3]$, and $Q \equiv [0.5, 0.5]$ be the coordinates of the positions of the balls. The previously derived equations DA (cf. Section 7.2.3) and dl (cf. Section 7.3.1) are used.

```
> X(t) :=  cos(t): Y(t) := 4/5*sin(t):
> Px := -3/5: Py := -3/10: Qx := 1/2: Qy := 1/2:
> DA := simplify(DAA);
```

FIGURE 7.5. *Graphical Solution for Circle.*

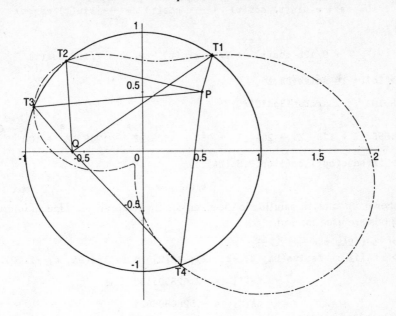

ALGORITHM 7.1. *Procedure* ResultPlot.

```
ResultPlot := proc(P1x, P1y, P2x, P2y, Xborder, Yborder,
                   Perturb, Start, End, Zerosvec, Nzeros)
 local i, n, Trajectories, AimPointX, AimPointY,
       PlotTraject, PlotPoints, PlotBorder, PlotPert;
 for i from 1 by 1 to Nzeros do
     AimPointX[i] := evalf(subs(t = Zerosvec[i], Xborder));
     AimPointY[i] := evalf(subs(t = Zerosvec[i], Yborder));
     Trajectories[i] := [P1x, P1y,
                         AimPointX[i], AimPointY[i],
                         P2x, P2y];
 od;
 PlotTraject := plot({seq(Trajectories[i], i = 1..Nzeros)},
                     style = LINE):
 PlotPoints := plot({[P1x, P1y], [P2x, P2y],
                     seq([AimPointX[i], AimPointY[i]],
                         i = 1..Nzeros)}, style=POINT):
 PlotBorder := plot([Xborder, Yborder, t = Start..End]):
 PlotPert := plot([Xborder*(1 + Perturb), Yborder*(1 + Perturb),
                  t = Start..End]):
 plot({PlotTraject, PlotPoints, PlotBorder, PlotPert});
 end;
```

$$DA := \frac{18}{625} \sin(t) \cos(t)^2 + \frac{369}{500} \cos(t)^2 + \frac{42}{125} \sin(t) \cos(t)$$

$$+ \; 9/125 \cos(t)^3 + 2/25 \sin(t) - 9/20 + 7/125 \cos(t)$$

```
> SolDA := solve(DA,t);
```

$$SolDA := 2 \; arctan(RootOf($$

$$556 \_Z + 128 \_Z^3 - 284 \_Z^5 + 260 - 1405 \_Z^2 - 1205 \_Z^4 + 100 \_Z^6))$$

```
> irreduc(op(1,op(1,op(2,SolDA))));
```

$$true$$

As shown, an analytic solution to the given cannot be obtained. Thus, numerical methods are used instead.

```
> plot(DA, t = -Pi..Pi);
>  tA[1] := fsolve(DA, t, -3..-2); tA[2] := fsolve(DA, t, -1..0);
```

$$tA[1] := -2.425591133$$

$$tA[2] := -.5260896824$$

```
> tA[3] := fsolve(DA, t, 1..2);    tA[4] := fsolve(DA, t, 2..3);
```

$$tA[3] := 1.038696884$$

$$tA[4] := 2.761693514$$

```
> tl[1] := fsolve(dll,t,-3..-2); tl[2] := fsolve(dll,t,-1..0);
```

$$tl[1] := -2.425591133$$

$$tl[2] := -.5260896824$$

```
> tl[3] := fsolve(dll,t,1..2);    tl[4] := fsolve(dll,t,2..3);
```

$$tl[3] := 1.038696884$$

$$tl[4] := 2.761693514$$

```
> Dan := DA/abs(evalf(subs( t = fsolve(diff(DA, t),
                                 t, -2..-1), DA))):
> dln := dll/abs(evalf(subs( t = fsolve(diff(dll, t),
                                 t, -2..-1), dll))):
> plot({Dan, dln}, t = 0..2*Pi);
> ResultPlot(Px, Py, Qx, Qy, X(t), Y(t), Dan, -Pi, Pi, tA, 4);
```

7.4.3   The Snail Billiard Table

A snail (or helix) shape of the cushion of a billiard table is rather unusual, but it can be used to further demonstrate the capabilities of MAPLE. The "snail shape

FIGURE 7.6. *Solution for Ellipse –* Dan *and* dln *Functions.*

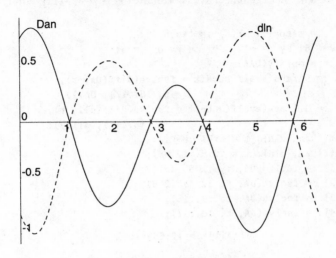

FIGURE 7.7. *Graphical Solution for Ellipse.*

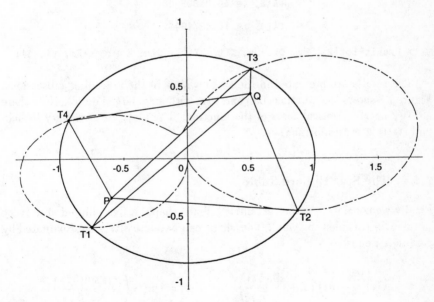

curve", or *the spiral of Archimedes*, is described best in the polar coordinate system by the function $\varrho = a\,\varphi$. The transformation the rectangular coordinates system gives us the parametric description of the spiral of Archimedes: $X(t) = t\cos(t)$, $Y(t) = t\sin(t)$, where $a = 1$. These equations are used to solve the snail billiard problem. Let the balls have coordinates $P \equiv [-6, -12]$, and $Q \equiv [7, 5]$.

```
> X(t) := t*cos(t): Y(t) := t*sin(t):
> Px := -6: Py := -12:   Qx := 7: Qy := 5:
> DA := simplify(DAA):
> Dan := DA/abs(evalf(subs(t = fsolve(diff(DA, t),
>                                    t, 15..17), DA))):
> dln := dll/abs(evalf(subs(t = fsolve(diff(dll, t),
>                                    t, 15..17), dll))):
> plot({Dan, dln}, t = 4*Pi..6*Pi);
> plot({Dan, dln}, t = 12.5..12.85);
> tA[1] := fsolve(DA, t, 12.5..12.6);
> tA[2] := fsolve(DA, t, 12.7..12.8);
> tA[3] := fsolve(DA, t, 14..15);
> tA[4] := fsolve(DA, t, 16..17);
```

$$tA[1] := 12.56987562$$

$$tA[2] := 12.75992609$$

$$tA[3] := 14.95803948$$

$$tA[4] := 16.82749442$$

```
> ResultPlot(Px, Py, Qx, Qy, X(t), Y(t), dln, 4*Pi, 6*Pi, tA, 4);
```

The results are presented in the same way as in the preceding subsections. Figure 7.8 shows the functions Dan and dln, with an enlarged detail. Note there are two nearly identical zeros of the function. The plots are necessary to help find starting values for fsolve.

7.4.4   The Star Billiard Table

Finally we consider a rather eccentric billiard shape, a five pointed star (very suitable for corpulent players). This shape can be successfully approximated by parametric equations

$$X(t) = \cos(t)\left(1 + \frac{\sin(5\,t)}{5}\right), \qquad Y(t) = \sin(t)\left(1 + \frac{\sin(5\,t)}{5}\right).$$

Let the ball coordinates be $P \equiv [-0.8, 0.2]$ and $Q \equiv [0.6, -0.8]$. Thus the balls are located close to the tops of the star corners (see Figure 7.13). We shall solve this example as shown previously. But we shall see, that there are many zeros

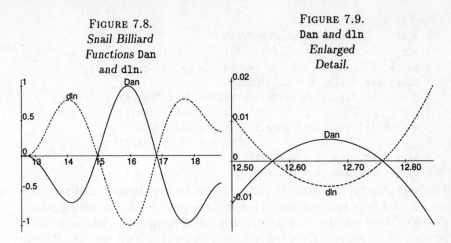

FIGURE 7.8.
*Snail Billiard
Functions* Dan
and dln.

FIGURE 7.9.
Dan *and* dln
*Enlarged
Detail.*

FIGURE 7.10. *Graphical Solution for Snail Billiard.*

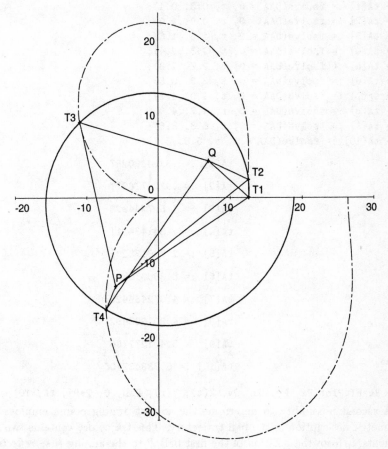

of the functions DA and dll.

```
> X(t) := cos(t)*(1 + sin(5*t)/5):
> Y(t) := sin(t)*(1 + sin(5*t)/5):
> Px := -4/5: Py := 1/5: Qx := 3/5: Qy := -4/5:
> plot({DAA, dll}, t = 0..2*Pi);
> Dan := DAA/evalf(abs(subs(t = fsolve(diff(DAA, t),
>                                 t, 1..1.5), DAA))):
> dln := dll/evalf(abs(subs(t = fsolve(diff(dll, t),
>                                 t, 1.6..2.2), dll))):
> plot({Dan, dln},t = 0..2*Pi);
> plot([Dan, dln, t = 0..2*Pi]);
```

Two final plots (cf. Figures 7.11 and 7.12) can be used to show that there are two different functions DAA and dll describing positions of the aiming points. As shown there are 10 aiming points but some of them may not be acceptable, because the trajectory of the ball is intersecting the billiard cushion. We can only find correct aiming points by examining the graphical solution.

```
> tA[1] := fsolve(DAA = 0, t, 0.3..0.4);
> tA[2] := fsolve(DAA = 0, t, 0.9..1.0);
> tA[3] := fsolve(DAA = 0, t, 1.5..1.6);
> tA[4] := fsolve(DAA = 0, t, 2.3..2.4);
> tA[5] := fsolve(DAA = 0, t, 2.7..2.8);
> tA[6] := fsolve(DAA = 0, t, 3.3..3.5);
> tA[7] := fsolve(DAA = 0, t, 4.0..4.2);
> tA[8] := fsolve(DAA = 0, t, 4.7..4.9);
> tA[9] := fsolve(DAA = 0, t, 5.3..5.5);
> tA[10] := fsolve(DAA = 0, t, 5.5..5.7);
```

$$tA[1] := .3824290257$$
$$tA[2] := .9324776977$$
$$tA[3] := 1.527744928$$
$$tA[4] := 2.341434311$$
$$tA[5] := 2.760135295$$
$$tA[6] := 3.396070545$$
$$tA[7] := 4.072484425$$
$$tA[8] := 4.807203452$$
$$tA[9] := 5.401272766$$
$$tA[10] := 5.638437106$$

```
> ResultPlot(Px, Py, Qx, Qy, X(t), Y(t), Dan, 0, 2*Pi, tA, 10);
```

A second possibility to determine the correct aiming points employs the parametric description of the ball trajectory. This trajectory contains two line segments, l_1 from the position of the first ball P to the aiming *(i.e. reflection)* point T_i on the billiard cushion and l_2 from T_i to the second ball position Q.

These line segments may be described parametrically using the parameter u.

$$l_1: \begin{aligned} x &= P_x + u\left(T_{i_x} - P_x\right) \\ y &= P_y + u\left(T_{i_y} - P_y\right) \end{aligned} \qquad l_2: \begin{aligned} x &= Q_x + u\left(T_{i_x} - Q_x\right) \\ y &= Q_y + u\left(T_{i_y} - Q_y\right) \end{aligned}$$

Now we can find points of intersection of lines l_1 and l_2 with the billiard cushion. We simply calculate the corresponding parameters $u_1, \ldots, u_2$. If their values satisfy $0 < u_i < 1$, it indicates that there is at least one other point of intersection on the line segment. So the trajectory which is located between the position of the ball and the reflection point cannot be used. Figure 7.13 shows that there are two unusable reflection points T_1 and T_7. We can use this to show that line segment QT_1 intersects with the billiard cushion inside:

```
> Tx[1] := evalf(subs(t = tA[1], X(t))):
> Ty[1] := evalf(subs(t = tA[1], Y(t))):
> eq1 := X(t) = Qx + u*(Tx[1] - Qx):
> eq2 := Y(t) = Qy + u*(Ty[1] - Qy):
> fsolve({eq1, eq2}, {u, t}, {u = 0..0.5, t=3*Pi/2..2*Pi});
```

$$\{t = 5.810766136, \ u = .3288529247\}$$

```
> fsolve({eq1, eq2}, {u, t}, {u = 0.33..0.8, t = 5.82..6.2});
```

$$\{u = .5576715283, \ t = 6.162750379\}$$

We see that line segment QT_1 intersects the billiard cushion twice between the points Q and T_1, corresponding to values of the parameter $u_1 = 0.3288529247$ and $u_2 = 0.5576715283$.

7.5 Conclusions

Using MAPLE we have solved the generalized billiard problem by two methods. The pictures and numbers indicate that the results of both methods are the same. It is more difficult to derive the final equation with the generalized reflection method than with the shortest trajectory method. But when all variables are substituted the final equation DA for the first method is simpler than dl, the result of the second method. Using the second method we must calculate square roots of various functions and their first derivatives. Therefore the final equation of the second method is more complicated. To what degree depends on the shape of boundary cushion. For some boundary functions it may happen that the result of the second method is simpler.

The first method can be generalized to an N-reflection trajectory. By this we mean that the first ball must first hit the cushion N times before colliding with the other ball. However the second method does not permit such a generalization. The property of shortest trajectory does not fulfill the reflection conditions in this case.

FIGURE 7.11.
Star Billiard
Functions Dan
and dln.

FIGURE 7.12.
Dan *and* dln
Parametric
Plot.

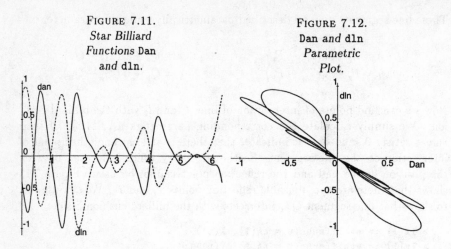

FIGURE 7.13. *Graphical Solution for Star Billiard.*

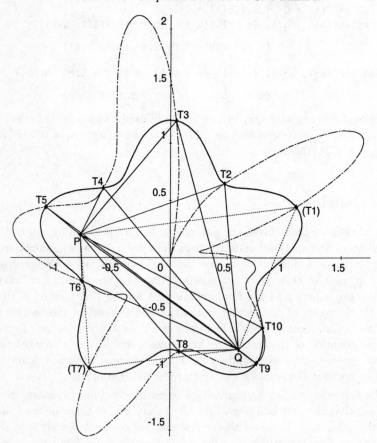

References

[1] W. GANDER AND D. GRUNTZ, *The Billiard Problem*, Int. J. Educ. Sci. Technol., 23, 1992, pp. 825 – 830.

[2] D. GRUNTZ, *Solution of the Billiard Problem using* MAPLE *geometry package*, MAPLE user's course, IFW – ETH, April 1993.

[3] R. G. LERNER AND G. L. TRIGG, *Encyclopedia of Physics*, VCH Publishers, New York, 1991.

[4] J. WALDVOGEL, *The Problem of the Circular Billiard*, El. Math., 47, 1992, pp. 108 – 113.

Chapter 8. Mirror Curves

S. Bartoň

8.1 The Interesting Waste

To solve the generalised billiard problem we used the generalised reflection method. This method is based on the calculation of M, the mirror image point of the position of the first ball. Point M moves as we move point T along the boundary of the billiard cushion shape, (see Chapter 7, Figure 7.2). M traces a *mirror curve*, which depends on the change of the tangent line at point T. This mirror curve is dependent on the position of point P and the shape of the billiard cushion.

In solving the generalised billiard problem it is not necessary to determine the shapes of the mirror curves. However, these curves are very interesting. It would be a pity not to examine them further. We may do so using MAPLE's graphical facilities.

8.2 The Mirror Curves Created by MAPLE

Because the position of the mirror point is given by two coordinates $M \equiv [M_x, M_y]$, both dependent on t, we obtain the mirror curve as a parametric function, see [1]. Its shape can be easily derived using part of the calculations perfomed to obtain equation DA, (see Chapter 7, Section 7.2.3 and Table 7.1). We show here only the necessary steps for the calculation of M_x, M_y. The result is

```
> E2 := solve({Cy - Py = k2*(Cx - Px),
>                 Cy - Y(t) = k1*(Cx - X(t))}, {Cx, Cy}):
> assign(E2);
> k1 := diff(Y(t),t)/diff(X(t),t):
> k2 := -1/k1:
> MX := normal(Px + 2*(Cx - Px)):
> MY := normal(Py + 2*(Cy - Py)):
```

$$M_x(t) = -\frac{\left(\frac{dY(t)}{dt}\right)^2 (P_x - 2X(t)) + 2\frac{dX(t)}{dt}\frac{dY(t)}{dt}(Y(t) - P_y) - P_x\left(\frac{dX(t)}{dt}\right)^2}{\left(\frac{dY(t)}{dt}\right)^2 + \left(\frac{dX(t)}{dt}\right)^2}$$

$$(8.1)$$

$$M_y(t) = \frac{\left(\frac{dX(t)}{dt}\right)^2(2Y(t) - P_y) + 2\frac{dX(t)}{dt}\frac{dY(t)}{dt}(P_x - X(t)) + P_y\left(\frac{dY(t)}{dt}\right)^2}{\left(\frac{dY(t)}{dt}\right)^2 + \left(\frac{dX(t)}{dt}\right)^2}.$$

$$(8.2)$$

Now we can create the mirror curves for a given pattern curve and a mirror point P. For example consider the parabola curve. Let the point P move along the y axis from the initial position $P_y = -3$, to the final position $P_y = 3$, with step $\Delta y = 1$, see Figure 8.1. We see the continuous deformation of the mirror curve as a function of P_y by looking at the 3d-plot, see Figure 8.2.

```
> X(t) := t: Y(t) := t^2/2:
> Px := 0: i := 0:
> Mx := simplify(MX):
> My := simplify(MY):
> PyStart := -3: PyEnd := 3:
> PyStep := 1:
> Tint := -3..3:
> for Py from PyStart by PyStep to PyEnd do;
>      i := i + 1;
>      P[i] := [Mx, My, t = Tint]:
> od:
> P[0] := [X(t), Y(t), t = Tint]:
> plot({seq(P[n], n = 0..i)});
> Py := 'Py':
> cond :=   axes = FRAME, orientation = [0,45],
>           labels = '['Py', 'Mx', 'My']';
> plot3d([Py, Mx, My], Py = PyStart..PyEnd, t = Tint, cond);
```

8.3   The Inverse Problem

The inverse problem – to find the original pattern curve for a known mirror curve and a fixed point, is very complicated. In this case $M_x = M_x(t), M_y = M_y(t)$, P_x, P_y are known, and we must solve the following system of differential equations for the functions $X(t)$, $Y(t)$ Equations (8.1) and (8.2). In general, this system of differential equations can not be solved analytically using MAPLE's dsolve function, so numeric methods must be used.

8.3.1   Outflanking Manoeuvre

However, it is very interesting that we can obtain an explicit analytic solution of the system of differential Equations (8.1) and (8.2) by using geometrical arguments! To solve the problem geometrically we consider Figure 8.3. It shows how to find the pattern curve for the given mirror curve and the mirror point. Let M_c be the given mirror curve, P_c be the pattern curve (*The original curve*), P be the given mirror point, M be a point on the mirror curve, M_1 and

FIGURE 8.1. *The Parabola's Mirror Curves.*

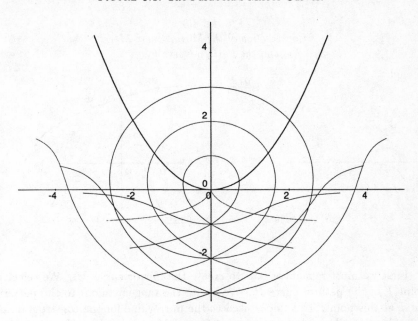

FIGURE 8.2.
Continuous Deformation of the Parabola's Mirror Curve.

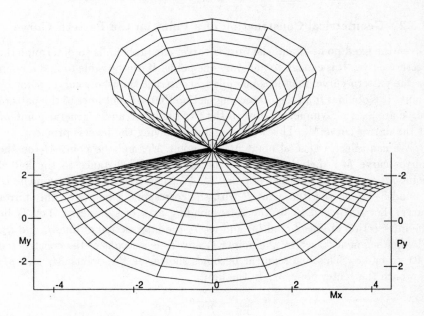

M_2 be points on the mirror curve to the left and right of M respectively, T be
a point on the pattern curve and l_t be the line tangent to P_c at point T.

FIGURE 8.3.
Construction of the Mirror Curve M_c
and the Pattern Curve P_c.

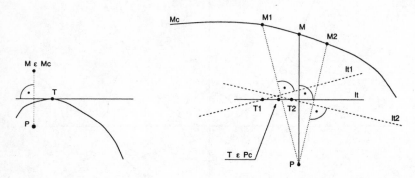

First we must remember how to create the mirror curve M_c. We select a
point T of the pattern curve P_c. We create the tangent line l_t to the pattern
curve at this point. This line is used as the mirror line for the construction of
point M, (l_t *is the axis of symmetry of P, and M. As the point T moves along
P_c, M traces the mirror curve M_c.

8.3.2   Geometrical Construction of a Point on the Pattern Curve

Given the fixed point P and the mirror curve, our problem is to determine the
pattern curve. It is enough to find only one point. If it is possible to find a point
on the pattern curve, then it is possible to construct the whole curve, point by
point. It is obvious from the preceeding section that tangent lines to the pattern
curve are axes of symmetry between the fixed point P and a general point M
at the mirror curve M_c. This will be useful in solving the inverse problem.

We can select a general point M, the point M_1, and the point M_2 on the
mirror curve M_c. Let the point M_1 be at a "small" distance to the left of
point M, and M_2 to the right of point M. We then construct line segments l_c,
l_{c1} and l_{c2} connecting the point P with the correspondig points on the mirror
curve. Let l_t, l_{t1} and l_{t2} be the corresponding axes of symmetry. Let T_1 be
the intersection of lines l_t and l_{t1}, and let T_2 the intersection of lines l_t and l_{t2}.
The line segment traced by the points T_1 and T_2 is a secant of the constructed
pattern curve. This line segment becomes shorter as the points M_1 and M_2
approach the center point M. In the limit

$$\lim_{\substack{M_1 \to M^- \\ M_2 \to M^+}} \overleftrightarrow{T_1 T_2} = 0$$

this line segment is converted to a point. This point is our point P_c on the pattern curve. Now we repeat the same process for the construction of the next point.

8.3.3 MAPLE Solution

The analytic solution of the inverse mirror problem is based on the previous geometrical construction. We can use Taylor's series to express the functions $M_{1_x}(t)$, $M_{1_y}(t)$, $M_{2_x}(t)$, $M_{2_x}(t)$, because the points M_1 and M_2 are at a "small" distances from the central point M.

To solve the inverse mirror problem we use the functions and variables from the Table 8.1.

TABLE 8.1.
List of Main Variables Used in the Inverse Problem.

Variable	Meaning
X(t), Y(t)	$X(t) = f(t)$ and $Y(t) = g(t)$: description of the mirror curve
Xx, Yy	$Xx = \varphi(t)$ and $Yy = \psi(t)$: calculated pattern curve
Px, Py	coordinates of the fixed point
dt	Δt, a "small" step of parameter t,
dX(t)	$X(t \pm \Delta t)/\Delta t$
dY(t)	$Y(t \pm \Delta t)/\Delta t$

```
> X(t) := 'X(t)': Y(t) := 'Y(t)': Px := 'Px': Py := 'Py':
> C1x   := (X1(t) + Px)/2: C1y := (Y1(t) + Py)/2:
> C2x   := (X2(t) + Px)/2: C2y := (Y2(t) + Py)/2:
> k1    := -1*(Px - X1(t))/(Py - Y1(t)):
> k2    := -1*(Px - X2(t))/(Py - Y2(t)):
> E1    := solve({Yy - C1y = k1*(Xx - C1x),
>                 Yy - C2y = k2*(Xx - C2x)}, {Xx, Yy}):
> assign(E1):
> X1(t) := X(t) - dX(t)*dt:   Y1(t) := Y(t) - dY(t)*dt:
> X2(t) := X(t) + dX(t)*dt:   Y2(t) := Y(t) + dY(t)*dt:
> Xx := normal(Xx);          Yy := normal(Yy);
```

$$Xx := (Px^2 \, dY(t) + Y(t)^2 \, dY(t) + Py^2 \, dY(t) - X(t)^2 \, dY(t)$$
$$- dX(t)^2 \, dt^2 \, dY(t) - dY(t)^3 \, dt^2 - 2 \, Py \, Y(t) \, dY(t)$$
$$- 2 \, Py \, X(t) \, dX(t) + 2 \, X(t) \, dX(t) \, Y(t))/\%1$$

```
        2           2                      2          2       2
Yy := -(Py  dX(t) + Px  dX(t) - dX(t) Y(t)  - dX(t) dt  dY(t)
        2                      3     2
      + X(t)  dX(t) - dX(t)  dt  - 2 Px Y(t) dY(t)

      + 2 X(t) Y(t) dY(t) - 2 Px X(t) dX(t))/%1

%1 := 2 (Px dY(t) - Py dX(t) - X(t) dY(t) + dX(t) Y(t))
```

The MAPLE expressions for Xx and Yy contain only terms dt^2, but no dt terms. If the expressions limit(x,dt=0) and limit(y,dt=0) are evaluated, the dt^2 terms approach zero, and the dX(t) and dY(t) terms become $dX(t)/dt$ and $dY(t)/dt$.

```
> Xx := limit(Xx,dt=0):  Yy := limit(Yy,dt=0):
> dX(t) := diff(X(t),t): dY(t) := diff(Y(t),t):
> Xx := simplify(Xx); Yy := simplify(Yy);
```

8.3.4 Analytic Solution

If the system of Equations (8.1) and (8.2) is in general too complicated for MAPLE to be solved by dsolve for $X(t)$ and $Y(t)$. But via our outflanking manoeuvre we could use MAPLE to derive explicit analytic solution for the general case.

The last step is to rewrite the equations Xx and Yy using standard mathematics language.

$$Xx(t) = \frac{\frac{dY(t)}{dt}\left(\left(Y(t)-P_y\right)^2+P_x^2-X(t)^2\right)+2X(t)\frac{dX(t)}{dt}\left(Y(t)-P_y\right)}{2\left(\frac{dX(t)}{dt}\left(Y(t)-P_y\right)+\frac{dY(t)}{dt}\left(P_x-X(t)\right)\right)}$$

$$Yy(t) = -\frac{\frac{dX(t)}{dt}\left(\left(X(t)-P_x\right)^2+P_y^2-Y(t)^2\right)+2Y(t)\frac{dY(t)}{dt}\left(X(t)-P_x\right)}{2\left(\frac{dX(t)}{dt}\left(Y(t)-P_y\right)+\frac{dY(t)}{dt}\left(P_x-X(t)\right)\right)}.$$

$$(8.3)$$

8.4 Examples

Now we can check our solution using Equations (8.3) for the pattern curve computation. The mirror curve for the computed pattern curve must be the same as the given mirror curve, which was used as input for the pattern curve computation.

8.4.1 The Circle as the Mirror Curve

We can find the pattern curve for the circle and a fixed point. Without loss of generality, we may assume that the mirror circle radius is 1, i.e. we are using a unit circle. Now for every position of the fixed point P we can rotate the coordinate system so that $P_y = 0$. The P_x coordinate can be variable. If P is located inside the circle, then $P_x < 1$. If $P_x > 1$, then P is placed outside the circle. When $P_x = 1$, the point P is on the circle.

FIGURE 8.4. *The Circle as Mirror Curve.*

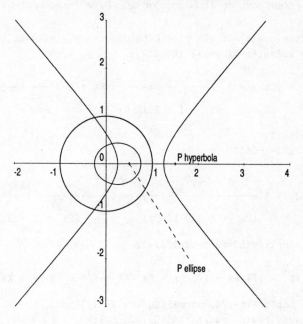

```
> X(t) := cos(t): Y(t) := sin(t):
> Px := 'Px': Py := 0:
> x := simplify(Xx); y := simplify(Yy);
```

$$x := 1/2 \ \frac{\cos(t) \ (Px^2 - 1)}{Px \ \cos(t) - 1}$$

$$y := 1/2 \ \frac{\sin(t) \ (Px^2 - 1)}{Px \ \cos(t) - 1}$$

```
> X(t) := x:  Y(t) := y:
> Mx := simplify(MX);  My := simplify(MY);
```

$$Mx := \cos(t)$$

$$My := \sin(t)$$

When the pattern curve x, y is substituted into the equations to calculate the mirror curve X(t), Y(t), the input and the output are equal. We can use this as a demonstration that the derivation of both systems of curves is correct.

Now we must find the equation of the pattern curve. Its parametrical description is:

$$x = \frac{\cos(t)\left(P_x^2 - 1\right)}{2\left(P_x\cos(t) - 1\right)}, \qquad y = \frac{\sin(t)\left(P_x^2 - 1\right)}{2\left(P_x\cos(t) - 1\right)}.$$

It looks like a conic section. To be sure we have to derive an analytic description of this curve.

```
> x := subs(cos(t)=Ct,x): y := subs(cos(t)=Ct,sin(t)=St,y):
> Sol := solve({x=XX,y=YY},{Ct,St});

                    XX                            YY
       Sol := {Ct = - 2 -----------------, St = - 2 -----------------}
                     2                          2
               Px  - 1 - 2 XX Px          Px  - 1 - 2 XX Px

> assign(Sol):
> EQ := St^2=1-Ct^2;

                    2                              2
                   YY                             XX
       EQ := 4 -------------------- = 1 - 4 --------------------
                 2             2              2             2
              (Px  - 1 - 2 XX Px)          (Px  - 1 - 2 XX Px)

> EQ := simplify(EQ*denom(St)^2/4);

            2      4       2       3                 2   2     2
   EQ := YY  = 1/4 Px - 1/2 Px - Px  XX + 1/4 + XX Px + XX  Px - XX

> EQ :=  map(t ->t+1/4, normal(EQ/(Px^2-1))):
> EQ := subs(rhs(EQ)=sqrt(rhs(EQ))^2, EQ):
> EQ := map(t->(t-rhs(EQ)-1/4)*(-4),EQ);

                     2
                    YY                    2
       EQ := - 4 ------- + (Px - 2 XX)  = 1
                   2
                 Px  - 1
```

As we see from the last equation EQ, the pattern curve for the unit circle is always a conic section. If the fixed point is inside the circle the pattern curve is an ellipse. The hyperbola results for a point outside the circle. The center C of the conic always has the coordinate $C_x = P_x/2$, $C_y = 0$. The major semiaxis of the conic is $a = 1/2$ and the minor semiaxis is $b = \sqrt{|P_x^2 - 1|}/2$. Where $e = \sqrt{a^2 - b^2}$ for the ellipse and $e = \sqrt{a^2 + b^2}$ for the hyperbola, e is the linear excentricity. We can calculate the distance between the focuses which is equal to $2e$ and to P_x. Because the center of the conic has coordinate $C_x = P_x/2$, the foci coordinates are always equal to $F_1 \equiv [0, 0]$ and $F_2 \equiv [P_x, 0]$. We plot some examples.

```
> X(t) := cos(t):    Y(t) := sin(t):
> Py := 0:    Px := 1/2:
> x1 := simplify(Xx):  y1 := simplify(Yy):
```

```
> Px := 3/2:
> x2 := simplify(Xx):  y2 := simplify(Yy):
> P10 := [X(t), Y(t), t=0..2*Pi]:
> P11 := [x1,y1,t=0..2*Pi],[1/2,0]:
> P12 := [x2,y2,t=0..2*Pi],[3/2,0]:
> plot({P10,P11,P12},-2..4,-3..3);
```

8.4.2 The Line as the Mirror Curve

Now let us consider the line as the mirror curve. Because this problem has translation symmetry, we can put the mirror line on the X axis of the coordinate system, and the fixed point P can be put on the Y axis, thus $P_x = 0$ and P_y is variable. Therefore we can compute the pattern curves as a function of P_y.

```
> X(t) := t: Y(t) := 0: Px := 0: Py := 'Py':
> x := simplify(Xx); y := simplify(Yy);
```

$$x := t$$

$$y := 1/2\ \frac{Py^2 + t^2}{Py}$$

```
> X(t) := x: Y(t) := y:
> Mx := simplify(MX); My := simplify(MY);
```

$$Mx := t$$

$$My := 0$$

```
> map(t->t*4*PY,YY=subs(t=XX,Py=PY*2,y));
```

$$4\ YY\ PY = 4\ PY^2 + XX^2$$

```
> subs(PY=Py/2,factor(map(t->t-4*PY^2,")));
```

$$-\ 2\ Py\ (-\ YY + 1/2\ Py) = XX^2$$

We obtain a family of parabolas depending on the parameter P_y. Let us try to find the envelope and plot some examples.

```
> E1 :="": E2:=YY=XX: E3:=YY=-XX:
> solve({E1,E2},{YY,XX}); solve({E1,E3},{YY,XX});
```

$$\{XX = Py,\ YY = Py\}$$

$$\{YY = Py,\ XX = -\ Py\}$$

FIGURE 8.5. *The Line as the Mirror Curve.*

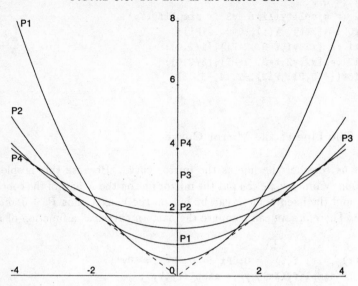

```
> i := 0:
> for Py from 1 by 1 to 4 do;
>       i := i + 1;
>       P[i] := [x,y,t=-4..4],[0,Py]:
> od:
> Li1 := [t,t,t=0..4]: Li2 := [t,-t,t=-4..0]:
> plot({seq(P[n],n=1..i),Li1,Li2});
```

We see that the pattern curve for the line is always a parabola equation. The top of the parabola is at the middle point of the line segment beginning at the point P and perpendicular to the mirror line. The focus point of the parabola coincides with the fixed point P. As the coordinate P_y changes its value, the parabolas fill the area defined by conditions $y \geq x$ and $y \geq -x$. These two lines create the envelope for the parabolas. Figure 8.5 shows this bounding of the parabolas.

8.5   Conclusions

The inverse mirror problem was successfully solved using MAPLE. It was possible to find a general shape of the pattern curve for both the circle and the line, as a function of the fixed point P. To do this it was necessary to solve a large system of equations, i.e. (8.1), (8.2) and (8.3) but we found the solution without difficulty.

We can demonstrate the pattern curve's continuos deformation as the function of the fixed (*mirror*) point. If we move with this point along any suitable curve, and the mirror curves corresponding to the fixed point's position in the

FIGURE 8.6. *Pattern Curves for the Hyperbola.*

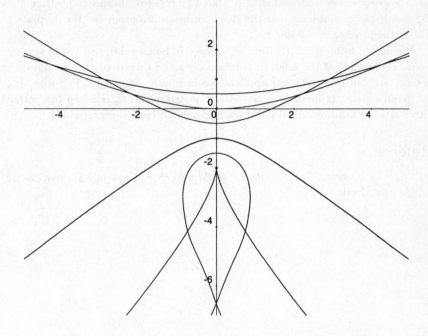

FIGURE 8.7.
*The Continuous Deformation of the Hyperbola Pattern
Curve.*

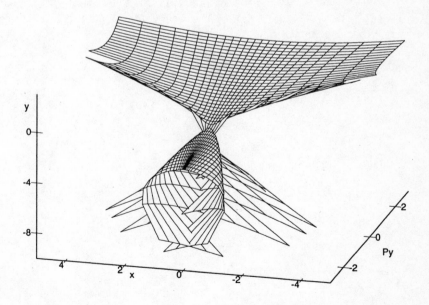

plane perpendicular to the given curve. The point of intersection of this plane and the given curve coincides with the fixed point's instantaneous position. Using the displacement length as the third cordinate we produced the 3d plots as shown the in Figures 8.6 and 8.7.

We do not know yet if the mirror curves will be useful in real world applications. It seems that the analytic solution obtained by our geometric argument is new. We can imagine some applications in physics, especially in optics. E.g. for given optical properties of an optical instrument *described by the pattern curve* one can find technical parameters *described by the mirror curve*.

References

[1] H. J. BARTSCH, *Taschenbuch Mathematischer Formeln*, Fachbuchverlag, Leipzig, 1991.

Chapter 9. Smoothing Filters

W. Gander and U. von Matt

9.1 Introduction

In many applications one is measuring a variable that is both slowly varying and also corrupted by random noise. Then it is often desirable to apply a smoothing filter to the measured data in order to reconstruct the underlying smooth function. We may assume that the noise is independent of the observed variable. Furthermore we assume that the noise obeys a normal distribution with mean zero and mean deviation δ.

In this chapter we will discuss two different approaches to this smoothing problem, the Savitzky-Golay filter and the least squares filter. We will analyse the properties of these two filters with the help of the test function

$$F(x) := e^{-100(x-1/5)^2} + e^{-500(x-2/5)^2} + e^{-2500(x-3/5)^2} + e^{-12500(x-4/5)^2}. \quad (9.1)$$

This function has four bumps of varying widths (cf. Figure 9.1).

In MATLAB we can generate a vector $\mathbf{f}$ of length $n = 1000$ consisting of measured data corrupted by random noise of mean deviation $\delta = 0.1$ by the statements of Algorithm 9.1. We get the sample data shown as Figure 9.2.

In the following sections we will denote the measured data by f_i, $i = 1, \ldots, n$, and the smoothed data by g_i, $i = 1, \ldots, n$.

9.2 Savitzky-Golay Filter

This approach to smoothing has been introduced by A. Savitzky and M.J.E. Golay in 1964 [10]. The original paper contains some errors that are corrected

ALGORITHM 9.1. *Generation of Noisy Data.*

```
n = 1000;
delta = 0.1;
x = [0:n-1]'/(n-1);
F = exp (- 100*(x - 1/5).^2) + exp (-  500*(x - 2/5).^2) + ...
    exp (-2500*(x - 3/5).^2) + exp (-12500*(x - 4/5).^2);
randn ('seed', 0);
f = F + delta * randn (size (x));
```

FIGURE 9.1. *Smooth Function $F(x)$.*

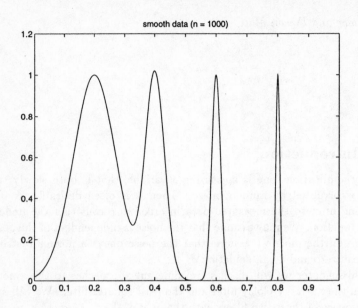

smooth data (n = 1000)

in [11]. The reader can also find another introduction to this subject in [8].

The key idea is that the smoothed value g_i in the point x_i is obtained by taking an average of the neighbouring data. The simplest method consists in computing a moving average of a fixed number of f_i's.

More generally we can also fit a polynomial through a fixed number of points. Then the value of the polynomial at x_i gives the smoothed value g_i. This idea is also shown as Figure 9.3, where n_L denotes the number of points to the left of x_i, and n_R denotes the number of points to the right of x_i. By $p_i(x)$ we denote a polynomial of degree M which is fit in the least squares sense through the $n_L + n_R + 1$ points. Then, we have $g_i = p_i(x_i)$.

9.2.1   Filter Coefficients

The polynomial $p_i(x)$ of degree M, which is to be fitted through the data f_i, can be written as

$$p_i(x) := \sum_{k=0}^{M} b_k \left(\frac{x - x_i}{\Delta x}\right)^k. \tag{9.2}$$

We assume that the abscissas x_i are uniformly spaced with $x_{i+1} - x_i \equiv \Delta x$. In order to fit $p_i(x)$ in the least squares sense through the measured data we have to determine the coefficients b_k such that

$$\sum_{j=i-n_L}^{i+n_R} \left(p_i(x_j) - f_j\right)^2 = \min. \tag{9.3}$$

FIGURE 9.2. *Noisy Function $f(x)$.*

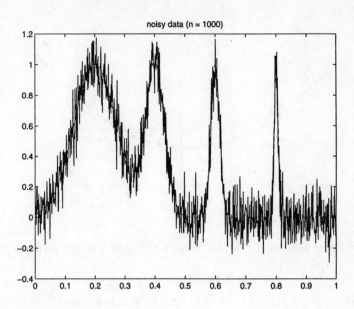

Let us define the matrix

$$A := \begin{bmatrix} (-n_L)^M & \ldots & -n_L & 1 \\ \vdots & & \vdots & \vdots \\ 0 & \ldots & 0 & 1 \\ \vdots & & \vdots & \vdots \\ n_R^M & \ldots & n_R & 1 \end{bmatrix} \in \mathbb{R}^{(n_L+n_R+1)\times(M+1)} \quad (9.4)$$

and the two vectors

$$\mathbf{b} := \begin{bmatrix} b_M \\ \vdots \\ b_1 \\ b_0 \end{bmatrix} \in \mathbb{R}^{M+1} \quad (9.5)$$

and

$$\mathbf{f} := \begin{bmatrix} f_{i-n_L} \\ \vdots \\ f_i \\ \vdots \\ f_{i+n_R} \end{bmatrix} \in \mathbb{R}^{n_L+n_R+1}. \quad (9.6)$$

It should be noted that the matrix A neither depends on the abscissa x_i nor on the stride Δx.

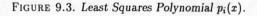

FIGURE 9.3. *Least Squares Polynomial* $p_i(x)$.

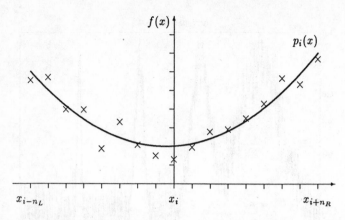

Using these definitions we can restate the least squares problem (9.3) in matrix terms as

$$\|Ab - f\|_2 = \min.\tag{9.7}$$

It would now be possible to solve (9.7) for $\mathbf{b}$ by means of the QR-decomposition of A (cf. [5, Chapter 5]). For our filtering purpose, however, we only need to know $g_i = p_i(x_i) = b_0$. The solution $\mathbf{b}$ of (9.7) can also be expressed as the solution of the normal equations

$$A^{\mathrm{T}}Ab = A^{\mathrm{T}}f.\tag{9.8}$$

Thus, we get

$$g_i = e_{M+1}^{\mathrm{T}}(A^{\mathrm{T}}A)^{-1}A^{\mathrm{T}}f,\tag{9.9}$$

where $\mathbf{e}_{M+1}$ denotes the $(M+1)$'st unit vector.

Obviously, we can represent g_i as a linear combination of the f_i's. We define the vector

$$\mathbf{c} := A(A^{\mathrm{T}}A)^{-1}\mathbf{e}_{M+1}\tag{9.10}$$

containing the filter coefficients $c_{-n_L}, \ldots, c_{n_R}$. Since $\mathbf{c}$ does not depend on x_i and Δx, it only needs to be evaluated once. Then, all the smoothed values g_i can be computed by the simple scalar product

$$g_i = \mathbf{c}^{\mathrm{T}}f = \sum_{j=i-n_L}^{i+n_R} c_{j-i}f_j.\tag{9.11}$$

The calculation of the vector $\mathbf{c}$ according to Equation (9.10) may be inaccurate for large values of M. This loss of accuracy can be attributed to the fact that the condition number of A is squared in forming $A^{\mathrm{T}}A$. On the other hand it is well-known that the least squares system (9.7) can be stably solved by means of the QR-decomposition

$$A = QR.\tag{9.12}$$

ALGORITHM 9.2. *Savitzky-Golay Smoothing Filter.*

```
function g = SavitzkyGolay (f, nl, nr, M)

A = ones (nl+nr+1, M+1);
for j = M:-1:1,
   A (:, j) = [-nl:nr]' .* A (:, j+1);
end
[Q, R] = qr (A);
c = Q (:, M+1) / R (M+1, M+1);

n = length (f);
g = filter (c (nl+nr+1:-1:1), 1, f);
g (1:nl) = f (1:nl);
g (nl+1:n-nr) = g (nl+nr+1:n);
g (n-nr+1:n) = f (n-nr+1:n);
```

By Q we denote an orthogonal $(n_L + n_R + 1)$-by-$(M + 1)$ matrix, and by R we denote an upper triangular $(M + 1)$-by-$(M + 1)$ matrix. If we substitute decomposition (9.12) into (9.10) we get for the vector $\mathbf{c}$ the expression

$$\mathbf{c} = \frac{1}{r_{M+1,M+1}} Q \mathbf{e}_{M+1}. \tag{9.13}$$

This is the numerically preferred way of computing $\mathbf{c}$. Amazingly enough, this has been pointed out neither in [8] nor in [10].

9.2.2 Results

We present the Savitzky-Golay smoothing filter as Algorithm 9.2. If we apply this algorithm to our initial smoothing problem from Figure 9.2, we get the smoothed curve in Figure 9.4. For easy reference we have also superimposed the graph of the function F from Equation (9.1). We have chosen the parameters $n_L = n_R = 16$ and $M = 4$ which seem to be optimal for this test case. The execution of Algorithm 9.2 needs about 0.13 seconds of CPU-time on a Sun Sparcstation 1+ equipped with a Weitek 3170 floating point unit running at 25 MHz.

The main advantage of a Savitzky-Golay filter is its speed. For given values of n_L, n_R, and M, the filter parameters $\mathbf{c}$ need to be evaluated only once. Then each filtered value g_i can be computed by the simple scalar product (9.11) of length $n_L + n_R + 1$. It is conceivable that this operation could even be implemented in hardware for special purpose applications.

It is a disadvantage that it is not obvious how to choose the filter parameters n_L, n_R, and M. In [1, 8, 13] some practical hints are given. But in many cases some visual optimization is needed in order to obtain the best results.

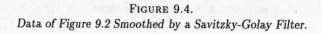

FIGURE 9.4.
Data of Figure 9.2 Smoothed by a Savitzky-Golay Filter.

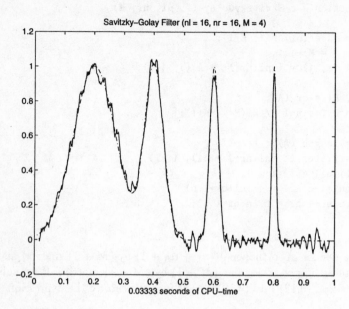

Finally, the boundary points represent yet another problem. They cannot be smoothed by a filter with $n_L > 0$ or $n_R > 0$. Either these boundary values are just dropped, as it is done in the case of Figure 9.4, or one constructs a special Savitzky-Golay filter with $n_L = 0$ or $n_R = 0$ for these special cases.

9.3   Least Squares Filter

Another approach to our filtering problem consists in requiring that the filtered curve $g(x)$ be as smooth as possible. In the continuous case we would require that

$$\int_{x_{\min}}^{x_{\max}} g''(x)^2 \, dx = \min. \tag{9.14}$$

Since the function $f(x)$ is only available as measured data f_i at discrete points x_i we will only compute the smoothed values g_i at the same points. Therefore, we must express the second derivative of $g(x)$ by a finite difference scheme. A popular choice is

$$g''(x_i) \approx \frac{g_{i+1} - 2g_i + g_{i-1}}{\Delta x^2}. \tag{9.15}$$

We could give similar stencils for non-equally spaced abscissas x_i. Consequently, condition (9.14) is replaced by the condition

$$\sum_{i=2}^{n-1} (g_{i+1} - 2g_i + g_{i-1})^2 = \min. \tag{9.16}$$

Besides this smoothness condition we also require that the function $g(x)$ approximates $f(x)$ within the limits of the superimposed noise. If we assume the f_i's to be corrupted by random noise of mean zero and mean deviation δ we require that

$$|g_i - f_i| \leq \delta \tag{9.17}$$

on the average. For n samples this condition can also be written as

$$\sum_{i=1}^{n} (g_i - f_i)^2 \leq n\delta^2. \tag{9.18}$$

Let us now define the matrix

$$A := \begin{bmatrix} 1 & -2 & 1 & & & \\ & 1 & -2 & 1 & & \\ & & \ddots & \ddots & \ddots & \\ & & & 1 & -2 & 1 \end{bmatrix} \in \mathbb{R}^{(n-2) \times n}. \tag{9.19}$$

Then, we can restate the optimization problem (9.16,9.18) in matrix notation as the minimization of

$$\|A\mathbf{g}\|_2 = \min \tag{9.20}$$

subject to the quadratic inequality constraint

$$\|\mathbf{g} - \mathbf{f}\|_2^2 \leq \alpha^2 := n\delta^2. \tag{9.21}$$

9.3.1 Lagrange Equations

Let us now study the solution of the optimization problem (9.20,9.21). First we assume that there are elements from the null space $\mathcal{N}(A)$ of the matrix A satisfying the constraint (9.21). In this case we want to determine the vector $\mathbf{g}$ which satisfies the constraint (9.21) best, i.e. we consider the minimization problem

$$\|\mathbf{g} - \mathbf{f}\|_2 = \min \tag{9.22}$$

subject to the linear equality constraint

$$A\mathbf{g} = \mathbf{0}. \tag{9.23}$$

It is not hard to show that the unique optimal solution in this case is given by

$$\mathbf{g} = \mathbf{f} - A^\mathrm{T}\mathbf{z}, \tag{9.24}$$

where $\mathbf{z}$ can be computed as the unique solution of the linear least squares problem

$$\|A^{\mathrm{T}}\mathbf{z} - \mathbf{f}\|_2 = \min. \tag{9.25}$$

The vector $\mathbf{z}$ can also be characterized as the solution of the normal equations

$$AA^{\mathrm{T}}\mathbf{z} = A\mathbf{f}, \tag{9.26}$$

which correspond to (9.25).

Now, let us assume that there is no element from the null space $\mathcal{N}(A)$ which is compatible with the constraint (9.21). In particular, this means that the vector $\mathbf{g} \in \mathcal{N}(A)$ defined by the Equations (9.24) and (9.25) satisfies

$$\|\mathbf{g} - \mathbf{f}\|_2 > \alpha. \tag{9.27}$$

We can study the least squares problem (9.20,9.21) by introducing the Lagrange principal function

$$\Phi(\mathbf{g}, \lambda, \mu) := \mathbf{g}^{\mathrm{T}} A^{\mathrm{T}} A \mathbf{g} + \lambda(\|\mathbf{g} - \mathbf{f}\|_2^2 + \mu^2 - \alpha^2), \tag{9.28}$$

where μ denotes a so-called slack variable. By differentiating Φ with respect to $\mathbf{g}$, λ, and μ we get the Lagrange equations

$$(A^{\mathrm{T}}A + \lambda I)\mathbf{g} = \lambda\mathbf{f}, \tag{9.29}$$

$$\|\mathbf{g} - \mathbf{f}\|_2^2 + \mu^2 = \alpha^2, \tag{9.30}$$

$$\lambda\mu = 0. \tag{9.31}$$

For $\lambda = 0$, we would have $A^{\mathrm{T}}A\mathbf{g} = \mathbf{0}$ or $A\mathbf{g} = \mathbf{0}$, since the matrix A has full rank. But according to our above assumption, the vector $\mathbf{g}$ cannot be an element of the null space $\mathcal{N}(A)$. Therefore we will assume $\lambda \neq 0$ from now on.

Because of $\lambda \neq 0$, we have $\mu = 0$ from Equation (9.31). Therefore, we can simplify the Lagrange Equations (9.29,9.30,9.31) to

$$(A^{\mathrm{T}}A + \lambda I)\mathbf{g} = \lambda\mathbf{f}, \tag{9.32}$$

$$\|\mathbf{g} - \mathbf{f}\|_2 = \alpha. \tag{9.33}$$

Since $\lambda \neq 0$, we can make use of Equation (9.32) to express $\mathbf{g}$ by

$$\mathbf{g} = \mathbf{f} - A^{\mathrm{T}}\mathbf{z}, \tag{9.34}$$

where

$$\mathbf{z} = \frac{1}{\lambda}A\mathbf{g}. \tag{9.35}$$

By substituting the expression (9.34) for $\mathbf{g}$ into (9.32,9.33), we get the dual Lagrange equations

$$(AA^{\mathrm{T}} + \lambda I)\mathbf{z} = A\mathbf{f}, \tag{9.36}$$

$$\|A^{\mathrm{T}}\mathbf{z}\|_2 = \alpha. \tag{9.37}$$

ALGORITHM 9.3.

Solution of the Constrained Least Squares
Problem (9.20,9.21).

Solve the linear least squares problem (9.25) for **z**.

if $\|A^{\mathrm{T}}z\|_2 > \alpha$ **then**

    Solve the secular equation (9.38) for the unique zero $\lambda > 0$.

    Solve the linear system (9.36) for **z**.

end

$g := f - A^{\mathrm{T}}z$

As soon as λ and **z** have been determined, we can compute **g** according to Equation (9.34).

In [3, 4] it is shown that there is a unique Lagrange multiplier $\lambda > 0$ and an associated vector **z** which solve the dual Lagrange Equations (9.36,9.37). Furthermore, the vector **g** from (9.34) will then solve the least squares problem (9.20,9.21).

The dual Lagrange Equations (9.36,9.37) have the advantage that the matrix $AA^{\mathrm{T}} + \lambda I$ is nonsingular for $\lambda \geq 0$. The Lagrange multiplier λ can be found by solving the nonlinear secular equation

$$s(\lambda) := \|A^{\mathrm{T}}(AA^{\mathrm{T}} + \lambda I)^{-1}Af\|_2^2 = \alpha^2. \qquad (9.38)$$

This will be discussed in more detail in Section 9.3.2.

As the result of our analysis we can present Algorithm 9.3 for the solution of the constrained least squares problem (9.20,9.21). The next sections will concentrate on the practical issues of the implementation in MATLAB.

9.3.2 Zero Finder

The solution of the secular Equation (9.38) for its unique zero $\lambda > 0$ represents the major effort of Algorithm 9.3. We show the graph of the secular function $s(\lambda)$ as Figure 9.5. Since $s(\lambda)$ is a nonlinear function an iterative method is needed to solve the secular Equation (9.38). A good choice would be Newton's method which is defined by the iteration

$$\lambda_{k+1} := \lambda_k - \frac{s(\lambda_k) - \alpha^2}{s'(\lambda_k)}. \qquad (9.39)$$

However, for our particular equation, Reinsch [9] has proposed the accelerated Newton iteration

$$\lambda_{k+1} := \lambda_k - 2\frac{s(\lambda_k)}{s'(\lambda_k)}\Big(\frac{\sqrt{s(\lambda_k)}}{\alpha} - 1\Big). \qquad (9.40)$$

If this iteration is started with $\lambda_0 = 0$ we get a strictly increasing sequence of λ_k's. Proofs of this key property can be found in [9] and in [12, pp. 65–66]. However, this mathematical property cannot be preserved in floating point

FIGURE 9.5. *Secular Function* $s(\lambda)$.

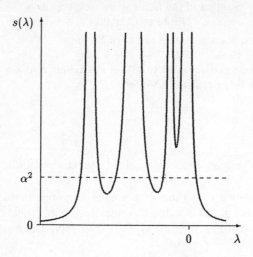

arithmetic. This observation leads to the numerical termination criterion

$$\lambda_{k+1} \leq \lambda_k. \tag{9.41}$$

9.3.3 Evaluation of the Secular Function

In order to use the iteration (9.40) to solve the secular Equation (9.38), we need a way to evaluate numerically the secular function $s(\lambda)$ and its derivative $s'(\lambda)$. The values of $s(\lambda)$ and $s'(\lambda)$ can be expressed by

$$s(\lambda) = \|A^{\mathrm{T}}\mathbf{z}\|_2^2, \tag{9.42}$$

$$s'(\lambda) = -2\mathbf{z}^{\mathrm{T}}(\mathbf{z} + \lambda\mathbf{z}'), \tag{9.43}$$

where $\mathbf{z}$ and $\mathbf{z}'$ satisfy the equations

$$(AA^{\mathrm{T}} + \lambda I)\mathbf{z} = A\mathbf{f} \tag{9.44}$$

and

$$(AA^{\mathrm{T}} + \lambda I)\mathbf{z}' = -\mathbf{z}. \tag{9.45}$$

The last two Equations (9.44) and (9.45) suggest that we have to solve linear systems involving the matrix $AA^{\mathrm{T}} + \lambda I$. However, we can also read Equation (9.44) as the normal equations corresponding to the linear least squares problem

$$\left\| \begin{bmatrix} A^{\mathrm{T}} \\ \sqrt{\lambda}I \end{bmatrix} \mathbf{z} - \begin{bmatrix} \mathbf{f} \\ \mathbf{0} \end{bmatrix} \right\|_2 = \min. \tag{9.46}$$

Similarly, we can compute $\mathbf{z}'$ as the solution of the least squares problem

$$\left\| \begin{bmatrix} A^{\mathrm{T}} \\ \sqrt{\lambda}I \end{bmatrix} \mathbf{z}' - \begin{bmatrix} \mathbf{0} \\ -\mathbf{z}/\sqrt{\lambda} \end{bmatrix} \right\|_2 = \min, \tag{9.47}$$

FIGURE 9.6. *First Stage of the QR-decomposition (9.48).*

$$
\begin{bmatrix}
\textcircled{1} & & & & \\
-2 & 1 & & & \\
1 & -2 & 1 & & \\
& 1 & -2 & 1 & \\
& & \ddots & \ddots & \ddots \\
\textcircled{σ} & & & & \\
& \sigma & & & \\
& & \sigma & & \\
& & & \sigma & \\
& & & & \ddots
\end{bmatrix}
\longmapsto
\begin{bmatrix}
\textcircled{r_{11}} & & & & \\
\textcircled{-2} & 1 & & & \\
1 & -2 & 1 & & \\
& 1 & -2 & 1 & \\
& & \ddots & \ddots & \ddots \\
0 & & & & \\
& \sigma & & & \\
& & \sigma & & \\
& & & \sigma & \\
& & & & \ddots
\end{bmatrix}
\longmapsto
$$

$$
\begin{bmatrix}
\textcircled{r_{11}} & r_{12} & & & \\
0 & r_{22} & & & \\
\textcircled{1} & -2 & 1 & & \\
& 1 & -2 & 1 & \\
& & \ddots & \ddots & \ddots \\
0 & & & & \\
& \sigma & & & \\
& & \sigma & & \\
& & & \sigma & \\
& & & & \ddots
\end{bmatrix}
\longmapsto
\begin{bmatrix}
r_{11} & r_{12} & r_{13} & & \\
0 & r_{22} & & & \\
0 & t & r_{33} & & \\
& 1 & -2 & 1 & \\
& & \ddots & \ddots & \ddots \\
0 & & & & \\
& \sigma & & & \\
& & \sigma & & \\
& & & \sigma & \\
& & & & \ddots
\end{bmatrix}
$$

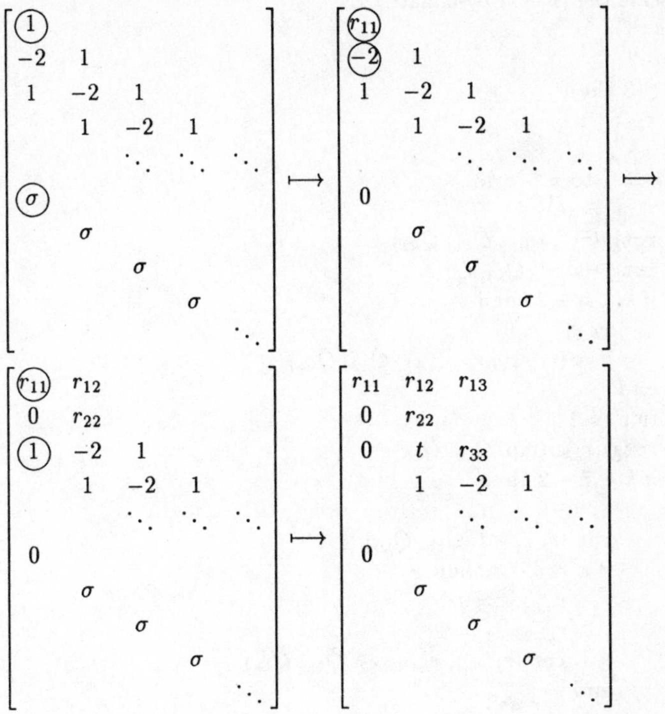

provided that $\lambda > 0$. It should be noted that for $\lambda = 0$ the vector $\mathbf{z}'$ is not needed to compute $s'(\lambda)$ in Equation (9.43). Numerically, we prefer computing $\mathbf{z}$ and $\mathbf{z}'$ from the two linear least squares problems (9.46,9.47) over solving the two linear systems (9.44,9.45).

We can solve the two least squares problems (9.46,9.47) with the help of the QR-decomposition

$$
\begin{bmatrix} A^{\mathrm{T}} \\ \sqrt{\lambda}I \end{bmatrix} = Q \begin{bmatrix} R \\ 0 \end{bmatrix},
\tag{9.48}
$$

where Q and R denote an orthogonal $(2n-2)$-by-$(2n-2)$ matrix, and an upper triangular $(n-2)$-by-$(n-2)$ matrix, respectively. In MATLAB we could compute this decomposition by the statement

```
>> [Q, R] = qr ([A'; sqrt(lambda)*eye(n-2)]);
```

However, this command does not take advantage of the special structure of the matrix, and its numerical complexity increases cubically with the size of A. Fortunately, we can devise an algorithm to compute the QR-decomposition (9.48) whose numerical complexity increases only linearly with the size of the matrix A. We can achieve this improvement by an appropriate sequence of Givens transfor-

ALGORITHM 9.4.
Calculation of the QR-decomposition (9.48).

Allocate the $(n-2)$-by-6 matrix $\bar{Q}$.
$r_{11} := 1$
$t := -2$
if $n > 3$ **then**
    $r_{22} := 1$
end
for $k := 1$ **to** $n - 2$ **do**
    $\text{tmp} := \sqrt{\lambda}$
    rotg $(r_{kk}, \text{tmp}, \bar{Q}_{k1}, \bar{Q}_{k2})$
    rotg $(r_{kk}, t, \bar{Q}_{k3}, \bar{Q}_{k4})$
    if $k < n - 2$ **then**
        $r_{k,k+1} := 0$
        rot $(r_{k,k+1}, r_{k+1,k+1}, \bar{Q}_{k3}, \bar{Q}_{k4})$
    end
    $\text{tmp} := 1$
    rotg $(r_{kk}, \text{tmp}, \bar{Q}_{k5}, \bar{Q}_{k6})$
    if $k < n - 2$ **then**
        $t := -2$
        rot $(r_{k,k+1}, t, \bar{Q}_{k5}, \bar{Q}_{k6})$
        if $k < n - 3$ **then**
            $r_{k,k+2} := 0$
            $r_{k+2,k+2} := 1$
            rot $(r_{k,k+2}, r_{k+2,k+2}, \bar{Q}_{k5}, \bar{Q}_{k6})$
        end
    end
end

mations. In Figure 9.6 we show the application of the first three Givens rotations when processing the first column. The quantity σ is an abbreviation for $\sqrt{\lambda}$. If we apply this step $n - 2$ times we get the desired QR-decomposition (9.48). We show the same procedure in pseudo-code as Algorithm 9.4. The construction and application of Givens rotations is described by calls of the BLAS routines `rotg` and `rot`. Their precise definition is given in [2, 6]. The actual implementation in MATLAB or in a conventional programming language like C or Fortran is now straightforward.

We stress that the matrix $\bar{Q}$ computed by Algorithm 9.4 is not identical to the matrix Q from the QR-decomposition (9.48). Rather the matrix $\bar{Q}$ contains the information on the Givens rotations needed to apply the matrix Q to a vector $\mathbf{x}$. We present the evaluation of the products $\mathbf{y} := Q\mathbf{x}$ and $\mathbf{y} := Q^{\mathrm{T}}\mathbf{x}$ as Algorithms 9.5 and 9.6.

ALGORITHM 9.5. *Evaluation of the Product* $\mathbf{y} := Q\mathbf{x}$.

$\mathbf{y} := \mathbf{x}$
for $k := n - 2$ **to** 1 **by** -1 **do**
  rot $(y_k, y_{k+2}, \bar{Q}_{k5}, -\bar{Q}_{k6})$
  rot $(y_k, y_{k+1}, \bar{Q}_{k3}, -\bar{Q}_{k4})$
  rot $(y_k, y_{n+k}, \bar{Q}_{k1}, -\bar{Q}_{k2})$
end

ALGORITHM 9.6. *Evaluation of the Product* $\mathbf{y} := Q^{\mathrm{T}}\mathbf{x}$.

$\mathbf{y} := \mathbf{x}$
for $k := 1$ **to** $n - 2$ **do**
  rot $(y_k, y_{n+k}, \bar{Q}_{k1}, \bar{Q}_{k2})$
  rot $(y_k, y_{k+1}, \bar{Q}_{k3}, \bar{Q}_{k4})$
  rot $(y_k, y_{k+2}, \bar{Q}_{k5}, \bar{Q}_{k6})$
end

9.3.4 MEX-Files

Since MATLAB is an interpreted language it is not well suited to run Algorithms 9.4, 9.5, and 9.6. The overhead introduced by its interpreter would be considerable. Rather our code performs much better when implemented in a conventional programming language like C or Fortran. Fortunately, MATLAB provides a means to execute separately compiled code—the so-called MEX-files.

Let us assume we have implemented Algorithms 9.4, 9.5, and 9.6 in the C programming language. If we want to execute this code from inside MATLAB we need an interface procedure for each of these algorithms. In MATLAB a function call has the general syntax

$$[l_1, l_2, \ldots, l_{\mathrm{nlhs}}] = \mathtt{fct}\ (r_1, r_2, \ldots, r_{\mathrm{nrhs}});$$

The l_i's are called output parameters, and the r_i's are called input parameters. If this function is to be implemented as an external C subroutine we need the following interface procedure:

```
#include "mex.h"

mexFunction (nlhs, plhs, nrhs, prhs)
    int    nlhs, nrhs;
    Matrix *plhs[], *prhs[];

{
    ...
}
```

The two parameters nlhs and nrhs give the number of left-hand side arguments and the number of right-hand side arguments with which fct has been called

ALGORITHM 9.7. *MEX-File for Algorithm 9.4.*

```
#include "mex.h"

#define max(A, B)  ((A) > (B) ? (A) : (B))
#define min(A, B)  ((A) < (B) ? (A) : (B))

#define n     prhs[0]
#define sigma prhs[1]

#define Qbar plhs[0]
#define R    plhs[1]

mexFunction (nlhs, plhs, nrhs, prhs)
  int    nlhs, nrhs;
  Matrix *plhs[], *prhs[];

{ int size, nnz;

  if (nrhs != 2) {
    mexErrMsgTxt ("spqr requires two input arguments.");
  } else if (nlhs != 2) {
    mexErrMsgTxt ("spqr requires two output arguments.");
  }

  if ((mxGetM (n) != 1) || (mxGetN (n) != 1) ||
      (*mxGetPr (n) < 3.0)) {
    mexErrMsgTxt ("n must be a scalar greater or equal 3.");
  }

  if ((mxGetM (sigma) != 1) || (mxGetN (sigma) != 1)) {
    mexErrMsgTxt ("sigma must be a scalar.");
  }

  size = (int) *mxGetPr (n);
  Qbar = mxCreateFull (size-2, 6, REAL);
  if (size == 3) {nnz = 1;} else {nnz = 3*size - 9;}
  R = mxCreateSparse (size-2, size-2, nnz, REAL);

  QR (size, *mxGetPr (sigma), mxGetPr (Qbar), R);
}
```

in MATLAB. The parameter plhs is a pointer to an array of length nlhs where we must put pointers for the returned left-hand side matrices. Conversely, the parameter prhs is a pointer to an array of length nrhs, whose entries point to the right-hand side matrices.

This interface routine should perform the following tasks:

1. It checks whether the proper number of input and output arguments has been supplied.

2. It makes sure that the dimensions of the input matrices meet their specification.

3. It allocates the storage for the output matrices.

4. It calls another subroutine to perform the actual calculation.

The included file mex.h contains the MEX-file declarations and prototypes. There are a number of auxiliary subroutines available that can be called by the interface routine. For details the reader is referred to the External Interface Guide of MATLAB.

As an example we present as Algorithm 9.7 the C code which serves as an interface to the QR-decomposition of Algorithm 9.4. A translation of the pseudo-code of Algorithm 9.4 into C is shown as Algorithm 9.8. We would also like to remind the reader that all the code is available in machine-readable form (see the preface for more information). In MATLAB we can now execute the statement

```
>> [Qbar, R] = spqr (n, sqrt (lambda));
```

to compute the sparse QR-decomposition (9.48).

In the same way we can implement Algorithms 9.5 and 9.6 by MEX-files. We can call them in MATLAB by the statements y = Qx (Qbar, x) and y = QTx (Qbar, x), respectively.

9.3.5 Results

We are now ready to present the implementation of the least squares filter as Algorithm 9.9. The matrix A from equation (9.19) is created as a sparse matrix. In this way only the nonzero entries of A need to be stored. This is accomplished by the function spdiags which defines a sparse matrix by its diagonals.

The QR-decomposition (9.48) is computed by a call of spqr which implements Algorithm 9.4 as a MEX-file. Similarly, a call of the function QTx executes the MEX-file corresponding to Algorithm 9.6.

If we apply Algorithm 9.9 to our test data represented in Figure 9.2 we get the smoothed curve from Figure 9.7. We have set $\delta = 0.1$, which corresponds to the mean deviation of the noise in the function $f(x)$.

From a visual point of view the least squares filter returns a smoother result than the Savitzky-Golay filter whose output has been presented as Figure 9.4.

ALGORITHM 9.8.
Calculation of the QR-decomposition (9.48) in C.

```
void QR (n, sigma, Qbar, R)
  int n;  double sigma, *Qbar;  Matrix *R;

{ int    i, j, k, nnz, n2, n3, n4, *ir, *jc;
  double co, *pr, si, t, tmp;

  nnz = mxGetNzmax (R);  n2 = n-2;  n3 = n-3;  n4 = n-4;
  ir = mxGetIr (R);  jc = mxGetJc (R);  pr = mxGetPr (R);
  /* diagonal of R */
  ir [0] = 0;  for (i = 1; i < n2; i++) {ir [3*i - 1] = i;}
  /* first upper off-diagonal of R */
  for (i = 0; i < n3; i++) {ir [3*i + 1] = i;}
  /* second upper off-diagonal of R */
  for (i = 0; i < n4; i++) {ir [3*i + 3] = i;}
  /* columns of R */
  jc [0] = 0;  jc [1] = 1;
  for (j=2; j < n2; j++) {jc [j] = 3*j - 3;}
  jc [n2] = nnz;

#define r(i, j) pr [k = jc [j], k + i - ir [k]]
  r (0, 0) = 1.0;  t = -2.0;  if (n > 3) {r (1, 1) = 1.0;}
  for (j = 0; j < n2; j++) {
    tmp = sigma;
    rotg (&r (j, j), &tmp, &Qbar [j], &Qbar [n2 + j]);
    rotg (&r (j, j), &t, &Qbar [2*n2 + j], &Qbar [3*n2 + j]);
    if (j < n3) {
      r (j, j+1) = 0.0;
      rot (&r (j, j+1), &r (j+1, j+1),
           Qbar [2*n2 + j], Qbar [3*n2 + j]);
    }
    tmp = 1.0;
    rotg (&r (j, j), &tmp, &Qbar [4*n2 + j], &Qbar [5*n2 + j]);
    if (j < n3) {
      t = -2.0;
      rot (&r (j, j+1), &t, Qbar [4*n2 + j], Qbar [5*n2 + j]);
      if (j < n4) {
        r (j, j+2) = 0.0;  r (j+2, j+2) = 1.0;
        rot (&r (j, j+2), &r (j+2, j+2),
             Qbar [4*n2 + j], Qbar [5*n2 + j]);
      }
    }
  }
#undef r
}
```

ALGORITHM 9.9. *Least Squares Smoothing Filter.*

```
function g = LeastSquares (f, delta)

n = length (f);
alpha = sqrt (n) * delta;
e = ones (n, 1);
A = spdiags ([e -2*e e], 0:2, n-2, n);

lambda = 0;
while 1,
  [Qbar, R] = spqr (n, sqrt (lambda));
  z = QTx (Qbar, [f; zeros(n-2, 1)]);
  z = R \ z (1:n-2);

  F = norm (A' * z)^2;
  if (F <= alpha^2), break; end;

  if (lambda > 0),
    zp = QTx (Qbar, [zeros(n, 1); -z/sqrt(lambda)]);
    zp = R \ zp (1:n-2);
    Fp = -2 * z' * (z + lambda * zp);
  else
    Fp = -2 * z' * z;
  end;

  lambdaold = lambda;
  lambda = lambda - 2 * (F / Fp) * (sqrt (F) / alpha - 1);
  if (lambda <= lambdaold), break; end;
end;
g = f - A' * z;
```

FIGURE 9.7.

Data of Figure 9.2 Smoothed by a Least Squares Filter.

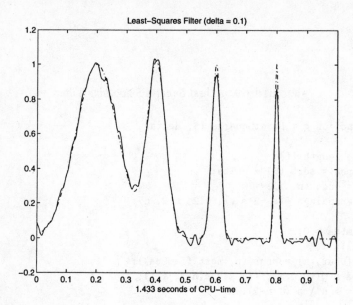

The results get even better when the number of points n is increased. On the other hand the CPU-times required to execute Algorithm 9.9 are substantially higher than those needed to execute the Savitzky-Golay filter from Algorithm 9.2. We have summarized these CPU-times for a number of different data sizes n as Table 9.1.

We conclude that a least squares filter can produce a smoother curve $g(x)$ than a Savitzky-Golay filter. However, we need to pay for this advantage with a more complex algorithm and with an increased CPU-time. A least squares filter has also the advantage that only one parameter, the mean deviation δ of the noise, has to be estimated. This quantity is more directly related to the physical data than the parameters n_L, n_R, and M from the Savitzky-Golay filter.

TABLE 9.1.

CPU-Times Corresponding to Different Data Sizes.

n	Savitzky-Golay Filter	Least Squares Filter
10^3	0.03 sec	1.4 sec
10^4	0.15 sec	17 sec
10^5	1.25 sec	237 sec

References

[1] M. U. A. BROMBA AND H. ZIEGLER, *Application Hints for Savitzky-Golay Digital Smoothing Filters*, Analytical Chemistry, 53 (1981), pp. 1583–1586.

[2] J. J. DONGARRA, C. B. MOLER, J. R. BUNCH AND G. W. STEWART, *LINPACK Users' Guide*, SIAM Publications, Philadelphia, 1979.

[3] W. GANDER, *On the Linear Least Squares Problem with a Quadratic Constraint*, Habilitationsschrift ETH Zürich, STAN-CS-78-697, Stanford University, 1978.

[4] W. GANDER, *Least Squares with a Quadratic Constraint*, Numer. Math., 36 (1981), pp. 291–307.

[5] G. H. GOLUB AND C. F. VAN LOAN, *Matrix Computations*, Second Edition, The Johns Hopkins University Press, Baltimore, 1989.

[6] C. L. LAWSON, R. J. HANSON, D. R. KINCAID AND F. T. KROGH, *Basic Linear Algebra Subprograms for Fortran Usage*, ACM Trans. Math. Softw., 5 (1979), pp. 308–325.

[7] W. H. PRESS, B. P. FLANNERY, S. A. TEUKOLSKY AND W. T. VETTERLING, *Numerical Recipes*, Cambridge University Press, Cambridge, 1986.

[8] W. H. PRESS AND S. A. TEUKOLSKY, *Savitzky-Golay Smoothing Filters*, Computers in Physics, 4 (1990), pp. 669–672.

[9] C. H. REINSCH, *Smoothing by Spline Functions. II*, Numer. Math., 16 (1971), pp. 451–454.

[10] A. SAVITZKY AND M. J. E. GOLAY, *Smoothing and Differentiation of Data by Simplified Least Squares Procedures*, Analytical Chemistry, 36 (1964), pp. 1627–1639.

[11] J. STEINIER, Y. TERMONIA AND J. DELTOUR, *Comments on Smoothing and Differentiation of Data by Simplified Least Square Procedure*, Analytical Chemistry, 44 (1972), pp. 1906–1909.

[12] U. VON MATT, *Large Constrained Quadratic Problems*, Verlag der Fachvereine, Zürich, 1993.

[13] H. ZIEGLER, *Properties of Digital Smoothing Polynomial (DISPO) Filters*, Applied Spectroscopy, 35 (1981), pp. 88–92.

Chapter 10. The Radar Problem

S. Bartoň and I. Daler

10.1 Introduction

The controlling system for a multiradar display, in an air traffic long-distance control center, receives different information from different kinds of radars on the globe. The information coming from each radar contains among others the coordinates x, y, z (with respect to the cartesian coordinate system of the given radar) of an airplane which is "seen" by the radar. The two–dimensional

FIGURE 10.1. *Airplane in two Radar Systems in Plane.*

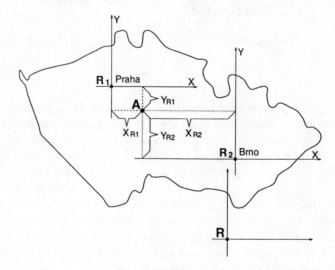

situation in the case of two radars R_1, R_2 is shown on Figure 10.1. We can see that the airplane is described by the coordinates $[x_{R_1}, y_{R_1}]$ of the radar R_1 and by the coordinates $[x_{R_2}, y_{R_2}]$ of the radar R_2. For the controlling system of the multiradar display it is necessary to work with the "absolute" coordinate system (with the origin R). The data from all the radars concerning the position of the airplane A are transformed into this system. That means that in this coordinate system the airplane A is described by several points which can be processed using appropriate criteria. *(For example, the airplane will be represented by the point which corresponds to its most probable position).* In the coordinate system with the origin R, the long-distance control is able to follow the relative position of airplanes from the visual information on the display. The controlling program for a multiradar display is then able to watch the whole region of operation of the airplane using chosen windows. For simplicity let the absolute coordinate system with the origin R be identical to the coordinate system of the radar R_2. For a multiradar display it is necessary to solve the following basic problem:

Let the radars R_1 and R_2 be situated at points P_1 and P_2 on the globe. An airplane A is "seen" by the radar R_1 in its local cartesian coordinate system $\mathbf{P_1}$ with the coordinates $[x_1, y_1, z_1] \equiv A(\mathbf{P_1})$, and it is necessary to find the coordinates $[x_2, y_2, z_2] \equiv A(\mathbf{P_2})$ of the airplane A in the cartesian coordinate system $\mathbf{P_2}$ of the radar R_2 (cf. Figure 10.2). The points P_1, P_2 on the globe

FIGURE 10.2. *Airplane in two Radar Systems.*

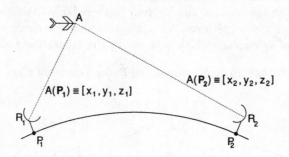

are given by the geographical coordinates $[f_1, l_1]$ and $[f_2, l_2]$, where f_1, f_2 are the geographical latitudes and l_1, l_2 are the geographical longitudes. These geographical coordinates $\mathbf{G} \equiv [f, l]$ are usually given in degrees, minutes, and seconds $(-90° \leq f \leq 90°, -180° \leq l \leq 180°)$. Also, let the cartesian coordinate systems $(P_1; +x_1, +y_1, +z_1) \equiv \mathbf{P_1}$, $(P_2; +x_2, +y_2, +z_2) \equiv \mathbf{P_2}$ have their origins in the points P_1, P_2 (cf. Figure 10.5). The $x_1 y_1$ plane is a tangent plane to the ellipsoid in the point P_1. The x_1-axis lies in the plane of the latitude f_1, the y_1-axis lies in the plane of the meridian l_1. The z_1-axis is positively oriented towards the earth's center. The x_1-axis and the y_1-axis, are oriented in the direction of increasing longitude and latitude, respectively. The axes of the coordinate system $\mathbf{P_2}$ are similarly oriented.

10.2 Converting Degrees into Radians

The geographical coordinates $[f, l]$ are usually given in degrees, minutes, seconds, and their decimal parts. For further calculations it is necessary to transform the angles f and l into radians. Since we will use this transformation several times, we design a MATLAB function deg2rad($\alpha°, [\,'\,], [\,''\,]$). The input variable α of this function will be a vector of 1 to 4 components (cf. Algorithm 10.1, Table 10.1 and Example 1).

ALGORITHM 10.1. *Function* deg2rad.

```
function rad = deg2rad(alpha)
%----------------------------
% conversion: alpha deg., min., sec.  -> radians
%
d = length(alpha);
if d > 4
   disp(alpha), error('invalid input list in function deg2rad')
end
alpha = [alpha(:); zeros(4-d,1)];
alpha(3) = alpha(3) + alpha(4)/100;
rad = pi/180*((alpha(3)/60 + alpha(2))/60 + alpha(1));
```

TABLE 10.1. *Data Organization of Angle* α.

Number of Components	Input Angle α
1	integer.decfrac°
2	integer° integer.decfrac′
3	integer° integer′ integer.decfrac″
4	integer° integer′ integer″ integer(decfrac)″

Example 1:

We test all the four possibilities for the input angle α as shown in Table 10.1. For the given input vectors we should always obtain the same value in radians:

```
>> format long
>> a = [16.641038888888888];      % 1 component
>> b = [16 38.462333333333333];   % 2 components
>> c = [16 38 27.74];             % 3 components
>> d = [16 38 27 74];             % 4 components
>> radians = [deg2rad(a) deg2rad(b) deg2rad(c) deg2rad(d)]

radians =

0.29044091956353 0.29044091956353 0.29044091956353 0.29044091956353
```

10.3 Transformation of Geographical into Geocentric Coordinates

In this section we develop a function to transform the geographical coordinates $[f, l]$ of a point P into geocentric cartesian coordinates: $(C; +x_c, +y_c, +z_c) \equiv \mathbf{C}$, with origin C in the earth's center. The z_c–axis goes through the earth's poles, with the positive orientation to the North Pole. The x_c–axis passes through the null and 180'th meridian, the positive orientation to the null meridian. The y_c–axis is perpendicular to the x_c–axis and to the z_c–axis, with positive orientation to the 90'th meridian (cf. Figure 10.5). For this transformation from the geographical coordinates $[f, l]$ into the geocentric cartesian coordinates $[x_c, z_c, y_c]$, (according to Figure 10.3), we will write the MATLAB function gg2gc(f, l). The shape of the Earth is a *geoid*, but for our purposes we will use

FIGURE 10.3.
*Transformation from Geographical to Geocentric
Coordinates.*

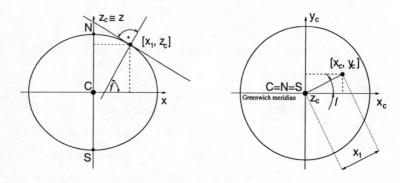

the approximation described by a circular ellipsoid. The axes of revolutions of both bodies are the same. The cross section of an ellipsoid is the (Krasovsky) ellipse, with the major semiaxis $A = 6378.245$ [km] and the minor semiaxis $B = 6356.863$ [km]. To derive the transformation equations it is convenient to use the parametric description of the ellipse (cf. Figure 10.4). It is important to remember that the geographical coordinates are not the spherical coordinates! The geographical latitude is determined by measuring the angle of an object *(sun, moon, known star)* in the sky above the horizon, i.e. the angle between a tangent plane to the earth's surface and the object. The usual parametric representation of the ellipse is

$$x(\varphi) = A\cos(\varphi), \qquad z(\varphi) = B\sin(\varphi).$$

In order to relate the angle f to x and z we first compute the normal vector $\vec{n}$ at $[x, z]$

$$\vec{t} \equiv \begin{pmatrix} \dot{x} \\ \dot{z} \end{pmatrix} = \begin{pmatrix} -A\sin(\varphi) \\ B\cos(\varphi) \end{pmatrix} \qquad \Longrightarrow \qquad \vec{n} \equiv \begin{pmatrix} -\dot{z} \\ \dot{x} \end{pmatrix} = \begin{pmatrix} -B\cos(\varphi) \\ -A\sin(\varphi) \end{pmatrix}.$$

Therefore,

$$\tan(f) = -\frac{\dot{x}}{\dot{z}} = \frac{A}{B}\tan(\varphi).$$

FIGURE 10.4.
An Ellipse Description by the Slope of the Normal Vector.

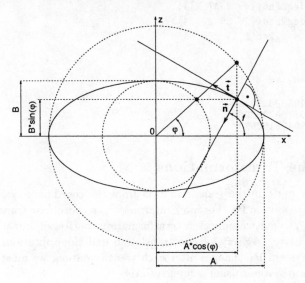

We are interested in obtaining $\sin(\varphi)$ and $\cos(\varphi)$. From $\tan(\varphi) = \frac{B}{A}\tan(f)$ we obtain:

$$\cos(\varphi) = \frac{1}{\sqrt{1 + \tan^2(\varphi)}}, \qquad \sin(\varphi) = \tan(\varphi)\cos(\varphi).$$

Now we can present the corresponding MATLAB function as Algorithm 10.2.

ALGORITHM 10.2. *Function* gg2gc.

```
function [P] = gg2gc(f, l)
%------------------------
%transformation geographic. -> geocentric. coordinates
% f, l in radians
%
A = 6378.245; B = 6356.863;    % Krasovsky ellipse
tanfi = B/A*tan(f);
cosfi = 1/sqrt(1 + tanfi^2);
sinfi = tanfi*cosfi;
P = [ A*cosfi*cos(l); A*cosfi*sin(l); B*sinfi ];
```

Let us now check both functions by computing the geocentric coordinates of Brno.

Example 2:

```
>> f = deg2rad([49 3 37 2]);
>> l = deg2rad([16 38 27 74]);
>> BRNO = gg2gc(f,l)

BRNO =

   1.0e+03 *

   4.01205896220355
   1.19917647308968
   4.79504251506287
```

10.4   The Transformations

We can now perform the transformation from the coordinate system $\mathbf{P_1}$ into the coordinate system $\mathbf{P_2}$. For more information on coordinate transformations, see e. g. [1, 2]. This complicated transformation consists of four partial transformations, more precisely, of one translation and three rotations. Since the coordinate system $\mathbf{P_1}$ changes after each transformation, we must distinguish the coordinate systems using a superscript:

$$\mathbf{P_1^i}, \quad i = 0, \cdots, 4, \quad \text{where } \mathbf{P_1^0} \equiv \mathbf{P_1}, \quad \mathbf{P_1^4} \equiv \mathbf{P_2}.$$

1. The Translation

The values of the displacement $[\Delta x, \Delta y, \Delta z] = P_2(\mathbf{P_1}) - P_1(\mathbf{P_1}) \equiv \vec{\Delta}_P$ are the coordinates of the point P_2 in the first coordinate system, i. e. we denote it by $P_2(\mathbf{P_1})$. The $\vec{\Delta}_P$ is known in the C system: $\vec{\Delta}_P(\mathbf{C}) = P_2(\mathbf{C}) - P_1(\mathbf{C})$. We must transform $\vec{\Delta}_P(\mathbf{C})$ into $\vec{\Delta}_P(\mathbf{P_1})$. This transformation is shown as Figure 10.5 and can be computed by the following steps:

1. Let us put the origin P_1'' of the coordinate system $\mathbf{P_1''}$ at the intersection of the equator and the Greenwich meridian. From Figure 10.5 we can see that the transformation is simply

$$\begin{pmatrix} \Delta x \\ \Delta y \\ \Delta z \end{pmatrix}_{\mathbf{P_1''}} = \begin{pmatrix} \Delta y \\ \Delta z \\ -\Delta x \end{pmatrix}_{\mathbf{C}} = M \times \begin{pmatrix} P_{2x} - P_{1x} \\ P_{2y} - P_{1y} \\ P_{2z} - P_{1z} \end{pmatrix}_{\mathbf{C}}, \text{ where } M = \begin{pmatrix} 0 & 1 & 0 \\ 0 & 0 & 1 \\ -1 & 0 & 0 \end{pmatrix}.$$

2. To move $\mathbf{P_1''}$ into $\mathbf{P_1'}$, we perform a rotation around the y''-axis with the angle l_1. This transformation can be described by the rotation matrix R_1:

$$\begin{pmatrix} \Delta x \\ \Delta y \\ \Delta z \end{pmatrix}_{\mathbf{P_1'}} = R_1 \times \begin{pmatrix} \Delta x \\ \Delta y \\ \Delta z \end{pmatrix}_{\mathbf{P_1''}}, \text{ where } R_1 = \begin{pmatrix} \cos(l_1) & 0 & \sin(l_1) \\ 0 & 1 & 0 \\ -\sin(l_1) & 0 & \cos(l_1) \end{pmatrix}.$$

FIGURE 10.5. $\vec{\Delta}_P(\mathbf{C}) \Longrightarrow \vec{\Delta}_P(\mathbf{P_1})$ Transformation
$\mathbf{C}$, $\mathbf{P_1}$ and $\mathbf{P_2}$ Definitions
Basic Transformations.

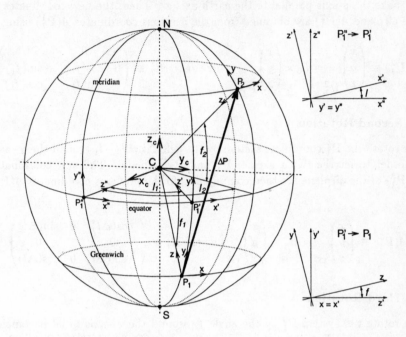

3. To move $\mathbf{P_1'}$ into $\mathbf{P_1}$, we use a rotation around the x'-axis with the angle f_1. This transformation is described by the matrix R_2:

$$\begin{pmatrix} \Delta x \\ \Delta y \\ \Delta z \end{pmatrix}_{\mathbf{P_1}} = R_2 \times \begin{pmatrix} \Delta x \\ \Delta y \\ \Delta z \end{pmatrix}_{\mathbf{P_1'}}, \text{ where } R_2 \equiv \begin{pmatrix} 1 & 0 & 0 \\ 0 & \cos(f_1) & \sin(f_1) \\ 0 & -\sin(f_1) & \cos(f_1) \end{pmatrix}.$$

4. Now the coordinate system $\mathbf{P_1}$ is in a general position. Summarizing steps 1 – 4, the translation vector $\vec{\Delta}_P(\mathbf{P_1})$ can be expressed by

$$\begin{pmatrix} \Delta x \\ \Delta y \\ \Delta z \end{pmatrix}_{\mathbf{P_1}} = R_2 \times R_1 \times M \times \begin{pmatrix} P_{2x} - P_{1x} \\ P_{2y} - P_{1y} \\ P_{2z} - P_{1z} \end{pmatrix}_{\mathbf{C}}.$$

We obtain the new coordinates $A(\mathbf{P_1^1})$ of the airplane from the previous coordinates $A(\mathbf{P_1})$ by using the relation

$$A(\mathbf{P_1^1}) \equiv \begin{pmatrix} x \\ y \\ z \end{pmatrix}_{\mathbf{P_1^1}} = A(\mathbf{P_1}) - \begin{pmatrix} \Delta x \\ \Delta y \\ \Delta z \end{pmatrix}_{\mathbf{P_1}}.$$

2. First Rotation

We rotate the $\mathbf{P}_1^1$ coordinate system around the x-axes by the angle f_1 in order to make the y-axis parallel to the earth axis z_c. Then, the new coordinates of the airplane $A(\mathbf{P}_1^2)$ are obtained from the previous coordinates $A(\mathbf{P}_1^1)$ using

$$A(\mathbf{P}_1^2) \equiv \begin{pmatrix} x \\ y \\ z \end{pmatrix}_{\mathbf{P}_1^2} = R_3 \times \begin{pmatrix} x \\ y \\ z \end{pmatrix}_{\mathbf{P}_1^1} , \text{ where } R_3 = R_2^T \equiv \begin{pmatrix} 1 & 0 & 0 \\ 0 & \cos(f_1) & -\sin(f_1) \\ 0 & \sin(f_1) & \cos(f_1) \end{pmatrix}.$$

3. Second Rotation

We rotate the $\mathbf{P}_1^2$ coordinate system by the agle $\Delta l = l_2 - l_1$ around the $y-$axis in order to let the two x-axes of $\mathbf{P}_1^2$ and $\mathbf{P_2}$ coincide. The new coordinates $A(\mathbf{P}_1^3)$ of the airplane are then computed from the previous coordinates $A(\mathbf{P}_1^2)$ by

$$A(\mathbf{P}_1^3) \equiv \begin{pmatrix} x \\ y \\ z \end{pmatrix}_{\mathbf{P}_1^3} = R_4 \times \begin{pmatrix} x \\ y \\ z \end{pmatrix}_{\mathbf{P}_1^2} , \text{ where } R_4 \equiv \begin{pmatrix} \cos(\Delta l) & 0 & \sin(\Delta l) \\ 0 & 1 & 0 \\ -\sin(\Delta l) & 0 & \cos(\Delta l) \end{pmatrix}.$$

4. Third Rotation

We rotate the system $\mathbf{P}_1^3$ by the angle f_2 around the $x-$axis to let it coincide with the system $\mathbf{P_2}$. Thus, the final coordinates $A(\mathbf{P_2}) \equiv A(\mathbf{P}_1^4)$ of the airplane A are obtained from the previous coordinates $A(\mathbf{P}_1^3)$ by

$$A(\mathbf{P_2}) \equiv \begin{pmatrix} x \\ y \\ z \end{pmatrix}_{\mathbf{P}_1^4} = R_5 \times \begin{pmatrix} x \\ y \\ z \end{pmatrix}_{\mathbf{P}_1^3} , \text{ where } R_5 \equiv \begin{pmatrix} 1 & 0 & 0 \\ 0 & \cos(f_2) & \sin(f_2) \\ 0 & -\sin(f_2) & \cos(f_2) \end{pmatrix}.$$

10.5   Final Algorithm

The above steps can be concatenated. By the using matrices $R_1 - R_5$ we get the over–all transformation

$$A(\mathbf{P_2}) \equiv \begin{pmatrix} x \\ y \\ z \end{pmatrix}_{\mathbf{P_2}} = R_5 \times R_4 \times R_2^T \times \left[A(\mathbf{P_1}) - R_2 \times R_1 \times M \times \begin{pmatrix} P_{2x} - P_{1x} \\ P_{2y} - P_{1y} \\ P_{2z} - P_{1z} \end{pmatrix}_{\mathbf{C}} \right].$$

This algorithm can be used as the basis for the MATLAB function transf, (see Algorithm 10.3).

$$A(\mathbf{P_2}) = \text{transf}(f_1, l_1, A(\mathbf{P_1}), f_2, l_2).$$

ALGORITHM 10.3. *Function* transf.

```
function [A2] = transf(f1, l1, A1, f2, l2)
%----------------------------------------
% the airplane radar position recalculation
% f, l = geographical radar positions in radians
% A1 = [x; y; z](P1) = position of airplane seen by radar at P1
%
M = [   0        1        0
        0        0        1         % M = almost permutations
       -1        0        0    ];   % matrix
%
R1 = [ cos(l1)    0     sin(l1)
         0        1        0        % R1 = Displacement
      -sin(l1)    0     cos(l1)];   %      1. rotation matrix
%
R2 = [   1        0        0
         0     cos(f1)  sin(f1)     % R2 = Displacement
         0    -sin(f1)  cos(f1)];   %      2. rotation matrix
%
P1c = gg2gc(f1, l1);               % 1. radar    geocentric
P2c = gg2gc(f2, l2);               % 2. radar    coordinates
%
DPc = P2c - P1c;                   % DPc - radar's displacement
%                                    (1. radar pos. [f=0, l=0])
T = R2*R1*M*DPc;                   % - radar's displacement
%                                    (1. radar pos. [f1, l1])
a = A1 - T;                        % A. pos. after translation
%
Dl = l2 - l1;                      % longitude difference
%
R4 = [ cos(Dl)    0     sin(Dl)
         0        1        0        % R4 = rotation matrix,
      -sin(Dl)    0     cos(Dl)];   %      rot. around y by l2-l1
%
R5 = [   1        0        0
         0     cos(f2)  sin(f2)     % R5 = rotation matrix,
         0    -sin(f2)  cos(f2)];   %      rot.  around x by f2
%
A2 = R5*R4*R2'*a;                  % A2 = [x; y; z](P2)
%                                    position of airplane
%                                    seen by radar at P2
% end of function
```

10.6   Practical Example

Our problem is now completely solved. We can check our solution with a practical example:

```
>> format long
>> f1 = deg2rad([49 45 18]);                % Praha
>> l1 = deg2rad([14 7 58]);                 %   position
>> f2 = deg2rad([49 3 37 2]);               % Brno
>> l2 = deg2rad([16 38 27 74]);             %   position
>> A1praha = [200; 140; -5.790];            % 1. A. seen from Praha
>> A2praha = [157; 397; -9.870];            % 2. A. seen from Praha
>> A1brno = transf(f1, l1, A1praha, f2, l2) % 1. A. seen from Brno

A1brno =

   1.0e+02 *

   0.23632088742730
   2.13625791235094
  -0.06831714145899

>> a1praha = transf(f2, l2, A1brno, f1, l1) % inv. transformation

a1praha =

   1.0e+02 *

   2.00000000000000
   1.40000000000000
  -0.05790000000000

>> A2brno = transf(f1, l1, A2praha, f2, l2) % 2. A. seen from Brno

A2brno =

   1.0e+02 *

  -0.10857206384904
   4.71937837075423
  -0.06683743260798

>> a2praha = transf(f2, l2, A2brno, f1, l1) % inv. transformation

a2praha =

   1.0e+02 *

   1.57000000000000
   3.97000000000000
  -0.09870000000000
```

Acknowledgments

The authors thank J. Hřebíček and W. Gander for their suggestions and help to improve this chapter.

References

[1] H. J. BARTSCH, *Taschenbuch Mathematischer Formeln*, Fachbuchverlag, Leipzig, 1991.

[2] D. G. ZILL AND M. R. CULLEN, *Advanced Engineering Mathematics*, PWS-KENT, Boston, 1992.

Chapter 11. Conformal Mapping of a Circle

H.J. Halin

11.1 Introduction

Mapping techniques are mathematical methods which are frequently applied for solving fluid flow problems in the interior and about bodies of nonregular shape. Since the advent of supercomputers such techniques have become quite important in the context of numerical grid generation [1]. In introductory courses in fluid dynamics students learn how to calculate the circulation of an incompressible potential flow about a so-called "Joukowski airfoil" [3] which represent the simplest airfoils of any technical relevance. The physical plane where flow about the airfoil takes place is in a complex $p = u + iv$ plane where $i = \sqrt{-1}$. The advantage of a Joukowski transform consists in providing a conformal mapping of the p plane on a $z = x + iy$ plane such that calculating the flow about the airfoil gets reduced to the much simpler problem of calculating the flow about a displaced circular cylinder. A special form of the mapping function $p = f(z) = u(z) + iv(z)$ of the Joukowski transform reads

$$p = \frac{1}{2}(z + \frac{a^2}{z}). \tag{11.1}$$

In this chapter we shall demonstrate how the mathematical transformations required in applying mapping methods can be handled elegantly by means of a language for symbolic computation and computer algebra. Rather than chosing a large physical problem that would be beyond the scope of this book, we select a very simple application of conformal mapping to illustrate the essential steps involved.

11.2 Problem Outline

It is suitable to express both x and y in terms of some parameter t such that $z(t) = x(t) + iy(t)$. Consequently also $p(z(t)) = f(z(t))$ holds. Inserting expression $z(t)$ into $p(z) = f(z(t))$ leads to

$$P(t) = U(t) + iV(t) = p(z(t)) \tag{11.2}$$

Twofold differentiation on either side of the equal sign with respect to t yields at next

$$\dot{P}(t) = p'(z(t))\dot{z}(t), \tag{11.3}$$

and subsequently

$$\ddot{P}(t) = p''(z(t))(\dot{z}(t))^2 + p'(z(t))\ddot{z}(t) \qquad (11.4)$$

where dots and primes denote derivatives with respect to t and z, respectively.

The relations outlined so far are needed for handling the following problem. We assume a mapping function p which results from solving the second order differential equation presented in [2]

$$z^2 p'' + z p' + (\alpha z^2 + \beta z + \gamma)p = 0 \qquad (11.5)$$

subject to the initial conditions $p'(0) = p_0'$ and $p(0) = p_0$.

Obviously the problem of mapping $z(t)$ on the domain $Y(t) = U(t) + iV(t)$ requires the solution of the complex second order differential equation specified by (11.5). This can be done by proceeding as follows: For the considered problem $z(t)$ is chosen as a circle of radius r, i.e. $z = re^{it}$. Hence, derivatives of $z(t)$ with respect to t can be readily evaluated. Inserting the complex expressions for $z(t)$, $\dot{z}(t)$, and $\ddot{z}(t)$, respectively, into Equations (11.2)-(11.5) permits one to completely eliminate any explicit appearance of z and its t-derivatives from all these equations. After this p' and p'' in (11.3) and (11.4) can be expressed only in terms of $\dot{P}(t)$ and $\ddot{P}(t)$. Finally, when using these expressions together with (11.2), our second order differential equation can be modified such that it only entails $P(t)$, $\dot{P}(t)$, and $\ddot{P}(t)$. Considering (11.2) we can simplify this complex differential equation by collecting the real and imaginary components. This yields a system of two coupled second order differential equations. The solution $U(t)$ and $V(t)$ can now be obtained by application of a standard numerical integration algorithm.

For the following two sets of initial conditions and values of parameter r illustrative solutions can be found:

$$
\begin{array}{llll}
r & = 1 & r & = 0.6 \\
U(0) & = -0.563 & U(0) & = -0.944 \\
\dot{U}(t) & = 0 & \dot{U}(t) & = 0 \\
V(0) & = 0 & V(0) & = 0 \\
\dot{V}(t) & = 0.869 & \dot{V}(t) & = 0.658
\end{array}
$$

In each of the two runs integration is done over the interval $(0 \le t \le 6\pi)$. Moreover, the following parameter values will be used $\alpha = 1$, $\beta = 0.5$, and $\gamma = -4/9$. Subsequently the latter three parameters will be referred to as a, b, and c.

11.3 MAPLE Solution

The solution steps outlined above are not very difficult to perform. Anyhow, since there are several manipulations required, deriving the formulas manually and programming them in any of the well known higher computer languages is error prone and time consuming. It will be shown in the following that an advanced mathematical computation tool such as MAPLE with its numerous symbolic, numeric, and graphical features, can be very helpful in making the solution process or at least parts of it more elaborate and elegant.

The first major task in dealing with the sample problem is to derive the two second order differential equations for $U(t)$ and $V(t)$, respectively. To do this we start with the definition of the parametric representation of the transformed circle $P(t) = p(z(t))$ in the complex $P = U + iV$ plane:

```
> p(z(t))=P(t):
```

Now we would like to express the first derivative of the as yet unknown function $p(z(t))$ with respect to t. For doing this we apply MAPLE's differentiation operator `diff` and solve for the first derivative with respect to z, i.e. $p'(t) = D(p)(z(t))$, which we denote as pprime.

```
> pprime:=solve(diff(",t),D(p)(z(t)));
```

$$
pprime := \cfrac{\dfrac{d}{dt} P(t)}{\dfrac{d}{dt} z(t)}
$$

Similarly, by a second application of the operator D to p we obtain an expression that can be solved for $p''(t)$ which we denote as p2prime.

```
> p2prime:=solve(diff("",t,t),D(D(p))(z(t)));
```

$$
p2prime := -\cfrac{D(p)(z(t))\left(\dfrac{d^2}{dt^2} z(t)\right) - \left(\dfrac{d^2}{dt^2} P(t)\right)}{\left(\dfrac{d}{dt} z(t)\right)^2}
$$

Since $D(p)(z(t))$ is by definition identically to $p'(t)$ we can make this replacement in the expression that yielded p2prime.

```
> D(p)(z(t)):=pprime;
```

$$
D(p)(z(t)) := \cfrac{\dfrac{d}{dt} P(t)}{\dfrac{d}{dt} z(t)}
$$

The new form of p2prime is

```
> p2prime;
```

$$
-\cfrac{\cfrac{\left(\dfrac{d}{dt}\,P(t)\right)\left(\dfrac{d^2}{dt^2}\,z(t)\right)}{\dfrac{d}{dt}\,z(t)} - \left(\dfrac{d^2}{dt^2}\,P(t)\right)}{\left(\dfrac{d}{dt}\,z(t)\right)^2}
$$

Now everything is available for insertion into the complex differential Equation (11.5) which will be named **ode**.

```
> ode:=z(t)^2*p2prime+z(t)*pprime+(a*z(t)^2+b*z(t)+c)*P(t);
```

$$
ode := -\,z(t)^2\,\cfrac{\cfrac{\left(\dfrac{d}{dt}\,P(t)\right)\left(\dfrac{d^2}{dt^2}\,z(t)\right)}{\dfrac{d}{dt}\,z(t)} - \left(\dfrac{d^2}{dt^2}\,P(t)\right)}{\left(\dfrac{d}{dt}\,z(t)\right)^2}
$$

$$
+\,\frac{z(t)\left(\dfrac{d}{dt}\,P(t)\right)}{\dfrac{d}{dt}\,z(t)} + (a\,z(t)^2 + b\,z(t) + c)\,P(t)
$$

So far the process of handling the problem has been strictly formal without taking note of the fact that $z(t)$ is a circle. Next this information is provided

```
> z(t):=r*exp(I*t):
```

so that we can specify $P(t)$ as a function depending only on t.

```
> P(t):=U(t)+I*V(t):
```

Our complex differential equation **ode** will now be split into two coupled ones **re** and **im** of the same order. All real components will be collected and allocated to re. Likewise all imaginary components will contribute to im. In either case we replace the complex exponential function of the circle by its well known trigonometric representation involving a sine and cosine function. This is accomplished by the argument trig in MAPLE's combine command combine(...,trig). The commands for doing the decomposition read in detail

```
> re:=combine(evalc(Re(ode)),trig);
```

$$
re := - \left(\frac{d^2}{dt^2} U(t) \right) + U(t)\, a\, r^2\, \cos(2\,t) + U(t)\, b\, r\, \cos(t)
$$

$$
+ U(t)\, c - V(t)\, a\, r^2\, \sin(2\,t) - V(t)\, b\, r\, \sin(t)
$$

```
> im:=combine(evalc(Im(ode)),trig);
```

$$
im := - \left(\frac{d^2}{dt^2} V(t) \right) + U(t)\, a\, r^2\, \sin(2\,t) + U(t)\, b\, r\, \sin(t)
$$

$$
+ V(t)\, a\, r^2\, \cos(2\,t) + V(t)\, b\, r\, \cos(t) + V(t)\, c
$$

As can be seen from the above lines the terms are not yet grouped optimally. Therefore we collect in re all coefficients of $U(t)$ and $V(t)$, respectively. This yields

```
> re:=collect(collect(re,U(t)),V(t))=0:
> im:=collect(collect(im,U(t)),V(t))=0:
```

For integration we will combine the differential equations for the real and imaginary components of $P(t)$ to form the overall system odes.

```
> odes:= re,im;
```

odes :=

$$
(-\, b\, r\, \sin(t) - a\, r^2\, \sin(2\,t))\, V(t)
$$

$$
+ (b\, r\, \cos(t) + c + a\, r^2\, \cos(2\,t))\, U(t) - \left(\frac{d^2}{dt^2} U(t) \right) = 0,
$$

$$
(b\, r\, \cos(t) + c + a\, r^2\, \cos(2\,t))\, V(t)
$$

$$
+ (b\, r\, \sin(t) + a\, r^2\, \sin(2\,t))\, U(t) - \left(\frac{d^2}{dt^2} V(t) \right) = 0
$$

A numerical solution of such a set of differential equations is feasible and thus potentially very time consuming especially since MAPLE's mode of operation is interpretative rather than doing number crunching executions on compiled programs. Moreover, at the present MAPLE offers just a single fourth-fifth order Runge-Kutta-Fehlberg algorithm. Since MAPLE permits output also in Fortran and C notation it would already be a tremendous saving to derive the above equations and get them automatically coded for further usage in a Fortran or C environment.

FIGURE 11.1.

$V(t)$ *over* $U(t)$ *for*   *first Set of Parameters* ———
                        second Set of Parameters – – –.

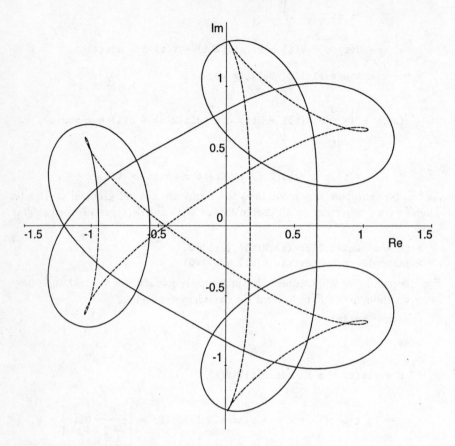

MAPLE is capable of offering a numeric solution to our problem by means of its 4-5th order Runge-Kutta-Fehlberg algorithm. Prior to applying this algorithm we specify the initial conditions for our first parameter set

```
> init:=V(0)=0,U(0)=-.563,D(V)(0)=.869,D(U)(0)=0:
```

With these initial conditions MAPLE's routine `dsolve` will give as a solution which we can look at as a procedure F that can be evaluated subsequently to give the numerical values of $U(t)$ and $V(t)$ for various arguments t. Of course we still need to specify the remaining parameters, i.e. a, b, c, and r.

```
> a:=1: b:=0.5: c:=-0.444444443: r:=1:
> F:=dsolve({odes, init}, {U(t),V(t)},numeric);

F := proc(rkf45_x) ... end
```

Since we want the solution in form of a graphic we will have to evaluate our procedure F at for instance 201 equally spaced points in the interval $(0 \leq t \leq 6\pi)$ and temporarily store the values of $U(t)$ and $V(t)$ in a list.

```
> Tend:=6*Pi: numpts:=200: step:=Tend/numpts: L:=[]:
> for j from 0 to numpts do
>      T:=j*step:
>      x:=F(T):
>      L:=[L[], subs(x, [U(t), V(t)])]:
> od:
```

where *numpts* is the number of points. L is a list of lists. Each time when invoking procedure F a new set of values of t, $U(t)$ and $V(t)$ will be added to the list. At the very end we use a MAPLE command to produce a plot, Figure 11.3, where $V(t)$ is plotted over $U(t)$, *(line ———)*

```
> plot(L);
```

By using the second set of initial conditions and a new value of parameter r we will get another solution which is also shown in Figure 11.3. *(line – – –)*.

```
> init:=V(0)=0,U(0)=-.944,D(V)(0)=.658,D(U)(0)=0:
> r:=0.6:
```

Of course the program could be readily modified to find solutions for both sets of initial conditions. This would only require embedding the program outlined above into an additional loop and a loop-controlled assignment of initial values. This also requires a new value of the radius.

References

[1] J. HÄUSER and C. TAYLOR, *Numerical Grid Generation in Computational Fluid Dynamics*, Pineridge Press, Swansea, U.K., 1986.

[2] J. HEINHOLD and U. KULISCH, *Analogrechnen*, BI-Hochschultaschenbücher Reihe Informatik, Bibliographisches Institut Mannheim / Zürich, 168/168a, 1968.

[3] W.F. HUGHES and J.A. BRIGHTON, *Fluid Dynamics*, Schaum's Outline Series, McGraw-Hill, USA, 1967.

Chapter 12. The Spinning Top

F. Klvaňa

12.1 Introduction

In this chapter we will study the motion of a spinning top – the well known children's toy. From the physical point of view we can represent it as a symmetric rigid rotor in a homogeneous gravitational field. Let O be the point at the tip of the top. Let (x, y, z) be an inertial coordinate system having its origin at the

FIGURE 12.1. *Coordinate Systems.*

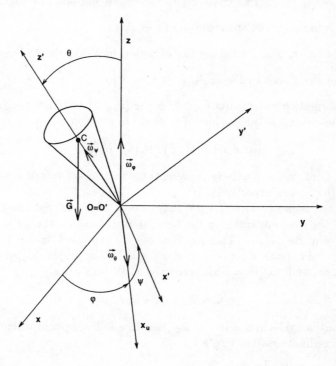

point O of the rotor where the z axis is oriented vertically (see Figure 12.1). Let $\vec{G} = (0, 0, -m\,g)$ be the weight of the rotor (acting at the center of mass), where m is the mass of the rotor and g is the gravitational acceleration. Then the kinetic energy of this rotor with angular velocity $\vec{\omega} = (\omega_1, \omega_2, \omega_3)$ is

$$T = \frac{1}{2} \sum_{i,j=1}^{3} I_{ij} \, \omega_i \, \omega_j. \qquad (12.1)$$

Notice that the vector $\vec{\omega}$ has the direction of the axis of rotation. I_{ij} is the tensor of inertia of the rotor (see [1, 2]). There exists at least one body-fixed coordinate system (x', y', z') with origin $O' = O$, in which the tensor of inertia is diagonal. In such a system the coordinate axes are called principal axes of inertia. For a symmetric rotor the axis of symmetry is one of the principal axes which we denote by z'. The two other principal axes are in the (x', y') plane orthogonal to z'. The kinetic energy has the form

$$T = \frac{1}{2} I_1 \left(\omega_{x'}^2 + \omega_{y'}^2 \right) + \frac{1}{2} I_3 \omega_{z'}^2, \qquad (12.2)$$

where I_1 and I_3 are the corresponding principal moments of inertia.

It is useful to describe the rotation of a body about the fixed point O by the Euler angles (φ, θ, ψ). Using them we express the transformation from the coordinate system (x, y, x) to (x', y', z') by successive rotations (see Figure 12.1):

1. about the z-axis by the angle φ $(x \to x_u)$,

2. about the x_u-axis (called the line of nodes) by the angle θ $(z \to z')$,

3. about the z'-axis by the angle ψ $(x_u \to x')$.

The transformation matrix $\hat{A}(\varphi, \theta, \psi)$ from the (x, y, z) system to the (x', y', z') system is expressed as the product of matrices of rotation,

$$\hat{A}(\varphi, \theta, \psi) = \hat{R}_z(\psi) \cdot \hat{R}_x(\theta) \cdot \hat{R}_z(\varphi), \qquad (12.3)$$

where $\hat{R}_x$, and $\hat{R}_z$, respectively, represents the matrices of rotations about the x-axis or the z-axis, respectively.

The Euler angles $(\varphi(t), \theta(t), \psi(t))$ may be used as generalized coordinates of the rotor. Let the rotor rotate in the time interval dt about the instantaneous axis by the angle $|\vec{\omega}| \, dt$. This rotation can be expressed as the succession of rotations about the z-, x_u-axis and z'- axis by the angles $|\vec{\omega}_\varphi| \, dt = \dot{\varphi} \, dt$, $|\vec{\omega}_\theta| \, dt = \dot{\theta} \, dt$, and $|\vec{\omega}_\psi| \, dt = \dot{\psi} \, dt$, respectively. We can write

$$\vec{\omega} = \vec{\omega}_\varphi + \vec{\omega}_\theta + \vec{\omega}_\psi. \qquad (12.4)$$

The angular velocities $\vec{\omega}_\phi$, $\vec{\omega}_\theta$, $\vec{\omega}_\psi$ have the following components in the rotating coordinate system $(x'y'z')$:

$$
\begin{aligned}
((\omega_\varphi)_{x'}, (\omega_\varphi)_{y'}, (\omega_\varphi)_{z'}) &= \hat{A}(\varphi, \theta, \psi) \cdot (0, 0, \dot{\varphi}) \\
((\omega_\theta)_{x'}, (\omega_\theta)_{y'}, (\omega_\theta)_{z'}) &= \hat{R}_z(\psi) \cdot (\dot{\theta}, 0, 0) \qquad (12.5) \\
((\omega_\psi)_{x'}, (\omega_\psi)_{y'}, (\omega_\psi)_{z'}) &= (0, 0, \dot{\psi}). \qquad (12.6)
\end{aligned}
$$

Using (12.2) and (12.5) we express the kinetic energy T as a function of the generalized coordinates $(\varphi(t), \theta(t), \psi(t))$ and the velocities $(\dot{\varphi}(t), \dot{\theta}(t), \dot{\psi}(t))$

$$T = \frac{1}{2} I_1 (\dot{\theta}^2 + \dot{\varphi}^2 \, sin^2\theta) + \frac{1}{2} I_3 (\dot{\psi} + \dot{\varphi} \, cos\,\theta)^2. \tag{12.7}$$

For the potential energy of the rotor we find

$$V = m\,g\,l \cdot cos\,\theta \tag{12.8}$$

where l is the distance between the center of mass C of the rotor and the fixed point O.

Our problem is well suited to be solved by the Lagrange formalism. Let $L = T - V$ be the Lagrangian and let $(q_1, ..., q_n)$ and $(\dot{q}_1, ..., \dot{q}_n)$ be the generalized coordinates and velocities of the system with n degrees of freedom. Then, the equations of motion are the Lagrange equations

$$\frac{d}{dt} \left(\frac{\partial L}{\partial \dot{q}_i} \right) - \frac{\partial L}{\partial q_i} = 0 \qquad i = 1, ..., n. \tag{12.9}$$

If L doesn't depend explicitly on some coordinate q_k (such a coordinate is called a cyclic coordinate) then the corresponding Lagrange equation is

$$\frac{d}{dt} \left(\frac{\partial L}{\partial \dot{q}_k} \right) = 0 \quad \Longrightarrow \quad \frac{\partial L}{\partial \dot{q}_k} = p_k = const, \tag{12.10}$$

which means, that the conjugate momentum p_k is a constant of motion.

Because of the relatively complicated nature of the system of the three Lagrange equations we will use MAPLE for its derivation and study.

12.2 Formulation and Basic Analysis of the Solution

In the MAPLE solution of our problem we use the vector formalism of the package linalg together with the following notation for the variables:

$$(\varphi, \theta, \psi) \longrightarrow \text{Euler} := [\text{phi,theta,psi}]$$
$$(\dot{\varphi}, \dot{\theta}, \dot{\psi}) \longrightarrow \text{dEuler} := [\text{dphi,dtheta,dpsi}].$$

```
> with(linalg):
> Euler   := vector([phi, theta, psi]):
> dEuler := vector([dphi, dtheta, dpsi]):
```

As the first step of our solution we will express the Lagrangian L in terms of Euler angles. To express the matrices R_x, R_z of rotation about the coordinate axes x and z, we define the matrix operators

$$\hat{R}_x = \begin{pmatrix} 1 & 0 & 0 \\ 0 & cos & sin \\ 0 & -sin & cos \end{pmatrix} \quad , \quad \hat{R}_z = \begin{pmatrix} cos & sin & 0 \\ -sin & cos & 0 \\ 0 & 0 & 1 \end{pmatrix} . \tag{12.11}$$

The transformation matrix A is then given by Equation (12.3),

$$A = R_z(\psi) \cdot R_x(\theta) \cdot R_z(\varphi). \tag{12.12}$$

```
> Rz := matrix([[cos, sin, 0], [-sin, cos, 0], [0, 0, 1]]):
> Rx := matrix([[1, 0, 0], [0, cos, sin], [0, -sin, cos]]):
> A  := evalm(Rz(psi(t)) &* Rx(theta(t)) &* Rz(phi(t))):
```

Using Equations (12.4) and (12.5), the angular velocity $\vec{\omega}$ in the coordinate system $(x'y'z')$ is given by

$$(\omega_{x'}, \omega_{y'}, \omega_{z'}) = A \cdot (0, 0, \dot{\varphi}) + R_z(\psi) \cdot (\dot{\theta}, 0, 0) + (0, 0, \dot{\psi}). \tag{12.13}$$

```
>              # vectors of angular velocities about Euler axis
> omega_phi := vector([0,0,dphi(t)]):
>              #rotation about axis z - dphi
> omega_theta := vector([dtheta(t),0,0]):
>              #rotation about the 1. xu  - dtheta
>              # vector of the resulting angular velocity
>              # Omega in (x',y',z')
> Omega := evalm(A &* omega_phi + Rz(psi(t)) &* omega_theta
>              + vector([0,0,dpsi(t)])));

  Omega := [

      sin(psi(t)) sin(theta(t)) dphi(t) + cos(psi(t)) dtheta(t),

      cos(psi(t)) sin(theta(t)) dphi(t) - sin(psi(t)) dtheta(t),

      cos(theta(t)) dphi(t) + dpsi(t) ]
```

Then, using Equations (12.2) and (12.8) we can write the Lagrangian as

$$L = T - V = \frac{1}{2} I_1 \left(\omega_{x'}^2 + \omega_{y'}^2 \right) + \frac{1}{2} I_3 \omega_{z'}^2 - m \, g \, l \cos \theta. \tag{12.14}$$

```
> T := 1/2*I1*(Omega[1]^2 + Omega[2]^2) + 1/2*I3*Omega[3]^2;
>              #kinetic energy

T := 1/2 I1 (
                                                                          2
    (sin(psi(t)) sin(theta(t)) dphi(t) + cos(psi(t)) dtheta(t))
                                                                          2
  + (cos(psi(t)) sin(theta(t)) dphi(t) - sin(psi(t)) dtheta(t))
                                                         2
  ) + 1/2 I3 (cos(theta(t)) dphi(t) + dpsi(t))
```

```
> V := M*g*L*cos(theta(t)):     #potential energy
> LF := T - V:       # Lagrangian
```

The second step is the development of the Lagrange equations for the rotor. For their derivation it will be useful to define the MAPLE function

```
LEq2( LagrFce, var, dva , indep)
```

(see Algorithm 12.1), where `LagrFce` is the Lagrangian, `var` and `dvar` are vectors of the generalized variables and velocities, and `indep` is the independent variable (time t). In the case of a cyclic coordinate, this function returns the Equation (see 12.10)

$$\frac{\partial L}{\partial \dot{q}_k} = IMq_k, \qquad (12.15)$$

where IMq_k (conjugate momentum to q_k) is a constant of motion. The function returns the equations as a set.

Because the standard function `diff(g,u)` differentiates only if u is a name, we will define a generalized differentiation function `sdiff(g,u)`, where u can be an expression.

To concatenate the string IM and the name of the cyclic variable q_k (by our definition a function $q_k(t)$), we should define a function `cname(name,fce)` which concatenates the name `name` and the name of function `fce`. The definitions of these functions are in Algorithm (12.1).

Since the coordinates φ and ψ are cyclic Function LEq2 returns two equations for the constants of motion p_φ (with name `IMphi`), and p_ψ (`IMpsi`) and the Lagrange equation corresponding to variable θ. For easier access to the right-hand sides of these equations we will transfer this set of equations into a table where the left-hand sides (`IMphi`, `IMpsi`, `0`) will be the indices for the corresponding right-hand sides.

```
>              # generation of the Lagrange equation, or integrals
>              # of motion (for phi and psi)
> LEqn := LEq2(LF,Euler(t),dEuler(t),t):
> LEqn := table([op(LEqn)]);
>              #transform the result from set to table

LEqn :=  table([
                                                         2
    IMphi = I1 dphi(t) - I1 dphi(t) cos(theta(t))

                2
      + I3 cos(theta(t))  dphi(t) + I3 cos(theta(t)) dpsi(t)
            / d        \
  0 = I1 |---- dtheta(t)|
            \ dt       /
                                     2
      - I1 cos(theta(t)) dphi(t)  sin(theta(t))

                                   2
      + I3 sin(theta(t)) dphi(t)  cos(theta(t))

      + I3 sin(theta(t)) dphi(t) dpsi(t) - M g L sin(theta(t))
    IMpsi = I3 cos(theta(t)) dphi(t) + I3 dpsi(t)           ])
```

The most important constant of motion is the energy $E = T + V$. Because $\omega_{z'}$ is proportional to the constant of motion p_ψ the quantity $E_c = E - 1/2 \, I_3 \, \omega_{z'}^2$ is also a constant of motion. We will use it instead of E for further study.

```
>              # Integrals of motion: IMphi,IMpsi and energy Ec
> Ec := simplify(T + V- 1/2*I3*Omega[3]^2);
```

ALGORITHM 12.1.
Functions for Generating a Lagrange Equations.

Function sdiff.

```
sdiff := proc(u,svar) local p;
    #differentiation of u with respect to expression svar
    subs(p = svar,diff(subs(svar = p,u),p))
end:
```


Function cname.

```
cname:= proc (nam,fce) local p;
    #add name of function  fce  to the name  nam
    if type(fce,function) then
        p:=op(0,fce); nam.p
     else
        nam.fce
     fi
end:
```


Function LEq2.

```
LEq2 := proc (LagrFce, var:vector,dvar:vector,indep:name)
        local  i,j,N,res;
    #the generation of the Lagrange equations or constants
    # of motion IM (for cyclic variables) for the Lagrange
    # function LagrFce and vector of generalized coordinates
    # var and velocities dvar and independent variable indep
    N:=vectdim(var);
    for i to N do
        res[i]:=simplify(sdiff(LagrFce,var[i]));
        if res[i]=0 then
            res[i] := cname('IM', var[i])
                    = sdiff(LagrFce, dvar[i])
        else
            res[i] := 0 = diff(sdiff(LagrFce, dvar[i]), indep)
                        - res[i]
        fi;
     od;
     {seq(simplify(res[i]), i=1..N)}
end:
```

$$\text{Ec} := -\ 1/2\ \text{I1 dphi(t)}^2\ \cos(\text{theta(t)})^2\ +\ 1/2\ \text{I1 dphi(t)}^2$$

$$+\ 1/2\ \text{I1 dtheta(t)}^2\ +\ \text{M g L }\cos(\text{theta(t)})$$

For simplification we will carry out the following steps:

1. Solving the equations for p_φ and p_ψ for the unknowns $\{\dot\varphi,\ \dot\psi\}$ and substituting them into E_c.

2. Introducing the parameters

$$b = \frac{p_\varphi}{I_1}, \quad a = \frac{p_\psi}{I_1}, \quad \beta = \frac{1}{2}\frac{I_1}{mgl}, \quad \alpha = \frac{2\,E_c}{I_1} \tag{12.16}$$

and solving the equation for E_c for the unknown $\dot\theta^2$.

3. Substitution of $u = cos\,\theta$ in the resulting equation.

As result we obtain the following differential equation for $u(t)$, which describes the so-called nutation of the rotor

$$\dot u^2 = y(u) := \beta\,u^3 - (\alpha + a^2)\,u^2 + (2\,a\,b - \beta)\,u + \alpha - b^2. \tag{12.17}$$

From the fact that $y(u) > 0$ it follows:

1. Because $\beta > 0$ we have $y(\pm\infty) = \pm\infty$ and $y(\pm 1) \leq 0$; so at least one root of $y(u)$ exists with $u > 1$.

2. Because $y(\pm 1) < 0$, two or zero roots have to be in the interval $[-1,1]$. For physically realistic conditions two roots should exist: $u_1 \leq u_2 \in [-1,1]$. Because $\dot\theta = 0$ for $\cos\theta_1 = u_1$ and $\cos\theta_2 = u_2$ we have $\theta(t) \in [\theta_2, \theta_1]$, so that the nutation angle of the top oscillates between θ_1 and θ_2.

```
>                # find dphi, dpsi with subs. IMpsi=a*I1, IMphi=b*I1
> dphipsi := solve({LEqn[IMphi] = b*I1, LEqn[IMpsi] =a *I1},
>           {dphi(t),dpsi(t)});

                     - b + cos(theta(t)) a
dphipsi := {dphi(t) = ---------------------,
                                       2
                      cos(theta(t))  - 1

                                                              2
dpsi(t) = - (- I3 cos(theta(t)) b + I3 cos(theta(t)) a

               2                      2
   - a I1 cos(theta(t))  + a I1) / ((cos(theta(t))  - 1) I3)}
```

```
> Econst := subs(dphipsi,Ec);
>                 # substitution for  dpsi and  dphi in  Ec
> dtheta2 := solve(subs(M = I1/(2*g*L)*beta,
>             Econst = I1*alfa/2),dtheta(t)^2):
>             # substitution
>             # cos(theta) = u -> -sin(theta)*dtheta = du
>             # then du2 = diff(u(t),t)^2
> du2 := simplify(subs(cos(theta(t)) = u,
>          dtheta2*(1-cos(theta(t))^2)));
```

$$du2 := beta\ u^3 - u^2\ a^2 - alfa\ u^2 + 2\ b\ u\ a - beta\ u + alfa - b^2$$

```
>                 # analysis of the solution due to the form of du2
> collect(du2,u);
```

$$beta\ u^3 + (-a^2 - alfa)\ u^2 + (2\ b\ a - beta)\ u - b^2 + alfa$$

```
> seq(factor(subs(u = i, du2)), i = {-1,1});
```

$$-(a + b)^2,\ -(a - b)^2$$

```
>             # so du2 (+-1) < 0 for b <> 0
```

The rotation of the top about the vertical z-axis (the so-called precession) is described by $\varphi(t)$ which is the solution of the differential equation (see the value of the variable dphipsi[1] above)

$$\dot{\varphi} = \frac{b - a\cos\theta}{sin^2\theta} \tag{12.18}$$

. Then we can classify the type of motion of the rotor by the sign of $\dot{\varphi}$ at the points θ_1, θ_2, where $\dot{\theta} = 0$. Let $\theta_1 \geq \theta_2 > 0$, so $u_2 = \cos\theta_2 > u_1$:

1. if $b/a > u_2$ or $b/a < u_1$, then $\dot{\varphi}$ doesn't change its sign (see Figure 12.2);

2. if $b - a\,u_2$ and $b - a\,u_1$ have opposite signs, then $\dot{\varphi}$ is periodically changing its sign (see Figure 12.3).

The differential Equation (12.17) may be solved in terms of elliptic functions. However, we will solve our problem numerically. The above form of the differential Equation (12.17) is not appropriate for the numerical solution, though.

12.3   The Numerical Solution

We will start from the Lagrange equations which were generated by MAPLE and saved under the variable LEq2 . The most important characteristics of the motion of the rotor are given by the time dependence of $\varphi(t)$ and $\theta(t)$ (the precession and nutation angles of the rotor), so we will restrict ourselves to find these variables.

Because we found the solution for $\dot\varphi$ and $\dot\psi$ (which are dependent on θ only and which are saved in the MAPLE variable dphipsi), we can use them to substitute $\dot\varphi$ and $\dot\psi$ in the last Lagrange equation connected with the variable θ. This equation together with the trivial equation diff(theta(t),t) = dtheta(t), and with the equation for $\dot\varphi$ (see 12.18) from dphipsi, form a system of three differential equations of first order for the variables phi(t), theta(t) and dtheta(t). We will now solve this system numerically.

```
>              # we substitute for dpsi and dphi
>              # in LEqn[0] (DE for theta)
> eqtheta := simplify(subs(dphipsi, LEqn[0])):
> eqtheta := simplify(eqtheta*I1*(cos(theta(t))^2 - 1)^2):
>              # simplify constant parameters in DE
> eqtheta := simplify(subs(M = I1/(2*g*L)*beta, eqtheta/I1^2));
```

$$eqtheta := \left(\frac{d}{dt} dtheta(t)\right) cos(theta(t))^4$$

$$- 2 \left(\frac{d}{dt} dtheta(t)\right) cos(theta(t))^2 + \left(\frac{d}{dt} dtheta(t)\right)$$

$$- cos(theta(t)) \, sin(theta(t)) \, b^2$$

$$+ cos(theta(t))^2 sin(theta(t)) \, b \, a + sin(theta(t)) \, b \, a$$

$$- sin(theta(t)) \, cos(theta(t)) \, a^2$$

$$- 1/2 \; beta \; sin(theta(t)) \; cos(theta(t))^4$$

$$+ beta \; sin(theta(t)) \; cos(theta(t))^2 - 1/2 \; beta \; sin(theta(t))$$

```
>              # DE for phi
> eqphi := diff(phi(t),t) = subs(dphipsi, dphi(t));
```

$$eqphi := \frac{d}{dt} phi(t) = \frac{- b + cos(theta(t)) \, a}{cos(theta(t))^2 - 1}$$

The system to be solved depends on the three parameters a, b and β, and on the three initial values $\varphi(0)$, $\theta(0)$ and $\dot\theta(0)$, respectively. Note that $\beta > 0$ while a and b can be chosen positive. Let us choose the initial conditions as

$$\varphi(0) = 0, \quad \theta(0) = \theta_0, \quad \dot\theta(0) = 0, \quad \text{where} \quad \theta_0 = 0.1, \tag{12.19}$$

and the parameters as

$$a = 1, \quad b = \lambda a \cos(\theta_0), \quad \beta = 1, \quad \text{where} \quad \lambda = 1.1. \tag{12.20}$$

F. Klvaňa

FIGURE 12.2. *Motion of the Top for* $\lambda = 1.1$.

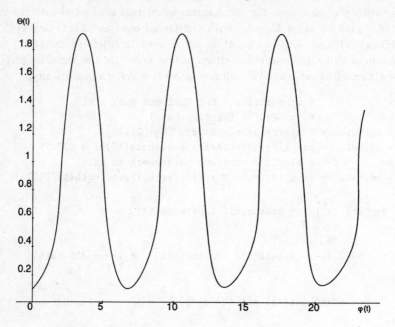

FIGURE 12.3. *Motion of the Top for* $\lambda = 0.96$.

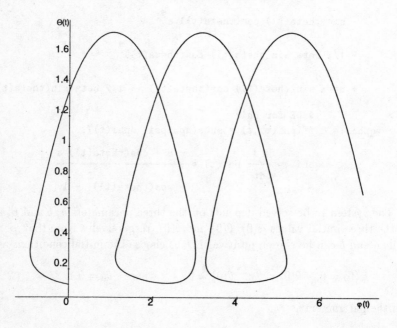

As follows from the discussion of Equation (12.18) two types of precession exist. If the constant $\lambda > 1$, as above, we obtain a solution with constant sign of $\dot{\varphi}$ giving the monotonic precession. For $\lambda < 1$ we obtain a solution with $\dot{\varphi}$ changing its sign corresponding to oscillatory precession.

The solution is illustrated using a parametric plot of $\varphi(t)$ over $\theta(t)$. Results are shown in Figure 12.2 ($\lambda = 1.1$) and Figure 12.3 ($\lambda = 0.96$), respectively.

```
>               #d definition of initial conditions
> theta0 := 0.1: #theta(0)
> initc := theta(0) = theta0, dtheta(0) = 0, phi(0) = 0:
>               # definition of parameters
> a := 1: beta := 1:
> lambda := 1.1:
> b := a*cos(theta0)*lambda:
>               # dependent variables of the system DE
> var := {phi(t),theta(t),dtheta(t)}:
>               # solving DE
> res := dsolve({eqtheta = 0, diff(theta(t), t) = dtheta(t),
>         eqphi, initc}, var, numeric);

  res := proc(t) 'dsolve/numeric/result2'(t,1928068,[1,1,1]) end

>               # resulting plot
> plot([seq([subs(res(i*0.5), phi(t)),
>               subs(res(i*0.5), theta(t))], i = 0..30)]);
```

References

[1] HERBERT GOLDSTEIN, *Classical Mechanics*, Addison-Wesley, 1980.

[2] M. R. SPIEGEL, *Theoretical Mechanics*, McGraw-Hill, 1980.

Chapter 13. The Calibration Problem

J. Buchar and J. Hřebíček

13.1 Introduction

When measuring gas pressure changes in a container, for example an engine cylinder or a gun, by means of a piezoelectric pressure transducer, highly relatively accurate values must be made available in order to obtain the specified absolute accuracy. For this special measuring and calibrating techniques are necessary, which allow the quantitative determination of the dynamic measuring properties of the transducer. The output from the transducer is in electric voltage. Therefore we must perform the calibration of the transducer so as to finally get the pressure. This is not difficult when we are working with a static pressure. The design of the equipment which enables well defined dynamic pressure measurement is much more complicated. This problem was solved by different authors by using a hydraulic pressure chamber, see [3]. For such a system we developed in our recent research project an experimental method for the dynamic pressure calibration. The essential problem connected with this method consists in the development of a physical model which allows a mathematical description of the hydraulic pressure pulses. This model enables us to calibrate a dynamic pulse pressure transducer in absolute pressure units. The schema of the experimental method is given in Figure 13.1. In the next chapter we will define a physical model using the results contained in [1].

13.2 The Physical Model Description

The pressure transducer is calibrated using hydrostatic pressure in a suitable chamber. For some applications; e.g. for the measurement of pressures in automobile engines or gun chambers, etc.; it is necessary to perform a dynamic calibration. For this purpose we suggest a simple experimental arrangement schematically drawn in Figure 13.1. A cylindrical chamber of is filled with a liquid of a given compressibility. The initial volume of this liquid is V_0. The piston has the same cross section S as the chamber and is loaded by the impact of the body of total mass M accelerated to the velocity $v_0 > 0$. The movement $x(t)$ of the piston leads to the volume change $\Delta V = Sx(t)$. This volume change corresponds to a pressure $p(t)$, which (for almost all compressible liquids) can

FIGURE 13.1. *Cross Section of Chamber.*

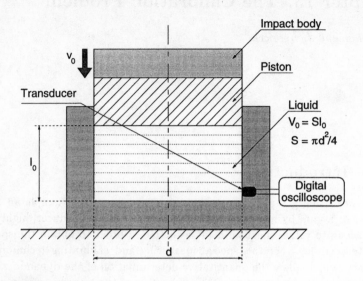

be obtained from the equation

$$p(t) = \alpha \frac{\Delta V}{V_0} + \beta \left(\frac{\Delta V}{V_0}\right)^2, \tag{13.1}$$

where $\alpha > 0$ and $\beta > 0$ are parameters of the given liquid.

Let us suppose that the impact velocity v_0 is limited to some reasonable value. We may then neglect the wave motion processes. The movement of the piston can be described by the differential equation

$$M\ddot{x} = -p(t)S, \tag{13.2}$$

with initial conditions

$$\begin{aligned} x(0) &= 0, \\ v = \dot{x}(0) &= v_0 \end{aligned} . \tag{13.3}$$

Substituting Equation (13.1) for the pressure $p(t)$ and $\Delta V = Sx(t)$ in Equation (13.2) results in:

```
> M*diff(x(t), t, t) = - (alpha*dV/V0 + beta*(dV/V0)^2)*S;
```

$$M \left(\frac{d^2}{dt^2} x(t)\right) = - \left(\frac{alpha\ dV}{V0} + \frac{beta\ dV^2}{V0^2}\right) S$$

```
> subs(dV = S*x(t), ")/S;
```

```
    /   2     \
    |  d       |
 M  |-----  x(t)|
    |   2      |                                          2      2
    \ dt     /        alpha S x(t)    beta S  x(t)
 --------------  = - ------------- - --------------
       S                 VO                 2
                                           VO
```

This is now simplified by using the formulas $S = \pi d^2/4$, $V_0 = \pi d^2 l_0/4$ and the constants

$$a = \sqrt{\frac{\alpha\pi}{4}\frac{d^2}{Ml_0}} \quad \text{and} \quad b = \frac{\beta\pi}{4}\frac{d^2}{Ml_0^2}.$$

```
> subs(S = Pi*d^2/4, VO = Pi*d^2*10/4, "):
> simplify(", {a^2*4*M*10 = alpha*Pi*d^2,
>                b*4*M*10^2 = beta*Pi*d^2}, [alpha, beta]);
```

```
      /   2     \
      |  d       |
   M  |-----  x(t)|
      |   2      |                          2
      \ dt     /        x(t) M (a  + b x(t))
 4  --------------- = - 4 ----------------------
          2                          2
        Pi d                       Pi d
```

```
> eq := "*Pi*d^2/4/M;
```

```
              2
             d                    2
   eq := ----- x(t) = - x(t) (a  + b x(t))
              2
             dt
```

```
> alpha*dV/VO + beta*(dV/VO)^2:
> subs(dV = S*x(t), S = Pi*d^2/4, VO = Pi*d^2*10/4, ");
```

```
                                     2
   alpha x(t)    beta x(t)
   ---------- + ----------
       10              2
                     10
```

We can now rewrite the initial value problem (13.2)-(13.3) as

$$\ddot{x}(t) + a^2 x(t) + bx(t)^2 = 0, \qquad (13.4)$$
$$x(0) = 0, \qquad (13.5)$$
$$\dot{x}(0) = v_0. \qquad (13.6)$$

Using the solution $x(t)$ of the above initial value problem we can evaluate the volume change $\Delta V = Sx(t)$. We obtain from (13.1) the value of the pressure $p = p(t)$ at time t

$$p(t) = \frac{x(t)}{l_0}\left(\alpha + \beta\frac{x(t)}{l_0}\right). \qquad (13.7)$$

When measuring the hydraulic pressure pulse we record the electrical voltage $U = U(t)$ of the transducer with a digital oscilloscope. We obtain an experimental record for the transducer for some time interval $T = [0, t_{max})$ – see Figure 13.1. For the same interval we have to find the solution $x(t)$ of the above initial value problem. Then we can compare the experimentally measured hydraulic pressure with the calculated pressure $p(t)$ from (13.7). For practical purposes it is enough to compare the measured and calculated pressures in the subinterval $T_m \subset T$, where the pressure increases up to its maximum.

The calibration of the transducer is very simple when $p(t) = kU(t)$, where k is a constant. If k is not constant we must use the method of Fourier Transform. The detailed analysis of this method is beyond the scope of this chapter.

13.3 Approximation by Splitting the Solution

Let us suppose that the solution $x(t)$ of the initial value problem (13.4 – 13.6) has the form

$$x(t) = x_a(t) + x_b(t)$$

where $x_a(t)$ is the solution of the initial value problem of the free undamped motion [4]

$$
\begin{aligned}
\ddot{x}_a(t) + a^2 x_a(t) &= 0, \\
x_a(0) &= 0, \\
\dot{x}_a(0) &= v_0.
\end{aligned}
$$

The above initial value problem has the analytic solution for $a \neq 0$ of

$$x_a(t) = \frac{v_0 \sin(at)}{a}. \tag{13.8}$$

Note that MAPLE could be used to derive this solution:

```
> deq := {diff(xa(t), t, t) + a^2*xa(t) = 0,
         xa(0) = 0, D(xa)(0) = v0}:
> dsolve(deq, xa(t));
```

$$
\mathtt{xa(t)} = \frac{\mathtt{v0\ sin(a\ t)}}{\mathtt{a}}
$$

The solution $x(t)$ of the initial value problem (13.4 – 13.6) has the form

$$x(t) = \frac{v_0 \sin(at)}{a} + x_b(t) \tag{13.9}$$

where it is assumed that $x_b(t)$ is a small perturbation of $x_a(t)$. Inserting $x(t)$ in (13.4) we obtain for $x_b(t)$ the initial value problem

$$
\begin{aligned}
\ddot{x}_b(t) + a^2 x_b(t) + b x_b(t)^2 + \frac{2 b v_0 \sin(at)}{a} x_b(t) + b \left(\frac{v_0 \sin(at)}{a} \right)^2 &= 0, \\
x_b(0) &= 0, \\
\dot{x}(0) &= 0.
\end{aligned}
$$

We will solve the differential equation for $x_b(t)$ in MAPLE, using its powerful tool for the solution of differential equations – the truncated power series. In our case the truncated power series is expanded at $t = 0$. It is applied to polynomials of degrees less or equal than the order N of the truncated power series. The MAPLE statements follow (we will use $\texttt{Order} = 12$)

```
>                   # initial value problem B
> eqb := diff(xb(t), t, t) + a^2*xb(t) + b*xb(t)^2
>         + 2*b*v0*sin(a*t)*xb(t)/a + b*(v0*sin(a*t)/a)^2 = 0;
```

$$
eqb := \left(\frac{d^2}{dt^2}\, xb(t)\right) + a^2\, xb(t) + b\, xb(t)^2
$$

$$
+ 2\, \frac{b\, v0\, \sin(a\, t)\, xb(t)}{a} + \frac{b^2\, v0^2\, \sin(a\, t)^2}{a^2} = 0
$$

```
> incondb := xb(0) = 0,D(xb)(0) = 0:
>             # determination of Order truncated power series
> Order := 12:
> solb := dsolve({eqb, incondb}, xb(t), series);
```

$$
solb := xb(t) = -\,1/12\, b\, v0^2\, t^4 + 1/72\, b^2\, a^2\, v0^2\, t^6
$$

$$
+ 1/252\, b^2\, v0^3\, t^7 - 1/960\, b\, a^4\, v0^2\, t^8 - 5/6048\, b^2\, v0^3\, a^2\, t^9
$$

$$
+ \left(\frac{17}{362880}\, b\, a^6\, v0^2 - 1/6048\, b^3\, v0^4\right) t^{10}
$$

$$
+ 1/12320\, b^2\, v0^3\, a^4\, t^{11} + O(t^{12})
$$

```
> polb := convert(rhs(solb), polynom):
```

The polynomial approximation of the truncated power series $s_N(t)$ given by MAPLE is equivalent to

$$
p_N(t) = -\frac{b v_0^2\, t^4}{12} \left(1 - \frac{a^2 t^2}{6} - \frac{v_0\, b t^3}{21} + \frac{a^4 t^4}{80} + \right.
$$
$$
\left. \frac{5 v_0\, a^2 b t^5}{504} + \frac{v_0^2\, t^6 b^2}{504} - \frac{17 t^6 a^6}{30240} - \frac{3 b a^4 v_0\, t^7}{3080} \cdots \right) \tag{13.10}
$$

The approximation of the solution $\tilde{x}_N(t) = x_a(t) + p_N(t)$ will enable us to determine the approximation $\tilde{p}_N(t)$ of the pressure $p(t)$ using $\tilde{x}_N(t)$ in Equation (13.7).

Prior to choosing the degree of the polynomial for obtaining a sufficiently accurate approximation of $x(t)$ we have to estimate the region of convergence of the truncated power series. For this we will use some simple heuristic arguments.

From the definition of the solution $x_a(t)$ and the pressure $p(t)$ it follows that the pressure pulse is positive for

$$t < t_a = \frac{\pi}{a}. \tag{13.11}$$

This is the first condition to determine the interval T where we will find the solution $x(t)$ and the pressure $p(t)$.

Let us suppose that each term in the parentheses in (13.10) has an absolute value less than 1. We can see that fourth and further terms in the parentheses in (13.10) are the combinations of the second and third term multiplied by a constant, which has an absolute value less than 1. Consequently only the second and the third term in the parentheses in (13.10) play a role. This assumption leads to the second condition

$$t < t_{coef} = \min\left(\left|\frac{a}{\sqrt{6}}\right|^{-1}, \left|\frac{v_0 b}{21}\right|^{-1/3}\right). \tag{13.12}$$

It is clear that for these values of t, the absolute value of the term in the parenthesis in (13.10) will be less than 1. If condition (13.12) is valid condition (13.11) is also true. From (13.8) follows that $|x_a(t)| \le v_0/a$, and the calibration makes sense for the pressure $p(t) > 0$. To obtain the positive approximation $\tilde{x}_N(t)$ the solution $x(t)$ from (13.8),(13.9) and (13.12), we use the third condition:

$$t < t_b = \left(\frac{abv_0}{12}\right)^{-1/4}. \tag{13.13}$$

The conditions (13.12) and (13.13) determine the maximum interval $[0,\ t_m)$, where $t_m = \min(t_{coef}, t_b)$. Where the truncated power series will convergence to the solution $x_b(t)$ and the approximation of the solution $\tilde{x}_N(t)$ will converge to the solution $x(t)$ of our problem.

How do we choose the degree of the truncated power series to obtain the given accuracy? We will apply the following criterion

$$|a_N| + |a_{N-1}| \le \varepsilon \left|\sum_{i=0}^{N} a_i\right|, \tag{13.14}$$

where a_i are the terms of the power series and ε denotes the maximum of the tolerable local relative approximation error [2]. This criterion uses the sum of the absolute values of the two last terms of the expression of the power series of order N as a measure of the truncation error, and relates it to the absolute value of the truncated power series. In our case, from the criterion (13.14) it follows that $\varepsilon = O(10^{-3})$ for the order of the power series equal to 12.

Example

To verify this approach we will solve the above initial value problem with the experimental values from the collection of J. Buchar $v_0 = 5\,[ms^{-1}]$, $\alpha =$

$3.8E9\,[Nm^{-2}]$, $\beta = 3E10\,[Nm^{-2}]$, $l_0 = 2E{-}2\,[m]$, $d = 1.5E{-}2\,[m]$, $M = 5\,[kg]$.
The following MAPLE program will plot graphs with the numerical solution and
solutions using polynomial approximation of truncated power series of different
degrees of the above initial value problem.

```
>                 # experimental constants
> alpha := 3.8*10^9:   beta := 30*10^9:  d   := 0.015:
> l0    := 0.02:       M    := 5:        v0 := 5:
>                 # determination of parameter a, b
>  a := sqrt(alpha*Pi*d^2/(4*M*l0)):  b := beta*Pi*d^2/(4*M*l0^2):
>                 # initial value problem B
>  eqb     := diff(xb(t), t, t) + a^2*xb(t) + b*xb(t)^2
>               + 2*b*v0*sin(a*t)*xb(t)/a + b*(v0*sin(a*t)/a)^2=0:
> incondb := xb(0) = 0, D(xb)(0) = 0:
>                 # numerical solution
> numsol := dsolve({eqb, incondb}, xb(t), numeric):
> sol     := x -> subs(numsol(x), xb(t) + v0*sin(a*t)/a):
> solp    := t-> (sol(t)/l0)*(alpha + beta*(sol(t)/l0))/10^9:
>                 # estimation of radius of convergence
> tm      := min(evalf(sqrt(6)/a),evalf(21/(v0*b))^(1/3),
>               evalf(21/(a*b*v0))^(1/4)):
>                 # saving graphs of numerical solution
> X[num] := plot(sol, 0..tm):
> P[num] := plot(solp, 0..tm):
>                 # analytic solution of first equation
> xa := v0*sin(a*t)/a:
>                 # Order of truncated power series approximation
>                 # and preparation of graphs
> ORD1 := [seq(i, i = 6..10), 12]:
> ORD2 := [seq(i, i = 6..10)]:
>                 # polynomial approximation of 5th - 9th
>                 # and 11th degree of  solution
> for ord in ORD1 do:
>     Order := ord:
>     sersol := dsolve({eqb, incondb}, xb(t), series):
>     pol := convert(rhs(sersol), polynom):
>     sol := pol + xa:
>     solp := (sol/l0)*(alpha + beta*sol/l0)/10^9:
>               # saving graphs
>     X[ord] := plot(sol, t = 0..tm):
>     P[ord] := plot(solp, t = 0..tm):
> od:
```

FIGURE 13.2.
*Numeric and Acceptable Polynomial Approximation of
Solution.*

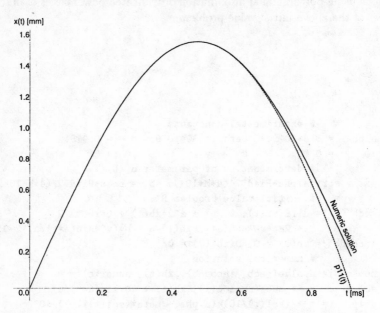

FIGURE 13.3.
*Numeric and Acceptable Polynomial Approximation of
Pressure.*

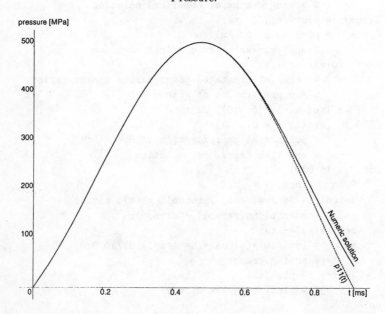

FIGURE 13.4.
Comparison of Numeric and Polynomial Approximations of Solutions.

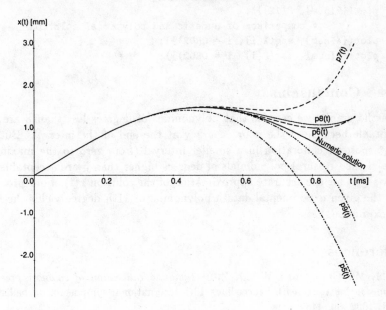

FIGURE 13.5.
Comparison of Numeric and Polynomial Approximations of Pressure.

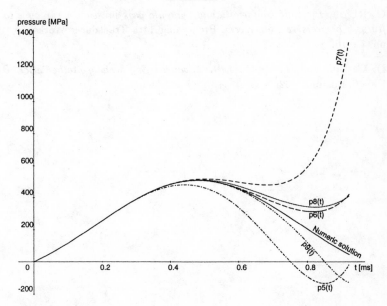

```
>               # display graphs of solutions and pressures
>               # numeric and acceptable power series solution
> plot({X[num], X[12]});
> plot({P[num], P[12]});
>               # comparison of numeric and polynomial solution
> plot({X[num], seq(X[i], i = ORD2)});
> plot({P[num], seq(P[i], i = ORD2)});
```

13.4   Conclusions

From the graphs we can see that polynomials of degrees less than 8 are not acceptable because of the poor accuracy at the end of the interval. But for the purpose of calibration in a smaller interval (from zero to the maximum value of the pressure) polynomials of degrees higher than 5 are acceptable. It follows that for the accurate approximation of the solution $x(t)$ of our problem with the given experimental data a polynomial of 11th degree yields the best approximation.

References

[1] M. W. CHANG and W. M. ZHU, *Dynamic calibration of chamber pressure measuring equipment*, Proceedings 13th international symposium on ballistics, 1, 1992, pp. 443 – 450.

[2] H. J. HALIN, *The applicability of Taylor series methods in simulation*, Proceedings of 1983 Summer Computer Simulation Conference, 2, 1983, pp. 1032 – 1076.

[3] G. RESCH, *Dynamic conformity and dynamic peak pressure accuracy – to new features of pressure transducers*, Proceeding 14th Transducer Workshop, 1987, pp. 1 – 10.

[4] D. G. ZILL and M. R. CULLEN, *Advanced Engineering Mathematics*, PWS-KENT, Boston, 1992.

Chapter 14. Heat Flow Problems

S. Bartoň and J. Hřebíček

14.1 Introduction

The heat flow problems are a very important part of thermodynamics. The solution of these problems influences many other technical problems. The most important equation describing heat flow rules, is the heat equation (Fourier equation)

$$a^2\left(\frac{\partial^2 T}{\partial x^2} + \frac{\partial^2 T}{\partial y^2} + \frac{\partial^2 T}{\partial z^2}\right) = \frac{\partial T}{\partial t}. \tag{14.1}$$

The difficulty of the solution of the Equation (14.1) depends on the difficulty of the boundary and initial conditions. We can differentiate two main groups of heat flow problems.

1. The steady state problems – in this case temperature T is not a function of the time t and Equation (14.1) becomes the Laplace equation. We shall solve this problem in the first part of this chapter.

2. Time dependent problems – these problems are usually solved numerically. We will show, that for the very simple one dimensional problem $T = T(x,t)$ with a constant boundary condition, $T(0,t) = $ const, and our initial condition of $T(x,0) = $ const, an analytical solution can be found.

14.2 Heat Flow through a Spherical Wall

Consider a hollow sphere of inner and outer radii r_1 and r_2 respectively. Let T_1 and T_2 be the constant temperatures over the inner and outer spherical surfaces respectively, and let k be the finite thermal conductivity of the wall material. We will find a steady state solution to the heat flow rate and temperature distribution as a function of the radius r.

Let x,y,z be the coordinates of the Euclidean space. If the center of the spherical body is at the origin $O(0,0,0)$, then the temperature $T = T(x, y, z)$ is a function of the position within the body. From the symmetry and the boundary conditions, it is clear that $T(x, y, z) = $ const for all the points (x, y, z) of the sphere $x^2 + y^2 + z^2 = r^2$, $r_1 \le r \le r_2$. Therefore, $T = T(r)$ is a function of r only, and our problem is one–dimensional. We shall solve it in MAPLE by two methods which differ by the physical model used.

FIGURE 14.1. *Cross Section of the Spherical Wall.*

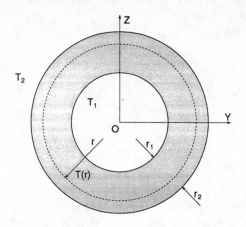

14.2.1   A Steady State Heat Flow Model

Let $\dot{q}$ be the heat flow density. According to the Fourier law

$$\dot{q} = -k\,\mathrm{grad}\,T \quad [Wm^{-2}; Wm^{-1}K^{-1}, K]. \tag{14.2}$$

Consider now the spherical surface with radius r, $r_1 \leq r \leq r_2$, with the center at the origin and area $A = 4\pi r^2$. Then the heat $\dot{Q}$ flowing through it is given by

$$\dot{Q} = \dot{q}A \quad [W]. \tag{14.3}$$

In steady state this quantity is independent of the radius r, because there are no heat sources inside the body. In the one-dimensional problem $\mathrm{grad}\,T$ can be replaced by dT/dr. Then from (14.2) and (14.3) we obtain

$$\dot{Q} = -k4\pi r^2 \frac{dT}{dr}. \tag{14.4}$$

Denoting

$$a = \frac{\dot{Q}}{4k\,\pi} \tag{14.5}$$

we get

$$\frac{dT}{dr} = -a\frac{1}{r^2}, \tag{14.6}$$

where the parameter a is unknown. The general solution of this equation is a function of the parameter a and that can be derived by hand.

$$T = T(r; a). \tag{14.7}$$

We now show how simple it is to solve Equation (14.6) analytically:

```
> sol := dsolve(diff(T(r), r) = -a/(r^2), T(r));
```

$$\text{sol} := T(r) = \frac{a + \_C1\ r}{r}$$

```
> T := unapply(rhs(sol), r);
```

$$T := r \to \frac{a + \_C1\ r}{r}$$

We shall use the initial conditions to determine a and _C1.

$$T(r_1) = T_1, \qquad T(r_2) = T_2 \tag{14.8}$$

```
> sol := solve({T(r1) = T1, T(r2) = T2}, {a, _C1});
```

$$\text{sol} := \{\_C1 = \frac{T1\ r1 - T2\ r2}{r1 - r2}, \ a = -\frac{r1\ r2\ (-\ T2 + T1)}{r1 - r2}\}$$

```
> assign(sol);
> normal(T(r));
```

$$\frac{r2\ r1\ T2 - r2\ r1\ T1 + r\ T1\ r1 - r\ T2\ r2}{(r1 - r2)\ r}$$

Now is the temperature function completely known. For the known temperatures on the outside and inside surfaces and their temperatures is the temperature inside the spherical wall function of r only.

Finally, we can compute the desired heat flow $\dot{Q}$ based on the definition of the parameter a using (14.5)

```
> Q := 4*k*Pi*a;
```

$$Q := -\ 4\ \frac{k\ Pi\ r1\ r2\ (-\ T2 + T1)}{r1 - r2}$$

14.2.2 Fourier Model for Steady State

In two dimensional steady state problems we have

$$\frac{\partial^2 T}{\partial x^2} + \frac{\partial^2 T}{\partial y^2} = 0, \tag{14.9}$$

or

$$\frac{\partial^2 T}{\partial r^2} + \frac{2}{r}\frac{\partial T}{\partial r} + \frac{\cos\varphi}{r^2 \sin\varphi}\frac{\partial T}{\partial \varphi} + \frac{1}{r^2}\frac{\partial^2 T}{\partial \varphi^2} = 0. \tag{14.10}$$

in polar coordinates r, φ.

Since in our case $T = T(r)$ is only a function of r, Equation (14.10) simplifies to

$$\frac{\partial^2 T}{\partial r^2} + \frac{2}{r}\frac{\partial T}{\partial r} = 0 \qquad (14.11)$$

with initial conditions (14.8). Solving (14.11) we obtain the temperature $T(r)$ as a function of the radius r:

```
> restart;
> inicon := T(r1) = T1, T(r2) = T2:
> deq := diff(T(r), r, r) + diff(T(r) ,r)*2/r = 0;
```

```
                / 2      \      d
                |  d      |    ---- T(r)
                | ----- T(r)|     dr
        deq := |-----      | + 2 --------- = 0
                |  2      |        r
                \ dr     /
```

```
> sol := simplify(dsolve({deq,inicon}, T(r)));
```

```
               r T2 r2 - r T1 r1 + r1 r2 T1 - r1 r2 T2
    sol := T(r) = - ---------------------------------------
                              (r1 - r2) r
```

By defining the distribution of the temperature $T = T(r)$ inside the spherical body for the given parameters r_1, T_1, r_2, T_2, we obtain the analytical solution of our problem by the Fourier model approach:

```
> T := unapply(rhs(sol), r);
```

```
             r T2 r2 - r T1 r1 + r1 r2 T1 - r1 r2 T2
    T := r -> - ---------------------------------------
                         (r1 - r2) r
```

which is the same as in the first approach. To get the desired heal flow $\dot{Q}$ we use (14.4)

```
> Q := simplify(-4*Pi*r^2*k*diff(T(r, r1, T1, r2, T2),r));
```

```
              Pi k r2 r1 (T1 - T2)
    Q := - 4 --------------------
                  r1 - r2
```

and again obtain the same result as with the first method.

14.2.3 MAPLE Plots

Let us plot now the distribution of the temperature $T = T(r; r_1, T_1, r_2, T_2)$, and print the heat flow $\dot{Q}$ for given values of the finite thermal conductivity of the wall material k, for inner and outer radii r_1 and r_2, and temperature T_1 and three different temperatures T_2. We will use:
$k = 12\ [Wm^{-1}K^{-1}]$, $T_1 = 400\ [K]$, $T_2 = 300, 200, 100\ [K]$, $r_1 = 0.1\ [m]$, $r_2 = 0.4\ [m]$.

We will compute the general analytical solution using the statements from the Section 14.2.1. We will then assign the values of k, T_1, r_1, r_2 and in a loop we will compute the three plots. Finally, we will plot all three graphs into one picture. Here is the complete MAPLE code for this job:

```
> r1 := 0.1: T1 := 400: r2 := 0.4: k := 12:
> TTs := [100, 200, 300]:
> for T2 in TTs do;
>     Tpl[T2] := T(r);
>     Qpl[T2] := evalf(Q);
> od:
> plot({seq(Tpl[T2], T2 = TTs)}, r = r1..r2);
```

FIGURE 14.2. *Temperature Distribution.*

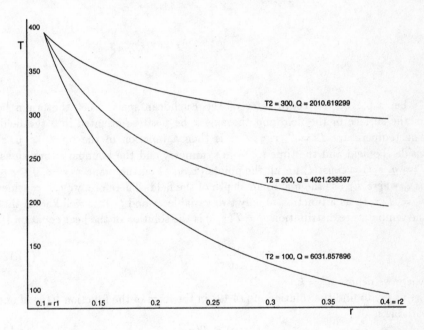

14.3 Non Stationary Heat Flow through an Agriculture Field

Consider a agriculture field that is being heated by the sun. Let us assume that at the beginning the temperature distribution in the field is given by T_f and the temperature T_s on the surface of the field is always constant (cf. Figure 14.3). Let $k > 0$ be the finite thermal conductivity of the field. The non stationary temperature distribution as function of the field depth x and the time t is to be determined.

FIGURE 14.3.
Boundary and Initial Condition for the Agricultural Field.

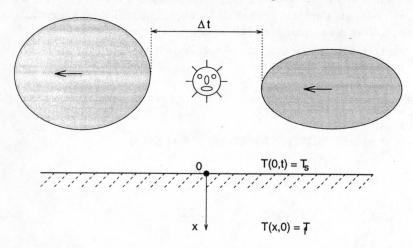

Let x, y, z be the coordinates of the Euclidean space. Let the origin be on the surface of the field and the axis x be positive oriented into the field. The temperature $T = T(x, y, z, t)$ is then a function of the point (x, y, z) inside the field and the time t. From symmetry and the boundary conditions, $T(x, y, z, t) = \text{const}(t)$ for all the points (x, y, z) on the plane $x = c$, $0 \leq c \leq d_{max}$ where d_{max} is the maximum depth of the field. Therefore, we can consider $T = T(x, t)$, as a function of only two variables x and t. It is well known that the temperature distribution $T = T(x, t)$ is the solution of the heat equation [1]

$$a^2 \frac{\partial^2 T}{\partial x^2} = \frac{\partial T}{\partial t} \tag{14.12}$$

where we denote $a^2 = k$.

Let us try to find the solution of (14.12) in the form of the function $V(u)$ of one variable u

$$V(u) = T(x, t) \tag{14.13}$$

where

$$u = u(x, t) = \frac{x}{2a\sqrt{t}}. \tag{14.14}$$

The Equation (14.14) substitutes two variables x and t by only one variable u. We can see, that this substitution converts the partial differential Equation (14.12) into a second order differential equation of one variable. This idea can be realized in MAPLE by:

```
>   restart;
>   Subs := u = x/(2*a*sqrt(t)):
>   T(x,t):=V(rhs(Subs));
```

$$T(x, t) := V(1/2 \ \frac{x}{a \ t^{1/2}})$$

```
> eq := a^2*diff(T(x,t), x, x) = diff(T(x, t), t);
```

$$eq := 1/4 \ \frac{D^{(2)}(V)(1/2 \ \frac{x}{a \ t^{1/2}})}{t} = - \ 1/4 \ \frac{D(V)(1/2 \ \frac{x}{a \ t^{1/2}}) \ x}{a \ t^{3/2}}$$

```
>  eq := subs(x = solve(Subs, x), eq)*t*4;
```

$$eq := D^{(2)}(V)(u) = - \ 2 \ D(V)(u) \ u$$

Thus we obtain a ordinary differential equation of the second order

$$\frac{d^2V(u)}{du^2} = -2u\frac{dV(u)}{du}, \tag{14.15}$$

which can be solved by hand using $\frac{dV(u)}{du} = W$.

$$\frac{d^2V(u)}{du^2} = -2u\frac{dV(u)}{du} \implies \frac{dW}{du} = -2uW$$

$$\implies \frac{dW}{W} = -2u \ du \implies \text{can be integrated}$$

$$\implies \ln|W| = -u^2 + C_1' \implies \frac{dV(u)}{du} = C_1 e^{-u^2}$$

$$\implies dV(u) = C_1 e^{-u^2} du \implies V(u) = C_1 \int_0^u e^{-p^2} dp + C_2.$$

The solution of (14.15) with MAPLE is

```
> Sol := dsolve(eq, V(u));
```

$$Sol := V(u) = \_C1 + \_C2 \ erf(u)$$

As we see, MAPLE is able to solve this equation. Both solutions are the same, because erf(u) (*The Gauss or error function*) is defined as

$$erf(u) = \frac{2}{\sqrt{\pi}} \int_0^u e^{-p^2} dp. \tag{14.16}$$

Now the variables x and t can be substituted back in the solution:

```
> T := unapply(rhs(subs(u=rhs(Subs),Sol)), x, t);
```

$$T := (x,t) \rightarrow \_C1 + \_C2 \ erf(1/2 \ \frac{x}{a \ t^{1/2}})$$

FIGURE 14.4.
Field Temperature for Depths 0.0, 0.01, 0.05, 0.1, 0.2, and 0.3[m].

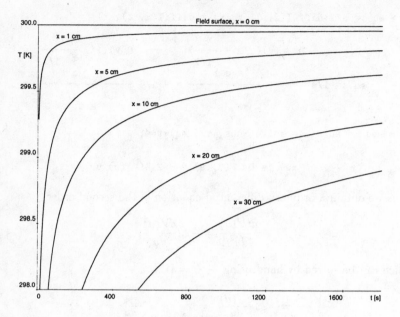

FIGURE 14.5.
Field Temperature as the Function of the Depth and Time.

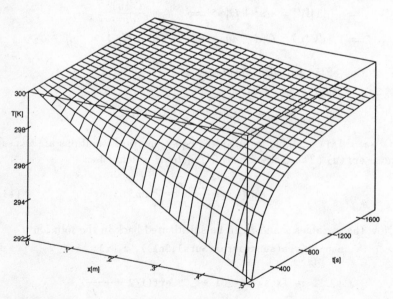

To determine the constants _C1 and _C2 the initial and boundary conditions (cf. Figure 14.3) are used. Let us prescribe the boundary condition $T(0,t) = \lim_{x \to 0_+} T(x,t) = T_s$ and the initial condition $T(x,0) = \lim_{t \to 0_+} T(x,t) = T_f$ i.e. at the temperature $t = O$ of the whole field is constant and equal to T_f. For MAPLE we assume $a \geq 0$ and $x \geq 0$.

```
> assume(a >= 0): assume(x >= 0):
> BounCon := Ts = limit(T(x,t), x = 0, right);
```

$$\text{BounCon} := \text{Ts} = \_C1$$

```
> IniCon := Tf = limit(T(x, t), t = 0, right);
```

$$\text{IniCon} := \text{Tf} = \_C2 + \_C1$$

```
> Sol := solve({IniCon, BounCon}, {_C1, _C2});
```

$$\text{Sol} := \{\_C1 = \text{Ts}, \_C2 = \text{Tf} - \text{Ts}\}$$

```
> assign(Sol);
> T(x,t);
```

$$\text{Ts} + (\text{Tf} - \text{Ts}) \ \text{erf}(1/2 \ \frac{x\tilde{}}{a\tilde{} \ t^{1/2}})$$

```
> evalb(diff(T(x,t),x,x)  - diff(T(x,t), t)/a^2=0);
```

$$\text{true}$$

By rewriting the final form is obtained,

$$T(x,t) = \frac{2(T_f - T_s)}{\sqrt{\pi}} \int_0^{\frac{x}{2a\sqrt{t}}} e^{-p^2} \, dp + T_s.$$

14.3.1 MAPLE Plots

Let us compute and plot the temperature distribution inside the agriculture field which has the maximum depth $d_{max} = 0.5[m]$ and the thermal conductivity $k = a^2 = 0.003[m^2 s^{-1}]$. The sun is shining for half an hour $\Delta t = 1800[s]$ during which the temperature on the surface of the field becomes $T_s = 300[K]$. The initial temperature of the field is $T_f = 285[K]$.

```
> Ts := 300: Tf := 285: a := sqrt(0.003):
> DVEC := [0, 0.01, 0.05, 0.1, 0.2, 0.5]:
> for d in DVEC do  Td[d] := T(d, t) od:
> plot({seq(Td[d], d = DVEC)}, t = 0..1800, 298..300);
> plot3d(T(x, t), x = 0..0.5, t = 0..1800);
```

References

[1] D. G. ZILL and M. R. CULLEN, *Advanced Engineering Mathematics*, PWS-KENT, Boston, 1992.

Chapter 15. Modeling Penetration Phenomena

J. Buchar and J. Hřebíček

15.1 Introduction

Penetration phenomena are of interest in numerous areas (cf. [3]). They are often associated with the problem of nuclear waste containment and with the protection of spacecraft or satellites from debris and/or meteorite impact. Formally the penetration is defined as the entrance of a projectile into the target without completing its passage through the body. The penetration phenomenon can be characterized according to the impact angle, the geometry and material characteristics of the target and the projectile and the striking velocity. In this chapter we limit our considerations to the normal incidence impact of a long rod on a semi-infinite target. This model corresponds for example to the situation in which a very thick armor is penetrated by a high kinetic energy projectile. The most efficient method for the solution of this problem is the numerical modeling by the finite elements method. Many finite elements computer programs are capable of handling very complex material constitutive relations. These programs are expensive and often require a substantial amount of execution time. This is the main reason why simple one-dimensional theories still have considerable value. Such theories also provide insight into the interactions between the physical parameters and their relationship to the outcome of the event. These interactions are usually difficult to ascertain from the computer analyses mentioned above. As a result, simple theories often provide the basis for the design of experiments, refining the areas in which numerical modeling by finite elements methods is applied. In this spirit, we will investigate some penetration models which are treated using MAPLE.

15.2 Short description of the penetration theory

The list of publications on the study of penetration is long, although the first models of this process were formulated during the sixties [8]. The model of the penetration of a semi-infinite target consists of the following four regimes:

1. Transient shock regime: On initial contact, shock waves are formed both in the target and the projectile as schematically shown in Figure 15.1. The material response is mainly governed by its compressibility and density.

FIGURE 15.1.
A scheme of wave pattern during the transient shock regime.

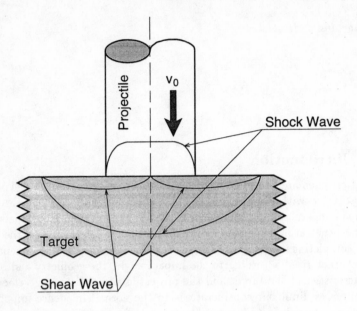

The shock pressures are usually high enough to cause extensive plastic flow, melting and vaporization.

2. Steady state regime: During this period of penetration the projectile erodes, while at the same time causing the formation of a crater. This stage is usually described by a modification of Bernoulli's equation.

3. Cavitation regime: After the complete consumption of the projectile, the crater continues to expand as a result of its own inertia and the energy trapped when the target pressures reduce to the order of the material strength. This reduction is a consequence of the multiple wave reflections [9].

4. Recovery regime: The dimension of the crater reduces slightly as a result of the elastic rebound. This rebound may produce tensile stresses high enough to cause spallation, as can be often observed on the recovered targets [5].

The main features of this model have been verified computationally [11]. The numerical simulation yields the most complex analysis of the penetration process. Simulation is extremely expensive because it requires many hours of CPU time on state-of-the-art machines. This procedure is thus neither convenient for the evaluation of series of ballistic experiments nor for an extensive study of the role of the penetration characteristics which were mentioned in the introduction. These facts strongly encourage the development of new analytical models of the penetration process. There are many analytical models of the penetration, for a summary cf. [2]. The most widely used is a one-dimensional model which is known as the Tate model [10] even if it was independently proposed by Alekseevskii [1]. The main features of this model which has become a standard reference for long-rod penetration of thick targets are reviewed in the following sections.

15.3 The Tate - Alekseevskii model

This model assumes that the projectile is rigid, except for a thin region near the target-projectile interface where erosion can occur. This region has no spatial extent but contains the interface between target and projectile. The behavior of this interface is described by a modification of the Bernoulli equation

$$\frac{1}{2}\rho_p(v-u)^2 + Y_p = \frac{1}{2}\rho_t u^2 + R_t \qquad (15.1)$$

where ρ_p and ρ_t are the projectile and target densities, respectively, v is the velocity of the rear part of the projectile, u is the penetration velocity, Y_p is the strength of the projectile and R_t is defined as the target resistance in the one-dimensional formulation.

The penetrated projectile is decelerated by a force transmitted from the interface along the length of the projectile. The deceleration is given by

$$\rho_p l \frac{dv}{dt} = -Y_p \qquad (15.2)$$

where $l = l(t)$ is the current length of the projectile. The change of the rod length in consequence of the erosion process is given by Newton's equation of motion for the undeformed section of the rod

$$\frac{dl}{dt} = -(v-u). \qquad (15.3)$$

Equations (15.1)–(15.3) represent a set of equations for the three unknown functions $l = l(t), v = v(t)$ and $u = u(t)$ with the initial conditions

$$v(0) = v_0, \qquad l(0) = L \qquad (15.4)$$

where v_0 is an impact velocity and L is the initial length of the projectile. The penetration velocity u can be obtained from Equation (15.1):

```
>       # Bernoulli equation
> eq := (1/2)*rhop*(v-u)^2+Yp=(1/2)*rhot*u^2+Rt:
> pen := solve(eq, u);

pen :=
```

```
   1/2 (rhop v +

                                  2
   (- 2 rhop Yp + 2 rhop Rt + rhot rhop v  + 2 rhot Yp - 2 rhot Rt)

   ^1/2)/(1/2 rhop - 1/2 rhot),

   1/2 (rhop v -

                                  2
   (- 2 rhop Yp + 2 rhop Rt + rhot rhop v  + 2 rhot Yp - 2 rhot Rt)

   ^1/2)/(1/2 rhop - 1/2 rhot)
```

```
>           # We take the second solution
>           # because of u < v and simplify it
> u_v[1] := simplify(pen[2]):
```

The value of u for the same density of the projectile and target, i.e. $\rho_p = \rho_t$, may be computed as follows

```
> simplify(series(u_v[1],rhop=rhot),symbolic):
> u_v[2] := subs({rhot=rho,rhop=rho},op(1,"));
```

$$
u\_v[2] := 1/2\ \frac{rho\ v^2 + 2\ Yp - 2\ Rt}{rho\ v}
$$

Thus, for $\rho_p \neq \rho_t$ the penetration velocity u is given by

$$
u = \frac{\rho_p v - \sqrt{2(R_t - Y_p)(\rho_p - \rho_t) + \rho_p \rho_t v^2}}{\rho_p - \rho_t} \tag{15.5}
$$

and for $\rho_p = \rho_t$ by

$$
u = \frac{\rho v^2 + 2(Y_p - R_t)}{2\rho v}. \tag{15.6}
$$

Inserting Equation (15.2) into (15.3) we obtain

$$
\frac{dl}{dv} = \frac{l(v)\rho_p(v - u)}{Y_p}. \tag{15.7}
$$

Integration of differential Equation (15.7) with the initial condition $l(v_0) = L$ by MAPLE

```
>           # Definition of initial value problem
> deq := diff(l(v), v)=l(v)*rhop*(v-u(v))/Yp:
> incond := l(v0) = L:
> len[1] := simplify (rhs (dsolve({deq, incond}, l(v))));
```

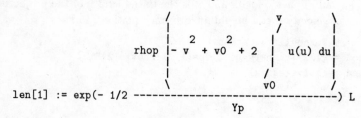

leads to the current length l of the projectile, which may be simplified for equal penetrator and target densities, i.e., $\rho_p = \rho_t$:

```
> subs(u=unapply(u_v[2],v),{rhop=rho,rhot=rho},len[1]):
> len[2] := simplify (expand ("));
```

```
len[2] :=

 /  - Rt + Yp\    /- Rt + Yp\
 |- ---------|    |---------|                  rho (- v + v0) (v0 + v)
 \    Yp    /     \   Yp    /                   -----------------------
v              v0             L exp(- 1/4               Yp             )
```

The penetration depth p of the rod at time T is

$$p = \int_0^T u(t)\, dt. \tag{15.8}$$

Using (15.2) yields

$$p = \frac{\rho_p}{Y_p} \int_{v(T)}^{v_0} u\, l\, dv . \tag{15.9}$$

Inserting the formulas for $u(v)$ and $l(v)$ into Equation (15.9), we obtain the general penetration equation

$$\frac{p}{L} = F(v_0, R_t, Y_p, \rho_t, \rho_p). \tag{15.10}$$

The above integral cannot be solved analytically in the general case, but we describe in the following subsections the exact solution of (15.10) for the choice of special parameter values.

15.3.1 Special case $R_t = Y_p$

For equal target resistance R_t and projectile strength Y_p, we compute $\lim_{T \to \infty} p(T)$. Obviously $T \to \infty$ corresponds to $v \to 0$.

```
> u_v[3] := simplify (subs(Rt=Yp, u_v[1]), symbolic):
> subs(u=unapply(u_v[3],v),len[1]):
> l := simplify(", symbolic):
> p := simplify(int(l*u_v[3], v=0..v0)):
```

The normalized penetration depth p/L is then given by

$$\frac{p}{L} = \frac{Y_p \left(\rho_p - \sqrt{\rho_p \rho_t}\right)}{\rho_p \left(\rho_t - \sqrt{\rho_p \rho_t}\right)} \left(-1 + e^{\frac{\rho_p \left(\rho_t - \sqrt{\rho_p \rho_t}\right) v_0^2}{2(\rho_p - \rho_t) Y_p}}\right). \tag{15.11}$$

For $\rho_p = \rho_t = \rho$, Equation (15.11) may be further simplified by

```
> simplify(limit(p,rhot=rhop),symbolic):
```

Thus we obtain

$$\frac{p}{L} = \frac{Y_p}{\rho} \left(1 - e^{-\frac{\rho v_0^2}{4 Y_p}}\right) . \tag{15.12}$$

15.3.2 Special case $\rho_p = \rho_t = \rho$

For equal penetrator and target densities, we distinguish following cases

Case 1: $R_t \geq Y_p$. According to (15.1), penetration occurs only if

$$\frac{1}{2}\rho_p v_0^2 + Y_p \geq R_t. \tag{15.13}$$

For $R_t = mY_p$, the velocity v ranges therefore from v_0 to v_m, where

$$v_m = \sqrt{\frac{2(m-1)Y_p}{\rho_p}}. \tag{15.14}$$

The normalized penetration depth can be determined as follows:

```
> vm := sqrt(2*(m-1)*Yp/rho):
> simplify (subs(Rt=m*Yp,len[2]*u_v[2])):
> p := (rho/Yp)*int(", v=vm..v0):
```

which may be neatly formatted as

$$\frac{p}{L} = \frac{v_0 L}{2Y_p} \int_{v_m}^{v_0} e^{-\frac{\rho(v_0-v)(v_0+v)}{4Y_p}} \left(\rho v^2 + 2Y_p - 2mY_p\right) \left(\frac{v}{v_0}\right)^m v^{-2} dv.$$

For $m \in \mathbb{N}$, the above expression may be further simplified, see for example p_1 and p_3:

```
> p1 := simplify(eval(subs(m=1, p)));

                / |          2  \                       2
                | |     rho v0  |                 rho v0
    p1 := L     |exp(1/4 -------) - 1| exp(- 1/4 -------)
                \ |        Yp        /                Yp

> p3 := simplify(eval(subs(m=3, p)));

              / |      2                       - 4 Yp + rho v0  2 \
              | |rho v0  - 8 Yp + 4 Yp exp(- 1/4 ---------------)|
              \ |                                      Yp         /
    p3 := L   ---------------------------------------------------------
                                          2
                                   rho v0
```

Case 2: $R_t < Y_p$. There are two velocity regimes with different penetration processes described by the inequalities

$$Y_p \geq \frac{1}{2}\rho_t u^2 + R_t, \qquad \text{for } u = v_0, \tag{15.15}$$

$$Y_p < \frac{1}{2}\rho_t u^2 + R_t, \qquad \text{for } u < v_0. \tag{15.16}$$

If (15.15) holds, then the rod penetrates like a rigid body with the impact penetration velocity v_0. Equality in (15.15) holds for the limit velocity

$$v_l = \sqrt{\frac{2(Y_p - R_t)}{\rho_t}}. \tag{15.17}$$

For $v_0 \leq v_l$ the decelerating pressure $\tilde{P}$ at the tip of the rod is given by $\tilde{P} = \frac{1}{2}\rho_t v_0^2 + R_t$. Inserting pressure $\tilde{P}$ into Equation (15.2) we obtain

$$\rho_p L \frac{dv}{dt} = -\left(\frac{1}{2}\rho_t v_0^2 + R_t\right). \tag{15.18}$$

Integration within boundaries v_0 and zero velocity leads to

$$p_r = L\left(\frac{\rho_p}{\rho_t}\right)^2 \ln\left(1 + \frac{\rho_t v_0^2}{2R_t}\right). \tag{15.19}$$

For $v_0 > v_l$ the penetration depth p_f is calculated by integrating (15.9) from v_0 to v_l. The total penetration p is then given by

$$p = p_r + p_f. \tag{15.20}$$

The basic Equations (15.1)–(15.3) of this penetration theory are highly non-linear. Generally, their solution can only be computed numerically. MAPLE enables us to obtain an approximation of the solution in the form of a series. A detailed analysis performed in [4] reveals that an approximation of the penetration velocity u by a 5th order polynomial u_{appr} is sufficient.

```
> restart:
>       # Bernoulli equation for same densities rho=rhot=rhop
> eqe := (1/2)*rho*(v(t)-u)^2+Yp=(1/2)*rho*u^2+Rt:
> u := solve(eqe,u):
> deqe1 := rho*l(t)*diff(v(t), t)=-Yp:
> deqe2 := diff(l(t), t)=-(v(t)-u):
> incond := l(0)=L, v(0)=v0:
> sol := dsolve({deqe1, deqe2, incond}, {l(t), v(t)}, series):
>       # Polynomial approximation of v(t) and l(t)
> v := op(2,op(select(x->op(1,x)='v(t)',sol))):
> l := op(2,op(select(x->op(1,x)='l(t)',sol))):
>       # Polynomial approximation of u(t)
> uappr := convert(series(v/2+(Yp-Rt)/(rho*v),t=0,6),polynom):
>       # First few coefficients of uappr
> series(uappr,t=0,2);
```

$$\left(\frac{1}{2}v0 + \frac{Yp - Rt}{rho\ v0}\right) + \left(-\frac{1}{2}\frac{Yp}{rho\ L} + \frac{(Yp - Rt)\ Yp}{rho^2\ v0^2\ L}\right)t + O(t^2)$$

We shall use this model in the following example

```
> rho := 7810: # Target and penetrator density
> L   := 0.25: # Length of rod
>       # Target resistance Rt = 900*10^6
>       # Strength of projectile Yp = 900*10^6
> u := subs(Rt=900*10^6,Yp=900*10^6,uappr):
> plot3d(u,t=0..0.0004,v0=1000..2500);
```

where the experimental data was taken from the shot No. B19, see [4]:
$\rho = \rho_t = \rho_p = 7810[kgm^{-3}]$, $L = 0.25[m]$, $R_t = Y_p = 9.10^8[Nm^{-2}]$. The

FIGURE 15.2.

Penetration velocity versus time and impact velocity v_0.

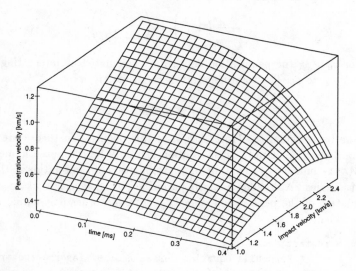

results of this computation (displayed in Figure 15.2) were compared with results of two-dimensional numerical simulations by the finite elements program AUTODYN 2D. It is shown in [4] that the results are essentially the same. The following penetration model takes into account especially the erosion processes at the rod nose.

15.4   The eroding rod penetration model

Assume that a cylindrical rod with initial cross-sectional area A_p, diameter d_p and length l_p, normally impacts the semi-infinite target with an impact velocity v_0 (cf. Figure 15.3). The target is made with a material of strength Y_t and density ρ_t, and the rod is made with a material of strength Y_p and density ρ_p. It was experimentally found that the rod erodes during the penetration. This erosion process occurs at the rod head, and leads to the decrease of the initial

FIGURE 15.3. *Penetration Process.*

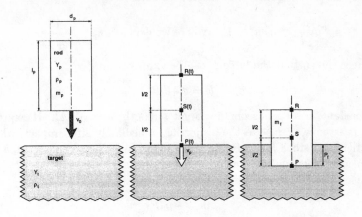

mass of the rod, $m_p = \rho_p A_p l_p$, and to the reduction of the rod length l_p. The mass of the rod lost per unit time can be expressed as

$$\dot{m} = \rho_p A_p \dot{l},$$

where $m(t)$ and $l(t)$ are the instantaneous mass and length of the rod, and the dots represent differentiation with respect to time t. Since $\dot{m} < 0$, the use of the symbol $\dot{m}_p = |\dot{m}|$ is convenient, i.e.

$$\dot{l} = -\frac{\dot{m}_p}{\rho_p A_p}. \tag{15.21}$$

Let $S(t)$ be the position of the center of the rod which is, at any time t, the middle point between the head position $P(t)$, and the rear position $R(t)$. Let us neglect the stress propagation phenomena in the impacting rod. The head and the rear velocity are given by

$$\dot{P} = \dot{S} + \frac{\dot{l}}{2} \;=\; \dot{S} - \frac{\dot{m}_p}{2\rho_p A_p}, \tag{15.22}$$

$$\dot{R} = \dot{S} - \frac{\dot{l}}{2} \;=\; \dot{S} + \frac{\dot{m}_p}{2\rho_p A_p}. \tag{15.23}$$

Consider the situation at the head of the rod. The mass Δm_p is lost while the velocity of the center of the rod, (the center of mass), becomes $\dot{S} + \Delta \dot{S}$. The momentum balance is

$$[(m - \Delta m_p)(\dot{S} + \Delta \dot{S}) + \dot{P}\Delta m_p] - m\dot{S} = -F\Delta t, \tag{15.24}$$

where F is the force exerted by the target opposing the motion of the rod. In the limit, for $\Delta t \to 0$, the Equation (15.24) has the form

$$m\frac{d\dot{S}}{dt} = (\dot{S} - \dot{P})\dot{m}_p - F. \tag{15.25}$$

Inserting Equation (15.22) into (15.25) we obtain

$$m\frac{d\dot{S}}{dt} = a_p\dot{m}_p^2 - F, \quad \text{where we denote} \quad a_p = \frac{1}{2\rho_p A_p}.$$

In [7] it is shown that the force F can be expressed as

$$F = a + b\dot{P}^2. \tag{15.26}$$

The constant, a, depends on the target strength, $a = 3Y_t A_p$. It express the target resistance against to the projectile immediately after impact, when the projectile head stops for a certain time period [6]. The second term, b, is the kinetic energy per unit volume or force per unit area, i.e., $b = \rho_t A_p/2$.

The erosion of the rod can be described, (see [4]), as

$$\dot{m} = -\mu_0 \dot{P} \tag{15.27}$$

or

$$\dot{m}_p = \mu_p \dot{P}, \tag{15.28}$$

respectively, where μ_p is an unknown parameter. Since the penetration depth $P(t)$ at $t = 0$ is zero, i.e. $P(0) = 0$, the solution of the differential Equation (15.27) is

$$m(t) = m_p - \mu_p P(t). \tag{15.29}$$

Let P_f be the final penetration depth of the rod head and let m_f be its residual mass at time t_f when the penetration is completed. Then the parameter μ_p has the value

$$\mu_p = \frac{m_p - m_f}{P_f}, \tag{15.30}$$

and it follows that the maximum value of μ_p is $\mu_{max} = m_p/P_f$. Putting Equation (15.28) into (15.22) we obtain

$$\dot{S} = (1 + \mu_p a_p)\dot{P} = k\dot{P}, \quad \text{where} \quad k = k(\mu_p) = 1 + \mu_p a_p. \tag{15.31}$$

Using Equations (15.26), (15.28), (15.29), and (15.31) the Equation (15.25) can be modified to the form

$$(m_p - \mu_p P)k\frac{d\dot{P}}{dt} = -(a + c\dot{P}^2), \quad \text{where} \quad c = c(\mu_p) = b - a_p\mu_p^2. \tag{15.32}$$

The solution of the differential Equation (15.32) with respect to the initial conditions

$$P(0) = 0, \tag{15.33}$$
$$\dot{P}(0) = v_p, \tag{15.34}$$

gives the time dependency of the penetration depth, i.e. $P = P(t)$. The initial penetration velocity v_p in (15.34) is determined according to Tate theory [6]

$$v_p = \frac{v_0}{2} + \frac{Y_t - Y_p}{\rho_t v_0}. \tag{15.35}$$

Because we cannot measure the function $P(t)$ experimentally it is necessary to look for some simplifications of Equation (15.32). If we take into account that

$$\frac{d\dot{P}}{dt} = \frac{d\dot{P}}{dP}\frac{dP}{dt}$$

the Equation (15.32) can be transformed to

$$-\frac{k}{a+c\dot{P}^2}\dot{P}\frac{d\dot{P}}{dP} = \frac{1}{m_p - \mu_p P}.$$

with the initial condition (15.34).

The above initial value problem can be easily solved by MAPLE.

```
> de := -k*DP(P)*diff(DP(P), P)/(a + c*DP(P)^2) =1/(mp - mu*P);

                    /  d        \
              k DP(P) |---- DP(P)|
                    \ dP        /                1
      de := - ---------------------  =  ---------
                               2          mp - mu P
                 a + c DP(P)

> ic := DP(0) = vp:
> pen := dsolve({de,ic},DP(P));

   pen :=
                                      /    c \              \1/2
                                      |2 ----|              |
                                      \  mu k/           2  |
                          (mp - mu P)          (a + c vp )  |
               |- 4 a + 4 ---------------------------------|
               |                    /    c \               |
               |                    |2 ----|               |
               \                    \  mu k/               /
                                      mp
      DP(P) = - 1/2 ------------------------------------------------,
                                      1/2
                                       c


                                      /    c \              \1/2
                                      |2 ----|              |
                                      \  mu k/           2  |
                          (mp - mu P)          (a + c vp )  |
               |- 4 a + 4 ---------------------------------|
               |                    /    c \               |
               |                    |2 ----|               |
               \                    \  mu k/               /
                                      mp
      DP(P) = 1/2 ------------------------------------------------
                                      1/2
                                       c

> sol := op(2,pen[2]);
```

```
       /                           /   c  \                        \1/2
       |                          |2 ----|                         |
       |                           \ mu k/                       2 |
       |                  (mp - mu P)              (a + c vp )|
       |- 4 a + 4 -----------------------------------------------|
       |                              /   c  \                     |
       |                             |2 ----|                      |
       \                              \ mu k/                     /
 sol := 1/2 ----------------------------------mp----------------------
                                       1/2
                                      c
```

```
> sol1 := subs(2*c/(mu*k)=1/e,sol);
```

```
        /                          (1/e)           2 \1/2
        |                (mp - mu P)      (a + c vp )|
        |- 4 a + 4 ----------------------------------|
        |                         (1/e)              |
        \                        mp                 /
 sol1 := 1/2 ----------------------------------------------
                              1/2
                             c
```

After some simple manipulations with the solution we obtain

$$\dot{P} = \sqrt{\frac{a}{c}\left((1 + \frac{c}{a}v_p{}^2)(1 - \frac{\mu_p}{m_p}P)^{1/\varepsilon} - 1\right)}, \tag{15.36}$$

where

$$\varepsilon = \varepsilon(\mu_p) = \frac{\mu_p k}{2c}$$

is the dimension-less erosion rate.

When the embedment occurs in a semi-infinite target, $\dot{P} = 0$ at time t_f, and from (15.36) it follows that

$$P_f = \frac{m_p}{\mu_p}\left(1 - (1 + \frac{c(\mu_p)}{a}v_p{}^2)^{-\varepsilon(\mu_p)}\right). \tag{15.37}$$

Equation (15.37) is more convenient for the evaluation of the parameter μ_p than Equation (15.30) because of the difficulties to determine the residual rod mass m_f. The data $[P_f, v_0]$ are then easily available during each terminal-ballistic experiment.

The simulation of the ballistic experiments involves the following steps:

1. The determination of the parameter μ_p. If the theory of penetration outlined in the this chapter is valid, then μ_p should be a constant for each rod-target material combination and independent of the striking velocity v_0. We will solve the Equation (15.37) in MAPLE for μ_p numerically and also evaluate the limit of (15.37) for $\mu_p \to 0$. This limit corresponds to the penetration of a rigid projectile. We will define the quantities k, c, and ε as functions of the variable μ. Also P_f is defined as a function of μ. We will denote μ_p the solution of the equation $P_f(\mu) = P_f$.

2. The evaluation of the velocity $\dot{P}$ as a function of P along the penetration path $P \in [0, P_f]$.

3. The solution of the initial value problem (15.32), (15.33), and (15.34) in order to obtain the function $P(t)$ and its graph.

4. The investigation of the influence of the target strength Y_t on the parameters and functions determined at points 1–3. The value of Y_t may be affected by the strain rate which is much higher than that occurring at a conventional test of materials.

15.5   Numerical Example

We will use the MAPLE for the solution of a concrete problem. Let us consider the following experimental data from the shot No. C06 from the collection of J. Buchar [4]: $m_p = 1.491$ $[kg]$, $v_0 = 1457.9$ $[ms^{-1}]$, $\rho_t = \rho_p = 7810$ $[kgm^{-3}]$, $d_p = 0.0242$ $[m]$, $Y_t = 9.7 \cdot 10^8$ $[Nm^{-2}]$, $Y_p = 15.81 \cdot 10^8$ $[Nm^{-2}]$, $P_f = 0.245$ $[m]$.

We now present the MAPLE program for the solution of the above example, and the four steps of the ballistics experiment analysis. In the first step we will find μ_p, and then we will plot the Figure 15.4, the graph of $P_f(\mu)$ on the interval $[0, \mu_{max}]$. In the second step we will plot the Figure 15.5, the graph of the penetration velocity $\dot{P}$ as a function of P and the determined parameter μ_p, see (15.37). In the third step we will solve the above initial value problem numerically and plot the Figure 15.6, the graph of the solution $P(t)$ in the chosen interval $(0, t_f)$, $t_f = 0.0006$. In the fourth step we will plot the Figure 15.7, the graph of the penetration depth as a function of Y_t and v_0.

```
>                   # Projectile and target data
>   rhot := 7810:      rhop := rhot:       mp := 1.491:
>   dp   := 0.0242:    Yt   := 9.70*10^8:  Yp := 15.81*10^8:
>   Ap   := Pi*dp^2/4: v0   := 1457.9:
>                   # the final penetration depth
>   pf := 0.245:

>                   # 1st step - Determination of mup and graph
                    # penetration depth vs erosion rate mu
                    # the definition of constants ap, a, b and
                    # initial penetration velocity
>   ap := 1/(2*rhop*Ap):   a   := 3*Yt*Ap:
>   b  := rhot*Ap/2:       vp  := v0/2+(Yt-Yp)/(rhot*v0):
>                   # The definition of functions k, c, eps and Pf of mu
>   k    := mu->1+ap*mu:            c := mu->b-ap*mu^2:
>   eps  := mu->mu*k(mu)/(2*c(mu)):
    Pf   := mu->mp*(1-(1+c(mu)*vp^2/a)^(-eps(mu)))/mu:
```

FIGURE 15.4.
The Influence of μ on the Penetration Depth.

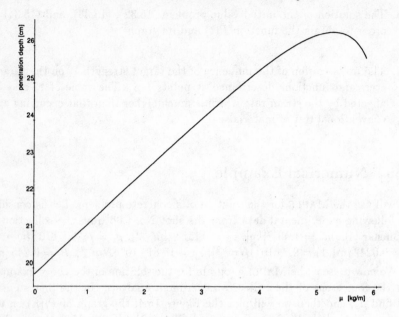

FIGURE 15.5.
Dependence of Penetration Velocity on Depth.

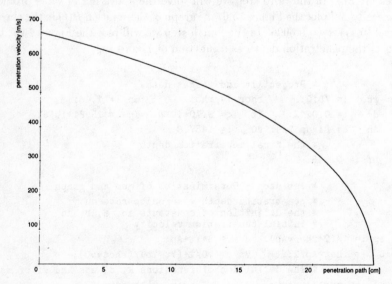

FIGURE 15.6. *Dependence of Depth on Time.*

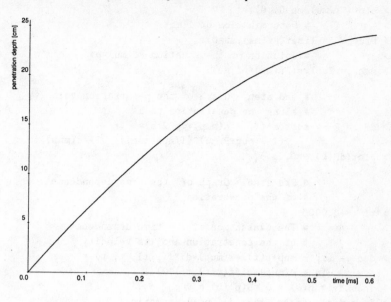

FIGURE 15.7.
The Influence of Target Strength and Impact Velocity.

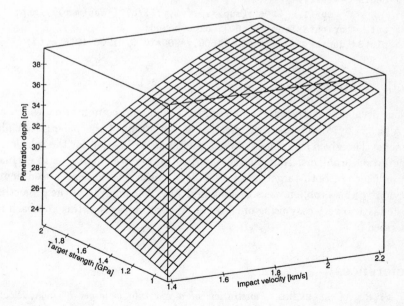

```
>                  # - Graph of influence of mu on the penetration depth
> plot(Pf(mu),mu=0..6);
>                  # Determination of limit
> Pfzero := limit(Pf(mu),mu=0):
>                  # Solution of the equation Pf(mu)=pf
> mup := fsolve(Pf(mu)=pf,mu):

>                  # 2nd step - Graph of the penetration velocity
                   # along the penetration path
> dP := P -> sqrt(a*((1 + c(mup)*vp^2/a)*
                   (1 - mup*P/mp)^(1/eps(mup)) - 1)/c(mup)):
> plot(dP(P),P=0..pf);

>                  # 3rd step - Graph of  the time dependence
                   # of the penetration
> tf := 0.0006:
>                  # The evaluation of the time dependence
                   # of the penetration and its velocity
> deq := (mp - mup*p(t))*k(mup)*diff(p(t), t, t) =
                   -(a + c(mup)*diff(p(t),t )^2):
> incond := p(0) = 0, D(p)(0) = vp:
> F := dsolve({deq, incond}, p(t), numeric):
> plots[odeplot](F, [t, p(t)], 0..tf);

>                  # 4th step - The evaluation of the influence
                   # of target strength and impact velocity
> vp1 := (vi,y) -> vi/2 + (y - Yp)/(rhot*vi):
> depth := (vi,y) ->
                   mp*(1 - (1 + c(mup)*vp1(vi,y)^2/a)^(-eps(mup)))/mup:
> opt := orientation=[-55,60], axes=boxed:
> plot3d(depth(v,y),vi=1400..1600,y=900*10^6..1200*10^6,opt);
```

15.6   Conclusions

It has been demonstrated that methods of symbolic computation which are
represented by Maple are very effective at the study of the penetration phenomena. The given examples show the usefulness of MAPLE for the solution of
penetration problems. Namely, the described procedure enables us to evaluate
the influence of both target and projectile strength on the penetration depth.
Previously, this problem was solved numerically. The analysis of the projectile's
erosion is also very easy using of MAPLE, other advantages of this approach are
described in [4].

References

[1] V. P. ALEKSEEVSKII, *Penetration of a rod into a target at high velocity*,
    Combustion, explosion and shock waves, 2, 1966, pp. 63 – 66.

[2] C. E. ANDERSON JR., S. R, BODNER, *Ballistic impact: the status of analytical and numerical modeling*, Int. J. Impact Engng., 7, 1988, pp. 9 – 35.

[3] Z. BÍLEK and J. BUCHAR, *The behavior of metals under high rates of strain (in Czech)*, Academia, Praha, 1984.

[4] J. BUCHAR, M. LAZAR, S. ROLC, *On the penetration of steel targets by long rods*, Acta Techn. CSAV 39, 1994, pp. 193 – 220.

[5] D. R. CHRISTMAN, J. W. GEHRING, *Analysis of high-velocity projectile penetration mechanics*, J. Appl. Phys., 27, 1966, pp. 63 – 68.

[6] J. D. CINNAMON ET AL., *A one - dimensional analysis of rod penetration*, Int. J. Impact Engng., 12, pp. 145 – 166, 1992.

[7] J.DEHN, *A unified theory of penetration*, Int. J. Impact Engng., 5, 1987, pp. 239 – 248.

[8] W. HERRMANN, J. S. WILBECK, *Review of hypervelocity penetration theories*, Int. J. Impact Engng., 5, 1987, pp. 307 – 322,

[9] V. K. LUK, M. J. FORRESTAL, D.E. AMOS, *Dynamical spherical cavity-expansion of strain-hardening materials*, J. Appl. Phys., 58, 1991, pp. 1 – 6.

[10] A. TATE, *A theory of the deceleration of long rods after impact*, J. Mech. Phys. Solids 15, 1967, pp. 287 – 399.

[11] J. A. ZUKAS, *High velocity impact dynamics*, Wiley Inter science, New York, 1990.

Chapter 16. Heat Capacity of System of Bose Particles

F. Klvaňa

16.1 Introduction

In this chapter we will study a system of Bose particles with nonzero mass, (for example He^4), in low temperature near absolute zero, when an interesting effect of superfluidity, (or also superconductivity for electrons) appears.

Let us consider a quantum system of N noninteracting boson particles, (particles with integer spin), with nonzero mass m. Let the system be in a volume V and in equilibrium with its surroundings, with absolute temperature T. Then the mean value of number of particles with energies in interval $[\epsilon, \epsilon + d\epsilon]$ is given by the eqn. [1, 2]

$$< n(\epsilon) > \cdot d\epsilon = \frac{g(\epsilon) \cdot d\epsilon}{e^{(\epsilon - \mu)/\theta} - 1}, \qquad \epsilon \in [0, \infty), \qquad (16.1)$$

where $< n(\epsilon) >$ has the meaning of an energy density of number of particles, $g(\epsilon)$ is a density of states, which in our case is given by eqn.

$$g(\epsilon) = g_0 V \frac{4\pi}{h^3} 2m^{3/2} \cdot \epsilon^{1/2} = \lambda \cdot \sqrt{\epsilon}, \qquad (16.2)$$

where $\theta = kT$, (k is the Boltzmann constant), is a statistical temperature.

The quantity $\mu = \mu(T, V, N)$ is the chemical potential, and its dependence on the thermodynamics parameters (T, V, N) is given by the normalization condition

$$N = \int_0^\infty < n(\epsilon) > d\epsilon = \lambda \int_0^\infty \frac{\epsilon^{1/2} d\epsilon}{e^{(\epsilon - \mu)/\theta} - 1} = \lambda \cdot \theta^{3/2} \int_0^\infty \frac{x^{1/2} \cdot dx}{e^{x - \mu/\theta} - 1} \qquad (16.3)$$

For a system of bosons it can be proved that $\mu \leq 0$ and $\mu = 0$ for $T = 0$.

But it follows from Equation (16.3) that $\mu = 0$ for $\theta = \theta_c > 0$ (θ_c is called critical temperature). So for $\theta = \theta_c$

$$N = \lambda \cdot \theta_c^{3/2} \int_0^\infty \frac{x^{1/2} \cdot dx}{e^x - 1}. \qquad (16.4)$$

Using a definition of the Riemann zeta function

$$\zeta(\nu) = \frac{1}{\Gamma(\nu)} \int_0^\infty \frac{x^{\nu-1}dx}{e^x - 1} \tag{16.5}$$

we can write (16.4) in the form

$$N = \lambda \cdot \Gamma\left(\frac{3}{2}\right) \cdot \theta_c^{3/2} \cdot \zeta\left(\frac{3}{2}\right) \tag{16.6}$$

For $\theta < \theta_c$ we have to use a different model for our system. In this case μ has to be zero and the normalization condition has the form

$$N - N' = \lambda \int_0^\infty \frac{\epsilon^{1/2}d\epsilon}{e^{\epsilon/\theta} - 1} \tag{16.7}$$

where N' is a number of particles, which are "condensed" in an one-particle ground state with $\epsilon = 0$. These condensed particles have a special behavior called *superfluidity*. So μ as a function of θ has two analytically different regions: $\mu = 0$ for $\theta \le \theta_c$ and for $\theta \ge \theta_c$, μ is given as a solution of Equation (16.3).

Our task will be to find temperature dependency of the constant volume heat capacity per particle C for such a system. By the definition

$$C = \frac{\partial E_p}{\partial T} = k \cdot \frac{\partial E_p}{\partial \theta} \tag{16.8}$$

where E_p is an internal energy per particle given by equation

$$E_p = \frac{\lambda}{N} \int_0^\infty \epsilon < n(\epsilon) > d\epsilon = \frac{\lambda}{N} \cdot \theta^{5/2} \int_0^\infty \frac{x^{3/2}dx}{e^{x-\mu/\theta} - 1}. \tag{16.9}$$

Let us define the function (usually called Bose-Einstein's integral – see [2])

$$F_{be}(z,\nu) = \frac{1}{\Gamma(\nu)} \int_0^\infty \frac{x^{\nu-1}dx}{e^{x+z} - 1}, \qquad z \ge 0, \quad \nu > 0; \tag{16.10}$$

as we can see, $F_{be}(0,\nu) = \zeta(\nu)$.

We can now formulate the following steps of solution for our problem:

1. Calculation of temperature dependence of μ:

   for $\theta \le \theta_c$: set $\mu = 0$,

   for $\theta \ge \theta_c$: μ is the solution of the Equation (16.3 and 16.6)

$$N = \lambda \cdot \theta_c^{3/2} \cdot \Gamma\left(\frac{3}{2}\right) \cdot \zeta\left(\frac{3}{2}\right) = \lambda \cdot \theta^{3/2} \cdot \Gamma\left(\frac{3}{2}\right) \cdot F_{be}\left(-\frac{\mu}{\theta}, \frac{3}{2}\right), \tag{16.11}$$

which leads to equation

$$F_{be}\left(-\frac{\mu}{\theta}, \frac{3}{2}\right) = \left(\frac{\theta_c}{\theta}\right)^{3/2} \cdot \zeta\left(\frac{3}{2}\right). \tag{16.12}$$

It is useful to transform the previous equation into canonical form using the dimensionless variables

$$y = \frac{\theta}{\theta_c}, \qquad \mu_d = \frac{\mu}{\theta_c}.$$

Then Equation (16.12) becomes

$$F_{be}\left(-\frac{\mu_d}{y}, \frac{3}{2}\right) = \frac{\zeta\left(\frac{3}{2}\right)}{y^{3/2}} \tag{16.13}$$

2. Calculation of the energy per particle, which is by (16.9) (and using 16.6) equal to

$$Ep = \frac{\Gamma\left(\frac{5}{2}\right)}{\Gamma\left(\frac{3}{2}\right)} \cdot \frac{\theta^{5/2}}{\theta_c^{3/2}} \cdot \frac{1}{\zeta\left(\frac{3}{2}\right)} \begin{cases} \zeta\left(\frac{5}{2}\right) & \text{for } \theta \le \theta_c \\ F_{be}\left(-\frac{\mu}{\theta}, \frac{5}{2}\right) & \text{for } \theta \ge \theta_c \end{cases} \tag{16.14}$$

Using a dimensionless quantity $\epsilon_d = E_p/\theta_c$ instead of E_p we can rewrite (16.14) in the form

$$\epsilon_d = \frac{\Gamma\left(\frac{5}{2}\right)}{\Gamma\left(\frac{3}{2}\right)} \cdot \frac{y^{5/2}}{\zeta\left(\frac{3}{2}\right)} \begin{cases} \zeta\left(\frac{5}{2}\right) & \text{for } y \le 1 \\ F_{be}\left(z, \frac{5}{2}\right) & \text{for } y \ge 1 \end{cases} \tag{16.15}$$

where $z = -\mu_d/y$ is given as a solution of Equation (16.13)

$$y^{3/2} \cdot F_{be}\left(z, \frac{3}{2}\right) = \zeta\left(\frac{3}{2}\right) \tag{16.16}$$

3. Calculation of heat capacity in units of k

$$c = \frac{C}{k} = \frac{d\epsilon_d}{dy} \tag{16.17}$$

Let us note, that for $y \gg 1$ a classical expression for energy per particle $E_p = 3\theta/2$ holds, from which follows $c = 3/2$.

16.2 MAPLE Solution

The basic problem for solution of our task is to represent the function

$$F_{be}(z, \nu) = \frac{1}{\Gamma(\nu)} \int_0^\infty \frac{x^{\nu-1} dx}{e^{x+z} - 1}, \qquad z \ge 0, \quad \nu > 0; \tag{16.18}$$

This function is a generalization of the Riemann zeta function and is not implemented in MAPLE. Because we are interested in the behavior of our system for low temperatures when $z \to 0$, we have to use the power expansion of F_{be}

ALGORITHM 16.1. *Function $F_{be}(z, \nu)$.*

```
'series/Fbe' := proc (z, nu:numeric, t) local n;
        # calculation of Bose-Einstein's  integral
        for nu noninteger
        1/GAMMA(nu)*int(x^(nu - 1)/(e^(z + x) - 1),
        x = 0..inf)
     if type(nu, integer) or not (nu > 1) then
        ERROR('2-nd arg. expect to be noninteger
              greater than 1 number')
      else
        # power expansion in z to order Order
        series((z)^(nu - 1)*GAMMA(1 - nu)
        + sum((-z)^n*Zeta(nu - n)/n!, n = 0..Order - 1)
        + O(t^Order), t)
     fi
   end;
```

in z. MAPLE cannot derive this expansion directly from Equation (16.18). We
have therefore to use the following expansion ([2, 3]) for noninteger $\nu > 1$:

$$F_{be}(z, \nu) = z^{\nu-1} \Gamma(1 - \nu) + \sum_{n=0}^{\infty} (-z)^n \frac{\zeta(\nu - n)}{n!} \qquad (16.19)$$

which is convergent for all $z \geq 0$. Let us define a function series/Fbe(z,nu,t)
(see Algorithm 16.1), which implements the evaluation of this series expansion
of $F_{be}(z, n)$ in t using the standard MAPLE function *series* (see Help in MAPLE).

The second problem is to compute functions like $\mu(\theta)$ or $E_p(\theta)$, which have
two analytically different regions. Physicists like to use one object to represent
one physical quantity. So for the definition of the above quantities the best way
is to define a functional analog of a statement $if - then - else$, for example of
the form

$$If(< relation >, < vthen >, < velse >),$$

which returns the expression $< vthen >$ or $< velse >$ depending on a
boolean value of the relation $< relation >$ (support of the definition of piecewise functions will be in the next version of MAPLE). Because we will need
to calculate derivatives of this function, it will be again a good idea to use the
standard functions *diff* by defining functions diff/If (see Help in MAPLE).
These functions are defined in Algoritm 16.2 .

The first step in the solution of our problem is to solve Equation (16.16) for
z. In this equation $F_{be}(z, 3/2)$ is expressed in the form of series in z, which
includes also the term $z^{1/2}$. But MAPLE can solve equations with pure power
series only. For this reason we should make transformation $z \to w^2$ and solve
the transformed equation

$$y^{3/2} \cdot F_{be}\left(w^2, \frac{3}{2}\right) = \zeta\left(\frac{3}{2}\right) \qquad (16.20)$$

ALGORITHM 16.2. *Functions for Evaluted If.*

```
# syntax of calling:  If(bool, vthen, velse)


'diff/If' := proc(bool, vthen, velse, x) ;
   If(bool, diff(vthen, x), diff(velse, x))
  end;


If:= proc(bool, vthen, velse)
        if type(bool, 'relation'(numeric)) then
          if bool then vthen else velse fi
        else 'If(args)'
      fi
    end;
```

for w. MAPLE can solve such equations and gives z as a series of $x = 1 - y^{-3/2}$. The chemical potential μ_d we can express then using the function If in the form

$$ If\,(y \leq 1, 0, -y * z). $$

A graph of this function is in Figure 16.1. The needed MAPLE statements follow :

```
>           # Basic equation for the chem. potential mud
>           # for y >= 1; z = -mud/y
> eqmu := series(Fbe(z, 3/2), z, 4) = y^(-3/2)*Zeta(3/2);

 eqmu :=

       1/2  1/2                                          2
 (- 2 z    Pi    + Zeta(3/2) - z Zeta(1/2) + 1/2 z  Zeta(-1/2)

          3                    4      Zeta(3/2)
    - 1/6 z  Zeta(-3/2) + O(z )) = ---------
                                      3/2
                                     y

>           # we choose the substition
>           # y^(-3/2) -> 1 - x  and z-> w^2
>           #  and invert the series
>  solw := solve(series(Fbe(w^2, 3/2), w, 7)
>           = (1 - x)*Zeta(3/2), w):
>           # then
> z := series(solw^2, x, 4);  # because  z = w^2 (z = -mu/th);
```

FIGURE 16.1.
Chemical Potential μ as a Function of $y = \theta/\theta_c$.

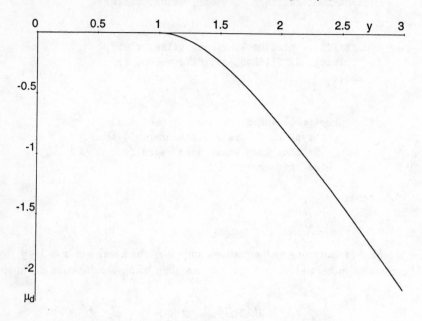

FIGURE 16.2. *Heat Capacity c as a Function of $y = \theta/\theta_c$.*

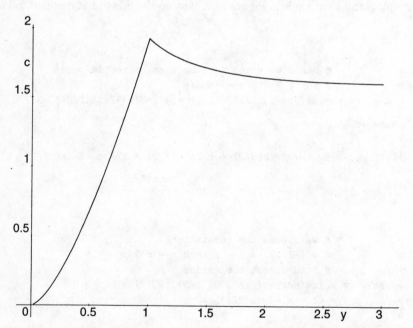

$$z := 1/4 \ \frac{\text{Zeta}(3/2)^2}{\text{Pi}} \ x^2 - 1/8 \ \frac{\text{Zeta}(3/2)^3 \ \text{Zeta}(1/2)}{\text{Pi}^2} \ x^3 + O(x^4)$$

```
> z:= convert(z, polynom): # for next evaluation
>              # graf of mud=-z*y on y
> plot(If(y <= 1, 0, -y*subs(x = 1 - y^(-3/2), z)), y = 0..3);
```

The dimensionless internal energy is given by Equation (16.15), which we can express in the form

$$\epsilon_d = \frac{3}{2} \frac{y^{5/2}}{\zeta\left(\frac{3}{2}\right)} \cdot If\left(y \le 1, \zeta\left(\frac{5}{2}\right), F_{be}\left(z, \frac{5}{2}\right)\right) \qquad (16.21)$$

where $F_{be}(z, 5/2)$ is given using z expressed in the previous step as a series in $x = 1 - y^{-3/2}$. Then the heat capacity c is given by Equation (16.17) and the graph of this function $c(y)$ is shown in Figure 16.2. As we should expect, the derivative of $c(y)$ has a discontinuity at point $y = 1$; this indicates, that this point ($\theta = \theta_c$) is a point of the phase transition of the second order. The rest of MAPLE's program follows:

```
>              # calculation of dimensionless internal energy
>              # per particle Ed, expansion of Fbe(z,5/2) in y
> Fy := subs(x = 1 - y^(-3/2),
>              convert(series(Fbe(z, 5/2), x, 4), polynom));
```

$$Fy := \text{Zeta}(5/2) - 1/4 \ \frac{\text{Zeta}(3/2)^3 \left(1 - \frac{1}{y^{3/2}}\right)^2}{\text{Pi}}$$

$$+ \left(1/6 \ \frac{\text{Zeta}(3/2)^3}{\text{Pi}} + 1/8 \ \frac{\text{Zeta}(3/2)^4 \ \text{Zeta}(1/2)}{\text{Pi}^2}\right)\left(1 - \frac{1}{y^{3/2}}\right)^3$$

```
>              # using the function If we can express energy for all y
> Ed := 3/2/Zeta(3/2)*y^(5/2)*If(y <= 1, Zeta(5/2), Fy):
>              #heat capacity is (in units of k)
> C := diff(Ed, y):
>              #and than we make graph of heat capacity
> plot(C, y = 0..3);
```

References

[1] C. KITTEL, *Elementary Statistical Physics*, John Wiley & Sons, Inc., 1958.

[2] F. LONDON, *Superfluids II.*, John Wiley & Sons, Inc., 1954.

[3] J.E. ROBINSON, *Note on the bose-einstein integral functions*, Physical Review, 83, 1951, pp. 678–679.

Chapter 17. Free Metal Compression

S. Bartoň

17.1 Introduction

Compression is a widely used basic process in metal forming. If compression is performed using two plane platens *(this is a special case of compression)* the lateral face is distorted (cf. Figure 17.1). This successive forming operation is called die forming, and it is necessary to predict the distortion in advance in order to provide enough space to fit the distorted body into a specific die.

FIGURE 17.1. *Free Compression.*

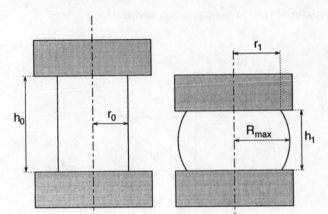

17.2 Disk compression

17.2.1 Mathematical and Physical Model

First we will construct a mathematical description of our problem. It will be necessary to make some simplifications in order to to obtain a solution. Assumptions:

1. We shall consider only the disk. Through the use of rotational symmetry we will reduce the complexity of the problem.

2. The material used is incompressible. This means that the volume of the material is constant, independent of the material's shape. This condition leads to the constant volume V: $dV/dp = 0 \iff V = \text{const}$.

3. We shall consider only a *ideal rigid* plastic material, i.e. we shall neglect the elasticity of the material.

4. Compression is so slow that at any time the flow of material is in equilibrium with the applied forces *(quasistationary process)* and the temperature of the material is in equilibrium with its surroundings *(isothermic process)*.

5. The axial section of the body (distorted surface) after the compression can be approximated by a parabolic curve, see [1, 4, 2]. This corresponds very well to results of practical experiments. We will determine the coefficients a, b and c of the parabola in the next section.

6. The base edges are sharp, i.e. the fillet radius F_r is equal to zero.

7. The material used is homogeneous and isotropic.

FIGURE 17.2. *Coordinates System.*

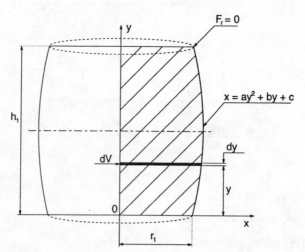

Due to the properties of the compressed material it will always have rotational symmetry, where the orientation of the axis of symmetry will always be constant. The shape of the body after the compression can be described by the perimeter of the axial section.

17.2.2 Parabolic Perimeter

In the following discussion we will refer to Figure 17.2 parabola. The perimeter has the equation $x = a\,y^2 + b\,x + c$. The coefficients a, b and c, are unknown, i.e. we need three equations to compute them. The first two equations are:

$$x\,(0) = r_1 \implies c = r_1 \tag{17.1}$$
$$x\,(h_1) = r_1 \implies a\,h_1^2 + b\,h_1 = 0. \tag{17.2}$$

The constant volume gives us a third equation. The initial volume is

$$V = V_0 = \frac{1}{4}\pi D_0{}^2$$

and must equal the volume of the body after the compression, which is calculated by

$$V = \pi \int_0^{h_1} y^2\,dy, \implies \frac{1}{4}\pi D_0{}^2 = \pi \int_0^{h_1} \left(a\,x^2 + b\,x + c\right)^2 dy. \tag{17.3}$$

Now we have a system of three Equations (17.1) – (17.3), so the unknowns a, b, c can be determined. We will use MAPLE to solve for them.

17.2.3 MAPLE Solution

```
> V0 := Pi*r0^2*h0:
> R := y -> a*y^2 + b*y + c:
> V1 := Pi*int(R(y)^2,y=0..h1);
                      2              3            4    2        2   5
V1 := Pi(c b h1  + 2/3 c a h1  + 1/2 b a h1  + c  h1 + 1/5 a  h1

            2   3
      + 1/3 b  h1 )
> eqns := {V1 = V0, R(0) = r1, R(h1) = r1}:
> Sol := solve(eqns, {a,b,c});
Sol := {c = r1,
                            3    2   5         2           2
    a = RootOf(- 10 r1 _Z h1  + _Z  h1  + 30 r1  h1 - 30 r0  h0),

                              3    2   5         2           2
    b = - RootOf(- 10 r1 _Z h1  + _Z  h1  + 30 r1  h1 - 30 r0  h0) h1}
```

As we see, our problem contains more than one solution set. There are exactly two since we solve a polynomial of degree two. We have to determine the correct one – the technically reasonable one.

To choose the correct solution we compute the maximal radius of the final body. Its y– coordinate is known: $y = h_1/2$. We can consider for example, that the rod will be stamped to $h_1 = h_0/4$, one fourth of its original height and that its base radius will be $r_1 = 2r_0$. The condition of the incompressibility of the material enables a determination of the maximal diameter Rmax in this case. Its value must be Rmax $= 2r_0$. It is not necessary to check all possible combinations of a and b, because the Equation (17.2) leads to $a = -b/h$. We can now select the suitable solution set.

```
> ax := subs(Sol, a):  bx := subs(Sol, b):
> a12 := allvalues(ax):  b12 := allvalues(bx):
> Sol1 := subs(ax = a12[1], bx = b12[1], Sol):
> Sol2 := subs(ax = a12[2], bx = b12[2], Sol):
> Rmax := simplify(subs(Sol1,r1 = 2*r0, h1 = h0/4, R(h1/2)),
>          symbolic);
                            Rmax := - 3 r0
> Rmax := simplify(subs(Sol2,r1 = 2*r0, h1 = h0/4, R(h1/2)),
>          symbolic);
                            Rmax := 2 r0
> Sol2 := subs(ax = a12[2], bx = b12[2], Sol);
 Sol2 := {c = r1,
```

$$a = \frac{1}{2} \frac{10\, r1\, h1^3 - 2\, 5^{1/2}\, h1^{5/2}\, (-r1^2\, h1 + 6\, r0^2\, h0)^{1/2}}{h1^5},$$

$$b = -\frac{1}{2} \frac{10\, r1\, h1^3 - 2\, 5^{1/2}\, h1^{5/2}\, (-r1^2\, h1 + 6\, r0^2\, h0)^{1/2}}{h1^4}\}$$

```
> assign(Sol2):
```

17.2.4 Base Radius as Function of Friction

In the preceding section the shape of the lateral face of the final body was derived as a function of the final height h_1 and base the radius r_1. But from the technical point of view it is known that r_1 depends on h_1 and on the initial dimensions h_0 and r_0. We try to find a suitable function for its description: $r_1 = F(h_0, r_0, h_1)$.

As a first step we assume no friction between the formed material and the platens. In the technical process this can be simulated by using plastic plates between the material and the platens or by specially preparing the bases of the disk [3]. In this case the formed material has always a cylindrical shape. r_1 can be determined simply by

$$r_1 = r_0 \sqrt{\frac{h_0}{h_1}}. \tag{17.4}$$

As a second step we assume unlimited friction between the material and the platens. Technically this can be simulated by countersinking the disk's basis into the platen's counter-bore. In this case

$$r_1 = r_0 = \text{const}, \tag{17.5}$$

and the lateral face curvature of the disk is the largest of all possible configurations

We can assume that in the usual case r_1 will satisfy the condition $r_0 \leq r_1 \leq r_0\sqrt{h_0/h_1}$. One of the simplest functions satisfying this condition is:

$$r_1 = r_0\left(1 + k\left(\sqrt{\frac{h_0}{h_1}} - 1\right)\right), \qquad \text{where} \qquad 0 \leq k \leq 1. \tag{17.6}$$

k is a "friction" coefficient. As we can see for $k = 0$ the Equation (17.6) becomes (17.5) and for $k = 1$ we obtain the Equation (17.4). The coefficient k can also be interpreted practically. If the disk is compressed by a conical platens with a specific top half angle the lateral face of the material is always cylindrical (cf. Figure 17.2.4). Using this we can determine $k = \sin(\varphi)$ (cf. Figure 17.2.4). The coefficient k depends on the properties of the formed material, the platen material, on the platen surface finish, and on the method of lubrification. In most cases we have $0.5 \leq k \leq 0.9$. The variable r1 can now be substituted into

FIGURE 17.3.
k *as Function of the Friction Angle,* $\mathbf{k} = \sin(\varphi)$.

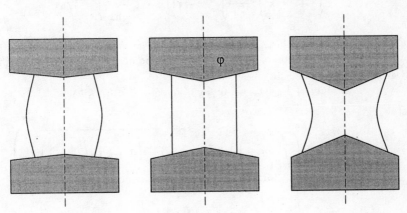

the variables a and b.

```
> r1 := r0*(1 + k*(sqrt(h0/h1) - 1)):
```

17.2.5 Simplification

We are not satisfied with our solution because it is too complicated. The variable b, for example, is the expression:

```
> b;
            /        /  1/2    \\
            |        |h0       ||   3
  - 1/2 (10 r0 |1 + k |----- - 1|| h1
            |        |  1/2    ||
            \        \h1       //
```

$$- 2\ 5^{1/2}\ h1^{5/2} \left(-r0 \left(1 + k\left(\frac{h0}{h1^{1/2}} - 1\right)\right)^2 \right)^{1/2} h1 + 6\ r0^2\ h0 \right)^{1/2} \right) \Big/\ h1^4$$

We shall try to simplify it. It will be necessary to use some substitutions and
back substitutions after simplification.

```
> b1 := subs(1+k*(sqrt(h0/h1)-1)=K,h0=N*h1,b):
> b2 := simplify(b1, power, symbolic):
> b3 := factor(simplify(subs(-5=-q^2, 5=q^2, b2), symbolic));
> b4 := subs(K=1+k*(sqrt(h0/h1)-1),N=h0/h1,q=sqrt(5),b3):
> b := b4;
```

$$b := -r0\ 5^{1/2}\left(\left(1 + k\left(\left(\frac{h0}{h1}\right)^{1/2} - 1\right)\right)5^{1/2}\right.$$
$$\left. - \left(-\left(1 + k\left(\left(\frac{h0}{h1}\right)^{1/2} - 1\right)\right)^2 + 6\frac{h0}{h1}\right)^{1/2}\right)\Big/h1$$

```
> a := -b/h1:
```

Thus the lateral face shape of the upset disk can be described by the following
function:

$$x = ay^2 + by + c, \qquad 0 \le y \le h_1, \qquad 0 < h_1 \le h_0,$$

where

$$b = -\frac{r_0\sqrt{5}\left(\left(1 + k\left(\sqrt{\frac{h_0}{h_1}} - 1\right)\right)\sqrt{5} - \sqrt{6\frac{h_0}{h_1} - \left(1 + k\left(\sqrt{\frac{h_0}{h_1}} - 1\right)\right)^2}\right)}{h_1},$$

$$a = -\frac{b}{h_1}, \qquad c = r_0\left(1 + k\left(\sqrt{\frac{h_0}{h_1}} - 1\right)\right).$$

17.2.6 Graphics

Let us consider a metal disk with initial radius $r_0 = 1$ and initial height $h_0 = 3$.
Let the final height h_1 be 1. *It is necessary to note here that compression
of disks with ratio $h_0/2r_0 > 2.5$ is dangerous because long disks may break!*
We compare the shapes after compression for several friction coefficients **k**: 0
(maximal friction) $\le$ k $\le$ 1 *(no friction)*. To compare the results at their best
we shall collect more results in one plot. Therefore we shall use procedure
BodyPlot, (see Algorithm 17.1), which allows us to show disk deformation in
Nsteps for more friction coefficients k. These coefficients must be collected in
the list Kvec. But first we must convert a function R(y) to function of other
parameters describing initial and final disk shape.

```
> Z := unapply(R(y),y,r0,h0,h1,k):
```

ALGORITHM 17.1. *Procedure* BodyPlot.

```
BodyPlot := proc(Shape, Rin, Hin, Hfin, Nsteps, Kvec)
#------------------------------------------------------
    local Nst, Rf, j, Kfr, i, n, Hi, F, Ls, Rs, Top, Bot,
        LeftSides, RightSides, TopSides, BottomSides;
    Nfr := nops(Kvec); Rf := 0;
    for j from 1 to Nfr do;
        Kfr := Kvec[j];
        Rf := Rf + 2*round(Shape(Hfin/2, Rin, Hin, Hfin, Kfr)+1);
        for i from 0 to Nsteps do;
            n := (j-1)*(Nsteps+1)+i;
            Hi := Hfin + (Hin-Hfin)*i/Nsteps;
            F(y) := Shape(y,Rin,Hin,Hi,Kfr);
            F(0) := Shape(0,Rin,Hin,Hi,Kfr);
            Ls[n] := [-F(y)+Rf, y, y=0..Hi];
            Rs[n] := [F(y)+Rf, y, y=0..Hi];
            Top[n] := [-F(0)+Rf, Hi, F(0)+Rf, Hi];
            Bot[n] := [-F(0)+Rf, 0, F(0)+Rf, 0];
        od:
    od;
    LeftSides   := seq(Ls[i], i=0..n):
    RightSides  := seq(Rs[i], i=0..n):
    TopSides    := seq(Top[i], i=0..n):
    BottomSides := seq(Bot[i], i=0..n):
    plot({LeftSides, RightSides, TopSides, BottomSides}):
end;
```

Now we can use the procedure BodyPlot and use it for visualization of the whole forming process.

```
> read('BodyPlot'):
> BodyPlot(Z, 1, 3, 1, 5, [0, 1/5]);
> BodyPlot(Z, 1, 3, 1, 4, [2/5, 3/5]);
> BodyPlot(Z, 1, 3, 1, 4, [4/5, 1]);
```

Finally we create a 3d–plot $R_{max} = R_{max}(h_1, k)$ for the same initial values h_0 and r_0, (cf. Figure 17.5).

```
> plot3d(Z(h1/2, 1, 3, h1, k), h1 = 1..3, k = 0..1,
>        axes=BOXED, orientation=[70,70]);
```

17.3   Compression of a metal prism

The method presented above can be generalized for the compression of a rectangular piece of metal. First we have to study the shape of the compressed

FIGURE 17.4.
Compressed Disk with Different Friction Coefficients.

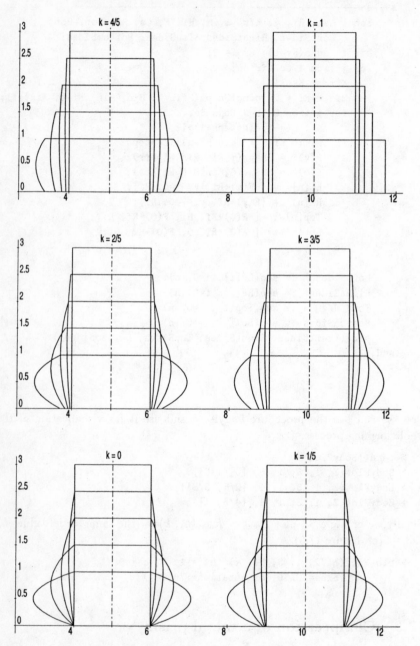

FIGURE 17.5. *Maximal Radius of the Final Shape.*

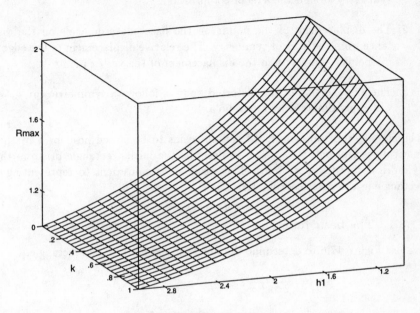

FIGURE 17.6.
The Rectangle in the Polar Coordinate System

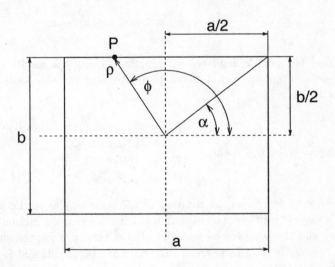

prism. As we can see, the distorted body fulfills the following conditions:

1. Each lateral surface is distorted. The distorted body keeps its partial symmetry around the axis of compression.

2. The displacement of the points on the base edges depends on the distance from the axes of symmetry. The relative displacement of the edge's midpoints is larger than the displacement of the vertex points.

3. The axial section of the distorted body is follows a symmetric curve, we will approximate it by a parabola.

Therefore cylindrical coordinate system seems to be suited best for a mathematical description. So we have to describe the initial rectangle prism in the cylindrical coordinate system. This problem is equivalent to representing a rectangle in the polar coordinate system.

17.3.1   The basic functions

We use Figure 17.6 to determine the function $\varrho = \varrho(\varphi)$ for the rectangle.

$$\varrho_1 = \frac{a}{2\cos(\varphi)}, \qquad -\alpha \leq \varphi \leq \alpha$$

$$\varrho_2 = \frac{b}{2\sin(\varphi)}, \qquad \alpha \leq \varphi \leq \pi - \alpha$$

$$\varrho_3 = \frac{a}{2|\cos(\varphi)|}, \qquad \pi - \alpha \leq \varphi \leq pi + \alpha$$

$$\varrho_4 = \frac{a}{2|\sin(\varphi)|}, \qquad \pi + \alpha \leq \varphi \leq 2\pi - \alpha \ .$$

Now we have to find the displacement function. Using the results from Section 17.6 we can find the simplest function satisfying the observation 2 from Section 17.3:

$$\Delta \varrho = \frac{1}{2} CkKU \ , \quad \text{where} \quad \begin{aligned} C &= \text{factor of proportionality} \\ k &= \text{friction angle} \\ K &= \sqrt{H/h} - 1 \\ U &= \sqrt{a^2 + b^2} \end{aligned}$$

First, we have to determine the constant C the same way as in the preceding part. Let's assume for the moment that $k = 1$, i.e. there is no friction between the platens and the compressed material. If the ratio of compression will be $H/h = 4$, then $K = 1$, and the area of the base has be to enlarged four times. For the area computation we shall use

$$S = \int_{\varphi_1}^{\varphi_2} \frac{\varrho^2(\varphi)}{2} \, d\varphi \ , \tag{17.7}$$

in our case (17.7) leads to

$$ab = \int_0^\alpha \left(\frac{a}{\cos(\varphi)} + CkKU\right)^2 d\varphi + \int_\alpha^{\pi/2} \left(\frac{b}{\sin(\varphi)} + CkKU\right)^2 d\varphi\,.$$

The proportionality factor C can be found with the help of MAPLE. We shall try to simplify the MAPLE results in order to obtain a better overview of the resulting formulas.

```
> Dr := C*k*K*U/2:
> rho[1] := a/2/cos(phi) + Dr;   rho[2] := b/2/sin(phi) + Dr;
> alpha := arctan(b/a):
> P1 := int(rho[1]^2/2, phi=0..beta):
> P2 := int(rho[2]^2/2, phi=beta..Pi/2):
> suB1 := ln((1+tan(beta)*cos(beta))/cos(beta))=B1:
> suB2 := ln(-(-1+cot(beta)*sin(beta))/sin(beta))=B2:
> P1a := expand(subs(suB1, P1));
```

$$P1a := \frac{1}{8}\frac{a^2\sin(beta)}{\cos(beta)} + \frac{1}{4}aCkKUB1 + \frac{1}{8}C^2k^2K^2U^2 beta$$

```
> P1b := op(1,P1a) + factor(sum(op(i,P1a), i=2..nops(P1a)));
```

$$P1b := \frac{1}{8}\frac{a^2\sin(beta)}{\cos(beta)} + \frac{1}{8}CkKU(beta\,UKkC + 2aB1)$$

```
> P2a := expand(subs(suB2, P2)):
> P2b := op(2,P2a) + factor(sum(op(i,P2a), i=1..nops(P2a))
>        - op(2, P2a)):
> Pc := factor(op(1, P1b) + op(1, P2b))
         + factor(op(2, P1b) + op(2, P2b));
```

$$Pc := \frac{1}{8}\frac{a^2\sin(beta)^2 + b^2\cos(beta)^2}{\cos(beta)\sin(beta)}$$
$$+ \frac{1}{16}CkKU(kKCU\,Pi + 4B1\,a - 4B2\,b)$$

```
> Pc := subsop(1=simplify(subs(beta=alpha, op(1, Pc))), Pc);
```

$$Pc := \frac{1}{4}ba + \frac{1}{16}CkKU(kKUC\,Pi + 4aB1 - 4B2\,b)$$

The base area Pc is described in terms of the input variables, where the variables B1 and B2 depend on a and b only.

```
> BsuB1 := simplify(subs(beta=alpha, rhs(suB1) = lhs(suB1)),
>          symbolic);
```

$$BsuB1 := B1 = \ln((a^2 + b^2)^{1/2} + b) - \ln(a)$$

```
> BsuB2 := simplify(subs(beta=alpha, rhs(suB2) = lhs(suB2)),
          symbolic);
```

$$BsuB2 := B2 = \ln((a^2 + b^2)^{1/2} - a) - \ln(b)$$

The variable C can be found using the condition that the volume remains constant. If $k = 0$, the lateral surface can be curved in the xy plane only. In this case the material volume fulfills the condition

$$Sh = abH, \quad \text{where} \quad \begin{aligned} S &= \text{Base area} \\ h &= \text{Height of the compressed body} \end{aligned} \tag{17.8}$$

If we select $H/h = 4$, then $K = 1$, and k must be implicitly 1, if we use (17.8). The base area Pc then must be four times larger than the initial base area. We continue in MAPLE.

```
> EC := 4*a/2*b/2 = subs(K=1, k=1, Pc);
```

```
  EC := b a = 1/4 b a + 1/16 C U (U C Pi + 4 a B1 - 4 B2 b)
```

```
> SC := solve(EC, C):
> subT := BsuB1, BsuB2, U=sqrt(a^2+b^2), a=8, b=6:
> C1t := evalf(subs(subT, SC[1]));
> C2t := evalf(subs(subT, SC[2]));
```

$$C1t := -2.331649897$$

$$C2t := .7863380120$$

```
> C2 := simplify(SC[2], symbolic);
```

$$C2 := -2 \frac{a\,B1 - B2\,b - (a^2\,B1^2 - 2\,a\,B1\,B2\,b + B2^2\,b^2 + 3\,Pi\,b\,a)^{1/2}}{U\,Pi}$$

```
> C2 := subs(op(1, op(2, op(3, op(2,C2)))) =
>            factor(op(1, op(2, op(3, op(2,C2)))) - 3*Pi*b*a)
>          + 3*Pi*b*a, C2);
```

$$C2 := -2 \frac{a\,B1 - B2\,b - ((a\,B1 - B2\,b)^2 + 3\,Pi\,b\,a)^{1/2}}{U\,Pi}$$

We obtain two roots, where only the positive value makes sense physically. The simplest selection of the correct one is by substitution of numeric values. Now we can plot some examples of distortion of the rectangular base during the stamping process.

```
> subvar := C=C2, Beta[1]=ln(B1), Beta[2]=ln(B2),
>           U=sqrt(a^2+b^2), K=sqrt(H/h)-1:
> subnum := a=8, b=6, H=4, k=1: i := 0:
```

```
> with(plots):
> for hh from 4 by -3/15 to 1 do:
>    F[i]:= polarplot(subs(subvar, subnum, h=hh, rho[1]),
>                     phi=0..subs(subvar, subnum, alpha)):
>    F[i+1]:= polarplot(subs(subvar, subnum, h=hh, rho[2]),
>                     phi=subs(subvar, subnum, alpha)..Pi/2);
>    i := i + 2;
> od:
> display({seq(F[j],j=0..i-1)});
> i := 'i':
```

FIGURE 17.7. *Basis distortion*

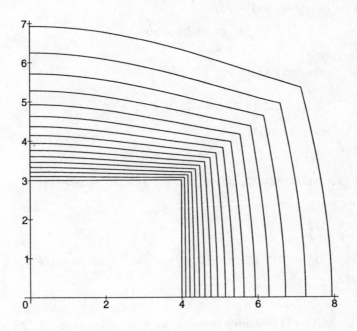

17.3.2   The lateral sides distortion

Let us assume that lateral distortion can be described by a parabolic curve. In the cylindrical coordinate system the shape of the lateral surface is given by

$$\varrho(\varphi, z) = Q_2(\varphi)z^2 + Q_1(\varphi)z + Q_0(\varphi) . \qquad (17.9)$$

According to the preceding part we can find 3 independent equations to determine $Q_2(\varphi)$, $Q_1(\varphi)$ and $Q_0(\varphi)$, cf. (17.2), (17.2) and (17.3).

$$\begin{aligned}
\varrho(\varphi, 0) &= Q_0(\varphi) \\
\varrho(\varphi, h) &= Q_0(\varphi) \\
\iiint dV &= abH .
\end{aligned} \qquad (17.10)$$

To solve (17.10) we use the similar approach as in the Section 17.3.1. We express $\iiint dV$ in cylindrical coordinates and split it into two parts for $0 \leq \varphi \leq \alpha$ and $\alpha \leq \varphi \leq \pi/2$.

$$\iiint dV = 2 \int_0^h \left(\int_0^\alpha \varrho_1(\varphi)^2 \, d\varphi + \int_\alpha^{\pi/2} \varrho_2(\varphi)^2 \, d\varphi \right) dz$$

We shall continue with MAPLE.

```
> Rz := Q2*z^2 + Q1*z + Q0;
```

$$Rz := Q2 \, z^2 + Q1 \, z + Q0$$

```
> E1 := subs(z=0, Rz) = r0;
```

$$E1 := Q0 = r0$$

```
> assign(E1);
> E2 := subs(z=h, Rz) = r0;
```

$$E2 := Q2 \, h^2 + Q1 \, h + r0 = r0$$

```
> Q1 := solve(E2, Q1);
```

$$Q1 := - \, Q2 \, h$$

```
> R3 := Int(Int(Rz^2/2, phi=0..Pi/2), z=0..h) = a*b*H/4;

R3 :=
```

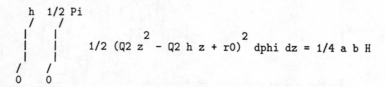

To find the value of the double integral, we first integrate for φ. As in Section 17.3.1 let us skip MAPLE's output.

```
> dV1 := int(subs(r0 = rho[1], Rz^2/2), phi=0..beta):
> dV1a := expand(subs(suB1, dV1)):
> dV1b := factor(sum(op(i, dV1a), i=1..nops(dV1a)-1))
>           + op(nops(dV1a), dV1a):
> dV2 := int(subs(r0 = rho[2], Rz^2/2), phi=beta..Pi/2):
> dV2a := expand(subs(suB2, dV2)):
> dV2b := factor(sum(op(i, dV2a), i=1..nops(dV2a)-1))
>           + op(nops(dV2a), dV2a):
> dV := factor(op(1, dV1b) + op(1, dV2b))
>           + factor(op(2, dV1b) + op(2, dV2b)):
> dV := subsop(2 = simplify(subs(beta = alpha, op(2, dV))), dV):
> R3 := collect(int(dV, z=0..h), h) = a*b*H/4;
```

$$R3 := 1/120\ Q2^2\ Pi\ h^5$$

$$+\ (1/12\ Q2\ B2\ b\ -\ 1/24\ C\ k\ K\ U\ Q2\ Pi\ -\ 1/12\ Q2\ a\ B1)\ h^3$$

$$+\ (-\ 1/4\ b\ C\ k\ K\ U\ B2\ +\ 1/16\ C^2\ k^2\ K^2\ U^2\ Pi$$

$$+\ 1/4\ a\ C\ k\ K\ U\ B1\ +\ 1/4\ b\ a)\ h\ =\ 1/4\ a\ b\ H$$

We solve this quadratic equation for Q2 and obtain two solutions. To select the correct one we substitute the predefined values subnum.

```
> i:= 'i': subnum := a=8, b=6, H=4, h=1, k=1:
> SQ2 := solve(R3, Q2):
> q1 := factor(SQ2[1]):
> q2 := factor(SQ2[2]):
> q1n = evalf(subs(subvar, subnum, q1)),
> q2n = evalf(subs(subvar, subnum, q2));
```

$$q1n\ =\ 77.94969775,\quad q2n\ =\ 0$$

```
> Q2 := q2;
```

$$Q2 := 1/2\ (5\ C\ k\ K\ U\ Pi\ h^3\ -\ 10\ B2\ b\ h^3\ +\ 10\ a\ B1\ h^3\ -\ 5^{1/2}\ ($$

$$h^5\ (-\ h\ C^2\ k^2\ K^2\ U^2\ Pi^2\ +\ 4\ h\ C\ k\ K\ U\ Pi\ B2\ b$$

$$-\ 4\ h\ C\ k\ K\ U\ Pi\ a\ B1\ +\ 20\ h\ B2^2\ b^2\ -\ 40\ h\ B2\ b\ a\ B1$$

$$+\ 20\ h\ a^2\ B1^2\ -\ 24\ h\ Pi\ b\ a\ +\ 24\ Pi\ a\ b\ H))\verb|^|1/2)\ /\ (Pi\ h^5)$$

The function Rz is well known, just note that the variable r0 must be substituted by a different function for each lateral side of the body. To plot the whole compressed body we have to add two new functions rho[3] and rho[4] for the remaining two sides. The system of functions R[i] describes the compressed body.

```
> rho[3] := abs(subs(subvar, a/cos(phi)/2 - Dr)):
> rho[4] := abs(subs(subvar, b/sin(phi)/2 - Dr)):
> for i from 1 to 4 do:
>    R[i] := subs(subvar, Q2*z^2 + Q1*z + rho[i]);
> od:
```

17.3.3 Graphics

The problem now has been solved analytically. For a graphical output let us select the following values: $a = 12$, $b = 8$, $H = 16$, $k = 1/2$. The body will be compressed in 5 steps, reducing its height in each step by the factor 3/4. The whole process will be shown in a 3-dimensional graphical output.

```
> subnum := A = a/2,  a = 12,  B = b/2,  b = 8,  C = H*step,
>             H = 16, step = 3/4,  k = 1/2:
> Alpha := evalf(subs(subnum, alpha));

                    Alpha := .5880026036

> i := 'i': Ni := 9: Nstep := 5:
```

Ni is the number of plotting points used as a parameter for graphical output.
Nstep is the number of the compressions.

```
> In[1] := [seq(-Alpha + 2*Alpha*i/Ni, i=0..Ni)]:
> In[2] := [seq(Alpha + (Pi - 2*Alpha)*i/Ni, i=0..Ni)]:
> In[3] := [seq(Pi - Alpha + 2*Alpha*i/Ni, i=0..Ni)]:
> In[4] := [seq(Pi + Alpha + (Pi - 2*Alpha)*i/Ni, i=0..Ni)]:
```

In[i] is the table of the angles used for drawing the base edges.

```
> phi := 'phi':
> Ia[1] := -Alpha..Alpha:
> Ia[2] := Alpha..Pi - Alpha:
> Ia[3] := Pi - Alpha..Pi + Alpha:
> Ia[4] := Pi + Alpha..2*Pi - Alpha:
```

Ia[i] is the table of the intervals of phi, they are used for plotting the lateral
sides.

```
> BRD := [-A, B, C]:    FRD := [A, B, C]:
> FRT := [A, B, H]:     BRT := [-A, B, H]:
> FLD := [A, -B, C]:    FLT := [A, -B, H]:
> BLD := [-A, -B, C]:   BLT := [-A, -B, H]:
> with(plots):
> Ip := polygonplot3d(subs(subnum, {[BRD, FRD, FRT, BRT],
>               [FRD, FLD, FLT, FRT], [BLD, FLD, FLT, BLT],
>               [BRD, BLD, BLT, BRT], [BLT, FLT, FRT, BRT],
>               [BLD, FLD, FRD, BRD]})):
> P4D := polygonplot3d(subs(subnum, [[-A, -B, 0], [-A, B, 0],
>               [A, B, 0], [A, -B, 0]])):
```

BRD, FRD, etc. are the coordinates of the corners of the uncompressed body,
(Front, Back, Right, Left, Top, Down). Ip shows the uncompressed body pro-
truding the level of the first compression. P4D draws the contour of the initial
body at the level of the stationary platens.

```
> for j from 1 to Nstep do:
>     h := subs(subnum, H*step^j):
>     for i from 1 to 4 do:
>         Rf[i] := evalf(subs(subnum, R[i])):
>     od:
>     L := [seq(seq([Rf[i]*cos(phi), Rf[i]*sin(phi), z],
>           phi=In[i]), i=1..4)]:
```

```
>      phi := 'phi':
>      PTB := polygonplot3d({subs(z=0, L), subs(z=h, L)}):
>      P4T := polygonplot3d(subs(subnum,[[-A,-B,h], [-A,B,h],
                                         [A,B,h], [A,-B,h]])):
>      for i from 1 to 4 do:
>          phi := 'phi':
>          Pl[i] := cylinderplot(Rf[i], phi=Ia[i],
                    z=0..h, numpoints=Ni^2):
>      od:
>      FP[j] := display({PTB, P4T, seq(Pl[i], i=[1,3,4])}):
>      print(FP[j]);
> od:
> display({Ip, P4D, seq(FP[j], j=1..5)}, axes=BOXED,
            title='Stamping of rectangle rod');
```

Rf[i] is the set of the substituted functions. L is the table of the coordinates of the base edges at heights $z = h$ and $z = 0$, which is plotted by PTB. P4T is the projection of the initial base edge to the current stamping level – it is used only for comparisons. Pl[i] is the separate plot of each lateral side, which collects FP[j], together with the plots of the bases and the projection of the initial bases shape. One side – Pl[2] is omitted to be able a look inside the body.

FIGURE 17.8.
Stamping of the rectangle rod
$a = 12$, $b = 8$, $H = 16$, $k = 1/2$, $h_i/h_{i+1} = 3/4$

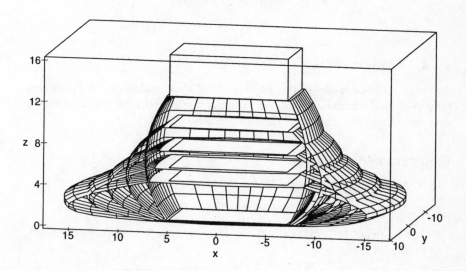

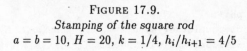

FIGURE 17.9.
Stamping of the square rod
$a = b = 10, H = 20, k = 1/4, h_i/h_{i+1} = 4/5$

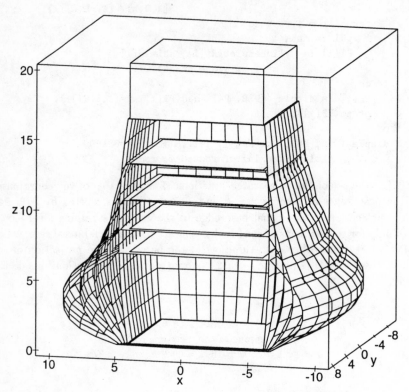

17.4   Conclusions

The mathematical model of the deformation of the metal body can be successfully used for technical calculations. The number of technical experiments can thus be reduced and this saves time and money.

References

[1] B. AVITZUR, *Metal Forming*, Marcel Dekker, New York, 1980.

[2] T. Z. BLAZYNSKI, *Metal Forming*, MacMillan Press LTD, London, 1976.

[3] A. FARLÍK and E. ONDRÁČEK, *Theory of the dynamic forming (in czech)*, SNTL, Praha, 1968.

[4] S. R. REID, *Metal Forming*, Pergamon Press, Oxford, 1985.

Chapter 18. Gauss Quadrature

U. von Matt

18.1 Introduction

In this chapter, we study how to compute Gauss quadrature rules with the help of MAPLE. We consider the integral

$$\int_a^b f(x)\omega(x)\,dx, \tag{18.1}$$

where $\omega(x)$ denotes a nonnegative weight function. We assume that the integrals

$$\int_a^b |x|^k \omega(x)\,dx \tag{18.2}$$

exist for all $k \geq 0$. Additionally, we assume that $\omega(x)$ has only a finite number of zeroes in the interval $[a,b]$ (cf. [20, p. 18]).

The purpose of Gauss quadrature is to approximate the integral (18.1) by the finite sum

$$\int_a^b f(x)\omega(x)\,dx \approx \sum_{i=1}^{m+n} w_i f(x_i), \tag{18.3}$$

where the abscissas x_i and the weights w_i are determined such that all polynomials to as high a degree as possible are integrated exactly.

We also consider the cases of Gauss-Radau and Gauss-Lobatto quadrature where m abscissas on the boundary of the interval $[a,b]$ are prescribed. We denote these prescribed abscissas by $x_1, \ldots, x_m$, where m can take the values $m = 0$, $m = 1$, and $m = 2$.

The theory of Gauss quadrature is a large and varied field. In this chapter we will concentrate on those parts that are necessary to derive the quadrature rules. The reader is also referred to the relevant literature [4, 20, 31].

Orthogonal polynomials play a key role Gauss quadrature. As soon as the three-term recurrence relationship of the orthogonal polynomials is known the abscissas and the weights of the Gauss quadrature rule can be computed by means of an eigenvalue decomposition. In Section 18.2 we will therefore derive two alternative ways of computing the orthogonal polynomials.

In the first case the interval $[a,b]$ and the weight function $\omega(x)$ have to be known explicitly. Then we can use the Lanczos algorithm to compute the three-term recurrence relationship of the orthogonal polynomials by symbolic integration.

In the other case only the moment corresponding to the interval $[a, b]$ and the weight function $\omega(x)$ need to be available. We present an algorithm to compute the three-term recurrence relationship of the orthogonal polynomials based on the Cholesky decomposition of the Gram matrix.

In Section 18.3 we prove a theorem which is fundamental to the calculation of Gauss quadrature rules. On the basis of this theorem we can give algorithms to compute Gauss, Gauss-Radau, and Gauss-Lobatto quadrature rules in Sections 18.4, 18.5, and 18.6. The calculation of the weights w_i is addressed in Section 18.7. Finally, we derive an expression for the quadrature error in Section 18.8.

The calculation of Gauss quadrature rules is a rewarding application of MAPLE. We can use its symbolic capabilities to compute the coefficients of the three-term recurrence relationship exactly. Since MAPLE also supports floating-point arithmetic with an arbitrary precision we can compute the abscissas and weights of the quadrature rules by an eigenvalue decomposition to any desired accuracy.

18.2   Orthogonal Polynomials

In this section we discuss several approaches to computing the orthogonal polynomials corresponding to the interval $[a, b]$ and the weight function $\omega(x)$.

DEFINITION 18.0.1. *We denote by*

$$(f, g) := \int_a^b f(x)g(x)\omega(x)\,dx \tag{18.4}$$

the inner product with respect to the weight function $\omega(x)$ and the interval $[a, b]$.

This inner product has also the important property that

$$(xf, g) = (f, xg), \tag{18.5}$$

which will be used frequently throughout this chapter.

DEFINITION 18.0.2. *The expression*

$$\mu_k := (x^k, 1) = \int_a^b x^k \omega(x)\,dx \tag{18.6}$$

is called the k'th moment with respect to the weight function $\omega(x)$.

Many books are concerned with calculating Gauss quadrature rules from these ordinary moments [1, 6, 28, 33]. This approach, however, is cursed with numerical instabilities, as Gautschi has shown in [9]. As a remedy, so-called modified moments are introduced (cf. [10, p. 245] and [27, p. 466]).

DEFINITION 18.0.3. *The expression*

$$\nu_k := (\pi_k, 1) = \int_a^b \pi_k(x)\omega(x)\,dx, \tag{18.7}$$

where π_k denotes a polynomial with exact degree k, is called the k'th modified moment with respect to the weight function $\omega(x)$.

We assume that the polynomials $\pi_0(x), \pi_1(x), \ldots$ satisfy the three-term recurrence relationship

$$x\pi_{k-1} = \hat{\gamma}_{k-1}\pi_{k-2} + \hat{\alpha}_k\pi_{k-1} + \hat{\beta}_k\pi_k, \qquad k = 1, 2, \ldots \qquad (18.8)$$

where $\hat{\gamma}_0 := 0$ and $\pi_{-1}(x) := 0$. The coefficients $\hat{\beta}_k$ are supposed to be non-zero.

The ordinary moments μ_k represent a special case of the modified moments ν_k. They can be obtained by setting $\pi_k(x) = x^k$. In this case the three-term recurrence relationship (18.8) is given by $\hat{\alpha}_k = \hat{\gamma}_k = 0$ and $\hat{\beta}_k = 1$.

DEFINITION 18.0.4. *We define the matrix*

$$M := \begin{bmatrix} m_{00} & \cdots & \cdots & m_{0,n-1} \\ \vdots & & & \vdots \\ \vdots & & & \vdots \\ m_{n-1,0} & \cdots & \cdots & m_{n-1,n-1} \end{bmatrix} \qquad (18.9)$$

to be the Gram matrix of order n, where each entry

$$m_{ij} := (\pi_i, \pi_j) \qquad (18.10)$$

is an inner product.

Not only is the matrix M symmetric, but because of

$$\mathbf{v}^T M \mathbf{v} = \sum_{i=0}^{n-1} \sum_{j=0}^{n-1} v_i m_{ij} v_j = \left(\sum_{i=0}^{n-1} v_i \pi_i, \sum_{j=0}^{n-1} v_j \pi_j \right) > 0$$

for $\mathbf{v} \neq \mathbf{0}$ it is also positive definite.

Now we show how the matrix M can be computed from the modified moments ν_k and the three-term recurrence relationship (18.8). A similar derivation can also be found in [10, pp. 255–256].

Since $\pi_0(x)$ is a constant, we immediately have

$$m_{i0} = (\pi_i, \pi_0) = \pi_0 \nu_i, \qquad m_{0j} = (\pi_0, \pi_j) = \pi_0 \nu_j. \qquad (18.11)$$

Consequently, we will assume $i > 0$ and $j > 0$ in the following. If we substitute in (18.10) the polynomial $\pi_j(x)$ by the recurrence relationship (18.8), we get

$$m_{ij} = (\pi_i, \pi_j) = \frac{1}{\hat{\beta}_j} (\pi_i, x\pi_{j-1} - \hat{\gamma}_{j-1}\pi_{j-2} - \hat{\alpha}_j\pi_{j-1})$$

$$= \frac{1}{\hat{\beta}_j} ((x\pi_i, \pi_{j-1}) - \hat{\gamma}_{j-1}m_{i,j-2} - \hat{\alpha}_j m_{i,j-1}).$$

Applying the recurrence relationship (18.8) once more for substituting $x\pi_i(x)$ one has

$$m_{ij} = \frac{1}{\hat{\beta}_j} ((\hat{\gamma}_i\pi_{i-1} + \hat{\alpha}_{i+1}\pi_i + \hat{\beta}_{i+1}\pi_{i+1}, \pi_{j-1}) - \hat{\gamma}_{j-1}m_{i,j-2} - \hat{\alpha}_j m_{i,j-1})$$

or

$$m_{ij} = \frac{1}{\hat{\beta}_j}(\hat{\gamma}_i m_{i-1,j-1} + (\hat{\alpha}_{i+1} - \hat{\alpha}_j)m_{i,j-1} + \hat{\beta}_{i+1}m_{i+1,j-1} - \hat{\gamma}_{j-1}m_{i,j-2}), \quad (18.12)$$

where $m_{i,-1} = 0$. Consequently, we have in (18.12) a recursive scheme to progressively build up the matrix M from the initial values (18.11).

The dependencies in (18.12) can also be described by the following stencil:

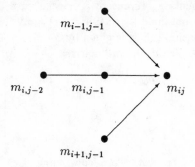

This picture indicates which entries of the matrix M have to be known before the value of m_{ij} can be computed. The calculation of the Gram matrix M is also shown in MAPLE as Algorithm 18.1.

DEFINITION 18.0.5. *The polynomials $p_0(x), p_1(x), \ldots$ are called orthogonal polynomials with respect to the inner product (18.4), if the following conditions are met:*

1. *$p_k(x)$ is of degree k.*

2. *The polynomial $p_k(x)$ satisfies the orthogonality condition*

$$(p_k, p) = 0 \qquad (18.13)$$

   for all polynomials $p(x)$ of degree less than k.

3. *The polynomial $p_k(x)$ satisfies the normalization condition*

$$(p_k, p_k) = 1. \qquad (18.14)$$

Because of condition (18.14) the polynomial p_0 must be a constant different from zero. Therefore a simple corollary of (18.13) consists in

$$(p_k, 1) = 0 \qquad (18.15)$$

for $k \geq 1$.

The following theorem ensures the existence of orthogonal polynomials with respect to the inner product (18.4), and it shows a first way of computing them.

THEOREM 18.1. *For any given admissible inner product there exists a sequence $\{p_k(x)\}_{k=0}^{\infty}$ of orthogonal polynomials.*

ALGORITHM 18.1.
Calculation of the Gram matrix M from Modified
Moments.

```
Gram := proc (pi0, alphahat, betahat, gammahat, nu, n)
  local i, j, M;

  M := array (symmetric, 0..2*n-1, 0..2*n-1);
  for i from 0 to 2*n-1 do
    M[i,0] := simplify (pi0 * nu[i]);
  od;
  for i from 1 to 2*n-2 do
    M[i,1] := simplify (
                (gammahat[i] * M[i-1,0] +
                (alphahat[i+1] - alphahat[1]) * M[i,0] +
                betahat[i+1] * M[i+1,0]) / betahat[1]);
  od;
  for j from 2 to n-1 do
    for i from j to 2*n-1-j do
      M[i,j] := simplify (
                  (gammahat[i] * M[i-1,j-1] +
                  (alphahat[i+1] - alphahat[j]) * M[i,j-1] +
                  betahat[i+1] * M[i+1,j-1] -
                  gammahat[j-1] * M[i,j-2]) / betahat[j]);
    od;
  od;

  RETURN (M);
end:
```

PROOF. According to a paper of Mysovskih [22], we set up $p_k(x)$ as

$$p_k(x) = \sum_{i=0}^{k} s_{ki}\pi_i(x). \tag{18.16}$$

We define the lower triangular matrix

$$S := \begin{bmatrix} s_{00} & & & \\ \vdots & \ddots & & \\ \vdots & & \ddots & \\ \vdots & & & \ddots \\ s_{n-1,0} & \cdots & \cdots & s_{n-1,n-1} \end{bmatrix}. \tag{18.17}$$

The orthogonality condition (18.13) implies

$$\Big(\sum_{i=0}^{k} s_{ki}\pi_i, \sum_{j=0}^{l} s_{lj}\pi_j\Big) = \sum_{i=0}^{k}\sum_{j=0}^{l} s_{ki}s_{lj}m_{ij} = 0 \tag{18.18}$$

for $k \neq l$. The normalization condition (18.14) means that

$$\left(\sum_{i=0}^{k} s_{ki}\pi_i, \sum_{i=0}^{k} s_{ki}\pi_i\right) = \sum_{i=0}^{k} \sum_{j=0}^{k} s_{ki}s_{kj}m_{ij} = 1. \tag{18.19}$$

In matrix terms conditions (18.18) and (18.19) can be represented by

$$SMS^{T} = I,$$

where M denotes the Gram matrix from (18.9). Because M is a symmetric and positive definite matrix we can compute the Cholesky decomposition

$$M = LL^{T} \tag{18.20}$$

with the lower triangular matrix L. Since the inverse of L is a lower triangular matrix as well, we have found the desired matrix S in $S := L^{-1}$. $\square$

In contrast to (18.16) the following representation of the orthogonal polynomials is usually more useful.

THEOREM 18.2. *The orthogonal polynomials* $p_0(x), p_1(x), \ldots$ *satisfy the three-term recurrence relationship*

$$xp_{k-1} = \beta_{k-1}p_{k-2} + \alpha_k p_{k-1} + \beta_k p_k, \qquad k = 1, 2, \ldots \tag{18.21}$$

with

$$\alpha_k = (xp_{k-1}, p_{k-1}), \tag{18.22}$$

$$\beta_k = (xp_{k-1}, p_k), \tag{18.23}$$

where $\beta_0 := 0$, $p_{-1}(x) := 0$, *and* $p_0(x) := \pm\sqrt{1/\mu_0} = \pm\sqrt{\pi_0/\nu_0}$.

PROOF. Obviously, xp_{k-1} can be written as

$$xp_{k-1} = \sum_{i=0}^{k} c_i p_i$$

with $c_i = (p_i, xp_{k-1}) = (xp_i, p_{k-1})$. Because of (18.13) we have $c_0 = \cdots = c_{k-3} = 0$. If we define α_k and β_k according to (18.22) and (18.23), we can immediately derive (18.21). $\square$

This theorem allows us to derive a first recursive algorithm for the calculation of the orthogonal polynomials. If the coefficients $\alpha_1, \ldots, \alpha_k$ and $\beta_1, \ldots, \beta_{k-1}$ as well as the polynomials $p_0, \ldots, p_{k-1}$ are known, then p_k is already determined up to a multiple due to Equation (18.21). We have

$$q_k := \beta_k p_k = (x - \alpha_k)p_{k-1} - \beta_{k-1}p_{k-2}. \tag{18.24}$$

The normalization condition (18.14) implies

$$\beta_k = \pm\sqrt{(q_k, q_k)}, \tag{18.25}$$

and thus $p_k = q_k/\beta_k$. Finally, the value of α_{k+1} is given by (18.22).

ALGORITHM 18.2. *Lanczos Algorithm.*

```
Lanczos := proc (iprod, alpha, beta, n)
  local k, p, q, x;

  alpha := array (1..n);
  if n > 1 then beta := array (1..n-1) else beta := 'beta' fi;

  p[0] := collect (1 / sqrt (iprod (1, 1, x)), x, simplify);
  alpha[1] := normal (iprod (x*p[0], p[0], x));
  q := collect ((x - alpha[1]) * p[0], x, simplify);
  for k from 2 to n do
    beta[k-1] := normal (sqrt (iprod (q, q, x)));
    p[k-1] := collect (q / beta[k-1], x, simplify);
    alpha[k] := normal (iprod (x*p[k-1], p[k-1], x));
    q := collect ((x - alpha[k]) * p[k-1] - beta[k-1]*p[k-2],
                  x, simplify);
  od;

  RETURN (NULL);
end:
```

This recursive scheme is also known as the Lanczos algorithm. We present its implementation in MAPLE as Algorithm 18.2. It should be noted that the inner product (18.4) is passed as the parameter iprod. As an example, we can use the statements

```
> a := 0;  b := infinity;
> omega := t -> exp (-t);
> iprod := (f, g, x) -> int (f * g * omega (x), x=a..b);
> n := 10;
> Lanczos (iprod, 'alpha', 'beta', n);
```

to compute the recurrence coefficients $\alpha_k = 2k - 1$ and $\beta_k = k$ of the Laguerre polynomials.

The Lanczos algorithm requires the capability of evaluating the inner product (18.4) with arbitrary polynomials. It is also possible to derive an alternative algorithm based only on the knowledge of the modified moments (18.7).

In the proof of Theorem 18.1 we have presented a way of computing the orthogonal polynomials which is based on the Cholesky decomposition (18.20) of the Gram matrix M. The matrix S, which is used to represent the p_k's in (18.16), has been obtained as the inverse of the Cholesky factor L. The direct evaluation of the Cholesky decomposition (18.20) requires $O(n^3)$ operations [17, Section 4.2]. However, we will now show that the entries of the matrix L satisfy a similar recurrence relationship as those of the Gram matrix M. This observation will allow us to devise a modified algorithm which only requires $O(n^2)$ operations.

Because of $S = L^{-1}$ we have

$$L = MS^{\mathrm{T}}$$

from (18.20). The entry l_{ij} of L can thus be written as

$$l_{ij} = \sum_{k=0}^{j} m_{ik}s_{jk} = \left(\pi_i, \sum_{k=0}^{j} s_{jk}\pi_k\right),$$

and because of (18.16) we get

$$l_{ij} = (\pi_i, p_j). \tag{18.26}$$

Due to (18.20) the value of l_{00} is given by

$$l_{00} = \sqrt{m_{00}}. \tag{18.27}$$

We will assume $i > 0$ in the following. If we substitute in (18.26) the polynomial π_i by means of the recurrence relationship (18.8), we get

$$l_{ij} = (\pi_i, p_j) = \frac{1}{\hat{\beta}_i}(x\pi_{i-1} - \hat{\gamma}_{i-1}\pi_{i-2} - \hat{\alpha}_i\pi_{i-1}, p_j)$$

$$= \frac{1}{\hat{\beta}_i}((x\pi_{i-1}, p_j) - \hat{\gamma}_{i-1}l_{i-2,j} - \hat{\alpha}_i l_{i-1,j}).$$

Now, we can use the recurrence relationship (18.21) to substitute the polynomial $xp_j(x)$ in the expression $(x\pi_{i-1}, p_j) = (\pi_{i-1}, xp_j)$. This leads to

$$l_{ij} = \frac{1}{\hat{\beta}_i}((\pi_{i-1}, \beta_j p_{j-1} + \alpha_{j+1}p_j + \beta_{j+1}p_{j+1}) - \hat{\gamma}_{i-1}l_{i-2,j} - \hat{\alpha}_i l_{i-1,j})$$

or

$$l_{ij} = \frac{1}{\hat{\beta}_i}(\beta_j l_{i-1,j-1} + (\alpha_{j+1} - \hat{\alpha}_i)l_{i-1,j} + \beta_{j+1}l_{i-1,j+1} - \hat{\gamma}_{i-1}l_{i-2,j}), \tag{18.28}$$

where $l_{-1,j} = 0$. We have derived a recurrence relationship for the elements of the matrix L. The dependencies in L can also be described by the following stencil:

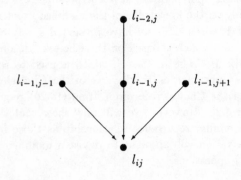

One should note, however, that the unknown coefficients α_k and β_k appear as well in Equation (18.28). Therefore, we cannot compute all the entries in L according to (18.28).

If $\alpha_1, \ldots, \alpha_{k-1}$ and $\beta_1, \ldots, \beta_{k-1}$ as well as all the l_{ij}'s with $i < k$ are known, we can use (18.28) to compute l_{kj} for $j = 0, \ldots, k-2$. The values of

$$l_{k,k-1} = \frac{1}{l_{k-1,k-1}}(m_{k,k-1} - \sum_{j=0}^{k-2} l_{kj}l_{k-1,j}) \qquad (18.29)$$

and

$$l_{kk} = \sqrt{m_{kk} - \sum_{j=0}^{k-1} l_{kj}^2} \qquad (18.30)$$

are available from the Cholesky decomposition (18.20) of M. On the other hand the recurrence relationship (18.28) gives the expression

$$l_{k,k-1} = \frac{1}{\hat{\beta}_k}(\beta_{k-1}l_{k-1,k-2} + (\alpha_k - \hat{\alpha}_k)l_{k-1,k-1}) \qquad (18.31)$$

for $l_{k,k-1}$. If we solve (18.31) for α_k we get

$$\alpha_k = \hat{\alpha}_k + \frac{\hat{\beta}_k l_{k,k-1} - \beta_{k-1}l_{k-1,k-2}}{l_{k-1,k-1}}. \qquad (18.32)$$

In the same way we get

$$l_{kk} = \frac{1}{\hat{\beta}_k}\beta_k l_{k-1,k-1} \qquad (18.33)$$

from (18.28), such that

$$\beta_k = \hat{\beta}_k \frac{l_{kk}}{l_{k-1,k-1}}. \qquad (18.34)$$

In [27] Sack and Donovan introduced a similar approach to computing the three-term recurrence relationship (18.21) from modified moments. They called it the "long quotient—modified difference (LQMD) algorithm". Gautschi presented in [10] a related algorithm based on the Cholesky decomposition (18.20) of the Gram matrix M. Unfortunately, he did not notice the recurrence relationship (18.28) of the entries in the Cholesky factor L. Although his presentation is much clearer than that by Sack and Donovan, the amount of work required by his algorithm is of the order $O(n^3)$.

Let us now present the implementation of our approach in MAPLE as Algorithm 18.3. For a given n, the constant polynomial π_0, the coefficients $\hat{\alpha}_k$, $k = 1, \ldots, 2n-1$, $\hat{\beta}_k$, $k = 1, \ldots, 2n-1$, and $\hat{\gamma}_k$, $k = 1, \ldots, 2n-2$, as well as the modified moments ν_k, $k = 0, \ldots, 2n-1$, must be supplied as input parameters. Then, Algorithm 18.3 builds up the Gram matrix M based on the recursive formulas (18.11) and (18.12). Afterwards, it uses Equations (18.27), (18.28), (18.29), (18.30), (18.32), and (18.34) to construct the Cholesky factor L as well

ALGORITHM 18.3.
Calculation of the Three-Term Recurrence
Relationship (18.21)
from Modified Moments.

```
SackDonovan := proc (pi0, alphahat, betahat, gammahat, nu, n,
                     alpha, beta)
  local j, k, L, M;

  M := Gram (pi0, alphahat, betahat, gammahat, nu, n);
  L := array (0..n, 0..n);
  alpha := array (1..n);
  if n > 1 then beta := array (1..n-1) else beta := 'beta' fi;
  L[0,0] := simplify (sqrt (M[0,0]));
  L[1,0] := simplify (M[1,0] / L[0,0]);
  alpha[1] := simplify (
                  alphahat[1] + betahat[1] * L[1,0] / L[0,0]);
  k := 1;
  while k < n do
    L[k,k] := simplify (
                  sqrt (M[k,k] - sum ('L[k,j]^2', 'j'=0..k-1)));
    beta[k] := simplify (betahat[k] * L[k,k] / L[k-1,k-1]);
    k := k+1;
    L[k,0] := M[k,0] / L[0,0];
    for j from 1 to k-2 do
      L[k,j] := simplify (
                    (beta[j] * L[k-1,j-1] +
                    (alpha[j+1] - alphahat[k]) * L[k-1,j] +
                    beta[j+1] * L[k-1,j+1] -
                    gammahat[k-1] * L[k-2,j]) / betahat[k]);
    od;
    L[k,k-1] := simplify (
                    (M[k,k-1] -
                    sum ('L[k,j] * L[k-1,j]', 'j'=0..k-2)) /
                    L[k-1,k-1]);
    alpha[k] := simplify (
                    alphahat[k] +
                    (betahat[k] * L[k,k-1] -
                    beta[k-1] * L[k-1,k-2]) / L[k-1,k-1]);
  od;

  RETURN (NULL);
end:
```

as the coefficients α_k, $k = 1, \ldots, n$, and β_k, $k = 1, \ldots, n - 1$ of the three-term recurrence relationship (18.21). The amount of work required by this algorithm is of the order $O(n^2)$.

The amount of storage needed by Algorithm 18.3 is also of the order $O(n^2)$. A more elaborate implementation, like that given by Sack and Donovan, could even get by with storage requirements proportional to n. For the sake of clarity we do not pursue this any further.

The reader should notice that the savings of Algorithm 18.3 over the algorithm given by Gautschi can only be attained in floating-point arithmetic. In a symbolic calculation, as it is performed in MAPLE, not only the number of operations but also the size of the operands affects the total execution time. Although Algorithm 18.3 needs less arithmetic operations compared to the algorithm by Gautschi the operands tend to be more complex. Consequently, we do not observe significant speedups by our algorithm over that given by Gautschi.

As a sample application of Algorithm 18.3 we consider the calculation of the orthogonal polynomials that correspond to the interval $[0, \infty]$ and the two weight functions

$$\omega_{\cos}(x) := e^{-x}(1 + \cos \varphi x), \tag{18.35}$$

$$\omega_{\sin}(x) := e^{-x}(1 + \sin \varphi x). \tag{18.36}$$

It is well-known that the Laguerre polynomials $L_n(x)$ are the orthogonal polynomials with respect to the same interval and the weight function $\omega(x) = e^{-x}$. Therefore, it is sensible to consider the modified moments

$$\nu_n^{\cos} := \int_0^\infty L_n(x)\omega_{\cos}(x)\,dx, \tag{18.37}$$

$$\nu_n^{\sin} := \int_0^\infty L_n(x)\omega_{\sin}(x)\,dx. \tag{18.38}$$

We now show how the modified moments $\nu_n^{\cos}$ and $\nu_n^{\sin}$ can be computed analytically.

THEOREM 18.3. *The polynomial*

$$L_n(x) := \sum_{k=0}^n (-1)^{n-k}\binom{n}{k}\frac{x^k}{k!} \tag{18.39}$$

is the n'th Laguerre polynomial.

PROOF. The Laguerre polynomials are known to satisfy the three-term recurrence relationship (18.21) with $p_0 = 1$, $\alpha_k = 2k - 1$, and $\beta_k = k$. Since the polynomials defined by (18.39) satisfy the same recurrence relationship they must be identical to the Laguerre polynomials. $\square$

For any complex constant c with $\Re(c) < 0$ we have

$$\int_0^\infty x^n e^{cx}\,dx = n!\left(\frac{-1}{c}\right)^{n+1}. \tag{18.40}$$

This identity can be proved by partial integration and by induction on n. Because of Equations (18.39) and (18.40) we can also show that

$$\int_0^\infty L_n(x)e^{cx}\,dx = (-1)^{n+1}\frac{(c+1)^n}{c^{n+1}}. \tag{18.41}$$

Consequently, we have

$$\int_0^\infty L_n(x)e^{-x}\cos\varphi x\,dx = \Re\Big(\int_0^\infty L_n(x)e^{(-1+i\varphi)x}\,dx\Big)$$

$$= (-1)^{n+1}\Re\Big(\frac{(i\varphi)^n}{(-1+i\varphi)^{n+1}}\Big)$$

$$= \frac{(-1)^n\varphi^n}{(1+\varphi^2)^{n+1}}\sum_{k=0}^{\lfloor\frac{n}{2}\rfloor}\binom{n+1}{2k+1}(-1)^k\varphi^{n-2k},$$

and

$$\int_0^\infty L_n(x)e^{-x}\sin\varphi x\,dx = \Im\Big(\int_0^\infty L_n(x)e^{(-1+i\varphi)x}\,dx\Big)$$

$$= (-1)^{n+1}\Im\Big(\frac{(i\varphi)^n}{(-1+i\varphi)^{n+1}}\Big)$$

$$= \frac{(-1)^n\varphi^n}{(1+\varphi^2)^{n+1}}\sum_{k=0}^{\lfloor\frac{n+1}{2}\rfloor}\binom{n+1}{2k}(-1)^k\varphi^{n+1-2k}.$$

We can now express the modified moments (18.37) and (18.38) by

$$\nu_0^{\cos} = 1 + \frac{1}{1+\varphi^2}, \tag{18.42}$$

$$\nu_n^{\cos} = \frac{(-1)^n\varphi^n}{(1+\varphi^2)^{n+1}}\sum_{k=0}^{\lfloor\frac{n}{2}\rfloor}\binom{n+1}{2k+1}(-1)^k\varphi^{n-2k}, \qquad n > 0, \tag{18.43}$$

$$\nu_0^{\sin} = 1 + \frac{\varphi}{1+\varphi^2}, \tag{18.44}$$

$$\nu_n^{\sin} = \frac{(-1)^n\varphi^n}{(1+\varphi^2)^{n+1}}\sum_{k=0}^{\lfloor\frac{n+1}{2}\rfloor}\binom{n+1}{2k}(-1)^k\varphi^{n+1-2k}, \qquad n > 0. \tag{18.45}$$

By the MAPLE statements

```
> N := 10;
> phi := 1;

> alphahat := array (1..2*N-1, [seq (2*k-1, k=1..2*N-1)]);
> betahat := array (1..2*N-1, [seq (k, k=1..2*N-1)]);
> gammahat := array (1..2*N-2, [seq (k, k=1..2*N-2)]);
> L := (n, x) -> sum ('(-1)^(n-k) * binomial (n,k) * x^k / k!',
>                      'k'=0..n);
```

TABLE 18.1. *Values of $\alpha_n^{\cos}$ and $\beta_n^{\cos}$ for $\varphi = 1$.*

n	$\alpha_n^{\cos}$	$\beta_n^{\cos}$
1	$\frac{2}{3} \approx 0.66667$	$\frac{\sqrt{5}}{3} \approx 0.74536$
2	$\frac{53}{15} \approx 3.5333$	$\frac{12}{5} \approx 2.4000$
3	$\frac{329}{80} \approx 4.1125$	$\frac{\sqrt{1655}}{16} \approx 2.5426$
4	$\frac{44489}{5296} \approx 8.4005$	$\frac{8\sqrt{29499}}{331} \approx 4.1511$
5	$\frac{26238754}{3254723} \approx 8.0617$	$\frac{5\sqrt{91073657}}{9833} \approx 4.8527$
6	$\frac{31146028765}{2705520451} \approx 11.512$	$\frac{18\sqrt{10403284501}}{275147} \approx 6.6726$
7	$\frac{41962386991493}{3493256406708} \approx 12.012$	$\frac{7\sqrt{123806905335947}}{12695964} \approx 6.1349$
8	$\frac{99084727782033173}{5712757228305564} \approx 17.344$	$\frac{8\sqrt{213374749185568311}}{449966401} \approx 8.2126$
9	$\frac{465045058223400793942}{30249445557756103921} \approx 15.374$	$\frac{15\sqrt{1585460418582456041029}}{67226009521} \approx 8.8845$

```
> nucos[0] := 1 + 1 / (1+phi^2):
> for n from 1 to 2*N-1 do
>   nucos[n] := (-1)^n * phi^n / (1+phi^2)^(n+1) *
>               sum ('binomial (n+1,2*k+1) *
>                   (-1)^k * phi^(n-2*k)', 'k'=0..floor (n/2));
> od:
> nusin[0] := 1 + phi / (1+phi^2):
> for n from 1 to 2*N-1 do
>   nusin[n] := (-1)^n * phi^n / (1+phi^2)^(n+1) *
>               sum ('binomial (n+1,2*k) * (-1)^k *
>                   phi^(n+1-2*k)', 'k'=0..floor ((n+1)/2));
> od:

> SackDonovan (L (0, x), alphahat, betahat, gammahat, nucos, N,
>               'alphacos', 'betacos');
> SackDonovan (L (0, x), alphahat, betahat, gammahat, nusin, N,
>               'alphasin', 'betasin');
```

we can compute the three-term recurrence relationship (18.21) of the orthogonal polynomials corresponding to the interval $[0, \infty]$ and the two weight functions $\omega_{\cos}$ and $\omega_{\sin}$. We get the results shown as Tables 18.1 and 18.2.

THEOREM 18.4. *The orthogonal polynomial $p_k(x)$ has exactly k distinct zeroes $a < x_1 < \cdots < x_k < b$.*

PROOF. The proof is by contradiction (cf. [20, p. 21]). Let us assume that the polynomial $p_k(x)$ has only $k' < k$ zeroes ζ_i with odd multiplicity in the interval $]a, b[$. Consequently, the polynomial

$$q(x) := \prod_{i=1}^{k'} (x - \zeta_i)$$

TABLE 18.2. Values of $\alpha_n^{\sin}$ and $\beta_n^{\sin}$ for $\varphi = 1$.

n	$\alpha_n^{\sin}$	$\beta_n^{\sin}$
1	$1 \approx 1.0000$	$\frac{\sqrt{6}}{3} \approx 0.81650$
2	$\frac{5}{2} \approx 2.5000$	$\frac{\sqrt{165}}{6} \approx 2.1409$
3	$\frac{127}{22} \approx 5.7727$	$\frac{18\sqrt{65}}{55} \approx 2.6386$
4	$\frac{2578}{429} \approx 6.0093$	$\frac{\sqrt{784190}}{195} \approx 4.5413$
5	$\frac{2747911}{278031} \approx 9.8835$	$\frac{830\sqrt{1365}}{7129} \approx 4.3015$
6	$\frac{14684038321}{1375127068} \approx 10.678$	$\frac{3\sqrt{176313765003}}{192892} \approx 6.5306$
7	$\frac{21638014309259}{1590195668348} \approx 13.607$	$\frac{16268\sqrt{11567141}}{8243969} \approx 6.7114$
8	$\frac{9020385319743068}{667514062758403} \approx 13.513$	$\frac{54\sqrt{165092626746123}}{80969987} \approx 8.5691$
9	$\frac{2469307519278826001}{131341029442952049} \approx 18.801$	$\frac{\sqrt{1615594742551806361 94}}{1622095227} \approx 7.8359$

has the same sign changes as $p_k(x)$ in this interval. This means that the product $p_k(x)q(x)$ has no sign change in the interval $]a, b[$, such that

$$(p_k, q) \neq 0,$$

which contradicts the orthogonality property (18.13) of $p_k(x)$. $\square$

The following theorem establishes a link between a sequence $\{p_k\}_{k=0}^n$ of polynomials, which are defined by the three-term recurrence relationship (18.21), on the one hand and the eigenvalue decomposition of the tridiagonal matrix T with the coefficients α_k and β_k on the other hand.

THEOREM 18.5. *A polynomial $p_n(x)$ of degree n, which can be represented by a three-term recurrence relationship (18.21) with $\beta_k \neq 0$, has as zeroes the eigenvalues $x_1 < \cdots < x_n$ of the tridiagonal matrix*

$$T_n := \begin{bmatrix} \alpha_1 & \beta_1 & & \\ \beta_1 & \ddots & \ddots & \\ & \ddots & \ddots & \beta_{n-1} \\ & & \beta_{n-1} & \alpha_n \end{bmatrix}. \qquad (18.46)$$

Furthermore, let

$$T_n = QXQ^{\mathrm{T}} \qquad (18.47)$$

be the eigenvalue decomposition of T_n, where X denotes the eigenvalue matrix with $x_1, \ldots, x_n$ as diagonal entries and Q denotes the orthogonal eigenvector matrix. Assume the definitions

$$P := \begin{bmatrix} p_0(x_1) & \cdots & p_0(x_n) \\ \vdots & & \vdots \\ p_{n-1}(x_1) & \cdots & p_{n-1}(x_n) \end{bmatrix} \qquad (18.48)$$

and

$$W := \frac{1}{p_0} \begin{bmatrix} q_{11} & & \\ & \ddots & \\ & & q_{1n} \end{bmatrix}. \tag{18.49}$$

Then, we have

$$Q = PW. \tag{18.50}$$

PROOF. The three-term recurrence relationship (18.21) can be written in matrix terms as

$$x \begin{bmatrix} p_0 \\ \vdots \\ \vdots \\ p_{n-1} \end{bmatrix} = \begin{bmatrix} \alpha_1 & \beta_1 & & \\ \beta_1 & \ddots & \ddots & \\ & \ddots & \ddots & \beta_{n-1} \\ & & \beta_{n-1} & \alpha_n \end{bmatrix} \begin{bmatrix} p_0 \\ \vdots \\ \vdots \\ p_{n-1} \end{bmatrix} + \begin{bmatrix} 0 \\ \vdots \\ 0 \\ \beta_n p_n \end{bmatrix}. \tag{18.51}$$

It is well-known [23, p. 124], that T_n possesses n real, distinct eigenvalues $x_1 < \cdots < x_n$. Let us now consider an individual eigenvector $\mathbf{q}$ corresponding to an eigenvalue λ:

$$T_n \mathbf{q} = \lambda \mathbf{q}. \tag{18.52}$$

This is equivalent to the n equations

$$\begin{aligned} \alpha_1 q_1 + \beta_1 q_2 &= \lambda q_1, \\ \beta_{k-1} q_{k-1} + \alpha_k q_k + \beta_k q_{k+1} &= \lambda q_k, \qquad k = 2, \ldots, n-1, \\ \beta_{n-1} q_{n-1} + \alpha_n q_n &= \lambda q_n. \end{aligned} \tag{18.53}$$

Therefore, the elements of the vector $\mathbf{q}$ satisfy the three-term recurrence relationship

$$\begin{aligned} q_2 &= \frac{\lambda - \alpha_1}{\beta_1} q_1, \\ q_{k+1} &= \frac{\lambda - \alpha_k}{\beta_k} q_k - \frac{\beta_{k-1}}{\beta_k} q_{k-1}, \qquad k = 2, \ldots, n-1, \end{aligned} \tag{18.54}$$

where q_1 is chosen so that $\|\mathbf{q}\|_2 = 1$. Since $\beta_k \neq 0$, it is clear that the first element of each eigenvector must be different from zero. Otherwise, the whole vector would consist of zeroes—an obvious contradiction to the definition of an eigenvector.

On the other hand, we define

$$\mathbf{p}(x) := \begin{bmatrix} p_0(x) \\ \vdots \\ p_{n-1}(x) \end{bmatrix}. \tag{18.55}$$

From (18.21) we can see that the elements of the vector $\mathbf{p}(\lambda)$ obey the three-term recurrence relationship

$$p_1(\lambda) = \frac{\lambda - \alpha_1}{\beta_1}p_0(\lambda),$$

$$p_k(\lambda) = \frac{\lambda - \alpha_k}{\beta_k}p_{k-1}(\lambda) - \frac{\beta_{k-1}}{\beta_k}p_{k-2}(\lambda), \qquad k = 2,\ldots,n, \tag{18.56}$$

which is indeed the same as (18.54) except for a different initial value. Consequently, the vectors $\mathbf{q}$ and $\mathbf{p}(\lambda)$ must be equal up to a scaling factor:

$$\mathbf{q} = \frac{q_1}{p_0}\mathbf{p}(\lambda). \tag{18.57}$$

Because of $\beta_n \neq 0$, Equation (18.51) implies $p_n(\lambda) = 0$. If we evaluate (18.57) for each eigenvalue x_k, we get (18.50). □

18.3   Quadrature Rule

Let us now consider the problem of constructing a quadrature rule

$$\int_a^b f(x)\omega(x)\,dx \approx \sum_{i=1}^{m+n} w_i f(x_i) \tag{18.58}$$

which integrates polynomials exactly up to the maximal degree possible. We assume that the m abscissas $x_1 < \cdots < x_m$ on the boundary of the interval $[a, b]$ are prescribed. Of course, m can only take the values $m = 0$, $m = 1$, and $m = 2$.

Let

$$r(x) := \prod_{i=1}^m (x - x_i) \tag{18.59}$$

be a polynomial of degree m with the prescribed abscissas as zeroes. Furthermore let

$$s(x) := \prod_{i=m+1}^{m+n} (x - x_i) \tag{18.60}$$

be the unknown polynomial of degree n with the abscissas $x_{m+1},\ldots,x_{m+n}$ as zeroes.

The following theorem represents the key for computing a Gauss quadrature rule (cf. [20, p. 161]).

THEOREM 18.6. *The Gauss quadrature rule (18.58) is exact for all polynomials p up to degree $m + 2n - 1$ if and only if the following two conditions are met:*

1. *The Gauss quadrature rule (18.58) is exact for all polynomials p up to degree $m + n - 1$.*

2. *The equation*

$$\int_a^b r(x)s(x)p(x)\omega(x)\,dx = 0 \qquad (18.61)$$

applies for all polynomials p up to degree $n-1$.

PROOF. First let the Gauss quadrature rule (18.58) be exact for all polynomials up to degree $m + 2n - 1$. Trivially it will be exact for all polynomials up to degree $m + n - 1$. The polynomial $r(x)s(x)p(x)$ is of degree $\leq m + 2n - 1$ and thus is integrated exactly:

$$\int_a^b r(x)s(x)p(x)\omega(x)\,dx = \sum_{i=1}^{m+n} w_i r(x_i)s(x_i)p(x_i) = 0.$$

On the other hand assume that the two conditions 1 and 2 are satisfied. A polynomial $t(x)$ of degree $\leq m + 2n - 1$ can be factored according to

$$t(x) = r(x)s(x)p(x) + q(x),$$

where p and q are polynomials of degrees $\leq n - 1$ and $\leq m + n - 1$ respectively. We have

$$\int_a^b t(x)\omega(x)\,dx = \int_a^b r(x)s(x)p(x)\omega(x)\,dx + \int_a^b q(x)\omega(x)\,dx$$

$$= \int_a^b q(x)\omega(x)\,dx.$$

But for polynomials of degree $\leq m + n - 1$ the quadrature rule is exact, and we have

$$\int_a^b q(x)\omega(x)\,dx = \sum_{i=1}^{m+n} w_i q(x_i) = \sum_{i=1}^{m+n} w_i t(x_i),$$

since $t(x_i) = q(x_i)$. Consequently

$$\int_a^b t(x)\omega(x)\,dx = \sum_{i=1}^{m+n} w_i t(x_i),$$

and the quadrature rule is exact for all polynomials up to degree $m + 2n - 1$. $\square$

Now, let us consider the construction of quadrature rules for the interesting cases $m = 0$, $m = 1$, and $m = 2$. To this end we have to determine the $m + n$ abscissas x_i in such a way that condition 2 of Theorem 18.6 is satisfied. This calls for a different procedure in each of the three cases.

After this we will have to determine the weights w_i such that condition 1 of Theorem 18.6 is satisfied. This problem is tackled in Section 18.7. The results are presented in MAPLE as Algorithms 18.4, 18.5, and 18.6.

18.4   Gauss Quadrature Rule

In the case of a Gauss quadrature rule no abscissa is prescribed, i.e. $m = 0$ and $r(x) = 1$. If we choose $s(x) = p_n(x)$ condition 2 of Theorem 18.6 is satisfied. Therefore, the zeroes of $p_n(x)$, i.e. the eigenvalues of the matrix T_n, represent the desired abscissas x_i (cf. [18]).

ALGORITHM 18.4. *Gauss Quadrature Rule.*

```
Gauss := proc (mu0, alpha, beta, n, x, w)
  local D, i, Q, T;

  T := array (1..n, 1..n, symmetric, [[0$n]$n]);
  for i from 1 to n do
    T[i,i] := alpha[i];
  od;
  for i from 1 to n-1 do
    T[i,i+1] := beta[i];
    T[i+1,i] := beta[i];
  od;

  D := evalf (Eigenvals (T, Q));
  x := array (1..n, [seq (D[i], i=1..n)]);
  w := array (1..n, [seq (evalf (mu0) * Q[1,i]^2, i=1..n)]);

  RETURN (NULL);
end:
```

18.5   Gauss-Radau Quadrature Rule

In the case of a Gauss-Radau quadrature rule we prescribe exactly one abscissa x_1 on the boundary of the interval $[a, b]$, i.e. $m = 1$ and $r(x) = x - a$ or $r(x) = x - b$. Instead of directly computing a polynomial $s(x)$ that satisfies condition 2 of Theorem 18.6, we construct the polynomial $\tilde{p}_{n+1}(x) = r(x)s(x)$ of degree $n + 1$. We will determine this polynomial from the following two requirements:

1. $\tilde{p}_{n+1}$ contains s as a factor:

$$\tilde{p}_{n+1}(x_1) = 0. \tag{18.62}$$

2. The equation

$$\int_a^b \tilde{p}_{n+1}(x)p(x)\omega(x)\,dx = 0 \tag{18.63}$$

applies for all polynomials p up to degree $n - 1$.

We start with the following implicit representation of $\tilde{p}_{n+1}$ (cf. [16]):

$$x \begin{bmatrix} p_0 \\ \vdots \\ \vdots \\ p_n \end{bmatrix} = \begin{bmatrix} \alpha_1 & \beta_1 & & \\ \beta_1 & \ddots & \ddots & \\ & \ddots & \alpha_n & \beta_n \\ & & \beta_n & \tilde{\alpha}_{n+1} \end{bmatrix} \begin{bmatrix} p_0 \\ \vdots \\ \vdots \\ p_n \end{bmatrix} + \begin{bmatrix} 0 \\ \vdots \\ 0 \\ \tilde{p}_{n+1} \end{bmatrix}, \tag{18.64}$$

where the value of $\tilde{\alpha}_{n+1}$ has yet to be determined.

First we demonstrate that this choice of $\tilde{p}_{n+1}$ satisfies (18.63) for an arbitrary $\tilde{\alpha}_{n+1}$. Because of the last Equation (18.64)

$$x p_n = \beta_n p_{n-1} + \tilde{\alpha}_{n+1} p_n + \tilde{p}_{n+1}$$

and the recurrence relationship (18.21)

$$x p_n = \beta_n p_{n-1} + \alpha_{n+1} p_n + \beta_{n+1} p_{n+1}$$

we can represent the polynomial $\tilde{p}_{n+1}$ as

$$\tilde{p}_{n+1} = (\alpha_{n+1} - \tilde{\alpha}_{n+1}) p_n + \beta_{n+1} p_{n+1}. \tag{18.65}$$

Obviously, the polynomial $\tilde{p}_{n+1}$ is a linear combination of p_n and p_{n+1} and always satisfies (18.63).

We only have to determine the value of $\tilde{\alpha}_{n+1}$ such that $\tilde{p}_{n+1}(x_1) = 0$, or, equivalently, that x_1 is an eigenvalue of the matrix in Equation (18.64). For this, consider the eigenvalue equation

$$x_1 \begin{bmatrix} \mathbf{y} \\ \eta \end{bmatrix} = \left[\begin{array}{c|c} T_n & \\ & \beta_n \\ \hline \beta_n & \tilde{\alpha}_{n+1} \end{array} \right] \begin{bmatrix} \mathbf{y} \\ \eta \end{bmatrix},$$

or, equivalently,

$$x_1 \mathbf{y} = T_n \mathbf{y} + \beta_n \eta \mathbf{e}_n, \tag{18.66}$$

$$x_1 \eta = \beta_n y_n + \tilde{\alpha}_{n+1} \eta. \tag{18.67}$$

From (18.66) we see that $\mathbf{y}$ is a multiple of $(T_n - x_1 I)^{-1} \mathbf{e}_n$. Therefore, let

$$\mathbf{y} := (T_n - x_1 I)^{-1} \mathbf{e}_n. \tag{18.68}$$

Then, it follows from (18.66) that

$$\eta = -\frac{1}{\beta_n}. \tag{18.69}$$

Note that the matrix $T_n - x_1 I$ is positive or negative definite depending on the choice of x_1. In each case the value of the vector $\mathbf{y}$ is uniquely determined.

After substituting (18.69) into (18.67) we get

$$\tilde{\alpha}_{n+1} = x_1 + \beta_n^2 y_n. \tag{18.70}$$

Consequently, we have determined the polynomial $\tilde{p}_{n+1}(x)$ whose zeroes represent the abscissas of the Gauss-Radau quadrature rule.

ALGORITHM 18.5. *Gauss-Radau Quadrature Rule.*

```
Radau := proc (mu0, alpha, beta, n, x1, x, w)
  local alpha1tilde, D, e, i, Q, T, y;

  T := array (1..n, 1..n, symmetric, [[0$n]$n]);
  for i from 1 to n do
    T[i,i] := alpha[i] - x1;
  od;
  for i from 1 to n-1 do
    T[i,i+1] := beta[i];
    T[i+1,i] := beta[i];
  od;

  e := linalg[vector] (n, 0);  e[n] := 1;
  y := linalg[linsolve] (T, e);
  alpha1tilde := simplify (x1 + beta[n]^2 * y[n]);

  T := array (1..n+1, 1..n+1, symmetric, [[0$n+1]$n+1]);
  for i from 1 to n do
    T[i,i] := alpha[i];
  od;
  T[n+1,n+1] := alpha1tilde;
  for i from 1 to n do
    T[i,i+1] := beta[i];
    T[i+1,i] := beta[i];
  od;

  D := evalf (Eigenvals (T, Q));
  x := array (1..n+1, [seq (D[i], i=1..n+1)]);
  w := array (1..n+1, [seq (evalf (mu0) * Q[1,i]^2, i=1..n+1)]);

  RETURN (NULL);
end:
```

18.6 Gauss-Lobatto Quadrature Rule

In the case of a Gauss-Lobatto quadrature rule we prescribe the two abscissas $x_1 = a$ and $x_2 = b$, i.e. $m = 2$ and $r(x) = (x - a)(x - b)$. Instead of computing a polynomial $s(x)$ that satisfies condition 2 of Theorem 18.6, we construct the polynomial $\tilde{p}_{n+2}(x) = r(x)s(x)$ of degree $n + 2$. We will determine this polynomial from the following two requirements:

1. $\tilde{p}_{n+2}$ contains s as a factor:

$$\tilde{p}_{n+2}(x_1) = \tilde{p}_{n+2}(x_2) = 0. \tag{18.71}$$

2. The equation

$$\int_a^b \tilde{p}_{n+2}(x)p(x)\omega(x)\,dx = 0 \tag{18.72}$$

applies for all polynomials p up to degree $n - 1$.

We choose for $\tilde{p}_{n+2}$ the polynomial which is defined implicitly by the matrix equation (cf. [16])

$$x \begin{bmatrix} p_0 \\ \vdots \\ \vdots \\ p_n \\ \tilde{p}_{n+1} \end{bmatrix} = \begin{bmatrix} \alpha_1 & \beta_1 & & & \\ \beta_1 & \ddots & \ddots & & \\ & \ddots & \ddots & \beta_n & \\ & & \beta_n & \alpha_{n+1} & \tilde{\beta}_{n+1} \\ & & & \tilde{\beta}_{n+1} & \tilde{\alpha}_{n+2} \end{bmatrix} \begin{bmatrix} p_0 \\ \vdots \\ \vdots \\ p_n \\ \tilde{p}_{n+1} \end{bmatrix} + \begin{bmatrix} 0 \\ \vdots \\ \vdots \\ 0 \\ \tilde{p}_{n+2} \end{bmatrix}, \tag{18.73}$$

where $\tilde{\beta}_{n+1} \neq 0$ and $\tilde{\alpha}_{n+2}$ are yet unspecified.

We now show that this choice of $\tilde{p}_{n+2}$ will meet condition (18.72) for any $\tilde{\beta}_{n+1}$ and $\tilde{\alpha}_{n+2}$. In view of (18.21) the penultimate equation of (18.73)

$$xp_n = \beta_n p_{n-1} + \alpha_{n+1}p_n + \tilde{\beta}_{n+1}\tilde{p}_{n+1}$$

defines the polynomial $\tilde{p}_{n+1}$ as a multiple of p_{n+1}:

$$\tilde{p}_{n+1} = \frac{\beta_{n+1}}{\tilde{\beta}_{n+1}}p_{n+1}. \tag{18.74}$$

By substituting (18.74) into the last equation of (18.73)

$$x\tilde{p}_{n+1} = \tilde{\beta}_{n+1}p_n + \tilde{\alpha}_{n+2}\tilde{p}_{n+1} + \tilde{p}_{n+2}$$

we get

$$x\frac{\beta_{n+1}}{\tilde{\beta}_{n+1}}p_{n+1} = \tilde{\beta}_{n+1}p_n + \tilde{\alpha}_{n+2}\frac{\beta_{n+1}}{\tilde{\beta}_{n+1}}p_{n+1} + \tilde{p}_{n+2}.$$

Due to

$$xp_{n+1} = \beta_{n+1}p_n + \alpha_{n+2}p_{n+1} + \beta_{n+2}p_{n+2}$$

we can represent the polynomial $\tilde{p}_{n+2}$ by

$$\tilde{p}_{n+2} = (\frac{\beta_{n+1}^2}{\tilde{\beta}_{n+1}} - \tilde{\beta}_{n+1})p_n + \frac{\beta_{n+1}}{\tilde{\beta}_{n+1}}(\alpha_{n+2} - \tilde{\alpha}_{n+2})p_{n+1} + \frac{\beta_{n+1}\beta_{n+2}}{\tilde{\beta}_{n+1}}p_{n+2}. \quad (18.75)$$

The main observation here is that $\tilde{p}_{n+2}$ is given by a linear combination of p_n, p_{n+1}, and p_{n+2}, so that Equation (18.72) is always satisfied.

Now we will determine the values of $\tilde{\beta}_{n+1} \neq 0$ and $\tilde{\alpha}_{n+2}$ such that $\tilde{p}_{n+2}(a) = \tilde{p}_{n+2}(b) = 0$. But this is equivalent to requiring that the matrix in (18.73) possesses the two eigenvalues a and b. Consider the eigenvalue equations

$$a\begin{bmatrix} \mathbf{y} \\ \hline \eta \end{bmatrix} = \begin{bmatrix} T_{n+1} & \\ & \tilde{\beta}_{n+1} \\ \hline \tilde{\beta}_{n+1} & \tilde{\alpha}_{n+2} \end{bmatrix}\begin{bmatrix} \mathbf{y} \\ \hline \eta \end{bmatrix}$$

and

$$b\begin{bmatrix} \mathbf{z} \\ \hline \zeta \end{bmatrix} = \begin{bmatrix} T_{n+1} & \\ & \tilde{\beta}_{n+1} \\ \hline \tilde{\beta}_{n+1} & \tilde{\alpha}_{n+2} \end{bmatrix}\begin{bmatrix} \mathbf{z} \\ \hline \zeta \end{bmatrix},$$

or, equivalently,

$$ay = T_{n+1}\mathbf{y} + \tilde{\beta}_{n+1}\eta\mathbf{e}_{n+1}, \quad (18.76)$$

$$a\eta = \tilde{\beta}_{n+1}y_{n+1} + \tilde{\alpha}_{n+2}\eta, \quad (18.77)$$

$$b\mathbf{z} = T_{n+1}\mathbf{z} + \tilde{\beta}_{n+1}\zeta\mathbf{e}_{n+1}, \quad (18.78)$$

$$b\zeta = \tilde{\beta}_{n+1}z_{n+1} + \tilde{\alpha}_{n+2}\zeta. \quad (18.79)$$

We can now see from the Equations (18.76) and (18.78) that the vectors $\mathbf{y}$ and $\mathbf{z}$ are multiples of $(T_{n+1} - aI)^{-1}\mathbf{e}_{n+1}$ and $(T_{n+1} - bI)^{-1}\mathbf{e}_{n+1}$, respectively. If we define $\mathbf{y}$ and $\mathbf{z}$ by

$$\mathbf{y} := (T_{n+1} - aI)^{-1}\mathbf{e}_{n+1}, \quad (18.80)$$

$$\mathbf{z} := (T_{n+1} - bI)^{-1}\mathbf{e}_{n+1}, \quad (18.81)$$

Equations (18.76) and (18.78) imply

$$\eta = \zeta = -\frac{1}{\tilde{\beta}_{n+1}}. \quad (18.82)$$

Furthermore $T_{n+1} - aI$ and $T_{n+1} - bI$ represent a positive and negative definite matrix, respectively. In particular we have the inequality

$$y_{n+1} > 0 > z_{n+1}. \quad (18.83)$$

After substituting (18.82) into (18.77) and (18.79), and after multiplying by $\tilde{\beta}_{n+1}$ we get the linear system

$$\begin{bmatrix} 1 & -y_{n+1} \\ 1 & -z_{n+1} \end{bmatrix}\begin{bmatrix} \tilde{\alpha}_{n+2} \\ \tilde{\beta}_{n+1}^2 \end{bmatrix} = \begin{bmatrix} a \\ b \end{bmatrix}. \quad (18.84)$$

ALGORITHM 18.6. *Gauss-Lobatto Quadrature Rule.*

```
Lobatto := proc (mu0, alpha, beta, n, x1, x2, x, w)
  local alphan2tilde, betan1tilde, D, e, i, Q, T, y, z;

  T := array (1..n+1, 1..n+1, symmetric, [[0$n+1]$n+1]);
  for i from 1 to n+1 do
    T[i,i] := alpha[i] - x1;
  od;
  for i from 1 to n do
    T[i,i+1] := beta[i];
    T[i+1,i] := beta[i];
  od;

  e := linalg[vector] (n+1, 0);  e[n+1] := 1;
  y := linalg[linsolve] (T, e);
  for i from 1 to n+1 do
    T[i,i] := alpha[i] - x2;
  od;
  z := linalg[linsolve] (T, e);
  alphan2tilde := simplify ((x2 * y[n+1] - x1*z[n+1]) /
                           (y[n+1] - z[n+1]));
  betan1tilde := simplify (sqrt ((x2-x1) / (y[n+1] - z[n+1])));

  T := array (1..n+2, 1..n+2, symmetric, [[0$n+2]$n+2]);
  for i from 1 to n+1 do
    T[i,i] := alpha[i];
  od;
  T[n+2,n+2] := alphan2tilde;
  for i from 1 to n do
    T[i,i+1] := beta[i];
    T[i+1,i] := beta[i];
  od;
  T[n+1,n+2] := betan1tilde;
  T[n+2,n+1] := betan1tilde;

  D := evalf (Eigenvals (T, Q));
  x := array (1..n+2, [seq (D[i], i=1..n+2)]);
  w := array (1..n+2, [seq (evalf (mu0) * Q[1,i]^2, i=1..n+2)]);

  RETURN (NULL);
end:
```

Because of (18.83) the linear system (18.84) has the unique solution

$$\tilde{\alpha}_{n+2} = \frac{by_{n+1} - az_{n+1}}{y_{n+1} - z_{n+1}}, \tag{18.85}$$

$$\tilde{\beta}_{n+1} = \sqrt{\frac{b-a}{y_{n+1} - z_{n+1}}} > 0. \tag{18.86}$$

This means that we have eventually determined the polynomial $\tilde{p}_{n+2}(x)$ whose zeroes represent the abscissas of the Gauss-Lobatto quadrature rule.

18.7   Weights

The procedure for computing the weights is the same for each of the above mentioned quadrature rules. We have to determine the weights $w_1, \ldots, w_{m+n}$ such that condition 1 of Theorem 18.6 is met. Equivalently, we may require that the polynomials $p_0, \ldots, p_n$ and $\tilde{p}_{n+1}, \ldots, \tilde{p}_{m+n-1}$ from (18.64) and (18.73) are integrated exactly:

$$\int_a^b p_k(x)\omega(x)\,dx = \sum_{i=1}^{m+n} w_i p_k(x_i) = \frac{1}{p_0}\delta_{k0}, \qquad k = 0, \ldots, \min(n, m+n-1),$$

$$\int_a^b \tilde{p}_k(x)\omega(x)\,dx = \sum_{i=1}^{m+n} w_i \tilde{p}_k(x_i) = 0, \qquad k = n+1, \ldots, m+n-1.$$

In matrix terms this can be written as

$$\begin{bmatrix} p_0(x_1) & \cdots & \cdots & p_0(x_{m+n}) \\ \vdots & & & \vdots \\ \vdots & & & \vdots \\ \tilde{p}_{m+n-1}(x_1) & \cdots & \cdots & \tilde{p}_{m+n-1}(x_{m+n}) \end{bmatrix} \begin{bmatrix} w_1 \\ \vdots \\ \vdots \\ w_{m+n} \end{bmatrix} = \begin{bmatrix} 1/p_0 \\ 0 \\ \vdots \\ 0 \end{bmatrix}$$

or $P\mathbf{w} = \mathbf{e}_1/p_0$. Because of Theorem 18.5 we have $Q = PW$, such that

$$\mathbf{w} = \frac{1}{p_0} W Q^{\mathrm{T}} \mathbf{e}_1.$$

From (18.14) and (18.6) it follows that

$$\int_a^b p_0^2(x)\omega(x)\,dx = p_0^2 \mu_0 = 1,$$

such that finally the weights w_i are given by

$$w_i = \mu_0 q_{1i}^2, \qquad i = 1, \ldots, m+n. \tag{18.87}$$

As an application we will now compute a Gauss-Lobatto quadrature rule corresponding to the interval $[1, 2]$ and the weight function

$$\omega(x) := \frac{1}{x}. \tag{18.88}$$

The following MAPLE statements compute the three-term recurrence relation-ship (18.21) of the orthogonal polynomials. Then, the quadrature rule is com-puted by a call of Algorithm 18.6:

```
> N := 11;
> Digits := 100;
> a := 1;
> b := 2;
> omega := x -> 1 / x;

> alphahat := array (1..2*N-1, [0$2*N-1]);
> betahat := array (1..2*N-1, [1$2*N-1]);
> gammahat := array (1..2*N-2, [0$2*N-2]);

> pi0 := 1;
> nu[0] := ln (b) - ln (a);
> for n from 1 to 2*N-1 do
>    nu[n] := (b^n - a^n) / n;
> od;
> mu0 := nu[0] / pi0;

> SackDonovan (pi0, alphahat, betahat, gammahat, nu, N,
>               'alpha', 'beta');
> Lobatto (mu0, alpha, beta, N-1, a, b, 'x', 'w');
```

The abscissas and weights are shown as Table 18.3. The results have been rounded to twenty decimal digits.

18.8   Quadrature Error

We will now consider the question how to express the quadrature error

$$E[f] := \int_a^b f(x)\omega(x)\,dx - \sum_{i=1}^{m+n} w_i f(x_i). \tag{18.89}$$

We assume that the integrand f is a $(m + 2n)$-times continuously differen-tiable function on the interval $[a, b]$. Furthermore, let $H(x)$ denote the uniquely determined polynomial of degree $\leq m + 2n - 1$, which satisfies the Hermite interpolation conditions (cf. [29, p. 44])

$$H(x_i) = f(x_i), \qquad i = 1, \ldots, m + n,$$
$$H'(x_i) = f'(x_i), \qquad i = m + 1, \ldots, m + n.$$

First, we examine how well the polynomial $H(x)$ approximates the given function $f(x)$ on the interval $[a, b]$.

THEOREM 18.7. *Let*

$$Q(x) := \prod_{i=1}^{m}(x - x_i) \cdot \prod_{i=m+1}^{m+n}(x - x_i)^2 \tag{18.90}$$

TABLE 18.3.
Abscissas and Weights of a Gauss-Lobatto Quadrature
Rule.

k	x_k	w_k
1	1.0000000000000000000	0.0073101161434772987648
2	1.0266209022507358746	0.043205676918139196040
3	1.0875753284733094064	0.070685480638318232547
4	1.1786507622317286926	0.088433599898292821869
5	1.2936151328648399126	0.096108531378420052625
6	1.4243072396520977438	0.095097966102219702354
7	1.5611522948208446896	0.087445652257865527102
8	1.6938824042052787649	0.075118353999491464492
9	1.8123676368833335432	0.059695944656549921510
10	1.9074586992416619710	0.042332113537812345903
11	1.9717495114038218100	0.023827527632972240207
12	2.0000000000000000000	0.0038862173963865060038

denote a polynomial of degree $m + 2n$. Then for each x in the interval $[a, b]$ there exists a ξ with $a < \xi < b$ such that

$$f(x) = H(x) + \frac{f^{(m+2n)}(\xi)}{(m+2n)!}Q(x). \tag{18.91}$$

PROOF. For $x = x_i$ equation (18.91) is trivially satisfied. Therefore we assume that $x \neq x_i$ and $x \in [a, b]$ in the following. Let us consider the function

$$F(t) := f(t) - H(t) - \frac{f(x) - H(x)}{Q(x)}Q(t). \tag{18.92}$$

Obviously, $F(t)$ possesses at least $m + 2n + 1$ zeroes in the interval $[a, b]$. As a consequence of Rolle's theorem $F^{(m+2n)}(t)$ has at least one zero ξ in the interior of $[a, b]$:

$$F^{(m+2n)}(\xi) = f^{(m+2n)}(\xi) - \frac{f(x) - H(x)}{Q(x)}(m+2n)! = 0.$$

But this establishes Equation (18.91). □

The reader is referred to [20, p. 49] and [29, p. 48] for similar proofs.

After these preparations we are in a position to give a quantitative expression for the quadrature error (18.89). See also [20, pp. 162–163] and [29, p. 134].

THEOREM 18.8. *The error of the quadrature rule (18.58) is given by*

$$E[f] = \frac{f^{(m+2n)}(\xi)}{(m+2n)!} \int_a^b Q(x)\omega(x)\,dx \tag{18.93}$$

with $a < \xi < b$.

PROOF. According to (18.91) we can represent the integrand $f(x)$ for $a \le x \le b$ by

$$f(x) = H(x) + \frac{f^{(m+2n)}(\xi(x))}{(m+2n)!}Q(x) \tag{18.94}$$

with $a < \xi(x) < b$. Because of

$$f^{(m+2n)}(\xi(x)) = (m+2n)!\frac{f(x) - H(x)}{Q(x)}$$

we have in $f^{(m+2n)}(\xi(x))$ a continuous function for $a \le x \le b$.

The integration of the representation (18.94) of $f(x)$ yields

$$\int_a^b f(x)\omega(x)\,dx = \int_a^b H(x)\omega(x)\,dx + \frac{1}{(m+2n)!}\int_a^b f^{(m+2n)}(\xi(x))Q(x)\omega(x)\,dx. \tag{18.95}$$

The interpolating polynomial $H(x)$ is of degree $\le m + 2n - 1$ and is therefore integrated exactly:

$$\int_a^b H(x)\omega(x)\,dx = \sum_{i=1}^{m+n} w_i H(x_i) = \sum_{i=1}^{m+n} w_i f(x_i). \tag{18.96}$$

On the other hand $Q(x)$ has a constant sign on $[a, b]$. This allows us to make use of the generalized mean value theorem of integral calculus [19, p. 477], giving

$$\int_a^b f^{(m+2n)}(\xi(x))Q(x)\omega(x)\,dx = f^{(m+2n)}(\xi)\int_a^b Q(x)\omega(x)\,dx \tag{18.97}$$

for $a < \xi < b$. After substituting (18.96) and (18.97) into (18.95) we get

$$\int_a^b f(x)\omega(x)\,dx = \sum_{i=1}^{m+n} w_i f(x_i) + \frac{f^{(m+2n)}(\xi)}{(m+2n)!}\int_a^b Q(x)\omega(x)\,dx$$

with $a < \xi < b$. This establishes Equation (18.93). □

References

[1] N. I. AKHIEZER, *The Classical Moment Problem*, translated by N. Kemmer, Oliver & Boyd, Edinburgh and London, 1965.

[2] J. BOUZITAT, *Sur l'intégration numérique approchée par la méthode de Gauss généralisée et sur une extension de cette méthode*, C. R. Acad. Sci. Paris, 229 (1949), pp. 1201–1203.

[3] E. B. CHRISTOFFEL, *Über die Gaussische Quadratur und eine Verallgemeinerung derselben*, J. Reine Angew. Math., 55 (1858), pp. 61–82.

[4] P. J. DAVIS AND P. RABINOWITZ, *Methods of Numerical Integration*, Academic Press, Orlando, 1984.

[5] R. N. DESMARAIS, *Programs for computing abscissas and weights for classical and non-classical Gaussian quadrature formulas*, NASA Report TN D-7924, NASA Langley Research Center, Hampton VA, 1975.

[6] A. ERDÉLYI ET AL., *Higher Transcendental Functions*, Bateman Manuscript Project, McGraw-Hill, New York, 1953.

[7] C. F. GAUSS, *Methodus Nova Integralium Valores per Approximationem Inveniendi*, Werke, Vol. 3, Göttingen, 1866, pp. 163–196.

[8] W. GAUTSCHI, *Computational aspects of three-term recurrence relations*, SIAM Review, 9 (1967), pp. 24–82.

[9] W. GAUTSCHI, *Construction of Gauss-Christoffel Quadrature Formulas*, Math. Comp., 22 (1968), pp. 251–270.

[10] W. GAUTSCHI, *On the Construction of Gaussian Quadrature Rules from Modified Moments*, Math. Comp., 24 (1970), pp. 245–260.

[11] W. GAUTSCHI, *Minimal Solutions of Three-Term Recurrence Relations and Orthogonal Polynomials*, Math. Comp., 36 (1981), pp. 547–554.

[12] W. GAUTSCHI, *A Survey of Gauss-Christoffel Quadrature Formulae*, in E. B. Christoffel, The Influence of His Work on Mathematics and the Physical Sciences, ed. P. L. Butzer and F. Fehér, Birkhäuser, Basel, 1981, pp. 72–147.

[13] W. GAUTSCHI, *An algorithmic implementation of the generalized Christoffel theorem*, in Numerical Integration, Internat. Ser. Numer. Math., ed. G. Hämmerlin, Birkhäuser, Basel, 57 (1982), pp. 89–106.

[14] W. GAUTSCHI, *Questions of numerical condition related to polynomials*, in Studies in Mathematics, Volume 24: Studies in Numerical Analysis, ed. G. H. Golub, Math. Assoc. Amer., Washington, 1984, pp. 140–177.

[15] W. GAUTSCHI, *Orthogonal polynomials—constructive theory and applications*, J. Comput. Appl. Math., 12&13 (1985), pp. 61–76.

[16] G. H. GOLUB, *Some Modified Matrix Eigenvalue Problems*, SIAM Review, 15 (1973), pp. 318–334.

[17] G. H. GOLUB AND C. F. VAN LOAN, *Matrix Computations*, Second Edition, The Johns Hopkins University Press, Baltimore, 1989.

[18] G. H. GOLUB AND J. H. WELSCH, *Calculation of Gauss Quadrature Rules*, Math. Comp., 23 (1969), pp. 221–230.

[19] H. HEUSER, *Lehrbuch der Analysis, Teil 1*, Teubner, Stuttgart, 1986.

[20] V. I. KRYLOV, *Approximate Calculation of Integrals*, translated by A. H. Stroud, Macmillan, New York, 1962.

[21] A. MARKOFF, *Sur la méthode de Gauss pour le calcul approché des intégrales*, Math. Ann., 25 (1885), pp. 427–432.

[22] I. P. MYSOVSKIH, *On the Construction of Cubature Formulas with Fewest Nodes*, Soviet Math. Dokl., 9 (1968), pp. 277–280.

[23] B. N. PARLETT, *The Symmetric Eigenvalue Problem*, Prentice-Hall, Englewood Cliffs, 1980.

[24] W. H. PRESS AND S. A. TEUKOLSKY, *Orthogonal Polynomials and Gaussian Quadrature with Non-classical Weight Functions*, Computers in Physics, 4 (1990), pp. 423–426.

[25] P. RABINOWITZ, *Abscissas and Weights for Lobatto Quadrature of High Order*, Math. Comp., 14 (1960), pp. 47–52.

[26] R. RADAU, *Étude sur les formules d'approximation qui servent à calculer la valeur numérique d'une intégrale définie*, J. Math. Pures Appl., Ser. 3, 6 (1880), pp. 283–336.

[27] R. A. SACK AND A. F. DONOVAN, *An Algorithm for Gaussian Quadrature given Modified Moments*, Numer. Math., 18 (1972), pp. 465–478.

[28] J. A. SHOHAT AND J. D. TAMARKIN, *The Problem of Moments*, Second Edition, American Mathematical Society, New York, 1950.

[29] J. STOER, *Einführung in die Numerische Mathematik I*, Springer-Verlag, 1983.

[30] J. STOER AND R. BULIRSCH, *Einführung in die Numerische Mathematik II*, Springer-Verlag, 1978.

[31] A. H. STROUD AND D. SECREST, *Gaussian Quadrature Formulas*, Prentice-Hall, Englewood Cliffs, New Jersey, 1966.

[32] G. SZEGÖ, *Orthogonal Polynomials*, American Mathematical Society, New York, 1939.

[33] H. S. WALL, *Analytic Theory of Continued Fractions*, van Nostrand, New York, 1948.

[34] J. C. WHEELER, *Modified moments and Gaussian quadratures*, Rocky Mountain J. of Math., 4 (1974), pp. 287–296.

Chapter 19. Symbolic Computation of Explicit Runge-Kutta Formulas

D. Gruntz

19.1   Introduction

In this chapter we show how MAPLE can be used to derive explicit Runge-Kutta formulas which are used in numerical analysis to solve systems of differential equations of the first order. We show how the nonlinear system of equations for the coefficients of the Runge-Kutta formulas are constructed and how such a system can be solved. We close the chapter with an overall procedure to construct Runge-Kutta formulas for a given size and order. We will see up to which size such a general purpose program is capable of solving the equations obtained.

The solution of the initial value problem

$$y'(x) = f(x, y(x)), \qquad y(x_k) = y_k \tag{19.1}$$

can be approximated by a Taylor series around x_k, which is obtained from (19.1) by repeated differentiation and replacing $y'(x)$ by $f(x, y(x))$ every time it appears.

$$
\begin{aligned}
y(x_k + h) &= \sum_{i=0}^{\infty} y^{(i)}(x_k) \frac{h^i}{i!} \\
&= y(x_k) + h f(x_k, y(x_k)) + \frac{h^2}{2} \left(\left. \frac{\partial}{\partial x} f(x, y(x)) \right|_{x=x_k} \right) + \cdots \\
&= y(x_k) + h \Big(f(x_k, y(x_k)) \\
&\qquad + \underbrace{\frac{h}{2} \big(f_x(x_k, y(x_k)) + f(x_k, y(x_k)) f_y(x_k, y(x_k)) \big) + \cdots \Big)}_{\Phi(x_k, y(x_k), h)}
\end{aligned}
$$

$$\tag{19.2}$$

A numerical approximation to the solution of (19.1) can be computed by using only a few terms of (19.2) with h sufficiently small and by repeating this computation from the point $x_{k+1} = x_k + h$.

The idea of the Runge-Kutta methods is to approximate the Taylor series (19.2) up to order m by using only *values* of $f(x, y(x))$ and no derivatives of it. For example, the Taylor series of the improved Euler method,

$$y_{k+1} = y_k + h f\left(x_k + \frac{h}{2}, y_k + \frac{h}{2} f(x_k, y_k)\right),$$ (19.3)

is the same as (19.2) up to the coefficient of h^2, i.e. up to the order $m = 2$. We will prove this statement later in this chapter.

The general scheme of a Runge-Kutta formula was formulated by Kutta [9] and has the following form: Let s be an integer (the "number of stages"), and let $a_{i,j}$, b_i and c_i be real coefficients. Then the method

$$
\begin{aligned}
k_1 &= f(x,y), \\
k_2 &= f(x + c_2 h, y + h\, a_{2,1}\, k_1), \\
&\vdots \\
k_s &= f\Big(x + c_s h, y + h \sum_{j=1}^{s-1} a_{s,j}\, k_j\Big), \\
\Phi(x,y,h) &= \sum_{i=1}^{s} b_i k_i, \\
y_{k+1} &= y_k + h\, \Phi(x_k, y_k, h),
\end{aligned}
$$

is called an *s-stage explicit Runge-Kutta method*. s is also the number of evaluations of f used to compute y_{k+1}. Such a Runge-Kutta scheme is defined by the $(s^2 + 3s - 2)/2$ variables $a_{i,j}$, b_i and c_i. It has become customary in the literature to symbolize such a method with the following table of coefficients:

$$
\begin{array}{c|ccccc}
0 & & & & & \\
c_2 & a_{2,1} & & & & \\
c_3 & a_{3,1} & a_{3,2} & & & \\
\vdots & \vdots & \vdots & \ddots & & \\
c_s & a_{s,1} & a_{s,2} & \cdots & a_{s,s-1} & \\
\hline
 & b_1 & b_2 & \cdots & b_{s-1} & b_s
\end{array}
$$

The derivation of an s-stage Runge-Kutta method of order m consists of two steps:

1. From the condition that the Runge-Kutta formula and the Taylor series of the solution must agree up to order m, a set of nonlinear equations for the parameters $a_{i,j}$, b_i and c_i can be constructed, and

2. this system of equations must either be solved or its inconsistency must be proven.

Of these two steps the second is by far the more difficult (see [11, 4, 2]). The problem of the generation of Runge-Kutta equations was also asked in the problem section of the SIGSAM Bulletin [8], but an answer never appeared.

In the next section, we will solve Step 1 and Step 2 with MAPLE for $s = 3$ and $m = 3$.

19.2 Derivation of the Equations for the Parameters

For the derivation of the system of equations for the parameters of a Runge-Kutta formula, we must be able to compute the Taylor series of the solution $y(x + h)$ and of the Runge-Kutta formula. MAPLE knows how to differentiate a function with two parameters that both depend on x, i.e.

```
> diff(f(x,y(x)),x);
```

$$D[1](f)(x, \ y(x)) + D[2](f)(x, \ y(x)) \left(\frac{d}{dx} \ y(x) \right)$$

where `D[1](f)(x, y(x))` stands for the derivative of f with respect to the first argument, i.e. $f_x(x, y(x))$. For an extended discussion of the D-Operator in MAPLE we refer the reader to [10].

The next problem is to replace $y'(x)$ by $f(x, y(x))$ whenever it appears. There are several ways of doing that. One possibility is to use the interface offered by the procedure `diff` which allows the user to install his own differentiation functions. (Note: Since `diff` remembers every function call, this will work only after restarting MAPLE.)

```
> restart;
> 'diff/y' := (a,x) -> f(a,y(a))*diff(a,x):
> diff(y(x),x);
```

$$f(x, \ y(x))$$

```
> diff(y(x),x$2);
```

$$D[1](f)(x, \ y(x)) + D[2](f)(x, \ y(x)) \ f(x, \ y(x))$$

Another possibility is to overwrite the derivative of the operator `y` by our own definition. Whenever D is called with the argument y, the user-defined procedure is returned. With this definition it is possible to compute the Taylor series of $y(x + h)$ around $h = 0$, and that is exactly what we need. We feel that this is the most elegant solution:

```
> D(y) := x -> f(x,y(x)):
> taylor(y(x+h),h=0,3);
```

$$y(x) + f(x, \ y(x)) \ h$$

$$+ \ (1/2 \ D[1](f)(x, \ y(x)) + 1/2 \ D[2](f)(x, \ y(x)) \ f(x, \ y(x))) \ h^2$$

$$+ \ O(h^3)$$

This series is correct but unfortunately not very easy to read, because of the complicated notation for the derivatives of $f(x, y(x))$. Therefore we introduce some `alias` definitions for the derivatives which will make the expressions readable. The first few derivatives of $y(x)$ will then have their well-known form:

```
> alias(F = f(x,y(x)), Fx = D[1](f)(x,y(x)), Fy = D[2](f)(x,y(x)),
>     Fxx = D[1,1](f)(x,y(x)), Fxy = D[1,2](f)(x,y(x)),
>     Fyy = D[2,2](f)(x,y(x))):
> diff(F,x);
```

$$Fx + Fy\ F$$

```
> diff(F,x$2);
```

$$Fxx + Fxy\ F + (Fxy + Fyy\ F)\ F + Fy\ (Fx + Fy\ F)$$

```
> taylor(y(x+h),h=0,3);
```

$$y(x) + F\ h + (1/2\ Fx + 1/2\ Fy\ F)\ h^2 + O(h^3)$$

For computing the Taylor series of the function Φ, which we defined in the general Runge-Kutta scheme, we must be able to compute the series of the expressions $k_i = f(x + c_i h, y + h \sum_{j=1}^{i-1} a_{i,j} k_j)$ around $h = 0$. This can be performed by simply using the `taylor` command as well. For multivariate Taylor series expansions, the function `mtaylor` could be used, but in our case, this is not necessary.

```
> taylor(f(x+h, y(x)+h), h=0, 3);
```

$$F + (Fx + Fy)\ h + (1/2\ Fxx + Fxy + 1/2\ Fyy)\ h^2 + O(h^3)$$

Now we have prepared the tools for computing the Taylor series of the solution $y(x)$ and of the Runge-Kutta formula. In the following we try to compute the coefficients of a Runge-Kutta scheme of order three $(m = 3)$ with three stages $(s = 3)$.

```
> m := 3:
> taylor(y(x+h),h=0,m+1);
```

$$y(x) + F\ h + (1/2\ Fx + 1/2\ Fy\ F)\ h^2$$

$$+ (1/6\ Fxx + 1/3\ Fxy\ F + 1/6\ Fyy\ F^2 + 1/6\ Fy\ Fx + 1/6\ Fy^2\ F)\ h^3$$

$$+ O(h^4)$$

```
> TaylorPhi := normal((convert(",polynom) - y(x))/h);
```

$$TaylorPhi := F + 1/2\ h\ Fx + 1/2\ h\ Fy\ F + 1/6\ h^2\ Fxx$$

$$+ 1/3\ h^2\ Fxy\ F + 1/6\ h^2\ Fyy\ F^2 + 1/6\ h^2\ Fy\ Fx + 1/6\ h^2\ Fy^2\ F$$

The `convert` command converts the Taylor series into a polynomial, i.e. it cuts off the O-term. The variable `TaylorPhi` corresponds to Φ in Equation (19.2).

For the Runge-Kutta scheme we get the following Taylor series. Note that we keep the parameters $a_{i,j}$, b_i and c_i as symbolic objects.

```
> k1 := taylor(f(x,        y(x)),                    h=0, m):
> k2 := taylor(f(x+c2*h, y(x)+h*(a21*k1)),           h=0, m):
> k3 := taylor(f(x+c3*h, y(x)+h*(a31*k1+a32*k2)),h=0, m):
> RungeKuttaPhi := convert(series(b1*k1+b2*k2+b3*k3,h,m), polynom);
```

RungeKuttaPhi := b1 F + b2 F + b3 F

     + (b2 (Fx c2 + Fy a21 F) + b3 (Fx c3 + Fy a31 F + Fy a32 F)) h

$$+ (b2 (1/2 \ Fxx \ c2^2 + c2 \ Fxy \ a21 \ F + 1/2 \ a21^2 \ F^2 \ Fyy) + b3 \ ($$

$$1/2 \ Fxx \ c3^2 + c3 \ Fxy \ a31 \ F + c3 \ Fxy \ a32 \ F + 1/2 \ a31^2 \ F^2 \ Fyy$$

$$+ a31 \ F^2 \ Fyy \ a32 + 1/2 \ a32^2 \ F^2 \ Fyy + Fy \ a32 \ Fx \ c2$$

$$+ Fy^2 \ a32 \ a21 \ F)) \ h^2$$

The difference d of the two polynomials `TaylorPhi` and `RungeKuttaPhi` should be zero. We consider d as a polynomial in the unknowns h, F, Fx, Fy, Fxx, etc. and we set the coefficients of that polynomial to zero. This gives us a nonlinear system of equations which must be solved (We will refer to it as equation (*)).

```
> d := expand(TaylorPhi-RungeKuttaPhi):
> eqns := {coeffs(d, [h,F,Fx,Fy,Fxx,Fxy,Fyy])};
```

eqns := {1/6 - b3 a32 c2, 1/6 - b3 a32 a21,

$$- b2 \ c2 + 1/2 - b3 \ c3, \ 1/6 - 1/2 \ b2 \ c2^2 - 1/2 \ b3 \ c3^2 ,$$

     1 - b2 - b3 - b1, - b2 a21 - b3 a32 + 1/2 - b3 a31,

     - b2 c2 a21 - b3 c3 a31 + 1/3 - b3 c3 a32,

$$- 1/2 \ b2 \ a21^2 - b3 \ a31 \ a32 - 1/2 \ b3 \ a32^2 + 1/6 - 1/2 \ b3 \ a31^2 \}$$

```
> vars := indets(eqns);
```

         vars := {c2, a21, a32, a31, c3, b3, b2, b1}

19.3   Solving the System of Equations

In this section we discuss the second step of the derivation of Runge-Kutta formulas, i.e. the question how to solve the system (*) of nonlinear equations. We note that we have to deal with a system of *polynomial* equations in the unknowns. Special algorithms exist for this type of problem.

We describe two algorithms which are used in computer algebra systems to solve systems of polynomial equations. The first is based on the theory of Gröbner bases for polynomial ideals, and the second uses polynomial resultants for performing nonlinear elimination steps. For a good introduction to both methods we refer the reader to [5].

But first, we give MAPLE's `solve` command a try. This command tries to solve the system of equations in a natural way using a substitution approach. For system (*) this approach is quite good, because the equations are almost in a triangular form as we will see later. The substitution algorithm used by MAPLE's `solve` command is described in detail in [6].

```
> sols := solve(eqns,vars);

sols :=
              - 1 + 2 b3 c3
  {a32 = 1/4 --------------------,
                            2
              b3 (- 1 + 3 b3 c3 )

                            2     3
               - 6 b3 c3 + 12 b3   c3  + 1
     a31 = 1/4 --------------------------,
                            2
               b3 (- 1 + 3 b3 c3 )

                          2
               - 1 + 3 b3 c3
     a21 = 2/3 --------------,
               - 1 + 2 b3 c3

                            2    2                              2
               1 - 4 b3 c3 + 4 b3  c3           - 1 + 3 b3 c3
     b2 = - 3/4 -----------------------, c2 = 2/3 --------------,
                            2                    - 1 + 2 b3 c3
               - 1 + 3 b3 c3

                              2
               - 1 + 12 b3 c3   - 12 b3 c3 + 4 b3
     b1 = 1/4 ----------------------------------, c3 = c3, b3 = b3}
                            2
               - 1 + 3 b3 c3

     ,
                                              2           2
  {b2 = 0, b3 = 3/4, a31 = 2/3 - a32, c2 = -----, a21 = -----,
                                          9 a32         9 a32

     c3 = 2/3, b1 = 1/4, a32 = a32}
```

Thus, for $s = 3$, we found two (parameterized) solutions which can be represented by the following coefficient schemes. Note that in the first solution, the unknowns c_3 and b_3 are free parameters, i.e. they can take on any value. This is indicated by the entries `c3 = c3` and `b3 = b3` in the solution set. For the second solution, $a_{3,2}$ is a free parameter (see also Figure 19.1). From the first solution we get the method of Heun of third order if we set $a_{3,2} = 2/3$.

We will now present two other methods to solve the system of equations.

FIGURE 19.1.

Three Step Runge-Kutta Methods of Order 3.

$$
\begin{array}{c|ccc}
0 \\
\dfrac{2}{3} & \dfrac{3 b_3 c_3{}^2 - 1}{2 b_3 c_3 - 1} \\[2ex]
c_3 & \dfrac{1 - 6 b_3 c_3 + 12 b_3{}^2 c_3{}^3}{4 b_3 (3 b_3 c_3{}^2 - 1)} & \dfrac{2 b_3 c_3 - 1}{4 b_3 (3 b_3 c_3{}^2 - 1)} \\[2ex]
\hline
& \dfrac{12 b_3 c_3{}^2 - 1 + 4 b_3 - 12 b_3 c_3}{12 b_3 c_3{}^2 - 4} & \dfrac{3}{4}\dfrac{(2 b_3 c_3 - 1)^2}{1 - 3 b_3 c_3{}^2} & b_3
\end{array}
$$

$$
\begin{array}{c|ccc}
0 \\
\dfrac{2}{9 a_{3,2}} & \dfrac{2}{9 a_{3,2}} \\[2ex]
\dfrac{2}{3} & \dfrac{2}{3} - a_{3,2} & a_{3,2} \\[2ex]
\hline
& \dfrac{1}{4} & 0 & \dfrac{3}{4}
\end{array}
$$

19.3.1 Gröbner Bases

A wide variety of problems in computer algebra involving polynomials may be formulated in terms of *polynomial ideals*. Examples of such problems are simplifications with respect to (polynomial) side relations or solutions of systems of (polynomial) equations.

We recall the definition of an ideal here. Given a (finite) set $F = \{f_1, f_2, \ldots, f_n\}$ of multivariate polynomials over a field $\mathbb{K}$, then the ideal $\langle F \rangle$ generated by the set F is defined as

$$
\langle F \rangle = \langle f_1, f_2, \ldots, f_n \rangle = \left\{ \sum_{i=1}^{m} h_i f_i \ \Big|\ h_i \in \mathbb{K}[x_1, \ldots, x_n] \right\},
$$

that is, $\langle F \rangle$ is the set of all the polynomials that can be constructed from combinations of the polynomials in F. The elements in F are called a *basis* for the ideal $\langle F \rangle$.

The method of Gröbner bases consists in transforming the given set F into a canonical basis G (called a Gröbner basis) first, such that $\langle G \rangle = \langle F \rangle$, and then in solving the problems with $\langle G \rangle$ rather than with $\langle F \rangle$. This transformation process is done by eliminating terms of the set of polynomials similar to the process of Gaussian elimination. New polynomials are formed from pairs of old ones f_1, f_2 as $p = \alpha f_1 + \beta f_2$ where α and β are properly chosen polynomials. By this process, variable by variable will be eliminated (according to a specified ordering). If the system has finitely many solutions, eventually a polynomial in one variable remains which can then be solved and substituted into the other elements of the Gröbner basis. This way one gets a generalization of the triangularization process of Gaussian elimination. We will not go into any details of the theory and the algorithm to compute Gröbner bases and refer the reader to [1] for an introduction. However, we will use the Gröbner bases algorithm implemented in the MAPLE system [3] to solve our system of equations:

```
> G := grobner[gbasis](eqns, [b1,b2,c2,a21,a31,a32,b3,c3], plex);

                   2
    G := [b1 - 6 a32 b3  c3 - 1 + b3 + 3 b3 a32,

                 2
         b2 + 6 a32 b3  c3 - 3 b3 a32, c2 - a21,
```

$$3\ a32\ a21\ +\ 6\ a32\ b3\ c3^2\ -\ c3\ -\ 2\ a32,$$

$$6\ a21\ b3\ c3\ -\ 3\ a21\ -\ 6\ b3\ c3^2\ +\ 2,\ a31\ +\ a32\ -\ c3,$$

$$1\ -\ 2\ b3\ c3\ -\ 4\ b3\ a32\ +\ 12\ b3^2\ c3^2\ a32]$$

The last equation contains three unknowns which means, that the system has two free parameters. We can solve this last equation with respect to $a_{3,2}$.

```
> a32 := normal(solve(G[7], a32));
```

$$a32 := 1/4\ \frac{-\ 1\ +\ 2\ b3\ c3}{b3\ (-\ 1\ +\ 3\ b3\ c3^2)}$$

This expression is only a solution, if the denominator is not zero. Let us first assume this case. The values for the other unknowns can be obtained by a back substitution process over the Gröbner bases *G*.

```
> a31 := normal(solve(G[6], a31));
```

$$a31 := 1/4\ \frac{-\ 6\ b3\ c3\ +\ 12\ b3^2\ c3^3\ +\ 1}{b3\ (-\ 1\ +\ 3\ b3\ c3^2)}$$

```
> a21 := normal(solve(G[5], a21));
```

$$a21 := 2/3\ \frac{-\ 1\ +\ 3\ b3\ c3^2}{-\ 1\ +\ 2\ b3\ c3}$$

```
> normal(G[4]);
```

$$0$$

```
> c2 := normal(solve(G[3], c2));
```

$$c2 := 2/3\ \frac{-\ 1\ +\ 3\ b3\ c3^2}{-\ 1\ +\ 2\ b3\ c3}$$

```
> b2 := factor(solve(G[2], b2));
```

$$b2 := -\ 3/4\ \frac{(-\ 1\ +\ 2\ b3\ c3)^2}{-\ 1\ +\ 3\ b3\ c3^2}$$

```
> b1 := normal(solve(G[1], b1));
```

$$b1 := 1/4 \; \frac{- \; 1 \; + \; 12 \; b3 \; c3^2 \; - \; 12 \; b3 \; c3 \; + \; 4 \; b3}{- \; 1 \; + \; 3 \; b3 \; c3^2}$$

and we get the same solution as with the `solve` command directly.

For $b_3 (3 \, b_3 \, c_3{}^2 - 1) = 0$ we arrive at another solution by adding the polynomial $3 \, b_3{}^2 \, c_3{}^2 - b_3$ to the ideal we obtained from the latter Gröbner basis computation. First we must clear the parameters $b_1, a_{3,1}$, etc., which we assigned above.

```
> b1 := 'b1': b2 := 'b2': b3 := 'b3': c2 := 'c2': c3 := 'c3':
> a21 := 'a21': a31 := 'a31': a32 := 'a32':
> grobner[gbasis]([G[], 3*b3^2*c3^2-b3],
>                          [b1,b2,c2,a21,a31,a32,b3,c3], plex);
   [4 b1 - 1, b2, c2 - a21, 9 a32 a21 - 2, 3 a31 + 3 a32 - 2,

    - 3 + 4 b3, 3 c3 - 2]
```

This corresponds to the second solution computed above with the `solve` command.

19.3.2 Resultants

The solution process using resultants is also similar to Gaussian elimination, because the resultant of two polynomials $f, g \in \mathbb{R}[x]$ is an eliminant, that is, $\mathrm{res}_x(f, g) \in \mathbb{R}$. The resultant of two polynomials $f, g \in \mathbb{R}[x]$ (written $\mathrm{res}_x(f, g)$) is defined to be the determinant of the Sylvester matrix of f, g (see any introductory algebra book, e.g. [12]). The following theorem (taken from [5]) shows how resultants may be used to solve systems of polynomial equations.

Let $\overline{F}$ be an algebraically closed field, and let

$$f = \sum_{i=0}^{m} a_i(x_2, \ldots, x_r) \, x_1^i, \quad g = \sum_{i=0}^{n} b_i(x_2, \ldots, x_r) \, x_1^i,$$

be elements of $\overline{F}[x_1, \ldots, x_r]$ of positive degrees in x_1. Then, if $(\alpha_1, \ldots, \alpha_r)$ is a common zero of f and g, their resultant with respect to x_1 satisfies

$$\mathrm{res}_{x_1}(\alpha_2, \ldots, \alpha_r) = 0.$$

Conversely, if $\mathrm{res}_{x_1}(\alpha_2, \ldots, \alpha_r) = 0$ then one of the following conditions holds:

$a_m(\alpha_2, \ldots, \alpha_r) = b_n(\alpha_2, \ldots, \alpha_r) = 0,$
$\forall \, x \in \overline{F} \; : \; f(x, \alpha_2, \ldots, \alpha_r) = 0,$
$\forall \, x \in \overline{F} \; : \; g(x, \alpha_2, \ldots, \alpha_r) = 0,$
$\exists \, \alpha_1 \in \overline{F} \;$ such that $\; (\alpha_1, \alpha_2, \ldots, \alpha_r) \;$ is a common zero of f and $g,$

where the last case is the interesting one for us.

We now try to use MAPLE's `resultant` function to transform the system of equations into triangular form. We first collect the equations in different sets B_j such that

$$B_j = \left\{ p \in \overline{F}[x_j, \ldots, x_r] - \overline{F}[x_{j+1}, \ldots, x_r] \right\}.$$

We consider in the sequel the equations as elements in $\mathbb{Q}[b_1, a_{3,1}, b_2, c_2, a_{2,1}, a_{3,2}, b_3, c_3]$ and define the sets B_j.

```
> X := [b1,a31,b2,c2,a21,a32,b3,c3]:
> for i to nops(X) do B[i] := {} od:
> for p in eqns do
>     for i while not has(p,X[i]) do od;
>     B[i] := B[i] union {primpart(p)}
> od:
```

Let us look at the sets B_i. Consider especially the number of elements in each of these sets.

```
> seq('B['.i.']' = B[i], i=1..nops(X));

B[1] = {1 - b2 - b3 - b1},

    B[2] = {- 2 b2 a21 - 2 b3 a32 + 1 - 2 b3 a31,

        - 3 b2 c2 a21 - 3 b3 c3 a31 + 1 - 3 b3 c3 a32,

                      2                          2              2
        - 3 b2 a21  - 6 b3 a31 a32 - 3 b3 a32  + 1 - 3 b3 a31 },

                                           2           2
    B[3] = {- 2 b2 c2 + 1 - 2 b3 c3, 1 - 3 b2 c2  - 3 b3 c3 },

    B[4] = {1 - 6 b3 a32 c2}, B[5] = {1 - 6 b3 a32 a21},

    B[6] = {}, B[7] = {}, B[8] = {}
```

Thus we can eliminate b_2 from the two elements in B_3 giving an additional element for the set B_4, which then has two elements too. Eliminating c_2 from these two equations yields a resultant in $\mathbb{Q}[a_{3,2}, b_3, c_3]$ which goes into B_6.

```
> primpart(resultant(B[3][1], B[3][2], b2));

      2        2                           2
   3 c2  - 6 c2  b3 c3 - 2 c2 + 6 c2 b3 c3

> B[4] := B[4] union {"}:
> primpart(resultant(B[4][1], B[4][2], c2));
                                    2    2
   1 - 2 b3 c3 - 4 b3 a32 + 12 b3  c3  a32

> B[6] := B[6] union {"}:
```

Since we know from the above computation that the whole system has two free parameters, we can stop the process and start back-substituting the solution. We will only construct the second solution, which is valid in the case $4 b_3 (3 b_3 c_3{}^2 - 1) \neq 0$.

```
> a32 := normal(solve(B[6][1],a32));
```

```
                    - 1 + 2 b3 c3
      a32 := 1/4 --------------------
                                   2
                  b3 (- 1 + 3 b3 c3 )
```

```
> a21 := normal(solve(B[5][1],a21));
```

```
                              2
                 - 1 + 3 b3 c3
      a21 := 2/3 --------------
                 - 1 + 2 b3 c3
```

```
> c2   := normal(solve(B[4][1],c2));
```

```
                             2
                - 1 + 3 b3 c3
      c2 := 2/3 --------------
                - 1 + 2 b3 c3
```

```
> b2   := normal(solve(B[3][1],b2));
```

```
                               2
                (- 1 + 2 b3 c3)
      b2 := - 3/4 ----------------
                               2
                - 1 + 3 b3 c3
```

```
> a31 := normal(solve(B[2][1],a31));
```

```
                             2   3
                - 6 b3 c3 + 12 b3 c3 + 1
      a31 := 1/4 -------------------------
                                   2
                  b3 (- 1 + 3 b3 c3 )
```

```
> b1   := normal(solve(B[1][1],b1));
```

```
                                2
               - 1 + 12 b3 c3 - 12 b3 c3 + 4 b3
      b1 := 1/4 --------------------------------
                                        2
                       - 1 + 3 b3 c3
```

and we obtain the same results as when using Gröbner basis.

19.4 The Complete Algorithm

In this section we compile all the MAPLE statements that we have used to derive the Runge-Kutta scheme for $s = 3$ into a single MAPLE procedure called RungeKutta(s,m). It computes the coefficients for an arbitrary Runge-Kutta method with s stages of order m. Instead of the names c1, c2, a21 etc. we use indexed names to represent the parameters. Unfortunately, for values of s greater than 3, the equations can no longer be solved by MAPLE and other Computer Algebra Systems directly. The system of polynomial equations has already become too complex. It can be simplified by adding the so-called symmetry conditions,

$$c_i = \sum_{j=1}^{i-1} a_{i,j}, \quad i = 2..s,$$

which we obtain by requiring that for the differential equation $y' = 1, y(0) = 0$ all the predictor values $y_i^* = y + h \sum_{j=1}^{i-1} a_{i,j}$ at position $x + c_i h$ are the same as the values obtained by inserting the exact solution $y(x) = x$. With these additional conditions, Runge-Kutta formulas can be computed for the order $m = 1, \cdots, 4$. The complete MAPLE code is shown in Algorithm 19.1.

ALGORITHM 19.1. *Procedure* RungeKutta.

```
RungeKutta := proc(s, m)
   local TaylorPhi, RungeKuttaPhi, d, vars, eqns, k, i, j;
   global a, b, c, h;

   # Taylor series
   D(y) := x -> f(x,y(x)):
   TaylorPhi := convert(taylor(y(x+h),h=0,m+1), polynom):
   TaylorPhi := normal((TaylorPhi - y(x))/h);

   # RK-Ansatz:
   c[1] := 0;
   for i from 1 to s do
      k[i] := taylor(f(x+c[i]*h,
                     y(x)+sum(a[i,j]*k[j], j=1..i-1)*h), h=0, m):
   od:
   RungeKuttaPhi := 0:
   for i from 1 to s do
      RungeKuttaPhi := RungeKuttaPhi + b[i] * k[i]:
   od:
   RungeKuttaPhi := series (RungeKuttaPhi, h, m):
   RungeKuttaPhi := convert(RungeKuttaPhi, polynom);

   d := expand(TaylorPhi - RungeKuttaPhi):
   vars := {seq(c[i], i=2..s),
            seq(b[i], i=1..s),
            seq((seq(a[i,j], j=1..i-1)), i = 2..s)
           };
   eqns := {coeffs(d, indets(d) minus vars)};
   # symmetry condition:
   eqns := eqns union
           {seq(sum(a[i,'j'], 'j'=1..i-1)-c[i], i=2..s)};
   solve(eqns, vars);
end:
```

19.4.1   Example 1:

We first test this procedure for the parameters $s = 2$ and $m = 2$

```
> RungeKutta(2, 2);
```

$$\{b[1] = 1 - b[2], \quad a[2, 1] = \frac{1}{2\ b[2]}, \quad c[2] = \frac{1}{2\ b[2]}, \quad b[2] = b[2]\}$$

Again we have one free parameter, namely b_2. In Figure 19.2 this result is shown in the table notation.

FIGURE 19.2. *General two Stage Runge-Kutta Schema.*

$$
\begin{array}{c|cc}
0 & & \\
\frac{1}{2b_2} & \frac{1}{2b_2} & \\
\hline
 & 1 - b_2 & b_2
\end{array}
$$

For $b_2 = 1$ we obtain the improved Euler method (see Equation (19.3)), and for the choice $b_2 = 1/2$ we get the rule

$$y_{k+1} = y_k + \frac{h}{2}\left(f(x_k, y_k) + f(x_k + h, y_k + h\,f(x_k, y_k))\right)$$

which is known as Heun's method.

19.4.2   Example 2:

In this example we compute the 4-stage Runge-Kutta formulas of order 4.

```
> RK4 := RungeKutta(4, 4):
> RK4[1];
```

$\{c[4] = 1,\ a[2, 1] = 1,\ b[3] = 2/3,\ b[1] = 1/6,\ c[2] = 1,$

$$c[3] = 1/2,\quad a[4, 1] = 1/4\,\frac{-1 + 4\ b[4]}{b[4]},\quad b[2] = -b[4] + 1/6,$$

$$a[4, 2] = -\frac{1}{12\ b[4]},\quad a[4, 3] = \frac{1}{3\ b[4]},\quad a[3, 1] = 3/8,$$

$a[3, 2] = 1/8,\ b[4] = b[4]\}$

We get two solutions, where the first one has b_4 as a free parameter and can be represented by the scheme shown in Figure 19.3.

The second solution has $a_{2,1}$ and $a_{3,2}$ as free parameters. Since the solution is rather complicated, we try to simplify it by aliasing the roots of a second degree polynomial by α. Furthermore we define $\beta = \alpha\,a_{3,2}\,a_{2,1}$. The % terms

FIGURE 19.3. *Simple Solution for s = 4 and m = 4.*

0				
1	1			
$\frac{1}{2}$	$\frac{3}{8}$	$\frac{1}{8}$		
1	$1 - \frac{1}{4b_4}$	$-\frac{1}{12b_4}$	$\frac{1}{3b_4}$	
	$\frac{1}{6}$	$\frac{1}{6} - b_4$	$\frac{2}{3}$	b_4

stand for common subexpressions and are displayed underneath the solution set.

```
> alias(alpha=RootOf( (-576*a[3,2]^2*a[2,1]^3-1152*a[3,2]^3
>     *a[2,1]^3+2304*a[3,2]^3*a[2,1]^4+576*a[3,2]^2*a[2,1]^2)*x^2
>     +(24*a[3,2]*a[2,1]^2-48*a[3,2]*a[2,1])*x+1, x)):
> S := subs(alpha=beta/a[3,2]/a[2,1], RK4[2]);
```

S := {c[4] = 1, c[2] = a[2, 1], a[2, 1] = a[2, 1],

$$a[3, 2] = a[3, 2], \quad b[3] = \frac{beta}{a[3, 2]\ a[2, 1]},$$

$$a[3, 1] = -1/24\ \frac{1 - 24\ beta + 24\ beta\ a[3, 2]}{beta},$$

a[4, 2] = 1/2 (- 168 %3 - 48 beta a[2, 1]

+ 384 beta a[3, 2]^2 a[2, 1]^4 + 264 %2

- 576 beta a[3, 2]^2 a[2, 1]^3 + 24 beta a[2, 1]^2 + 2 a[2, 1]

- a[2, 1]^2 + 4 a[2, 1]^3 a[3, 2] - 5 %6 + 24 beta - 96 %1

+ 192 beta a[3, 2]^2 a[2, 1]^2 - 1 + %5)

$$\Big/ \ (a[3, 2]\ \%4\ a[2, 1]^2),$$

a[4, 1] = 1/2 (1 + 3 %6 - %5 + 552 %3 - 72 beta a[2, 1]^2

- 2 a[2, 1] - 1728 beta a[3, 2]^2 a[2, 1]^4

+ 960 beta a[3, 2]^2 a[2, 1]^3 - 192 beta a[3, 2]^2 a[2, 1]^2

$$- 24\ \text{beta} + 96\ \%1 - 408\ \%2 + a[2,\ 1]^2 + 72\ \text{beta}\ a[2,\ 1]$$

$$+ 24\ \text{beta}\ a[2,\ 1]^3 - 288\ \text{beta}\ a[3,\ 2]\ a[2,\ 1]^4$$

$$+ 1152\ a[3,\ 2]^2\ a[2,\ 1]^5\ \text{beta})\ /\ (a[3,\ 2]\ \%4\ a[2,\ 1]^2),$$

$$b[4] = 1/288\ \frac{\%4}{(-\ a[2,\ 1] + 1 + 4\ \%6 - 2\ \%5)\ \text{beta}\ (a[2,\ 1] - 1)},$$

$$c[3] = 1/24\ \frac{-\ 1 + 24\ \text{beta}}{\text{beta}},$$

$$b[2] = -\ 1/576\ \frac{96\ \%1 - 24\ \text{beta} + 1}{(a[2,\ 1] - 1)\ \text{beta}\ a[3,\ 2]\ a[2,\ 1]^2},$$

$$a[4,\ 3] = 12\ \text{beta}$$

$$(-\ a[2,\ 1]^2 + 2\ a[2,\ 1] - 1 + 4\ a[2,\ 1]^3\ a[3,\ 2] - 6\ \%6 + 2\ \%5)$$

$$/(a[3,\ 2]\ a[2,\ 1]\ \%4),$$

$$b[1] = 1/576\ \frac{288\ \%2 - 96\ \%1 - 24\ \text{beta}\ a[2,\ 1] + 24\ \text{beta} - 1}{\text{beta}\ a[3,\ 2]\ a[2,\ 1]^2}\}$$

$$\%1 := \text{beta}\ a[3,\ 2]\ a[2,\ 1]$$

$$\%2 := \text{beta}\ a[3,\ 2]\ a[2,\ 1]^2$$

$$\%3 := \text{beta}\ a[3,\ 2]\ a[2,\ 1]^3$$

$$\%4 := 120\ \text{beta}\ a[2,\ 1] + 576\ \%3 - 96\ \text{beta}\ a[2,\ 1]^2 - 672\ \%2$$

$$- 48\ \text{beta} + 192\ \%1 - 1 + 2\ a[2,\ 1]$$

$$\%5 := a[3,\ 2]\ a[2,\ 1]$$

$$\%6 := a[3,\ 2]\ a[2,\ 1]^2$$

From this solution we obtain the classical Runge-Kutta method of order 4 by setting $a_{2,1} = 1/2$ and $a_{3,2} = 1/2$. α is then defined to be the root of $18x^2 - 9x + 1$. If we take the root $\alpha = 1/3$ we get the following parameters with $\beta = 1/12$.

```
> subs(beta=1/12,a[2,1]=1/2,a[3,2]=1/2, S);
```

$\{c[4] = 1,\ b[1] = 1/6,\ c[3] = 1/2,\ b[4] = 1/6,\ a[4,\ 1] = 0,$

$1/2 = 1/2,\ c[2] = 1/2,\ b[3] = 1/3,\ b[2] = 1/3,\ a[4,\ 2] = 0,$

```
    a[4, 3] = 1, a[3, 1] = 0}
```

If we set $a_{2,1} = 1/3$ and $a_{3,2} = 1$ we get the polynomial $2304x^2 - 1080x + 81$ which defines two formulas. If we take the root $\alpha = 3/8$ we get the so-called 3/8-Rule.

```
> subs(beta=1/8,a[2,1]=1/3,a[3,2]=1, S);
{c[4] = 1, 1 = 1, c[3] = 2/3, a[4, 3] = 1, 1/3 = 1/3,
    c[2] = 1/3, a[4, 1] = 1, b[1] = 1/8, b[4] = 1/8, b[2] = 3/8,
    a[3, 1] = -1/3, a[4, 2] = -1, b[3] = 3/8}
```

The coefficient schemes of these two methods are shown below:

FIGURE 19.4. *classical Runge-Kutta method*   FIGURE 19.5. *3/8-Rule*

$$
\begin{array}{c|cccc}
0 & & & & \\
\frac{1}{2} & \frac{1}{2} & & & \\
\frac{1}{2} & 0 & \frac{1}{2} & & \\
1 & 0 & 0 & 1 & \\
\hline
 & \frac{1}{6} & \frac{1}{3} & \frac{1}{3} & \frac{1}{6}
\end{array}
\qquad\qquad
\begin{array}{c|cccc}
0 & & & & \\
\frac{1}{3} & \frac{1}{3} & & & \\
\frac{2}{3} & -\frac{1}{3} & 1 & & \\
1 & 1 & -1 & 1 & \\
\hline
 & \frac{1}{8} & \frac{3}{8} & \frac{3}{8} & \frac{1}{8}
\end{array}
$$

19.5   Conclusions

We have demonstrated that MAPLE is a great help in deriving the equations which define an explicit Runge-Kutta formula. We note that we have made no attempt to simplify these equations. Techniques for doing so are well-known. The equations we constructed are the result of brute force formula manipulations, and, consequently, only Runge-Kutta formulas of up to order 4 can be derived. The equations corresponding to higher order formulas are still too big to be solved by today's computer algebra systems.

As early as 1966 Moses conjectured in [11] that the known inconsistency of the system of equations which corresponds to the five-stage Runge-Kutta method of order five could not be established using a computer algebra system. This is still valid for today's computer algebra systems and hence the algorithms to solve systems of polynomial equations must still be improved. One research direction is to take advantage of symmetries in the equations.

This chapter also justifies the mathematicians' efforts to simplify the systems in order to construct Runge-Kutta formulas of up to order 10 (17 stages) [7].

References

[1] B. BUCHBERGER, *Gröbner Bases: An Algorithmic Method in Polynomial Ideal Theory*, in Progress, directions and open problems in multidimensional systems theory, ed. N.K. Bose, D. Reidel Publishing Co, 1985, pp. 189-232.

[2] J.C. BUTCHER, *The non-existence of ten Stage eight Order Explicit Runge-Kutta Methods*, BIT, 25, 1985, pp. 521-540.

[3] S. CZAPOR and K. GEDDES, *On Implementing Buchbergers's Algorithm for Gröbner Bases*, ISSAC86, 1986, pp. 233-238.

[4] G.E. COLLINS, *The Calculation of Multivariate Polynomial Resultants*, Journal of the ACM,18, No. 4, 1971, pp. 512-532.

[5] K.O. GEDDES, S.R. CZAPOR, and G. LABAHN, *Algorithms for Computer Algebra*, Kluwer, 1992.

[6] G.H. GONNET and M.B. MONAGAN, *Solving systems of Algebraic Equations, or the Interface between Software and Mathematics*, Computers in mathematics, Conference at Stanford University, 1986.

[7] E. HAIRER, S.P. NØRSETT and G. WANNER, *Solving Ordinary Differential Equations I*, Springer-Verlag Berlin Heidelberg, 1987.

[8] R.J. JENKS, *Problem #11: Generation of Runge-Kutta Equations*, SIGSAM Bulletin,10, No. 1, 1976, p. 6.

[9] W. KUTTA, *Beitrag zur näherungsweisen Integration totaler Differentialgleichungen*, Zeitschrift für Math. u. Phys., Vol. 46, 1901, pp. 435-453.

[10] M. MONAGAN and J.S. DEVITT, *The D Operator and Algorithmic Differentiation*, Maple Technical Newsletter, No. 7, 1992.

[11] J. MOSES, *Solution of Systems of Polynomial Equations by Elimination*, Comm. of the ACM,9, No. 8, 1966, pp. 634-637.

[12] B.L. VAN DER WAERDEN, *Algebra I*, Springer-Verlag, Berlin, 1971.

Chapter 20. Transient Response of a Two-Phase Half-Wave Rectifier

H.J. Halin and R. Strebel

20.1   Introduction

Electronic circuits are typically governed by linear differential equations with constant or time-dependent coefficients. The numerical simulation of such systems in the time-domain can be quite demanding, especially if the systems are very large and if they feature widely distributed eigenvalues. Methods for the analysis of electronic circuits have been presented in several textbooks, e.g. [2]. There are also a number of different packages for computer-aided analyses on the market with programs which are offsprings of codes such as ECAP [3] or SPICE2 [5]. These programs employ fully numerical methods and have therefore well known pros and cons.

In what follows we would like to take advantage of the analytical capabilities and the accuracy of MapleV [1] in order to elegantly solve a small but tricky sample problem from the area of electronic circuits. It will be outlined why the problem, the simulation of the transient response of a two-phase half-wave rectifier, is a demanding problem in many ways. This will be explained below in more detail.

For the numerical solution by means of conventional programs a straight-forward implementation of the mathematical model would not be sufficient. Instead some 'tricks' would have to be used to overcome the several numerical difficulties to be discussed later on. This is why an unexperienced analyst most likely would not immediately succeed in performing this simulation study.

20.2   Problem Outline

The problem to be investigated is the simulation of the electrical transient in a two-phase half-wave rectifier after two alternating voltage sources which act as external driving functions have been put in the circuit. This problem has originally been described in [4]. The structure of the model is illustrated in figure 20.1 The system is composed of two ideal diodes D_1 and D_2, two resistances and two impedances R_1, R_2, L_1, and L_2, respectively, the two open-circuit voltages $u_1(t)$, $u_2(t)$, and a load expressed by the resistance R_3 and the impedance L_3. The currents flowing through the diodes are $i_1(t)$ and $i_2(t)$,

FIGURE 20.1. *Structure of the Rectifier System*

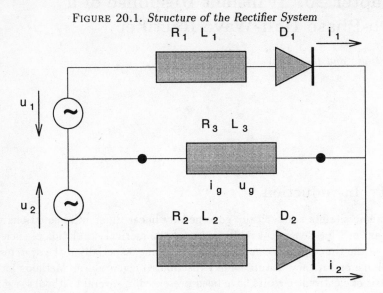

respectively. $i_g(t)$ is the rectified current, while $u_g(t)$ is the rectified voltage. Time is represented by t.

Depending on which diode is conducting three different cases can be distinguished. Which of the three cases applies will depend on the logical values of two time-dependent variables $diod_1$ and $diod_2$. We will define these variables later on but we would like to emphasize already that we use them only for didactic reasons. In the listing of the program that follows these variables do not show up explicitly.

1 Only diode D_1 is conducting. This case applies if $diod_1 = true$ and $diod_2 = false$:

$$\frac{d}{dt}i_1(t) = \frac{u_1 - i_1 R_{13}}{a_2} \qquad (20.1)$$

$$\frac{d}{dt}i_2(t) = 0 \qquad (20.2)$$

2 Only diode D_2 is conducting. This case applies if $diod_1 = false$ and $diod_2 = true$:

$$\frac{d}{dt}i_1(t) = 0 \qquad (20.3)$$

$$\frac{d}{dt}i_2(t) = \frac{u_2 - i_2 R_{23}}{a_1} \qquad (20.4)$$

3 Diode D_1 and diode D_2 are conducting. This case applies if $diod_1 = true$ and $diod_2 = true$:

$$\frac{d}{dt}i_1(t) = \frac{a_1u_1 - L_3u_2 - z_1i_1 - z_2i_2}{b} \tag{20.5}$$

$$\frac{d}{dt}i_2(t) = \frac{a_2u_2 - L_3u_1 - z_3i_2 - z_4i_1}{b} \tag{20.6}$$

where

$$
\begin{aligned}
a_1 &= L_2 + L_3 \\
a_2 &= L_1 + L_3 \\
b &= L_1L_2 + L_1L_3 + L_2L_3 \\
R_{13} &= R_1 + R_3 \\
R_{23} &= R_2 + R_3 \\
z_1 &= a_1R_1 + L_2R_3 \\
z_2 &= L_2R_3 - L_3R_2 \\
z_3 &= a_2R_2 + L_1R_3 \\
z_4 &= L_1R_3 - L_3R_1
\end{aligned}
$$

Note that only one of these three cases will hold at any time and that the fourth case where both variables are *false* is not meaningful except in the steady state situation when the voltage sources are disconnected. The necessary conditions on which one of the three cases is relevant at a given time will be discussed later on when introducing the conditions for the values of $diod_1$ and $diod_2$.

The rectified voltage $u_g(t)$ and the rectified current $i_g(t)$ are given by

$$u_g(t) = R_3(i_1 + i_2) + L_3\left(\frac{d}{dt}i_1(t) + \frac{d}{dt}i_2(t)\right) \tag{20.7}$$

$$i_g(t) = i_1 + i_2, \tag{20.8}$$

respectively.

The voltages $u_1(t)$ and $u_2(t)$ read

$$u_1(t) = U sin(\omega t) \tag{20.9}$$

$$u_2(t) = -u_1(t). \tag{20.10}$$

where

$$U = \sqrt{2}U_{eff} \tag{20.11}$$

and

$$\omega = 2\Pi\nu. \tag{20.12}$$

In this U_{eff} is the effective voltage while ν is the frequency.

In order to specify which of the diodes is conductive, we had already introduced the two logical variables $diod_1$ and $diod_2$. At any time t the logical values of these variables are governed by the following relations:

$$diod_1 = \begin{cases} true & \text{if } i_1 > 0 \text{ or } u_1 > u_g, \\ false & \text{otherwise} \end{cases} \qquad (20.13)$$

$$diod_2 = \begin{cases} true & \text{if } i_2 > 0 \text{ or } u_2 > u_g, \\ false & \text{otherwise} \end{cases} \qquad (20.14)$$

The transient will now be studied during a time interval $t_{start} \leq t \leq t_{final}$, where t_{start} and t_{final} denote the lower and the upper value of simulation time. For the study the following numerical values will be used:

$$R_1 = 2[\Omega] \qquad (20.15)$$
$$R_2 = 2[\Omega] \qquad (20.16)$$
$$R_3 = 10[\Omega] \qquad (20.17)$$
$$L_1 = 0.04[H] \qquad (20.18)$$
$$L_2 = 0.04[H] \qquad (20.19)$$
$$L_3 = 0.20[H] \qquad (20.20)$$
$$U_{eff} = 100[V] \qquad (20.21)$$
$$\nu = 50[Hz]. \qquad (20.22)$$

As initial conditions we choose

$$i_1(0) = 0 \qquad (20.23)$$
$$i_2(0) = 0. \qquad (20.24)$$

20.3 Difficulties in Applying Conventional Codes and Software Packages

When using an integration algorithm such as Runge-Kutta for solving the problem outlined above the user needs to write a main program or a driver routine from which an integrator is invoked. These calls are embedded in a do-loop and are such that the program runs under control of the integrator until the integration over a specified interval of the independent variable is completed. When program control is returned to the main program the solution at the end of the last interval is available and can be used for output. After this the integrator is called again for doing the integration over the next interval while using the last values of the solution as initial conditions.

When performing an integration step the integrator will call a routine that needs to be provided by the user for doing a so-called 'function evaluation'. In this the present value of the independent variable t, the number of first order ODEs and the solution vector at t are transferred to the referencing routine. This routine would essentially contain the code of the differential equations, i.e.

(20.1-20.5) together with mechanisms for making constants, such as (20.15), locally available, which were introduced in the main program. It is then possible to evaluate the right-hand sides of the differential equations and to return a vector of the time-derivatives of the solution to the integrator.

Prior to doing a 'function evaluation' of our problem it is necessary to determine the logical values of the variables $diod_1$ and $diod_2$ from (20.13) in order to decide which of the three forms of our system of two ODEs applies. Since the value of u_g, (20.13), is needed for doing the evaluation of $diod_1$ and $diod_2$ we obviously have an implicit relation. For evaluating $\frac{d}{dt}i_1$ and $\frac{d}{dt}i_2$ the rectified voltage u_g must be known. Thereafter $diod_1$ and $diod_2$ can be found and subsequently $\frac{d}{dt}i_1$ and $\frac{d}{dt}i_2$ from the case that applies momentarily.

In order to deal with this difficulty, Jentsch proposes in [4] the usage of a value of u_g which is delayed by τ seconds, where τ is some small amount of time. The delayed value u_{gd} to be used in (20.13) is given by

$$u_{gd}(t) = \begin{cases} u_g(t-\tau) & \text{if } t > \tau \\ u_g(0) & \text{if } t \leq \tau \end{cases}$$

Note that this is equivalent to

$$u_{gd}(s) = e^{(-\tau s)} u_g(s)$$

when using a standard engineering technique for linear problems by applying a Laplace transform.

In a numerical computation $u_{gd}(t)$ is found by interpolation between some values $u_g(t_i)$ and $u_g(t_{i+1})$, $(i = 1, 2, \ldots)$ where $(t_i \leq t - \tau \leq t_{i+1})$. $u_g(t_i)$ and $u_g(t_{i+1})$ are the values of u_g at the end of the $(i-1)$-th and i-th integration step, respectively.

Yet another difficulty arises at the beginning of the very first integration step at time $t_0 = t_{start}$. Since the initial conditions (20.23), i.e. $i_1(t_0)$, and $i_2(t_0)$ and the two voltages, which act as excitations, (20.9), i.e. $u_1(t_0)$, $u_2(t_0)$, $u_g(t_0)$ are all zero it follows $diod_1 = diod_2 = false$, so that it cannot be decided which case applies.

Even when arbitrarily assuming one of the three cases to be valid it turns out that $\frac{d}{dt}i_1(t_0) = \frac{d}{dt}i_2(t_0) = 0$. Clearly, from a physical point of view at least one of the diodes must become conductive, since $u_1(t)$ has a positive derivative and likewise $u_2(t)$ a negative derivative at $t = t_0$. This implies that one of the two logical variables must be *true*. Therefore at $t = t_0$ the evaluation of $diod_1$ and $diod_2$, respectively, has to be done on the basis of derivatives of $u_1(t)$, $u_2(t)$, and $u_g(t)$.

The decision can be also made when doing the initial evaluation of $diod_1$ and $diod_2$ at some location $t_0 + \epsilon$, where ϵ is a small positive number, rather than at t_0.

20.4   Solution by Means of Maple

In solving the sample problem by means of MapleV [1] the numerical difficulties mentioned above can be avoided elegantly.

In the following a program is presented which is suited for computing the transient response of the rectifier.

The program is composed of three files deqns.map, data.map, and procs.map, respectively.

The program starts by referencing the file deqns.map. After a restart we read and load from within deqns.map a library routine for the later usage of an unassign-statement. After this the files data.map and procs.map will be read. This is followed by assigning values to t_{start} and t_{final} so as to specify the range of the independent variable t.

Example calling sequence in deqns.map

```
#***********************************************************#
#        Example calling sequence                          #
#***********************************************************#

restart;
interface(plotdevice=x11):
readlib (unassign):
read ('data.map');
read ('procs.map');
tstart := 0:
tfinal := 0.050:
ddata := rectify_solve (array(1..2,[0,0]), tstart..tfinal):

plot (t->function_piecewise_apply (ddata[1], t), tstart..tfinal,
        title='Plot 1: i1(t)');
plot (t->function_piecewise_apply (ddata[2], t), tstart..tfinal,
        title='Plot 2: i2(t)');
plot (t->function_piecewise_apply (ddata[1], t)+
        function_piecewise_apply (ddata[2], t), tstart..tfinal,
        title='Plot 3: ig(t)');
plot (t->R.3*(function_piecewise_apply (ddata[1], t)+
            function_piecewise_apply (ddata[2], t))+
        L.3*(function_piecewise_diff (ddata[1], t)+
            function_piecewise_diff (ddata[2], t)),
    tstart..tfinal, title='Plot 4: ug(t)');
```

The integration of our differential equations is initiated by referencing procedure rectify_solve. This procedure which is listed at the very end of file procs.map serves as "main program". For the moment it is sufficient to mention that rectify_solve returns the analytic solutions $i_1(t)$ and $i_2(t)$ as elements of the two-dimensional vector ddata. Since analytic solutions can be found in piecewise form only each element itself is representing a list. Note that the initial conditions of the two state variables and the range of the simulation time are also entered when referencing rectify_solve. The plots that follow at the end of file deqns.map will be described at the end of this chapter.

Note that subscripts in equations (20.1-20.24) are represented throughout the program by a period followed by the subscript, e.g. R_3 in one of the equations will be denoted as R.3 in the program.

In file data.map the external forcing functions $u_1(t)$ and $u_2(t)$ are given first. After this some necessary parameters for our problem are introduced. In this nof_cases and nof_states represent the number of different cases to be encountered during the operation of the rectifier and the number of state variables, respectively.

Solution of the differential equations in data.map

```
#*************************************************************#
#        input                                               #
#*************************************************************#

u[1] := t ->  U*sin(Omega*t):
u[2] := t -> -U*sin(Omega*t):


#*************************************************************#
#        parameters                                          #
#*************************************************************#

U := sqrt(2)*100:
nu := 50:
Omega := 2*Pi*nu:

R.1 := 2:
R.2 := 2:
R.3 := 10:
L.1 := convert(0.04,rational):
L.2 := convert(0.04,rational):
L.3 := convert(0.2,rational):
a.1 := L.2 + L.3:
a.2 := L.1 + L.3:
b := L.1*L.2 + L.1*L.3 + L.2*L.3:
R.13 := R.1 + R.3:
R.23 := R.2 + R.3:
z.1 := a.1*R.1 + L.2*R.3:
z.2 := L.2*R.3 - L.3*R.2:
z.3 := a.2*R.2 + L.1*R.3:
z.4 := L.1*R.3 - L.3*R.1:


#*************************************************************#
#        equations                                           #
#*************************************************************#

nof_cases := 3:
nof_states := 2:

vars := {seq(j[k](t), k=1..nof_states)}:
deqn := array (1..3, [
  { diff(j[1](t),t) = j[1](t)*(-R.13/a.2) + u[1](t)/a.2,
    diff(j[2](t),t) = 0,
    j[1](t0) = j10,
    j[2](t0) = j20
```

```
    },
    { diff(j[1](t),t) = 0,
      diff(j[2](t),t) = j[2](t)*(-R.23/a.1) + u[2](t)/a.1,
      j[1](t0) = j10,
      j[2](t0) = j20
    },
    { diff(j[1](t),t) = j[1](t)*(-z.1/b) + j[2](t)*(-z.2/b)
                + 1/b*(a.1*u[1](t) - L.3*u[2](t)),
      diff(j[2](t),t) = j[1](t)*(-z.4/b) + j[2](t)*(-z.3/b)
                + 1/b*(a.2*u[2](t) - L.3*u[1](t)),
      j[1](t0) = j10,
      j[2](t0) = j20
    }]):

#************************************************************#
#        minimal distance for state change
#************************************************************#

eps := 1/nu*1.0e-6; # get some 'relative' gap
Digits := 14;

#************************************************************#
#        solve the system for all cases
#************************************************************#

unassign ('k','t0','j10','j20'):
for k from 1 to nof_cases do
  dsol[k] := simplify (dsolve (deqn[k], vars)):
  assign (dsol[k]);
  for n from 1 to nof_states do
   i[k][n] := unapply (j[n](t), t, t0, j10, j20):
  od:
  unassign ('j[1](t)','j[2](t)'):
od:
```

This is followed by the formulation of the three sets of differential equations for the three cases possible and by their subsequent formal solution. Note that neither the starting time t0 nor the initial conditions j10 and j20 have been specified numerically so far.

For finding roots of the state variables $i_1(t)$ and $i_2(t)$, respectively, at some location t it will be necessary to provide some tolerance e.g. $\epsilon = 1.0e - 6$. Since the length of time intervals in which each of the three cases applies depends in some way on the wavelength $1/\nu$ of the external forcing functions $u_1(t)$ and $u_2(t)$ it is more appropriate to introduce a "relative" tolerance $\epsilon = 1.0e - 6/\nu$.

The last file procs.map contains the "main program" and some procedures and functions for doing the numerical computations.

Procedure definitions in procs.map

```
#************************************************************#
#        Utilities                                         #
#************************************************************#
```

```
## return sign of val. 0 if val = 0.

sign_zero := proc (val: numeric)
  if (val > 0) then RETURN (1);
  elif (val = 0) then RETURN (0);
  else RETURN (-1);
  fi;
end:

## return sign of f(t+)

sign_rightof := proc (f, t: numeric)
  global eps;
  local r, s, x;
  if (type (t, rational)) then
    s := simplify (series (f(x), x=t));
    r := op(1,s);
    if    (is (r > 0)) then RETURN (1);
    elif (is (r = 0)) then RETURN (0);
    elif (is (r < 0)) then RETURN (-1);
    fi:
  fi:
  RETURN (sign_zero (evalf (f(t+eps))));
end:

## return smallest zero in [r]. NULL if none.

fsolve_smallest := proc (f, r: range)
  global eps;
  local tfrom, tto, s, sprev, t;
  tfrom := op(1,r); tto := op(2,r);
  sprev := NULL;
  while (true) do
    s := fsolve (f(t), t, t=tfrom..tto);
    if (whattype(s) <> float) then RETURN (sprev); fi;
    tto := s-eps;
    sprev := s;
  od;
end:

## Applies piecewise represented function.
## Implemented as sorted list of [left-border, function, ...].

function_piecewise_get := proc (f: list(list), t: numeric)
  local a, b, g, m, res;
  a := 1; b := nops (f) + 1;
  while (a < b-1) do
    m := round ((a+b)/2);
    if (f[m][1] >= t) then b := m;
    else a := m;
    fi;
  od;
  RETURN (f[a][2]);
end:

function_piecewise_apply := proc (f: list(list), t: numeric)
  local g;
  g := function_piecewise_get (f, t);
  RETURN (evalf(g(t)));
```

```
end:

function_piecewise_diff := proc (f: list(list), t: numeric)
  local g, h, x;
  g := function_piecewise_get (f, t);
  h := unapply (diff(g(x),x), x);
  RETURN (evalf(h(t)));
end:

#***********************************************************#
#           Get next interval                              #
#***********************************************************#

case[1,0] := 1: # i[2] = 0
case[0,1] := 2: # i[1] = 0
case[1,1] := 3:

## returns case that follows point t0.

next_case := proc (t0: numeric, j: array)
  global eps, case;
  RETURN (case[sign_rightof(j[1],t0), sign_rightof(j[2],t0)]);
end:

## returns currents for next interval. In VAR_case next case.

next_interval := proc (t0: numeric, i0: array, VAR_case)
  local t, j, s, case;
  for s from nof_cases by -1 to 1 do
    j := array(1..2);
    j[1] := unapply (i[s][1](t,t0,i0[1],i0[2]), t);
    j[2] := unapply (i[s][2](t,t0,i0[1],i0[2]), t);
    case := next_case (t0, j);
    if (s = case) then VAR_case := s; RETURN (j); fi;
  od;
  ERROR ('Continuation failed');
end:

## smallest zero of f in ]r] (without left border).
## right(r) if (f == 0) or (f(t) <> 0) in r.

crit_smallest := proc (f, r: range(numeric))
  global eps;
  local s, tfrom, tto;
  tfrom := op(1,r); tto := op(2,r);
  if (f = 0) then RETURN (tto); fi;
  s := fsolve_smallest (f, tfrom+eps..tto);
  if (whattype(s) <> float) then RETURN (tto); fi;
  RETURN (s);
end:

## returns next critical point.
## In VAR_i current i[] at this point.

next_crit := proc (j: array, r: range(numeric),
                   case: integer, VAR_i)
  local t, ug, ud, crit, tcrit, i;
  ug := unapply (evalf(R.3*(j[1](t) + j[2](t)) +
        L.3*(diff(j[1](t),t)+diff(j[2](t),t))), t);
```

```
 ud[1] := unapply (u[1](t) - ug(t), t);
 ud[2] := unapply (u[2](t) - ug(t), t);
 if (case = 1) then
    crit[1] := crit_smallest (j[1], r);
    crit[4] := crit_smallest (ud[2], r);
    tcrit := min(crit[1], crit[4]);
 elif (case = 2) then
    crit[2] := crit_smallest (j[2], r);
    crit[3] := crit_smallest (ud[1], r);
    tcrit := min(crit[2], crit[3]);
 elif (case = 3) then
    crit[1] := crit_smallest (j[1], r);
    crit[2] := crit_smallest (j[2], r);
    crit[3] := crit_smallest (ud[1], r);
    crit[4] := crit_smallest (ud[2], r);
    tcrit := min(crit[1], crit[2], crit[3], crit[4]);
 fi;
 i := array (1..2, [j[1](tcrit), j[2](tcrit)]);
 if (crit[1] = tcrit) then i[1] := 0; fi;
 if (crit[2] = tcrit) then i[2] := 0; fi;
 VAR_i := i;
 RETURN (tcrit);
end:


#***************************************************************#
#         Main program                                         #
#***************************************************************#

## returns array of list of [time, current, case].
## One list per current. One entry per interval.

rectify_solve := proc (i0: array(numeric), r: range(numeric))
  global nof_states;
  local tfrom, tto, tcur, scur, j, i, res, k;
  tfrom := op(1,r); tto := op(2,r);
  res := array (1..nof_states);
  for k from 1 to nof_states do res[k] := NULL; od;
  tcur := tfrom; i := i0;
  while (tcur < tto) do
    unassign ('scur');
    j := next_interval (tcur, i, scur);
    for k from 1 to nof_states do
      res[k] := res[k], [tcur, j[k], scur];
    od;
    unassign ('i');
    tcur := next_crit (j, tcur..tto, scur, i);
  od;
  for k from 1 to nof_states do res[k] := [res[k]]; od;
  RETURN (res);
end:
```

The "main program" in file procs.map is the procedure that governs most of the execution. The procedure uses the initial values of the state variables and the value of the independent variable at the beginning of each interval for which one of the three possible states holds. By making successive references to procedure next_interval it will be determined first which of the three cases applies.

In doing this, procedure `next_case` needs to be invoked which itself will call procedure `sign_rightof`. Of course the solutions in analytic form found already in file `deqns.map` will be used throughout. As can be seen in `sign_rightof`, the determination of the case that applies is done in analytical form at $t = t_{start}$ by evaluation of higher derivatives of the state variables $i_1(t)$ and $i_2(t)$ up to an order where they do not vanish any more. Otherwise the determination is done by looking for the states at some location $t + \epsilon$, where t denotes the last location of a change of the case of operation. Once the case is determined information regarding the results will be stored in lists in the "main program". After this the next interval will be considered until the whole range of the independent variable is covered.

The solution is illuminated by a number of plots for displaying the currents $i_1(t)$, $i_2(t)$, the rectified current $i_g(t)$, and the rectified voltage $u_g(t)$ over time.

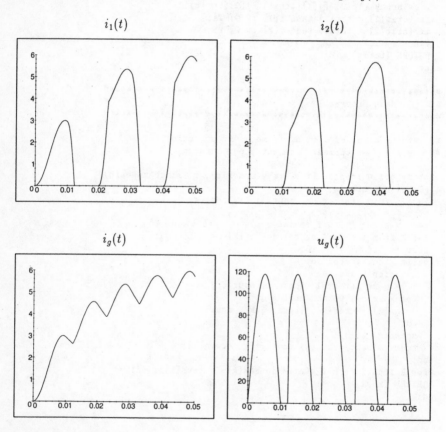

References

[1] B.W. Char, K.O. Geddes, G.H. Gonnet, B.L. Leong, M.B. Monagan, and S.M. Watt, Maple *Language/Reference Manual*, Springer Verlag, New

York, 1991.

[2] L.O. CHUA AND P.-M. LIN, *Computer-Aided Analysis of Electronic Circuits: Algorithms and Computational Techniques*, Prentice-Hall, Englewood Cliffs, N.J., 1975.

[3] R.W. JENSEN AND M.D. LIEBERMAN, *IBM Electronic Circuit Analysis Program*, Prentice-Hall, Englewood Cliffs, N.J., 1968.

[4] W. JENTSCH, *Digitale Simulation kontinuierlicher Systeme*, Oldenbourg Verlag, München und Wien, 1969.

[5] L.W. NAGEL, *SPICE2: A Computer Program to Simulate Semiconductor Circuits*, University of California, Ph.D. Dissertation, Berkeley, California, 1975.

Chapter 21. Circuits in Power Electronics

J. Waldvogel

21.1 Introduction

Over the last few years high power semi-conductor devices with intrinsic turn-off capability have become available. These devices, called gate turn-off (GTO) thyristors, consist of several layers of silicon with appropriate dotations; they are able to turn off currents of 1000 Amperes at thousands of volts within microseconds. In circuits used in power electronics the usual resistive, inductive and capacitive circuit elements are combined with thyristors which may simply be considered as switches. This technology is still an active field of research, and it has many important applications such as AC/DC conversion (both ways), speed control of locomotives and electric cars, control of power stations and power networks, etc.

For every fixed state of the thyristor switches Kirchhoff's laws must be satisfied, and therefore the dynamical behavior of such a circuit is described by a system of linear ordinary differential equations with constant coefficients, assuming linearity of the circuit elements. If the switches change their positions the structure of the circuit changes, but the final state of the currents in the circuit before switching determines the initial conditions after the switching.

Therefore the mathematical model of a circuit in power electronics is a system of linear differential equations with piecewise constant coefficients if the switching times are neglected. We assume the dynamics of the circuit to be described by n continuous functions of time t, which are represented by the vector $\mathbf{x}(t) \in \mathbb{R}^n$ of dependent variables. By using matrix notation the model may be written as

$$\dot{\mathbf{x}} = A(t)\mathbf{x} + \mathbf{p}(t) \qquad (21.1)$$

where dots denote derivatives with respect to time, $A(t)$ is a step function, i.e., a given piecewise constant $n \times n$ matrix, and $\mathbf{p}(t) \in \mathbb{R}^n$ is a given forcing function. In the environment of AC (alternating current) circuits $\mathbf{p}(t)$ and $A(t)$ are often periodic functions. With no loss of generality the period will be normalized to 2π, and in view of the Fourier decomposition of $\mathbf{p}(t)$ we will use the first harmonic as a model case. Usually the solution $\mathbf{x}(t)$ is specified by initial conditions $\mathbf{x}(0) = \mathbf{x}_0$, but other specifications, e.g. periodicity of $\mathbf{x}(t)$, will be considered in Section 21.3.

The initial value problem of systems of linear differential equations with

FIGURE 21.1. *Simplified SVC circuit*

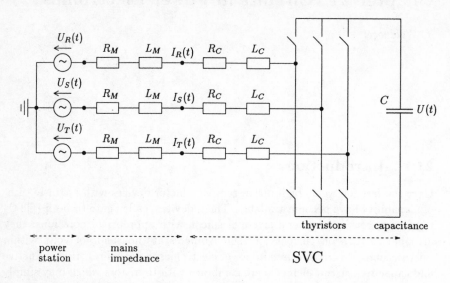

Description of the SVC circuit

Variable	Description
$U_R(t), U_S(t), U_T(t)$	AC voltages generated by the power station
R_M, L_M	Resistance and inductance of the mains
R_C, L_C, C	Resistance, inductance and capacitance of the SVC
$I_R(t), I_S(t), I_T(t)$	Currents injected in the mains
$U(t)$	Voltage across the DC capacitance of the SVC

a constant matrix A is a topic of elementary calculus (cf. [1]) and may be handled via the eigenvalues and eigenvectors of A or via the matrix exponential e^{At}. Even if the matrix $A(t)$ is piecewise constant the explicit solution of the initial value problem is straight-forward, although quite laborious if $A(t)$ has many discontinuities.

It turns out that the features of MATLAB allow a very elegant construction of the solution $\mathbf{x}(t)$ of this initial value problem. Also, periodic solutions may be easily calculated and plotted. In this article we will use a specific device from the field of electric power network control, the so-called Static Var Compensator (SVC) to explain the use of MATLAB in power electronics. Var stands for Volt-Ampere reactive.

SVCs are used in electric power networks to compensate for the voltage drop due to the losses in the power lines and due to a variable user load. In the usual three-phase AC system six switching operations per period are needed, in order to transfer an impulse of reactive power from one phase to another during an appropriate time interval in each period.

In Figure 21.1 a simplified SVC circuit including the mains is shown, the thyristors being represented by switches. For simplicity, no loads of the electric network are taken into consideration. In each circuit corresponding to a single phase only one switch may be closed at any time. For the circuit of Figure 21.1 it is sufficient to choose $n = 3$ independent variables, e.g.

$$x_1(t) = U(t), \quad x_2(t) = I_R(t), \quad x_3(t) = \frac{1}{\sqrt{3}}(I_S(t) - I_T(t)) \qquad (21.2)$$

Then the dynamics of the circuit is described by Equation (21.1) with

$$\mathbf{p}(t) = \frac{1}{L}(0, \cos t, \sin t)^T, \quad L = L_M + L_C, \quad R = R_M + R_C \qquad (21.3)$$

and

$$A(t) = B(\varphi(t)), \quad B(\varphi) = \begin{bmatrix} 0 & \frac{1}{C}\cos\varphi & \frac{1}{C}\sin\varphi \\ -\frac{2}{3L}\cos\varphi & -\frac{R}{L} & 0 \\ -\frac{2}{3L}\sin\varphi & 0 & -\frac{R}{L} \end{bmatrix}. \qquad (21.4)$$

The switching angle $\varphi(t)$ is a given piecewise constant function that controls the operation of the thyristors. In the 6-pulse SVC it is chosen as

$$\varphi(t) = \frac{\pi}{3}\text{round}\left(\frac{3}{\pi}(t - \tau)\right), \qquad (21.5)$$

where the shift τ is a parameter of the SVC to be chosen in $|\tau| \leq R$. Typical values of the parameters C, L, R, expressed in normalized units such that the period of the AC (often 0.02 sec) becomes 2π are

$$C = 0.2, \quad L = 0.15, \quad R = 0.005. \qquad (21.6)$$

The practical orders of magnitude of C, L and R are 150nF, 2Hy and 20Ω respectively. For more technical details the reader is referred to the textbooks [2], [3].

21.2 Linear Differential Equations with Piecewise Constant Coefficients

We consider the differential equation (21.1),

$$\dot{\mathbf{x}} = A(t)\mathbf{x} + \mathbf{p}(t),$$

for the unknown function $\mathbf{x}(t) \in \mathbb{R}^n$. For simplicity the given 2π-periodic forcing function $\mathbf{p}(t)$ is assumed to contain the first harmonic only,

$$\mathbf{p}(t) = \mathbf{b}e^{it} + \bar{\mathbf{b}}e^{-it}, \quad \mathbf{b} \in \mathbb{C}^n. \qquad (21.7)$$

The use of complex notation turns out to be advantageous since it greatly simplifies the equations, and it is fully supported by MATLAB. The piecewise constant real matrix $A(t)$ is assumed to be 2π-periodic as well. Therefore the $m + 1$ (possible) discontinuities (jumps) t_k of $A(t)$ will be introduced as

$$0 = t_0 < t_1 < t_2 < \dots < t_{m-1} < t_m = 2\pi,$$

and the discrete values of the matrix are denoted by

$$A(t) = A_k \text{ in } t_k \le t < t_{k+1}, \quad k = 0, \dots, m - 1. \tag{21.8}$$

Given initial conditions $x(0) = x_0$, Equation (21.1) has a unique solution $x(t)$; its values at the jumps are denoted by

$$x_k := x(t_k), \quad k = 0, \dots, m.$$

First, we construct the explicit solution $x(t)$ of (21.1) in the k-th subinterval $t \in [t_k, t_{k+1}]$ satisfying the appropriate differential equation and the initial condition:

$$\left. \begin{array}{l} \dot{x}(t) = A_k x(t) + p(t), \quad t \in [t_k, t_{k+1}] \\ x(t_k) = x_k \end{array} \right\} \quad k = 0, \dots, m - 1. \tag{21.9}$$

As usual we use the decomposition

$$x(t) = y(t) + z(t) \tag{21.10}$$

into a conveniently chosen particular solution $z(t)$ and the solution $y(t)$ of the homogeneous problem satisfying

$$\dot{y}(t) = A_k y(t), \quad y(t_k) = x_k - z(t_k). \tag{21.11}$$

Using the well-known matrix exponential we obtain

$$y(t) = e^{A_k t} c_k \tag{21.12}$$

with c_k determined from the second equation of (21.11).

The computation of the matrix exponential is a non-trivial problem with a long history, as is seen from the title of the survey paper [4], "Nineteen Dubious Ways to Compute the Exponential of a Matrix". In the MATLAB command expm the "least dubious" way, the method of Padé approximation, is implemented and works reliably, accurately and quickly in almost all cases. It is an expensive operation, however, requiring up to $30n^3$ flops for an $n \times n$ matrix.

If the matrix B is diagonalizable e^B may easily be computed via the eigenvalue factorization $B = TDT^{-1}$, $D = \text{diag}(\lambda_1, \dots, \lambda_n)$ as

$$e^B = Te^D T^{-1}, \quad e^D = \text{diag}(e^{\lambda_1}, \dots, e^{\lambda_n}), \tag{21.13}$$

where λ_j is the j-th eigenvalue of B.

In the case of the matrix $A(t) = B(\varphi(t))$ defined in (21.4) the eigenvalues turn out to be independent of φ and may be written explicitly as

$$\lambda_1 = -r, \quad \lambda_{2,3} = -r/2 \pm i\omega \tag{21.14}$$

where

$$r = -R/L, \quad \omega = \sqrt{\frac{2/3}{LC} - \frac{R^2}{4L^2}}.$$

Therefore, $\lambda_1, \lambda_2, \lambda_3$ are also the eigenvalues of all the matrices A_k for any choice of the switching times t_k. This is seen by means of the similarity relation

$$B(\varphi) = S(\varphi)B(0)S(\varphi)^{-1}$$

with the orthogonal matrix

$$S(\varphi) = \begin{bmatrix} 1 & 0 & 0 \\ 0 & \cos(\varphi) & -\sin(\varphi) \\ 0 & \sin(\varphi) & \cos(\varphi) \end{bmatrix}.$$

We then have

$$e^{B(\varphi)} = S(\varphi)e^{B(0)}S(\varphi)^{-1},$$

with the great advantage that $e^{B(0)}$ has a simple explicit representation due to the block diagonal structure of $B(0)$:

$$e^{B(0)} = e^{r/2}\begin{bmatrix} \cos(\omega)I + \sin(\omega)/\omega\, B_0 & 0 \\ 0 & e^{r/2} \end{bmatrix}.$$

Here I is the 2×2 unit matrix, B_0 is the upper left 2×2 block of $B(0)$, and r, ω are defined above. The reader is invited to derive or verify these relations by means of MAPLE. An implementation of $e^{B(\varphi)}$ is possible with about 30 elementary operations and 6 function calls (such as exp or sin).

To complete the construction of the solution in the k-th time interval a particular solution $z(t)$ of (21.9) has to be chosen. The simplest choice is a harmonic oscillation of the same frequency as $p(t)$, i.e.

$$\mathbf{z}(t) = -\mathbf{u}_k e^{it} - \bar{\mathbf{u}}_k e^{-it} \tag{21.15}$$

where the complex vector $\mathbf{u}_k \in \mathbb{C}^n$ must be determined such that (21.9) is satisfied. Inserting (21.15) into (21.9) yields the condition

$$(A_k - iI)\mathbf{u}_k = \mathbf{b}, \tag{21.16}$$

a system of linear equations in $\mathbb{C}$ for $\mathbf{u}_k$, where I is the $n \times n$ unit matrix. Therefore, the necessary and sufficient condition for the existence of a solution of the form (21.15) is $\det(A_k - iI) \neq 0$, i.e. $\pm i$ must not be an eigenvalue of A_k. From (21.14) there follows that this is satisfied as long as

$$R \neq 0 \quad \text{or} \quad \frac{2\,L}{3\,C} - \frac{R^2}{4} \neq L^2, \tag{21.17}$$

which is true for the specific data given in (21.6). The resonant case (Condition (21.17) violated) may be handled by augmenting (21.15) with terms such as $v_k t e^{it}$, but this case will not be pursued further.

Finally, combining (21.10), (21.12) and (21.15) yields the explicit solution

$$\mathbf{x}(t) = e^{A_k t} \mathbf{c}_k - 2 \operatorname{Re}(\mathbf{u}_k e^{it}), \quad t \in [t_k, t_{k+1}] \tag{21.18}$$

with

$$\mathbf{u}_k = (A_k - iI)^{-1} \mathbf{b} \tag{21.19}$$

and

$$\mathbf{c}_k = e^{-A_k t_k}(\mathbf{x}_k + 2 \operatorname{Re}(\mathbf{u}_k e^{it_k})), \tag{21.20}$$

as follows from (21.18) with $t = t_k$. Putting $t = t_{k+1}$ in (21.18) yields the value of $\mathbf{x}(t)$ at the next jump,

$$\mathbf{x}_{k+1} = e^{A_k t_{k+1}} \mathbf{c}_k - 2 \operatorname{Re}(\mathbf{u}_k e^{it_{k+1}}). \tag{21.21}$$

For evaluating $\mathbf{x}(t)$ at many points it is best to pre-compute and store $\mathbf{u}_k$, $\mathbf{c}_k$, $\mathbf{x}_{k+1}$ according to Equations (21.19), (21.20) and (21.21) in a loop running over $k = 0, \ldots, m - 1$. Then (21.18) yields $\mathbf{x}(t)$ involving at most one matrix exponential.

21.3   Periodic Solutions

In technical applications such as SVCs one is often interested in periodic solutions of the corresponding differential equations. However, periodic solutions are of practical significance only if they are attractive; then they arise naturally after a long time from an arbitrary initial state in their basin of attraction.

In linear problems such as (21.1) the principle of superimposition holds; therefore the stability of periodic solutions is determined by the corresponding homogeneous problem defined by $\mathbf{p}(t) = 0$ or $\mathbf{b} = 0$ (see Equation (21.7)). From Equations (21.19), (21.20), (21.21) with $\mathbf{b} = 0$ and $\mathbf{x}_k$ replaced by $\mathbf{y}_k$ we obtain

$$\mathbf{y}_{k+1} = e^{A_k(t_{k+1}-t_k)} \mathbf{y}_k \tag{21.22}$$

since the matrices $A_k t_{k+1}$ and $A_k t_k$ commute. Here $\mathbf{y}_k$ denotes the value of a solution of the homogeneous equation at the jump $t_k(k = 0, \ldots, m)$. Therefore, after a full period $t_m = 2\pi$, the value of $\mathbf{y}_m$ is given by the linear map

$$\mathbf{y}_m = M \mathbf{y}_0, \tag{21.23}$$

where

$$M = \prod_{k=0}^{m-1} e^{A_k(t_{k+1}-t_k)} \tag{21.24}$$

(the product taken from right to left) is the so-called monodromy matrix. There follows that a periodic solution of (21.1) is globally attractive if $|\mu_j| < 1$ holds for all eigenvalues μ_j of M.

It turns out that for the 6-pulse SVC given by the matrix (21.4) and the switching function (21.5) the eigenvalues μ_j are independent of the shift τ. In the example (21.6) the values

$$\mu_1 = 0.84311362558494 \tag{21.25}$$

$$\mu_{2,3} = -0.77497080502505 \pm 0.42379742896324i \tag{21.26}$$

are obtained; hence if a periodic solution exists it is globally attractive.

To construct such a solution $\mathbf{x}(t) = \mathbf{x}_P(t)$, an initial value vector $\mathbf{x}_0 \in \mathbb{R}^n$ has to be found such that

$$\mathbf{x}_m = \mathbf{x}_0 \quad \text{or} \quad \mathbf{f}(\mathbf{x}_0) := \mathbf{x}_m - \mathbf{x}_0 = 0 \tag{21.27}$$

in the notation of (21.21). Due to the linearity of the problem the vector valued function $\mathbf{f}$ defined in (21.27) is itself linear. Hence it suffices to compute $n + 1$ values of $\mathbf{f}$ in order to define the system of linear equations (21.27). This is necessary because $\mathbf{f}$ is defined only indirectly by means of the rather complicated algorithm described at the end of Section 21.2.

The $n + 1$ points of evaluation are conveniently chosen as the origin and the n unit points $\mathbf{e}_j = (0, \ldots, 0, 1, 0, \ldots, 0)^T$, where the non-vanishing component is in position j, $(j = 1, \ldots, n)$. If we denote

$$\mathbf{f}_0 := \mathbf{f}(0), \quad \mathbf{f}_j := \mathbf{f}(\mathbf{e}_j), \quad (j = 1, \ldots, n) \tag{21.28}$$

the linear function $\mathbf{f}(\mathbf{x})$ is explicitly given by

$$\mathbf{f}(\mathbf{x}) = \mathbf{f}_0 + \sum_{j=1}^{n} (\mathbf{f}_j - \mathbf{f}_0)\, x_j \tag{21.29}$$

where $\mathbf{x} = (x_1, \ldots, x_n)^T$. The initial value $\mathbf{x}_0$ satisfying $\mathbf{f}(\mathbf{x}_0) = 0$ is therefore obtained from the linear system

$$F\mathbf{x}_0 = \mathbf{f}_0 \tag{21.30}$$

where F is the matrix

$$F = [\mathbf{f}_0 - \mathbf{f}_1, \ldots, \mathbf{f}_0 - \mathbf{f}_n]. \tag{21.31}$$

A unique periodic solution exists if the matrix F is regular. In the numerical example (21.6) we obtain for all $\tau \in [-R, R]$ $\text{cond}(F) \doteq 11.74$, hence in this case F is far away from a singular matrix.

21.4 A MATLAB Implementation

In this section we will present a complete MATLAB program capable of carrying out the tasks listed below for the example of the 6-pulse SVC. It is based on the explicit solution of $n = 3$ linear differential equations with piecewise constant coefficients as described in the previous sections.

(a) The periodic solution $\mathbf{x}_P$ discussed in Section 21.3 is generated, and its values at the $m + 1$ jumps of $A(t)$ are stored. Possible near-degeneracies may be detected by means of $\text{cond}(F)$.

ALGORITHM 21.1. *Function* matrix.

```
function [A] = matrix(k)
% generates the matrix A[k], k=0,...,m-1
%
  global m C L R

  phi = k*2*pi/(m-1);
  A   = [
                     0, cos(phi)/C, sin(phi)/C
    -cos(phi)/1.5/L,      -R/L,         0
    -sin(phi)/1.5/L,        0,        -R/L
  ];

end % matrix
```

(b) Computation of the monodromy matrix M associated with x_P together with its eigenvalues for discussing the stability of x_P.

(c) Efficient tabulation and plotting of x_P (dense output).

(d) Fourier analysis of the periodic solution x_P.

The program is kept general as much as possible although some particular features of the specific example necessarily appear. This will enable the reader to adapt the program to any other problem involving linear ODEs with piecewise constant coefficients. The main objectives of the code are efficiency and simplicity, not luxury of the input and output. However, compared to the shortness of the program a fair amount of luxury and a high degree of reliability is achieved.

The core of the program is the function f = solution(x0) given in Algorithm 21.2. It solves (21.1) with the initial vector x0 $= x_0$ and returns the value $f = f(x_0)$ of the function defined in (21.27). According to the number nargout of output arguments in the actual call (a permanent variable of MATLAB) the matrices xx, uu, M are also computed. The matrices A_k specific to this example (see Equations (21.4), (21.5)) are generated by the function A = matrix(k) in Algorithm 21.1. Table 21.1 describes the variables which are passed as global parameters for convenience.

On exit from solution, xx will contain the values x_k, uu the intermediate results u_k and M the monodromy matrix. These variables are initialized in the first lines of solution. In the subsequent loop over k we first generate the matrix A_{k-1} by calling the function matrix. Then Equations (21.19), (21.20) and (21.21) are evaluated as described at the end of Section 21.2. The only modification is that c_k in (21.21) has been substituted by the expression in (21.20). This halves the number of matrix exponentials to be computed. Furthermore, it turns out that storing the vectors c_k can be avoided at almost no cost.

ALGORITHM 21.2. *Function* solution.

```
function [f, xx, uu, M] = solution(x0)
%SOLUTION        Solves the SVC problem over a period.
%               f == 0 <=> periodic solution
%
  global m n tt b

  if (nargout > 1), uu = []; xx = x0; end;
  if (nargout > 3), M  = eye(n); end;
  x = x0;
  for k = 1:m,
    A = matrix(k-1);
    E = expm(A*(tt(k+1)-tt(k)));
    u = (A-i*eye(n))\b;
    x = E*(x+2*real(u*exp(i*tt(k))))-2*real(u*exp(i*tt(k+1)));
    if (nargout > 1), uu = [uu,u]; xx = [xx,x]; end;
    if (nargout > 3), M  = E*M; end;
  end;
  f = x - x0;

end % solution
```

TABLE 21.1. *Description of Global Variables*

Variable	Description
m, n	Dimensional parameters
C, L, R	System parameters
b	Inhomogeneity **b** from Equations (21.7),(21.3)
tt(1:m+1)	Array of jumps, tt(1+k)=t_k, $(k = 0\ldots m)$

Since the MATLAB indices are ≥ 1 the loop index k has been shifted by 1. The newly computed vectors $u = u_k$, $x = x_{k+1}$ are stored by appending them to the matrices uu and xx, respectively. In the same loop the partial product M is updated according to (21.24). The final statement defines the function value (21.27).

In Algorithm 21.3 the main program per.m performing the tasks (a) through (d) by means of calls to the function solution is given. After initializing some global variables, the input of the shift τ is done via a program request. In this way the sensitive dependence of the circuit's behavior on τ may easily be studied. In the next statement the array of the jumps tt(1:m+1) (with the index shifted by 1) is defined:

$$\begin{aligned}
\texttt{tt(1)} &= 0 \\
\texttt{tt(1+k)} &= t_k = \tau + (k - \tfrac{1}{2})\frac{\pi}{3}, \quad (k = 1,\dots,6) \\
\texttt{tt(8)} &= 2\pi
\end{aligned}$$

(see (21.5)). Then the periodic solution x_P together with its initial value $\texttt{x0} = x_0$ is computed. The program closely follows Equations (21.28) through (21.31) and is self-explanatory.

In the next section of the program $x_P(t)$ is tabulated with step $\Delta = 2\pi/N$:

$$\texttt{xtab}(:,j) = x_P((j-1)\Delta), \quad j = 1,\dots,N.$$

In view of the subsequent fast-Fourier analysis N must be a power of 2. The algorithm is organized to work efficiently if $N \gg m$ as follows. Given a value of t, the index k is such that $t \in [t_k, t_{k+1})$. If $t \in [t_k, t_{k+1})$ is the first evaluation point in this interval, $x_P(t)$ must be calculated according to Equation (21.18). Hence we begin by computing the first term of (21.18) as

$$\texttt{aux} := e^{A_k t} c_k = e^{A_k(t - t_k)}(x_k + 2\,\mathrm{Re}\,(u_k e^{it_k})),$$

where the vectors x_k and u_k are taken from the arrays xx and uu, respectively. Furthermore, the matrix $E := e^{A_k \Delta}$ is computed and stored at this point, thus avoiding its frequent re-computation at later points in the same interval. Otherwise, it suffices to update aux as aux := E*aux.

In the final sections of the program the first component of $x_P(t)$, i.e. $U(t)$ (the voltage across the capacitance C) is plotted versus $j = 1 + t/\Delta$ as MATLAB Figure 1. The second and third components, which are both variable currents, are simultaneously plotted as MATLAB Figure 2. Finally, the 3 components of x_P are separately Fourier-analyzed by means of the MATLAB command fft that requires a column vector as its argument. The matrix cc serves for printing the first 32 complex Fourier coefficients of the three components of $x(t)$.

The data (21.6) in the three cases $\tau = -R$, $\tau = -0.375R$ and $\tau = R$ produce the plots presented in Figure 21.2. The sensitivity to small changes in τ is obvious. Ideally, the currents $x_2(t)$, $x_3(t)$ should be sinusoidal. One goal of research in this field is to reduce the disturbances due to the higher harmonics present in the periodic solution x_P.

ALGORITHM 21.3. *Script* per.

```
global m n C L R tt b

m = 7; n = 3;
C = 0.2; L = 0.15; R = 0.005;
b = [0;1;-i]/2/L;
N = 512;

tau = input('tau = ');
tt  = [0, 2*pi/(m-1)*[1/2:(m-3/2)]+tau, 2*pi];

f0 = solution(zeros(n,1));
F = []; for x = eye(n),
  F = [F, f0 - solution(x)];
end;
x0 = F\f0;
[ff, xx, uu, M] = solution(x0);

delta = 2*pi/N;
k = 0; xtab = [];
for j = 0:N-1,
  t = j*delta;
  if (tt(k+1) <= t),
    k = k+1;
    A = matrix(k-1);
    aux = expm(A*(t-tt(k)))*(xx(:,k)+2*real(uu(:,k)*exp(i*tt(k))));
    E = expm(A*delta);
  else
    aux = E*aux;
  end;
  xtab = [xtab, aux-2*real(uu(:,k)*exp(i*t))];
end;

figure(1); plot(xtab(1,:)');
figure(2); plot(xtab(2:3,:)');

cc = fft(1/N*xtab'); cc(1:32,:)
```

FIGURE 21.2. *Voltage and currents in an SVC*

Parameters: $C = 0.2$, $L = 0.15$, $R = 0.005$ according to Equation (21.6). The three cases of the shifts $\tau = -R$, $-0.375R$, R are shown. In the left-hand figures the voltage $x_1(t) = U(t)$ is plotted versus time t, whereas the currents $x_2(t) = I_S(t)$ (solid line) and $x_3(t) = (I_S(t) - I_T(t))/\sqrt{3}$ (dashed line) are plotted in the right-hand figures.

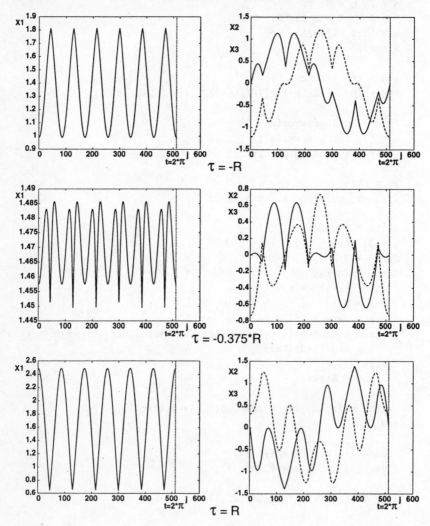

21.5 Conclusions

A computer simulation of a technical process is a research tool useful in designing and optimizing the process. The above specialized circuit simulator is more than ten times faster than a general-purpose simulator on the same problem, and it produces highly accurate approximations (14 decimals) to the exact solutions of the mathematical model. This enables the user to obtain reliable spectra of periodic solutions to high order, which, in turn, enable the designer to eliminate some of the unwanted harmonics.

Clearly, the success of this simulation is largely due to the high standards of the MATLAB software. Best results are obtained, however, if good software is combined with a careful mathematical analysis.

The author is indebted to Gerald Scheuer of the Institute of Power Electronics (ETH Zürich) for providing the differential equations of the SVC. Helpful comments by Rolf Strebel are gratefully acknowledged.

References

[1] M. BRAUN, *Differential Equations and their Applications, Fourth ed.*, Springer, New York, 1993, 578 pp.

[2] M. MEYER, *Leistungselektronik*, Springer, Berlin, 1990, 349 pp.

[3] T. J. E. MILLER, *Reactive Power Control in Electric Systems*, J. Wiley and Sons, New York, 1982, 381 pp.

[4] C.B. MOLER AND C.F. VAN LOAN, *Nineteen Dubious Ways to Compute the Exponential of a Matrix*, SIAM Review 20, 1978, pp. 801–836.

Index

air traffic control, 141
automatic differentiation, 44, 45

ballistic experiment, 204
BLAS routines, 132
Boltzmann constant, 211
  statistics, 59
Bose-Einstein's integral, 212

Cholesky decomposition, 242, 245
circuit, 299
conic section, 116
coordinate system, 142, 161
  transformations, 146
coordinates, geocentric, 143
  geographical, 143

differential equation, 1, 2, 37, 154,
    167, 174, 203, 285, 299, 301
  system, 4, 8, 16, 18, 267
  heat, 183
  Laplace, 183
  Poisson, 59
  dsolve(..., series), 177
  dsolve, 17, 19, 158, 203
  ode23 or ode45, 5, 21, 39, 49
diode, 285
discontinuity, 300
distance, 25, 69, 70, 81, 83
  aiming error, 91

eigenvalue, 303
electrical transient, 285
electronic circuit, 285
equations of motion, 38, 44
error function, 189

Euler method, improved, 268
Euler angles, 162

Fermi potential, 59
force, drag, 15
  Magnus, 15
  weight, 15
Fourier analysis, 308
Frobenius norm, 82

Gaussian elimination, 273
  for tridiagonal systems, 62
generalized reflection method, 89, 109
Givens rotation, 132
Gröbner basis, 273
gradient, 30, 47
Gram matrix, 239

Hamiltonian formalism, 42, 44
heat equation, 183
Hessian, 30
hidden line removal, 85

impedance, 285
inverse interpolation, 22

Jacobian, 61
Joukowski airfoil, 153

Krasovsky ellipse, 144

Lagrange equations, 128, 163
  formalism, 163
  principal function, 128
Laguerre polynomial, 243, 247
Lanczos algorithm, 243
Laplace equation, 183

D. Redfern

The Maple Handbook

Maple V Release 3

1994. V, 531 pp. 16 figs. ISBN 3-540-94331-5

The Maple Handbook: Maple V Release 3 is an essential reference tool for all users of the Maple system. It provides a complete listing of every command in the Maple language, categorized into logical categories and explained in the context of those categories. If a Maple command has different purposes in different categories, it is included more than once as appropriate. A short introductory tutorial starts the Handbook, and each category begins with a brief introduction to the related subject area. The Handbook is well referenced, with an alphabetical index of commands, and pointers to appropriate sections of the official Maple documentation (published by Springer-Verlag). This new approach to reference materials for Maple enhances the material found in Maple's on-line help files and provides a much more organized, intuitive resource for all users of the Maple system. The Handbook improves the efficiency of Maple users by supplying them with the information they need – at their fingertips. This new edition is comprised of the Maple V Release 3 symbolic computation language.

F. Stenger

Numerical Methods Based on Sinc and Analytic Functions

1993. XV, 565 pp. 8 figs. (Springer Series in Computational Mathematics, Vol. 20) ISBN 3-540-94008-1

Many mathematicians, scientists, and engineers are familiar with the Fast Fourier Transform, a method based upon the Discrete Fourier Transform. Perhaps not so many mathematicians, scientists, and engineers recognize that the Discrete Fourier Transform is one of a family of symbolic formulae called Sinc methods. Sinc methods are based upon the Sinc function, a wavelet-like function replete with identities which yield approximations to all classes of computational problems. Such problems include problems over finite, semi-infinite, or infinite domains, problems with singularities, and boundary layer problems. Written by the principle authority on the subject, this book introduces Sinc methods to the world of computation. It serves as an excellent research sourcebook as well as a textbook which uses analytic functions to derive Sinc methods for the advanced numerical analysis and applied approximation theory classrooms.
Problem sections and historical notes are included.

Tm.BA95.01.27c

B. Mishra

Algorithmic Algebra

1993. XII, 416 pp. 9 figs. (Monographs in Computer Science)
ISBN 3-540-94090-1

Algorithmic Algebra studies some of the main algorithmic tools of
computer algebra, covering such topics as Gröbner bases, charac-
teristic sets, resultants, and semialgebraic sets. The main purpose of the
book is to acquaint advanced undergraduate and graduate students in
computer science, engineering, and mathematics with the algorithmic
ideas in computer algebra so that they could do research in computational algebra or understand the algorithms underlying many popular
symbolic computational systems: Mathematica, Maple or Axiom, for
instance. Also, researchers in robotics, solid modeling, computational
geometry and automated theorem proving community may find it useful
as symbolic algebraic techniques have begun to play an important role
in these areas. The book, while being self-contained, is written at an
advanced level and deals with the subject at an appropriate depth.

The book is accessible to computer science students with no previous
algebraic training. Some mathematical readers, on the other hand, may
find it interesting to see how algorithmic constructions have been used
to provide fresh proofs for some classical theorems. The book also
contains a large number of exercises with solutions to selected
exercises, thus making it ideal as a textbook or for self-study.

Springer